Strawberry Fields

A volume in the series

Anthropology of Contemporary Issues

EDITED BY ROGER SANJEK

A full list of titles in the series appears at the end of the book.

Strawberry Fields

POLITICS, CLASS, AND WORK IN CALIFORNIA AGRICULTURE

Miriam J. Wells

Cornell University Press

Ithaca and London

First published 1996 by Cornell University Press.

Printed in the United States of America

♾ The paper in this book meets the minimum requirements of the American National Standard for Information Sciences—Permanence of Paper for Printed Library Materials, ANSI Z39.48-1984.

Library of Congress Cataloging-in-Publication Data

Wells, Miriam J., 1945–
Strawberry fields : politics, class, and work in California agriculture / Miriam J. Wells.
p. cm. — (The Anthropology of Contemporary Issues)
Includes bibliographical references and index.
ISBN 0-8014-3172-7 (cloth : alk. paper). — ISBN 0-8014-8279-8 (pbk. : alk. paper)
1. Strawberry industry–California. 2. Strawberry industry–California–Employees. 3. Agricultural laborers—California. 4. Agriculture—Economic aspects—California. I. Title II. Series.
HD9259.S83U648 1996
338.1'7475'09794—dc20 96-2613

This book is dedicated to my father,
my earliest and most enduring
intellectual inspiration.

Industrialized agriculture has its fullest development in California.
—Paul Taylor and Dorothea Lange, *An American Exodus,* 1939

In the harvest seasons, the orchards are peopled with thousands of workers; and, in the great fields, an army of pickers can be seen trudging along, in the dazzling heat, in the wake of a machine. The impression gained is one of vast agricultural domains, huge orchard and garden estates, without permanent occupants. . . . Here a new type of agriculture has been created: large-scale, intensive, diversified, mechanized.
—Carey McWilliams, *Factories in the Field,* 1935

Agriculture in California is peculiarly well suited to accommodate and usefully employ labor of almost any description. The market is without any structure of job rights or preferences. Not only are unions virtually nonexistent, but there is literally no relationship between employer and employee upon which any claims to recurrent employment might be built. To the employer the harvest hand is anonymous; he has not even a social security number for identification. To be sure, the farmer has preferences, but these are racial preferences.
—Lloyd H. Fisher, *The Harvest Labor Market in California,* 1953

Contents

Illustrations

Figures

Plates

Tables

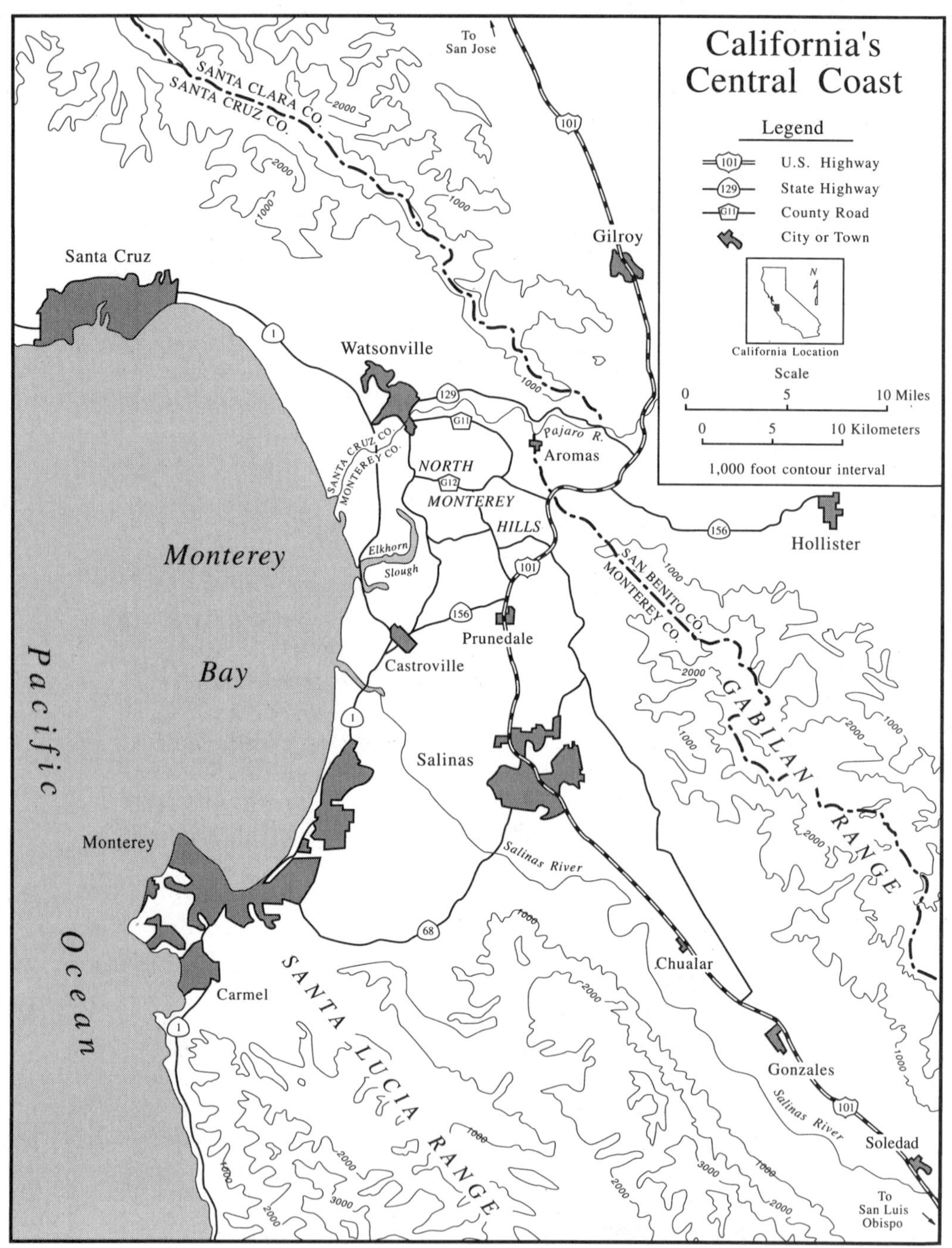

Figure 1. California's central coast region

Preface: The Ethnography of an Industry

This book is about social conflict and economic restructuring, and the play of political forces in the relationship between the two. I came to its argument not through an abstract engagement with broad theories of economic change but through my concrete, sustained study of a particular industry, region, and time—California's central coast strawberry industry in the post–World War II period. In the course of this investigation, I discovered that dominant portrayals of economic restructuring fail to adequately characterize the experience of this industry—not because of peculiarities of the industry itself, but because of shortcomings in the prevailing theories. Most tend to privilege global causes over local, structure over agency, and technological and market forces over social and political influences. I show here how substantially these neglected dimensions shape the processes of late twentieth-century economic change. In particular, I demonstrate that economic reconfigurations—too often portrayed as the inevitable and value-neutral outcomes of changing global economic structure—may instead be primarily the result of local sociopolitical conflicts.

My goal in this book is not only to engage and develop social theory through the causal analysis of a particular case, but to increase understanding of a fascinating and little-known world: the social system of strawberry growers and workers on California's central coast. This is a story of class formation and interethnic conflict. It unfolds along the back roads of a region famous as a tourist destination, but generally unknown for the inner workings of its agricultural economy. My choice of methods stemmed from my graduate training in social anthropology: primarily, participant observation and interviewing; secondarily, surveys and documentary analysis. It was clear from the start that my investigation would take me from the libraries and offices that compiled and assembled written records into the daily lives of people in the industry. Some of these contacts, such as in-depth and special-purpose interviews, were structured. Others, such as spontaneous conversations and various sorts of observation and participation, were free-flowing. I endeavored, through the fine mesh of ethnographic inquiry, to capture the rich detail of daily life in ways not possible through more removed techniques. Following the canons of qualitative fieldwork, I let the experience of my subjects inform me, rather than assuming the nature and primacy of broader influences. Although I employed hypotheses throughout the project to test and sharpen interpretations, the key causal variables in my analysis and the ultimate shape of my generalizations emerged from the process of inquiry.

My hope has been to develop an understanding of the local industry that embraces the experiences of both farmers and farm workers and to weave them into a fabric in which the development of labor processes makes sense. As I listened to individuals telling their stories, I soon learned that the social field of the industry was not unitary. Rather, it contained several relatively distinct spheres of activity, divided along lines of ethnicity, position in the occupational structure, and locality of dominant involvement. This differentiation was true for farmers as well as farm workers. It meant that neither group could be treated as homogeneous and that most individuals understood only their own part of the bigger picture. To capture this internal complexity, I conducted interviews with participants in all segments of the regional system. That there was no single set of meanings among them, but rather several patterns of understanding, helped me resist impulses to assert simple answers as to "what it all meant." For my part, I became increasingly convinced of the value of looking at a social system by exploring it from all angles, turning it like a gem to catch light from facets previously shaded.

This project had two phases. The first began in 1976, when I went to the central coast to study several strawberry production cooperatives that had been organized by former sharecroppers and farm workers and funded by public and private agencies as a means of combating rural poverty. The second phase, which overlapped somewhat with the first, began in the late 1970s, as I shifted my focus to the regional industry and its labor processes. The site for the study was California's central coast, which for the purposes of this book encompasses Santa Cruz and Monterey Counties, with their respective urban centers, Watsonville and Salinas (see Figure 1). It is bounded on the north by the San Francisco Bay metropolitan nexus and on the east by the increasingly urban counties of Santa Clara and San Benito.

To the south, mountainous barriers separate it from another berry-producing enclave in Santa Barbara and San Luis Obispo Counties.

My access to the field was relatively easy because the central coast is less than two hundred miles south of Davis, where I teach and reside. Over the years I traveled regularly to the area for four-day stints during fall and spring quarters and for up to two weeks between quarters and during the winter quarter, when I had no teaching obligations. Although interviews and documentary research have continued into the early 1990s, my most intensive fieldwork was conducted from 1976 through 1988. During that period I spent a substantial portion of most summers in the field. From June 1986 to January 1987 I lived and conducted fieldwork on the central coast. At first I stayed in motels. Then I rented a room in Salinas and later a room and then an apartment in Watsonville. These locations provided easy access to my subjects as well as a chance to participate in the daily life of these agricultural communities. As my friendships in the region deepened, individuals and families began to offer me a couch or a spare room. My most frequent haven was a small trailer parked under a spreading oak tree in the driveway of a cooperative staff member in the north Monterey County hamlet of Aromas. Staying in people's homes provided support, contacts, insights, and perspectives that would otherwise have been difficult to gain. My travels ranged from the town of Gilroy on the north to Gonzales and Soledad to the south. Most of my time, however, was spent on farms and in offices and homes in the environs of Watsonville and Salinas.

Days in the field were long and intense. Interviews and observation on farms could start as early as seven in the morning and continue until as late as eleven or twelve at night. Mornings after the day's work had been set in motion were often best for talking with farmers. Mornings were also good for office workers such as agricultural commissioners, extension agents, state employment officials, lawyers, and marketing organization and border patrol personnel. Many growers preferred to talk in the evening, however, and all interviews with workers were conducted after work and on the weekends. I discovered early on that, because labor is so politically charged for growers, and because workers are so aware of their own legal and economic vulnerability, most of my subjects were reluctant to be taped. I therefore took notes in shorthand during interviews, filled them in by hand immediately afterward in private, and transcribed them within a day.

The first phase of my research emphasized the problems and processes of planned economic development. It focused particularly on the cooperatives' internal organization and dynamics, the role of the U.S.-Mexico population flow, and the determinants of cooperative success and failure, with special attention to the ways that the cooperatives were linked to external sources of technical and financial support (see, for example, Wells 1982). This phase involved participant observation, unstructured interviewing, and a structured survey of members that dealt with the organization and functioning of the farms, members' life and work histories, and members' evaluations of cooperative farming. I volunteered in project offices, attended meetings, accompanied staff members on errands, took children to the dentist and hospital, translated documents, and helped unravel problems with officials. I relished long Sunday dinners in homes and brief bag lunches at the edges of fields, shared salsa recipes and helped cook, and attended birthdays, saint's day celebrations, christenings, weddings, and fiestas.

As often as I could, I picked strawberries. Many days ended for me with an aching back, stained hands, and dusty, sunburned arms and neck. It was clear that my economic contribution to the families I helped was marginal. I never mastered the dispatch and dexterity with which my cohorts filled their baskets. I did earn a fair amount of goodwill for my persistence, however, and (I learned) for my good-humored response to their gentle teasing about my snail's pace. Those days in the fields—the jokes, companionable silences, personal confidences, and shared exhaustion—are some of my warmest memories of the field.

In the course of my research on the cooperatives, I began to observe that the industry within which they were embedded did not fit scholarly predictions of how capitalist agriculture should be organized. Intrigued by this discrepancy, I shifted my focus to the industry and its labor processes: the second phase of my research. To construct a picture of the local farming system, I identified the key categories of actors and institutions involved in the industry and its surrounding support structure. Drawing on commodity systems theory (Friedland 1984a; Goldberg 1980, 1981) and my own prior fieldwork, I categorized the major dimensions of the system, including the generation and application of technology, farm supply inputs, the labor market, production practices, labor processes, grower and worker organizations, and marketing and distribution networks. I then began to interview key informants involved in each, including university researchers, county farm advisers, agricultural commissioners, labor commissioners, local and state employment and immigration officials, staff from local housing, health, and poverty agencies, farming input suppliers (e.g., nurseries, chemical and machinery companies, companies that fumigate the soil and install drip irrigation), marketing agents (e.g., individual brokers, marketing cooperatives, and sole grower-shippers), strawberry processors, agricultural lenders, union staff members and rank and file activists, lawyers dealing with labor rights and protections, and representatives of farmer interest groups. These interviews continued into the early 1990s.

At the same time, I began to gather written data on the industry and region. The historical societies and libraries of Santa Cruz and Monterey Counties, and the Giannini and Bancroft Libraries at the University of California, Berkeley, provided rich historical material, as did several in-depth regional studies (FitzSimmons 1983; Lydon 1985; Seivertson 1969; Wallick 1969). Climatic, hydrologic, and groundwater data published annually by the county flood control and water conservation districts, along with detailed county land-use maps published every several years by the State Department of Water Resources, helped me map the natural resources of the region. Land ownership and leasehold data by parcel obtained from the Santa Cruz County agricultural commissioner and assessor and the Monterey County agricultural commissioner helped clarify land tenure arrangements. The U.S. Census and the Census of Agriculture provided invaluable information on demography, marketing patterns, and production organization and trends, despite their shortcomings (FitzSimmons 1983:332–33). Several other sources helped reconstruct temporal changes in production: the *Annual Crop Reports* published by the agricultural commissioners' offices list the acreage, volume, and market value of farm commodities produced in the county; the Federal-State Market News Service publishes annual market reports on the various crop industries in the state, by region; and the California Strawberry Advisory Boards issue periodic and annual reports of production, acreage, and marketing.

I quickly realized that in order to understand how industry characteristics affected labor processes and class relations, I would need to become thoroughly versed in the technicalities of strawberry production. I found many resources in my own backyard. My colleagues at the Davis and Berkeley campuses of the University of California are international leaders in strawberry research and have produced some excellent treatises on strawberry production (Bain and Hoos 1963; California Gene 1982; Childers 1980; Darrow 1966; Kader et al. 1985; Thomas 1939; Thomas and Goldsmith 1945; Wilhelm and Sagen 1974). Also useful were the annual reports issued by the California Strawberry Advisory Board regarding the research it has sponsored through the University of California's Agricultural Experiment Station and Cooperative Extension. The circulars on production practices, costs, and returns issued by county agricultural agents since the early 1950s identified economic trends in the industry. Any shortcomings of interpretation or understanding are, of course, my own.

Some written sources have provided particular insight into the politics of California agriculture. From 1976 through 1990 I regularly read the

Packer, the weekly business newspaper of the Western Growers and Shippers Association; *California Farmer,* the major trade magazine of California agribusiness; and *California Agriculture,* the journal of University of California's Agricultural Experiment Station. Articles in the *Salinas Californian* and the Watsonville *Register-Pajaronian* provided useful descriptions of local agriculture and its leaders. They also documented public struggles over the wages and working conditions of farm laborers.

In 1986 and 1987, in order to characterize the grower and worker populations more systematically and to explore critical aspects of labor resistance and labor process change, I designed and administered two sets of in-depth interview schedules: one for growers; and one for labor-suppliers, including wage laborers and sharecroppers. In June 1986 I rented an apartment in Watsonville behind the Buddhist temple. From that base—at the mouth of the Pajaro Valley, a short ten minutes by car from the North Monterey County Hills and twenty minutes from the Salinas Valley floor—my research assistant and I completed interviews over the ensuing eight months of from 2.5 to 5 hours long each with forty-five berry growers and seventy wage laborers and sharecroppers.

I identified the grower population from the Pesticide Use Reports on file in the county agricultural commissioners' offices. Growers were of Japanese, Mexican, and European American descent. I generated a sample of potential interviewees representing the critical axes of the local system (see Appendix to Chapter 4) and developed personal networks through which to approach them. I made initial contact for the grower interviews directly by telephone. In all cases I was able to mention growers or other influential individuals in the industry (e.g., farm advisers, agricultural commissioners, officials from marketing companies and producer organizations, university researchers, farm supply dealers) who had recommended my speaking with that individual. All but two of the interviews with Mexican growers were conducted in Spanish, at the interviewees' request. The other interviews were conducted in English. Most interviews took place in growers' homes in the evenings, providing additional insights into ethnic contrasts. Others took place in dusty, paper-piled field offices, on the backs of flatbed trucks, and in tastefully decorated corporate offices.

Each interview was followed by a ranch visit of from one to four hours. These visits permitted direct observation of growers' resource levels and production practices, as well as of the labor process itself. The content of observations varied, depending on whether the grower was present and on what was taking place on the ranch. Through these visits and my earlier participant observation on the cooperatives, I observed the full annual cycle of production, from ground preparation and planting to picking and transport to market. I was present when extension agents arrived to advise farmers about pest problems, when marketing company field men came by to monitor the quality of picking, and when workers scattered into thickets and gullies as the border patrol pulled up in its van. I observed exchanges among growers, foremen, checkers, and pickers. I conversed informally with all players. Many of these talks provided leads for subsequent inquiry.

The generation of the worker sample was particularly challenging, since random sampling was impossible for this population and type of interview. The workers in this local system were of Mexican origin or descent. Most were immigrants and monolingual Spanish speakers; many were undocumented and highly mobile. There were no reliable written records of their numbers or characteristics. Their precarious economic position and illegal immigration status intensified their mistrust of individuals not personally known or vouched-for. To obtain agreement to an interview, much less to ensure its being given, and to get full, honest responses to politically and personally sensitive questions required considerable groundwork.

Most important to this end was my use of personal recommendations and connections to establish contact in each case. I had the good fortune, for the 1986–87 interviews, to secure the assistance of a reliable and well-connected intermediary. Sabino Lopez had been a farm laborer in the region for years and was, when I hired him, a community outreach worker for California Rural Legal Assistance, a legal services law firm in Salinas. His help was invaluable. Drawing on his personal acquaintances and on contacts developed over years of community outreach work, Sabino generated an extensive list of potential interviewees. Meanwhile, I asked members of the farm worker cooperatives for the names of friends, relatives, and acquaintances who performed field labor in the industry. I also recruited interviewees during ranch visits, then returned later to explain the project and secure an agreement to an interview.

I categorized each individual according to gender, the employing farm size and location, the employer's ethnicity, and the individual's role in the labor process (wage-paid field laborer, sharecropper, supervisor, or other employee). With an eye to proportional representation along these axes, I selected a pool of potential interviewees. To increase the breadth and reliability of response, I chose not to contact workers through their employers and not to conduct interviews on the job. I made every effort to ensure privacy and anonymity to interviewees. No two individuals from the same nuclear family were interviewed, and every attempt was made to diversify representation of kinship and acquaintance networks. Each interview was preceded by at least two contacts: one to explain the project and obtain agreement to participate, another to reconfirm the time and place of the interview. Since most workers lacked telephones, preinterview contacts were almost always made in person. All worker interviews were conducted in Spanish.

The fieldwork for this project evoked strains and required precautions not associated with more distant methodologies. Because we qualitative fieldworkers are directly involved in our fields of study, our own roles and perceptual leanings can color the interpretation and even the reality of our findings. Recognizing this possibility, I did my best to identify, understand, and mitigate my own impact. I approached the field as a genuinely interested (and, some interviewees commented, unexpectedly informed) student of my subjects' lives, a topic about which they were the undisputed experts. I presented myself as an agricultural anthropologist, a university researcher interested in the social aspects of agricultural change. I explained that I was studying postwar changes in the industry and wanted to understand them from the points of view of farmers as well as of farm workers. I dressed in the attire typical of the agricultural extension agents and production scientists with whom many were familiar: khaki or blue cotton trousers, heavy-soled shoes, a plaid shirt, often a duck-billed cap, and a heavy sweater or jacket to fend off the morning chill.

As an Anglo professor, I was an anomaly in the world of my subjects. There was no question of my passing as a farm worker, although I was familiar with aspects of their backgrounds through my travels and training as a Latin American anthropologist and my doctoral dissertation fieldwork on Mexican farm workers in the Midwest. Nor could I pass as a grower, although I felt a strong resonance with their world from my youth spent in a farming community in the Pacific Northwest, from my appetite for physical work developed in the process of building a log cabin with my family, and from my enthusiasm (or as one friend puts it, ferocity) for gardening. My subjects found me hard to place because I was a woman interested in topics that both growers and workers saw as "male": politics and economics. Rather than reducing my opportunities to learn about the industry, though, I think that my atypicality expanded them. Because I was an Anglo, farm workers tended to grant me more freedom of movement and expression than was customarily accorded to Mexican women in the same settings. Because I was assumed to be ignorant of the economics, politics, and technicalities of production agriculture, my subjects took special care to explain them to me. They discussed controversial aspects of the industry with a candor that was both unexpected and notably absent in the public conversations I observed in a variety of contexts. Though it is impossible to unravel all the components of trust in ethnographic field situations, I believe that my gender and outsider status, which reinforced the perception that I had no vested interest in local controversies, were contributing factors.

If my gender conferred some advantages, it imposed some limits as well. I was not entirely exempt from Mexican cultural restrictions on the behavior of women. During the cooperative research, a number of older women advised me in a motherly manner about measures I could take to protect my reputation. Interviews required my presence in contexts that farm workers considered inappropriate for a respectable woman: conversing alone with men in fields, in apartments and old houses, and in remote labor camps. Whenever possible, I encouraged wives or children to accompany me during conversations with male farm workers. As I built close friendships and acquaintanceships with worker and cooperative member families, and as I developed a reputation of dignity within certain circles of the regional farm worker community, I found that supportive gossip helped dispel concerns of impropriety. It was impossible to avoid all strain, however. Several times I found myself in gatherings where the profanity used by one man would spur another to protect my honor. These exchanges—two of them in the field and one in a bar—started with verbal challenges but could have progressed to physical violence. In such contexts I could not win. If I permitted my "protection," I lost my ability to maintain connections with all parties in the field. If I protested that I was not offended, my honor was cast in question. In such cases, I chose to make my farewells quickly and quietly.

The aid of a male research assistant from spring 1986 through spring 1987 was invaluable in this regard. Bruce Zanin was a former Peace Corps volunteer with a master's degree in agricultural economics and international agricultural development. Bruce contributed an insightful economist's eye to the construction of the interview schedules. He was an enthusiastic, talented, and tireless partner in the 1986–87 interviews. He provided me with a "respectable" escort and helped me assess possible gender bias in the data we received. As a matter of propriety and to encourage openness on family matters, I interviewed all the women workers, except in the case of one fairly acculturated young woman. Since there were more men in our sample, as in the strawberry labor force itself, we both interviewed men. I conducted all interviews with Japanese growers myself, because I was most familiar with their local history and cultural backgrounds. We both interviewed Mexican and Anglo growers.

We traveled to most worker interview sites together in a van. One of us would conduct an interview in the van; the other would interview in the residence, which was usually too small and crowded to accommodate more than one private conversation at once. Although my interviews were considerably longer, we observed no significant gender bias in the information we received. Young men did go into more enthusiastic detail with Bruce about their close scrapes with the Border Patrol and their illicit strategies for filling berry crates rapidly. I heard more from all workers about the personal strains of life north of the border. Gender also affected demeanor: workers gave me the limp handshake reserved for women, whereas Bruce often got a vigorous version of the Brown Power grip.

I find it interesting to reflect on the discrepancy between how hard I thought it would be to get information about farm labor and how much cooperation and information I actually received. Before I began the 1986–87 interviews, university colleagues warned me that most growers and workers would be too busy and mistrustful to talk with me. Any workers who did talk, these doubters predicted, would not give more than an hour and would most certainly not discuss labor. In point of fact, only two growers and a handful of workers refused interviews. Although over half of the questions dealt with labor, the length and depth of the responses far exceeded my expectations. I attribute some of this bounty to my gender, but my personal demeanor, my subjects' generosity, and the fact that I established interpersonal networks of recommendation probably also helped. In fact, I was disarmed to find that many of my subjects thanked *me* heartily after the interview. It is clear to me that the qualitative fieldworker's form of bearing witness—that of being a genuinely interested audience to our subjects' lives—may indeed be the main gift we have to offer.

I could not close this preface without acknowledging that this endeavor has been personally taxing. In the course of interviews and observations, I found myself empathizing with individuals whose mutual differences and grievances were considerable and legitimate. I struggled with feelings of disloyalty, sometimes with a desire to mute facets of the situation that cast unfavorable light on one participant or another. At times I longed for the comparatively removed and apparently less stressful modes of investigation to which my early graduate training in history and Latin American anthropology would have led me. At times I wished I had securely ensconced myself on the side of growers or of workers. Yet, in the end, I believe that these strains are major strengths of the study and well worth the effort. I accept that to tell this story in its entirety is to tell a story that will please no one completely.

So many people have helped bring this project to fruition that I cannot possibly do them all justice. To those who make their living from strawberries on the central coast—to growers and workers and the range of individuals who surround and support them, I owe an immense debt for their letting me into their lives. In the field, Bill Alvarado-Greenwood, Marshall

Ganz, Obdulia Hernandez, Steve Huffstutlar, and Sabino Lopez were repeated sources of inspiration and companionship in my efforts to comprehend the big picture. Bruce Zanin was an indefatigable partner in the 1986–87 interviews. Our debriefing runs at the base of the Pajaro Hills are some of my fondest memories of the field. My heartfelt appreciation goes to the various individuals who have provided research assistantship to me over the course of this long process. I am especially indebted to Sharon Blaha, Beverly Lozano, Betsy MacLean, Maureen Plas, Bernadette Tarallo, Sheri Wright, and Aaron Zazueta. At Davis, my colleague and jogging partner Ben Orlove has shared the twists and turns of this project twice a week for nigh on fifteen years. His patience and intellectual inspiration are woven into this book. I am grateful, too, for thoughtful exchanges over the years with Peggy Barlett, Arnold Bauer, Michael Burawoy, Gary Hamilton, Daniel Mountjoy, Arnold Strickon, Stefano Varese, Don Villarejo, and John Walton. Jeffrey Escoffier's encouragement and editorial assistance were invaluable in helping me develop the ideas and delivery of the book. Jane Adams, William Boyd, Bill Friedland, Craig Jenkins, Jack Kirby, Beverly Lozano, James McCarthy, Bob Thomas, Michael Watts, and an anonymous reviewer from Cornell University Press did me the tremendous favor of reading the entire manuscript and giving me detailed and challenging comments. I was fortunate to receive financial support for this project from the Agricultural Experiment Station of the University of California at Davis, which gave me faculty research grants each year, from the National Science Foundation, whose Sociology and Anthropology Programs jointly funded my research from June 1986 through June 1989, and from the Ford Foundation, which funded it from September 1986 through December 1989. I especially want to thank Peter Agree and Roger Sanjek, my editors at Cornell University Press, for their sage advice and unwavering enthusiasm for this project. I feel fortunate, indeed, to have received Roger's incisive suggestions on the final polishing of the manuscript. Finally, I am deeply grateful to my family: to my parents and brother for their support; to Krista and Andrea, for their interest and generous acceptance of my absorption in this project; and to my husband, Michael, whose belief in me and the book has often outweighed my own.

MIRIAM J. WELLS

Davis, California

Strawberry Fields

The Salinas Valley is in Northern California. It is a long narrow swale between two ranges of mountains, and the Salinas River winds and twists up the center until it falls at last into Monterey Bay.

I remember my childhood names for grasses and secret flowers. I remember where a toad may live and what time the birds awaken in the summer—and what trees and seasons smelled like—how people looked and walked and smelled even. The memory of odors is very rich.

I remember that the Gabilan Mountains to the east of the valley were light gay mountains full of sun and loveliness and a kind of invitation, so that you wanted to climb into their warm foothills almost as you want to climb into the lap of a beloved mother. They were beckoning mountains with a brown grass love. The Santa Lucias stood up against the sky to the west and kept the valley from the open sea, and they were dark and brooding—unfriendly and dangerous. I always found in myself a dread of west and a love of east. Where I ever got such an idea I cannot say, unless it could be that the morning came over the peaks of the Gabilans and the night drifted back from the ridges of the Santa Lucias. It may be that the birth and death of the day had some part in my feeling about the two ranges of mountains.

—John Steinbeck, *East of Eden,* 1952

[1]

Class Relations and the Organization of Work

I spent well over a decade studying class relations in California's central coast strawberry industry. Most mornings in the field found me on the road by seven o'clock, driving from the small trailer in the North Monterey Hills where I most often stayed, to the farm, office, or home where I was to conduct my first interview or field observation. Often, on those morning drives, I was struck by the contrasts of the Salinas Valley—its legendary productivity, the promise of its morning light, and the rugged, precarious course of the lives that are lived out in it. A sense of sanctuary enveloped those early hours, as wisps and billows of ocean fog sealed the valley off from the outside world. But as the fog burned off in late morning, it revealed line after wavering line of dusty, stoop-backed workers tending row upon row of lettuce, broccoli, and strawberries. Clearly, the nurture promised by the first light of day did not embrace the lives of those who tilled the soil. Or perhaps their toil was one realization of that early promise: the nurture of product, rather than process; the generation of an income greater than possible in their Mexican homeland, earned at the cost of back-breaking labor. Despite this apparent disparity for the first few hours of each day, the Salinas Valley felt like the promised land—a place where seekers would be led toward the fulfillment of their dreams.

Not only workers' dreams were at stake, I came to learn. Growers, too, invested their sweat in the harvest. Berry growers were not the absentee owners of huge "factories in the field"—to use Carey McWilliams's memorable characterization of California agriculture ([1935] 1971). Indeed, their farms were relatively small. Most rose with their workers and spent their days in the fields. Most came from immigrant stock themselves—Japanese,

European, and Mexican. Strawberry farming was their shot at the American dream. It was the joining of the paths of growers and workers, as they came together in the process of producing strawberries, which became the subject of my study.

I first went into the field in 1976, inspired by sociologists' renewed interest in capitalist labor processes and by historians' fine-grained explorations of workers' worlds and sources of resistance.[1] Virtually all of these early studies, I observed, neglected agricultural workers and work. Most wrote from one side or the other of the labor-capital relationship, slighting the other and the relations between them. With this project, I hoped to bring agriculture into the evolving debates about capitalist labor processes. I wanted to do so in a way that linked the worlds of the two classes. The terrain for my inquiry was the state of California, where capitalist agriculture has reached a developmental apex. California has one of the most technologically sophisticated, productive, and concentrated agricultural systems in the world. In many ways, its dominant agricultural pattern approximates the conditions of industrial capitalism. Here, the historical base of Spanish land-grant holdings and sustained surpluses of cheap immigrant labor have fostered large factorylike farms that are highly seasonal in labor demand and unprotected in labor use. Historically, scholars have portrayed the California harvest labor market as archetypically unstructured and competitive, with production relations that are particularly distant and impersonal and workers who are unskilled, undifferentiated, and dispensable (Burawoy 1976; Doeringer and Piore 1971; Fisher 1953; Fuller 1939; McWilliams [1935] 1971). In short, given its characteristics and portrayal, California may be the premier place to study agricultural labor processes in advanced capitalism.

Two early, unexpected empirical discoveries challenged my preconceptions and stimulated the reformulations that led to this book. My reading led me to anticipate two features of the economic system I had come to study. First, I expected wage labor to be the organizational form through which farm work would be accomplished. Second, I expected workers' resistance to be negligible, except among skilled workers and in situations where the newly ascendant United Farm Workers union was involved. Neither expectation was borne out. First, instead of the rationalized and impersonal system of mobile wage labor generally anticipated under capi-

[1] E. P. Thompson ([1963] 1966, 1967, 1971, 1975) and Harry Braverman (1974) initially inspired my interest. The works of Aminzade (1981, 1984), Burawoy (1979, 1985), Friedman (1977), Gordon, Edwards, and Reich (1982), Hobsbawm (1964, 1984), Montgomery (1979, 1987), Piore and Sabel (1984), Sabel ([1982] 1985), Scott (1985), and Tilly (1978) have provided fuel and helped me refine my analysis.

talism and widely portrayed in California agriculture, I found that a substantial and growing proportion of the strawberry crop was produced by sharecroppers. Instead of hiring crews of laborers who were paid a piece-rate wage, growers delegated planting, maintenance, and harvest to families who were paid a share of the market returns. Although sharecropping had been common in this industry before World War II, it virtually disappeared thereafter, as berry farming matured into a highly profitable business and crews of Mexican wage laborers were hired to bring in the crop. After the mid-1960s, however, many growers switched back to sharecropping. By the mid-1970s, when I came on the scene, about half of the acreage and the producers in the two-county region were involved in sharecropping. As my tenure in the field stretched into the early 1980s, the tide turned again and, by the end of the decade, only about 10 to 20 percent of the regional acreage was sharecropped.

Second, instead of the impotence the literature had led me to expect of unskilled workers, and in spite of the virtual absence of union contracts in the industry, I found that wage workers often intervened to shape the rewards and terms of their labor. For the most part, to be sure, their interventions did not take the form of extended strikes, picketing, or other grand gestures of polarization. Their opposition was usually more brief and hidden, couched in efforts at reconciliation. Nonetheless, at certain predictable points in each season and to varying degrees in different parts of the region, workers intervened to correct felt injustices in their relationships of employment.

These two unanticipated findings started me on the path to this book. The journey has taken me far beyond the explication of two perplexing developments in a minor segment of the agricultural economy: it has led me to challenge some of the most widely held assumptions regarding the causes and forms of economic development. Most important, it has led me to a new appreciation of the role of political forces in economic relationships, and it has deepened my understanding of the complexity underlying hegemonic economic patterns. Before I go further with this argument, however, let me explain why my initial discoveries surprised me.

The Organization of Capitalist Enterprise: Wage Labor vs. Sharecropping

Traditional economic theories saw sharecropping as inefficient and likely to disappear in advanced capitalism. Classical economists based this expectation on the incentive effects of share contracts (Marshall [1890] 1964;

Mill [1848] 1915; Smith [1869] 1937). John Stuart Mill argued that the share tenant "has less motive to exertion than the peasant proprietor since only half the fruits of his industry, instead of the whole, are his own" ([1848] 1915:22). Alfred Marshall thought that sharecroppers would thus tend to underinvest labor: "For, when the cultivator has to give his landlord half of the returns to each dose of capital and labor that he applies to the land, it will not be to his interest to apply any doses the total return to which is less than twice enough to reward him" ([1890] 1964:535–36). By the same token, he thought, landlords will underinvest capital.

Similarly, Marx and Lenin saw sharecropping as distinctly "precapitalist." They based this belief, however, not on a conceptual analysis of the incentive effects of share contracts, but on their empirical study of the transition from feudalism to capitalism in Europe. To them, sharecropping was a transitional economic form linking the closed, backward "natural economy" of feudalism with the competitive, efficient, market economy of capitalism (Lenin [1899] 1956); Marx [1894] 1977). Because European sharecroppers controlled the tools and methods of production and were constrained by attachment to a subsistence plot of land and personal dependence on a landowner, sharecropping prevented the mobility of labor and its separation from the means of production, which Marx and Lenin thought were required by capitalism. Lenin argued that production techniques in such systems are stagnant, because they are in the hands of "small peasants crushed by poverty and degraded by personal dependence and ignorance" ([1899] 1956:192). As a result, both authors expected sharecropping to disappear, because its low productivity could not compete with that of capitalist firms and its exploitation would convert peasants into farm laborers (Lenin [1899] 1956:202, 207–13; Marx [1894] 1977:3:802–13). Marx expressed his conviction of its incompatibility with capitalism in no uncertain terms: where sharecropping persists, he declared, it "is a mere tradition carried over from an obsolete mode of production and managing to prolong its existence as a survival. Its contradiction to the capitalist mode of production is shown by its disappearance . . . and its being forcibly shaken off as an anachronism" ([1894] 1977:3:789). This argument has been applied to other regions and periods as well.[2]

In sum, both traditional Marxist and classical economists believed that sharecropping would give way to direct rent and free markets in wage

[2]For example, in his analysis of sharecropping in Peru, Jose Mariategui argues that it "is a kind of servitude in politically and economically backward villages that has prolonged feudalism into our capitalist age" ([1927] 1974:63). Similarly, Harriet Friedmann argues that sharecropping is a form of precapitalist rent that survives where product and factor markets are undeveloped (1980:178).

labor. As capitalism developed, they predicted, labor would be loosed from its social moorings and replaced by more "rational" instrumental links of superordination and subordination. At the same time, workers' realms of skill and autonomy would be constricted to increase profits and control over labor. According to Marx, this process would affect class dynamics: as the objective rights and obligations of capitalists and laborers diverged, class structures would become increasingly simplified, and class relations would become progressively oppositional ([1867] 1977:vol.1).

The resurgence and subsequent decline of strawberry sharecropping, then, challenged these unilinear notions of development. Instead of a steady increase in wage labor, this industry witnessed a return to sharecropping after years of profitably employing wage workers. Instead of increasingly impersonal employment relations and reduced worker autonomy, it witnessed a broadening of labor providers' realms of control and a reintroduction of production relations based on personal connection. Finally, instead of increasingly simple and bipolar class dynamics, class structure and relations became more fragmented and complex. In essence, sharecropping created an intermediate category of direct producer which shared some of the prerogatives and interests of capital, and some of the dependency and concerns of labor. How was I to explain this development?

The Bases of Labor Resistance

My second unanticipated discovery had to do with the extent and sources of labor resistance and control. On the whole, the sociological and historical literature on work has emphasized the individual worker's skill-based essentiality at the point of production and the unionized workforce's collective vision, actions, and contracts with management as the major sources of workers' leverage (Braverman 1974; Edwards 1979; Friedman 1977; Gordon, Edwards, and Reich 1982; Haydu 1988; Littler 1982; Littler and Salaman 1984; Montgomery 1979, 1987; Wood 1983). The emphasis on skill is rooted in Marx's notion that a person's role in the productive process determines his or her power in the employment relationship. Thus while wage workers are fundamentally disempowered because they do not own the means of production, they do have some (and varying) degrees of potency if they command the specialized knowledge and abilities associated with skill. Much of the work stimulated by—and including—Harry Braverman's recent reconsideration of capitalist labor processes, as well as that encompassed by the "new social history," is concerned with the impact of workers' skill on their power at work (Braverman 1974; Brighton 1977;

Montgomery 1979, 1987; Zimbalist 1979). Whereas skill is seen as the major source of individual worker's leverage, work-based organizations—primarily unions but also associations such as guilds—are considered the major basis for their collective influence (Burawoy 1979; Clawson 1980; Dawley 1976; Edwards 1979; Foster 1974; Friedman 1977; Gordon, Edwards, and Reich 1982; Gutman [1966] 1977; Haydu 1988; Hobsbawm 1964, 1984; Littler 1982; Littler and Salaman 1984; Montgomery 1979, 1987; Wood 1983). Although some theorists examine the roles of wider societal institutions and associations (Dawley 1976; Gutman 1977; Thompson [1963] 1966), most emphasize the power accorded workers by their skill and organizations on the job.

Farm workers received short shrift in traditional labor studies, most of which examined skilled workers in the industrial core of the economy.[3] Agricultural workers were assumed by implication or explicit characterization to be unskilled, poorly organized, and relatively powerless (Friedman 1977; Edwards 1979). Yet the circumstances of farm labor in California have changed substantially in recent decades, altering many of the conditions thought to undermine the power of farm workers. In the late 1960s, the most powerful agricultural labor union in the nation's history, the United Farm Workers, built a labor-citizen alliance that won major contract victories in the California grape industry. In 1970 it turned its attention to the central coast, and throughout that decade labor relations in the region were embattled. Even allowing for the intensification of union mobilization in the state and its focus on the central coast, however, I still could not account for the resistance I encountered: workers in the California strawberry industry were neither skilled nor protected by union membership or contract. How, then, was I to explain the existence, efficacy, and—what is more—unevenness of resistance by relatively unskilled, nonunionized workers?

The Political Economy of Workplace Change

In the chapters to come, I argue that the politicization of economic relationships has transformed the forms, contexts, and outcomes of work-based class struggles in this industry, rendering an apparently precapitalist production form of renewed advantage to capitalist producers. The result is a restructuring of capitalist enterprise, due not only to the influence of political pressures, but also to the nature of the industry and locality.

[3]Such works as Friedland and Barton 1975, Friedland, Barton, and Thomas 1981, and Thomas 1985 are important exceptions to this tendency.

With regard to economic restructuring, I suggest that this readoption of sharecropping was a response to the changing political context of production: to a shift in border policy, an increase in union mobilization, and an extension of protective labor laws to seasonal farm workers. These changes altered the regional balance of power between strawberry growers and workers, motivating the reintroduction of an allegedly outmoded form of production. The "atavism" of this economic restructuring was only apparent, however. Not only are empirical forms of sharecropping highly diverse in general, but this particular form differed in important ways from those critiqued by Marx and Mill. I hope to show that the causes and functions of strawberry sharecropping were fully contemporary. It was one permutation of a wider process that is reconfiguring the national and global economies—the pervasive trend toward the apparent downsizing of firms and the distancing and casualizing of employment relations. This trend has increased the relative proportion of contractors and subcontractors, leased, temporary, and part-time employees, and small entrepreneurs—workers who generally lack job security and fall outside the protective laws of the state. Currently, these sorts of jobs may engage as many as 25 percent of U.S. workers (Berch 1985; Callaghan and Hartmann 1992; Dillon 1987). This development is widely attributed to such economic factors as increasing global competition, floating interest rates, and rising raw material and labor costs (Harvey 1989; Piore and Sabel 1984), but I maintain that in certain cases locally experienced political pressures may be as, or more, determinant.

With regard to workers' resistance, meanwhile, the emphasis on skill and unionization presents an overly simplistic view of the objective sources of strawberry workers' power, and it neglects the important matter of the subjective construction of protest. I show that the political construction of the regional labor market was the major regional determinant of workers' leverage, but that the industry and locality created spatial and temporal variance in their ability and willingness to resist. That is, over the course of each year, the strawberry production cycle engendered seasonal shifts in the balance of workplace power and seasonal crises in the legitimacy of employment relationships. Workers' responses to these swings, however, and to the changes in their leverage in the labor market, depended strongly on the immediate interpersonal, communal, and cultural contexts in which they operated. In this case, strawberry growing was localized in three microregions, which had differing historically evolved conventions regarding the issue of workplace justice. These microregional systems, which I call the "local organization of production," filtered the impact of regional political pressures and shaped workers' perceptions of and responses to injustice.

Politics and the World of Work

The argument developed here challenges the overly schematic, economistic, and deterministic perspective that guides much of the research on work (Braverman 1974; Brighton 1977; Burawoy 1979; to a lesser extent Edwards 1979; Edwards, Reich, and Gordon 1975; Friedman 1977; Gordon, Edwards, and Reich 1982; Montgomery 1979; Zimbalist 1979). Reflecting the influence of Marx's early claim that only economic relations are objective when it comes to class struggles ([1867] 1977), this latter approach represents economic structure as the primary determinant of class struggles and workplace change, the point of production as the terrain in which workplace contests are determined and played out, and the evolution of capitalist production systems as largely uniform and unilinear. From this point of view, the vector of causality leads outward from the structure of the capitalist firm, establishing the shape and broader rhythms of politics, social relations, ideologies, and even the national and international economies.

Without denying that these studies have furthered our understanding and while acknowledging the important modifications made by some, I believe the insistence on production-based causality mischaracterizes the contemporary transformations of work. It not only impedes explanation of the diverse ways in which economic systems evolve, but—especially in the case of the more schematic of these analyses (e.g., Braverman 1974; Edwards, Reich, and Gordon 1975)—it underestimates the impact of sociopolitical influences on work. "Capitalist" firms tend to be treated generically in these studies, aside from the minimal elaboration provided by the core-periphery sectoral distinction. As a result, we develop little insight into other sorts of differentiation within or between economic sectors. Even where core-periphery disjunctures are acknowledged, they tend to devolve into bifurcated unilinear predictions, hampering explication of fluctuations and reversals in form within each sector. Moreover, because these studies focus on the broad structural transformations of economic systems, we gain little sense of how capitalists and laborers might actually engage, and potentially transform, such structures. Indeed, certain macrostructural trends in work organization and class relations would appear to be universal. These studies also obscure the impact of politics. Because they treat workers and owners primarily in terms of their positions in the productive process, they isolate work from the totality of class experience. They do not inform us about the full range of institutions and processes that determine the relative leverage and interests of laborers and capitalists. We are far removed from work as they experience it: from how each class actually perceives its goals and alternatives, from how the interests and resources of different segments of capital and different populations of workers might vary, and from how—or whether—sociopolitical factors might intervene to shape the relations between them. Finally, we have little insight into the evolving interplay between social structure and human agency—into the ways that sociopolitical as well as economic structures might permit and constrain individual action, and into the ways that individuals' initiatives might reciprocally shape the structures that surround them.

In this book, I develop an alternative approach to the study of class mobilization and labor process change which also has roots in the Marxist tradition. This approach acknowledges the significance of civil society and the state, and it portrays the process of economic development as inherently uneven (Gramsci 1971; Kautsky [1899] 1989; Poulantzas [1974] 1979; Trotsky [1932] 1937). It reinforces the accumulating historical evidence that ideology, politics, and communal values and organization have long shaped the relations of production.[4] It also benefits from the "new political economy of agriculture" (Friedland et al. 1991), especially studies conducted by William Friedland, Amy Barton, and Robert Thomas on the California-Arizona lettuce and tomato industries (Friedland and Barton 1975; Friedland, Barton, and Thomas 1981; Thomas 1985). Because these works treat a time period and region that overlap with the present study, they offer fruitful material for the comparative analysis of agricultural commodity systems.

My argument builds on the work of Michael Burawoy, who has entered the most important and far-reaching critique of economism in the labor process literature to date (1985). Burawoy argues that different stages of capitalist development encourage different forms of state intervention, which in turn impose different kinds of regulatory pressures on class struggles at work. Burawoy's analysis significantly challenges the facile separation between economic base and sociopolitical superstructure, and it provides a useful comparative framework for relating the two in different times and places. Burawoy is most concerned, however, with the broad structural transformations of political-economic systems, and he does not inform us sufficiently about the actual relations between economy and society. To put it another way, although he argues persuasively *that* politics make a difference, he does not show us exactly *how* they make a difference: how they impinge on the point of production and how they affect the con-

[4]See, for example, Aminzade 1981, 1984; Bulmer 1975; Clawson 1980; Dawley 1976; Foster 1974; Gutman 1977; Hahn and Prude 1985; Hobsbawm 1964, 1984; and Thompson [1963] 1966, 1967, 1971, 1975.

crete processes of class formation, class struggle, and labor process change. Nor do we see how struggles arising from the workplace might in turn shape political constraints. Burawoy acknowledges that state apparatuses and production organizations evolve in a contingent manner, but he does not specify the systematic sources of contingency or of uneven economic development. Moreover, because he concentrates on employment in the industrial core of the economy, he leaves us with underpoliticized and undifferentiated notions of work in the periphery.

My central objective in this book is to rethink the relationship between economy and society. If we want to explain changes in the organization and relations of production in advanced capitalist societies, I believe, we must examine the crucial roles played by political structures and conflicts. Although such influences have been widely treated as "outside" the fundamental dynamics of economic systems, in fact they have long structured workplace activity in the United States and elsewhere. They have grown in consequence, moreover, as capitalism has been consolidated over the course of the twentieth century: governments have become increasingly involved in guaranteeing the profitability of capitalist enterprise and in regulating and muting its discontents. This politicization of workplace relations means that two realms that are generally considered in isolation—the economic and the political—must be examined as interconnected. It means as well that prevalent assumptions about the primacy of economic influences must be challenged and the reciprocal impacts of the two explored.

To understand the dynamics of class relations at work, then, we must challenge the ontological priority of economic events. We must be more catholic in the range of influences we acknowledge and less fixed in our expectations of the forms that socioeconomic systems will assume. Our inquiries must delve below the level of structural abstraction but reach above the level of daily action. Although economic forces must retain a central role in our analyses, we must broaden our notions of the inherent tendencies of capitalist economic structure, including the pulls toward opposition and conflict generated by workers' and owners' diverging interests in the quality of work and the disposition of surplus value, as well as the pulls toward cooperation and compliance generated by workers' dependence on their jobs and owners' interest in workers' effort. Even more to the point, economic forces must take their place in the minds of scholars beside the other influences on daily life. Social classes and their relations do not unfold mechanically from places and tensions within the system of production: these structural forces are only part of the contexts in which actors coalesce their intentions and their alternatives. As a result, we cannot anticipate the transformations of economic systems or the contributions of each class to constructing those changes from the inherent dynamics of capitalism alone.

We must also bring work and politics closer. It is not enough to study the two abstractly or from afar—for example, by charting the different types of political regimes that regulate production (Burawoy 1985) or the different developmental stages through which economies evolve (Braverman 1974; Edwards 1979; Gordon, Edwards, and Reich 1982). We must also look at how political structures and conflicts permeate daily work life, how they affect the options, perceptions, and initiatives of class actors in certain industries and localities. We cannot assume that political structures and statuses are generated by economic power relations, as do instrumental Marxists, or "produced external to participation in economic organizations," as do some proponents of substantial relative autonomy (Thomas 1985:27). Rather, we must explore the ways economic and political systems shape one other and how people acting at the local level reciprocally shape the structures around them.[5]

In this book, I explore the bases of class mobilization and labor process change in California's central coast strawberry industry.[6] I am particularly concerned with the conditions underlying workers' tendencies to challenge the terms set down by employers and owners' tendencies to reconfigure employment relationships to increase their control over labor. I will show that the initiatives of both vary in form and intensity in ways not attributable to a constant economic structure. This variance has to do not only with localized differences in the forces constraining their capacities and opportunities to mobilize, but also with differences in the factors shaping their willingness to do so. Although random individual variability is not a problem for systematic analysis, patterned variability that distinguishes different groups *is* consequential, because it affects the broad contours of change. I show that in this case, as in others (Moore 1978; Sabel [1982] 1985; Scott 1985), workers' opposition was not an inevitable response to the existence of what an observer might call injustice. Instead, it involved their subjective processing of objective facts in light of the aspirations and notions of workplace justice they brought to and developed in their work, and in terms of locally available alternatives and potentials for success. Nor

[5]Though Thomas expresses interest in showing how labor processes and social institutions "structure one another," in practice he emphasizes the ways that the labor process is influenced by "social relations and social processes external to it" (1985:9), especially the ways that managers utilize such processes, rather than the ways they are used by workers.

[6]I began to develop my analysis of the politicization of strawberry labor processes in the early 1980s. See Wells 1981, 1984a, 1984b, 1987a, 1987b, 1990, 1991 for earlier and partial articulations of the argument developed in this book.

are all capitalists equivalent. Producers in different industries and in different regional sectors of the same industry vary in the economic and social challenges they experience and in the means available to them to increase profitability. Even producers in the same industry and region may diverge in backgrounds, values, and goals. The economic "meaning" and utility of political statuses, statutes, and institutions may therefore vary considerably.

The Approach

This book explores the relationship among political pressures, economic organization, and class relations in agriculture. Its focus is on class struggle at work—its determinants as well as its outcomes. Although the study is grounded in the intensive exploration of a single case, the central coast California strawberry industry in the post–World War II period, its aim is to inform and refine broad theories of social change. My inquiry reflects a particular theoretical base: I proceed from the belief that class relations are structurally influenced but not structurally determined—that they are hammered out in the interactions between social classes in concrete historical contexts. It is, I contend, through the analysis of such contexts—their limits and their variations—that the preceding paradoxes can best be unraveled and our conceptions of the laws of social change advanced.

Here I combine purposive, actor-oriented models that focus on the immediate interests, costs, and rewards of individuals with Marxist structural models that focus on the interests of various classes and the transformations of economic systems. I am particularly concerned with the balance of power between farmers and farm workers, that is, with the conditions under which labor has an opening and the ways in which the bargain with capital can be struck differently. Empirically, I relate the circumstances in which strawberry growers and workers have found themselves in the postwar period to the large-scale changes of twentieth-century capitalism. The microlevel focus provides insight into the alternatives actually available to and desired by participants. The macrolevel location relates localized struggles to wider societal trends. In this case, the broad structural development that has most affected local actors is the expansion of the capitalist state, which has increased its involvement in the relations between economic actors.

In this book, I conceive of social classes as formed in the process of struggle. I hold that their concomitantly economic, sociopolitical, and ideological context as a whole defines the realm of possibilities and constraints for class choices at any moment in time (Przeworski 1985). The realm of politics, as I refer to it here, is the arena of struggles over the distribution of public resources. It includes the interest groups, institutions, and policies involved in establishing that distribution. It refers not simply to a certain allocation of benefits and costs in society or to certain relations of domination and subordination, but to the legitimation of these social arrangements in the eyes of the state and to the elaboration of regulations and institutions that implement this vision of social justice. In practice, politics defines the societally legitimate terms for the relations of production. It involves contests over the classification of the participants in production and over the prerogatives and limitations attached to each category. This definition of politics differs intentionally from those that view all struggles surrounding relations of structured domination as political, without regard to the kinds of resources they mobilize or to the legitimation of the right to those resources in the eyes of the state (Burawoy 1985:253). Equating politics with struggle is useful for certain purposes, but it does not attend to the origins of class resources or the terrains of class contests—concerns that are central to this book. My definition distinguishes between class dynamics that mobilize power sources inherent in the production process and those that engage and respond to sociopolitical forces and audiences beyond the point of production. It highlights the differences between struggles waged on the job and those waged in the legislative halls or courts, showing that whereas contests waged in one arena and with reference to one type of resource or audience help establish the terms for those in the other, there are important distinctions between them. Nonetheless, in practice, political and economic forces are thoroughly intertwined, interactive, and inseparable: together they structure the arenas of contest that generate social classes.

This analysis demonstrates that the forms and directions of workplace change are highly contingent and are critically shaped by sociopolitical forces. To explain these causes and processes of contemporary economic restructuring, we must consider the roles of three critical influences beyond the structure of capitalism itself: those of politics, the industry, and the locality. The first of these is the most inclusive and determinant. The second and third are increasingly particular and limited.

The Political Construction of the Labor Market

To acknowledge that the forces shaping class relations are not confined to the point of production is to acknowledge that other arenas of activity may be at least as important in shaping the transformations of work. I hope to demonstrate that, under circumstances familiar to capitalist agriculture, political influences shaping class leverage in the labor market may be more consequential for workplace struggles than are economic power sources inherent in the organization of production. To this end, I relate the evident politicization of California agriculture's production context, engendered by changing border policies, expanded labor protections, and increased union mobilization, to the immediate settings in which growers and workers engage over work. Although economic structure at the level of production provided a necessary substratum for the determination of class power, it was the increased leverage and exchange value of workers in the labor market that enhanced their potency at the point of production and provided the sufficient motivation for labor process change. Not only was labor market power the central determinant of labor process trans- [illegible] cantly shaped by politi- [illegible] se conflict and support [illegible] f workers to assert their [illegible] icroeconomic assump- [illegible] be equalized across the [illegible] t significantly constrain [illegible] wage that represents a [illegible] Even as it reinforces the [illegible] es and structures in eco- [illegible] tion of net advantages [illegible] 50), it recasts theories of labor market segmentation which see [illegible] ces of these divisions as economic (Edwards, Reich, and Gordon 1975; Edwards 1979; Gordon, Edwards, and Reich 1982).

In the ensuing analysis, I refer to the configuration of political constraints on a labor market at any given point in time as a "labor market regime." Such regimes both reflect and affect class interests, resources, and strategies at the level of production. They significantly shape the relative advantage to each class of particular labor processes. Because many class resources are politically established, political definitions, sanctions, and benefits often become the focus of workplace struggles. In the process, class contests may become displaced from the point of production, challenging the broader distribution of social power in the labor market. Through the course of such challenges, political structures, economic organization, and class relations may all be transformed. In short, far from being epiphenomenal, superstructural, or subsidiary to the contests waged on the job, sociopolitical forces are an integral—and sometimes determining—part of such struggles.

The Role of Industry

Although some of the variance in class relations and work organization comes from the different political contexts in which they unfold, industry characteristics also importantly differentiate the wider economy. This level of complexity is neglected by many labor process analysts, who allude generically to the "capitalist firm" and the "capitalist labor process."[7] This book reinforces earlier and recent evidence that the features of particular industries significantly restrict the ways that work can be organized and the social relations that surround it (Blauner 1964; Chandler 1969; Friedland 1984a; Friedland and Barton 1975; Friedland, Barton, and Thomas 1981; Goldberg 1980, 1981; Gouldner 1954; Griffith 1993; Hightower 1972; Hobsbawm 1964; Littler and Salaman 1984; Thomas 1985; Wells 1984a). It shows that commodity characteristics limit the technologies, the division of labor, and the production organization that a firm can employ. Product and product market characteristics affect such matters as the centrality of labor to profits, producers' alternative means of increasing productivity, their desire and ability to rationalize the production process, their interest in workers' cooperation, flexibility, and effort, the advantage to them of autonomy-expanding labor processes, and the longevity and stability of the employment relationship. Albeit some of these features may be viewed as a result of the sectoral involvement of the firm—as in the case of Edwards' analysis of bureaucratic control structures in the economic core and periphery (1979)—I suggest that both industrial and sectoral contrasts are at work.

Industrial production processes also vary in the leverage they accord workers which cannot be reduced to the component of skill. For example, in some industries the dispersed, periodically executed, or otherwise hidden nature of the tasks and the dependence of profits on workers' care and effort can increase the relative power of workers in the production relationship (Yarrow 1979). Agricultural industries vary greatly in this regard because of their dependence on natural processes and the diversity of crop characteristics. As I demonstrate here, industry-specific production processes may also establish crucial temporal junctures at which the legitimacy of authority relations is challenged and at which the relative power of the participants in production shifts. In addition, changes in an industry's

[7]Braverman (1974) and Burawoy (1979), for example, base their generalizations on the study of monopoly sector manufacturing industries and project that the concerns and the sources of power and vulnerability experienced by the participants in production in such firms prevail throughout the economy. Edwards (1979), Gordon, Edwards, and Reich (1982), and Littler and Salaman (1984) inquire into the contrasts in economic capacities and challenges experienced by industries in the core, as opposed to the periphery of the economy, but they do not inquire into industrial differentiation within these sectors.

market conditions, such as intensified product demand, can increase an employer's desire to minimize opposition (Friedman 1977), as can the impossibility of mechanizing or relocating production. The size of the firm and the nature of production tasks affect workers' interactions with each other and with their employers, and thus they affect the social ties among them (Bell and Newby 1975; Lockwood 1975).

Industries may also be differentially affected by world economic swings. We cannot assume that macroeconomic changes will have a uniform impact on an entire national economy or even on one of its segments, for human agency and additional contextual pressures intervene to construct a more varied, contingent pattern. Some industry-based complexity comes from the physical location of the industry. Industries situated in a particular region share risks and opportunities deriving from climatic conditions, from the governmental and social environment, and from the level of grassroots political mobilization and class struggle. Industries vary in their vulnerability to local conditions and in the impact of local pressures on profits. These sorts of industry characteristics can change over time, both constraining and permitting the development of class relations.

The Local Organization of Production

If the political construction of the labor market establishes the overarching balance of class power, and if industry characteristics further shape the options of social classes, the locality establishes a third, and most particular, structure of constraint on class relations at work. This level of complexity is largely ignored by the research on commodity systems or *filieres*—the systems of social, economic, and technical relations that surround the production and marketing of particular commodities (Friedland 1984a; Goldberg 1980, 1981). The literature has generally portrayed growers, workers, and social relations in a system as internally homogeneous. I show, however, that commodity systems may develop internally differentiated "local organizations of production" as class populations, employment opportunities, and production relations become differentially distributed across space and over time. The term "local organization of production" as used here encompasses the dimensions of locality (the climatic, historical, and physical features of certain geographical settings) and of social organization (the localized character of class composition, economic activity, and social relationships). There is nothing necessary about the forms of the local organization of production: they emerge from the conjuncture of contingent processes unfolding in particular locales.

The site of my research, California's central coast, shares a distinctive climate, production season, and array of agricultural producers, regulators, and servicers (e.g., farm supply companies, purveyers of production information, sales agents, processors, government agencies). It also exhibits a characteristic pattern of labor demand and composition and a distinctive structure of labor supply. Significantly, too, since 1970 the region has been the primary focus of agricultural union mobilization. These conditions are consequential because of growers' and workers' longstanding commitment to the region, which is the primary geographic focus for the economic activity of the individuals studied here. In the case of growers, though several farming corporations also have grower members in San Luis Obispo and Santa Barbara Counties to the south, no individual operated in both regions at the time of this study. The families of some growers have farmed berries on the central coast since the turn of the century. Santa Clara and San Benito Counties were part of the Salinas-Watsonville berry-growing nexus before World War II, but since the war urban encroachment on agricultural land and high summer temperatures inland that truncate the harvest have concentrated berry growing on the coast. Most berry growers here operate family farms or are members of family farming corporations. They are deeply embedded in community institutions and relationships. Many industry organizations are based in Santa Cruz and Monterey Counties, and growers interact in a variety of contexts. For the workers studied here, the central coast is familiar terrain as well. Their history with the industry begins after World War II. Many current workers have relatives who picked berries here in the 1950s and 1960s. Most date their direct involvement to the 1970s and after. In this case, as in California agriculture more generally (Gonzalez 1985; Martin 1987, 1988; Massey et al. 1987; Thomas 1985), workers have developed ongoing networks of job acquisition and security that focus on this particular crop and region. Although some pickers range out of the area before and after the harvest, or when they cannot find work, for most, the central coast strawberry industry comprises the centerstone of their livelihoods.

For strawberry growers and workers, the central coast is also an internally differentiated context of activity. Strawberries are grown in three distinct parts of the region: the Salinas Valley, the Pajaro Valley, and the North Monterey Hills. Distinctive segments of the grower and worker populations, forms of economic activity, and patterns of production relations have evolved in these three microregions. For workers, the boundaries between these microregions are semipermeable. That is, movement between them is possible, but more difficult and less common than movement within them. As a result, these contexts vary in ways that permit or even encourage—or alternatively dampen or undermine—class conflict at work. The organization of these localized production environments filters the influence of political constraints, enhancing the impact of some, dissipating the impact of others, and shaping class relations at work.

The ensuing analysis, then, explores the evolving relationship among political pressures, economic organization, and class relations in California's central coast strawberry industry. It attends particularly to the interplay between class relations in the labor process and those in the labor market.

[2]

The California Strawberry Industry and the Centrality of Labor

California's central coast strawberry industry evolved in a period of dramatic macrolevel change. Since World War II, the structure of U.S. agriculture has been transformed, and wide swings in the national and global economies have reconfigured farm labor processes. Yet the impact of macroeconomic change and the reshaping of agricultural systems have not been uniform, and swings in the world economy cannot account for labor process change in this industry. This chapter explores the conditions underlying the exceptional stability of profits in California's central coast strawberry industry despite the instability in the wider system. It shows that worldwide competitive advantages have concentrated market power in the hands of California berry producers, buffering them from the most severe macroeconomic downturns. The organization of the industry has reinforced the economic viability of relatively small scale producers who specialize in strawberries and operate in a single region. At the same time, distinctive features of the commodity, its technologies, and its production processes have restricted the strategic options of growers, with the result that control over harvest labor has become the key to profitability.

The U.S. Farm Economy and World Economic Swings

Scholars have long remarked on the long waves or cycles of capital accumulation that the international economy has exhibited since the Industrial Revolution (Burawoy 1985; Gordon, Edwards, and Reich 1982; Kondratieff

1925; Littler and Salaman 1984; Mandel 1978; Schumpeter 1939). These waves last roughly fifty years and exhibit two phases: one of relatively high profit rates and overall economic expansion, and another of falling profit rates and economic contraction. Some analysts argue that these systemic rhythms of capitalism stimulate changes in labor processes: that when the economy expands, technologies and institutional arrangements such as labor processes that facilitate capital accumulation tend to be consolidated, and that when it contracts, established technologies and markets become saturated, institutions undergirding capital accumulation disintegrate, and research and experimentation are initiated into new technologies and institutions that could improve returns. Whereas the conflicts between labor and capital can often be disguised in expansionary periods, stagnation stimulates employers to squeeze more from their workers, thus surfacing their differences, provoking labor unrest, and necessitating new means of cheapening and controlling labor (Ehrensaft 1980; Gordon, Edwards, and Reich 1982; Kondratieff 1925; Schumpeter 1939).

This argument raises the question of whether labor process shifts on California strawberry farms—from wage labor to sharecropping in the mid-1960s and back to wage labor in the early 1980s—can be attributed to swings in the world economy. Two queries must precede our assessment of this issue: did the contractions and expansions of the world economy coincide temporally with strawberry labor process transformations, and, if they did, were they likely to have been transmitted to the U.S. farm economy in general and to this industry in particular?

First, we must note that the rhythms of the international economy do not mirror those of the U.S. agricultural economy. The world economy entered a growth phase at the start of World War II which lasted through the early 1970s, when it took a sharp downturn that continues into the present. The U.S. farm economy followed the expansive course of the world system until the early 1950s, as the foreign demand created by the military and the domestic demand generated by overall prosperity provided outlets for increasing agricultural production (Buttel 1987; Cochrane 1979; Ehrensaft 1980).[1] Then it began a series of fluctuations that reflect its distinctive response to national and international change. By the mid-1950s, the demand for agricultural commodities generated by World War II, by postwar

[1]This was a period of rapid technological change in agriculture: new and more efficient farm machinery, crop strain hybridization, and intense applications of petrochemical inputs raised productivity and production by one-fourth (Cochrane 1979:128, 137). Agricultural marketing and input systems also matured, and advances in transportation and handling supported an increasingly national and international scope of distribution.

relief, and by the Korean War had faded. Agricultural productivity and production continued to expand, however, generating chronic surpluses and falling profits and prices into the early 1970s (Cochrane 1979:122–49).[2]

At that point, policy shifts and unusual economic conditions increased the demand for U.S. exports, stimulating an upswing in its farm economy that continued into the early 1980s. Contributing factors included policy changes that eliminated the aid-based world food regime of the 1950s and 1960s and made the world and U.S. agricultural economies more vulnerable to market conditions, as well as the world shortfall in oil, seed, and grain production in 1972 and the Russian wheat deal with U.S. producers, which drove down international supply and increased international demand. The world economic contraction also initially fostered global demand for U.S. farm exports, because the movement of First World firms to Third World countries to obtain cheap labor temporarily stimulated Third World economies and enabled them to purchase farm commodities. Moreover, the drop in interest rates and in the value of the U.S. dollar improved the terms on which foreigners could borrow or use cash to purchase U.S. crops. This option was made even more attractive by the Arab oil embargo, which increased the cost of petrochemical inputs (Buttel 1987; Friedmann 1991; McMichael 1994; Frobel 1980).

As a result, world demand, prices, and U.S. farm exports rose substantially over the 1970s, leading optimistic American farmers to expand export production and farm operations. Much of this expansion was accomplished through debt financing, encouraged by inflating farm values and very low real interest rates. Thus U.S. farmer debt almost doubled over the course of the 1970s, despite price drops toward the middle and end of the decade signaling international market saturation and economic instability (Shepard and Collins 1982). In 1981, prices peaked, then plummeted. Between 1981 and 1986, rising debt loads, overcapacity (crop surpluses and declining prices and profits), and the decapitalization of agriculture through declining land and other asset values engendered a crisis among U.S. farmers. The policy environment of the 1970s and 1980s and swings in the world economy contributed to this crisis (Buttel 1987; Leistritz and Murdock 1988). Between 1981 and 1986, U.S. farm export value fell from $44 billion to $26 billion, and the prices of most major commodities also dropped sharply (Petrulis et al. 1987; Runsten et al. 1987:49). Highly leveraged agricultural producers were forced to liquidate their assets. Although

[2]The agricultural downturn of this period was not as severe as it might have been, because of the buoyant world economy and countercyclical government policies (Buttel 1987:7; Friedmann 1991; Wessel 1983).

the 1985 Farm Bill slowed the downslide of land and product prices by substantially reinforcing net farm incomes, the economic condition of many U.S. farmers remained precarious in the late 1980s (Johnson et al. 1987; Leistritz and Ekstrom 1988:93–95; USDA 1986).

In sum, the mid-1960s—when strawberry sharecropping was reintroduced—were not an economic watershed for the U.S. farm economy. These years did not exhibit the sharp shift in profitability expected to stimulate labor process change. Rather, they were the midpoint of a twenty-year gradual downslope. Although the second period of labor process change—the early 1980s—was indeed an era of developing crisis in the national farm economy, that crisis was not shared proportionally by California or its central coast strawberry industry.

The Place of California Agriculture

Swings in the global and national farm economies have encouraged economic rationalization and structural change in U.S. agriculture over the course of the twentieth century (Carter and Johnston 1978; Raup 1985; Rodefeld 1978; Tweeten 1981; USDA 1979). Although California has shared in some of these transformations, in other ways its experience has been unique.

Structural Change

Perhaps the most striking change nationally has been the radical increase in the scale and concentration of production as measured in land area, value of products sold, and fixed capital investment. Within this pattern, the number of small, subcommercial farmers who augment farm incomes with off-farm work has grown, and viable, medium-sized family farms have become a "disappearing middle." The result is a trend toward a more dualistic farm structure (Barlett 1993; Buttel 1987; OTA 1986). This process is especially advanced in California, where agricultural production and sales have long been particularly concentrated and have become even more so since World War II (Fisher 1953; Goldschmidt [1947] 1978; McWilliams [1935] 1971; Villarejo 1980, 1985). Thus the largest 2.5 percent of California farms operate 60 percent of the state's cropland, and net farm incomes are 2.5 times the national average (U.S. Bureau 1984a). In 1987 the 3 percent of California farms with annual gross sales exceeding $1 million accounted for 60 percent of all sales, the 7 percent with annual sales over $500,000 accounted for 74 percent, and the 79 percent with annual sales under $100,000 accounted for only 8 percent (U.S. Bureau 1989:9, Table 2). Workers are concentrated on the largest farms, which are buffered from market swings and local pressures by their expansion to different parts of the nation and world (Hightower 1972; Thomas 1985; Villarejo and Redmond 1988).

The second important change is the differentiation of agricultural production and distribution into separate economic subsystems, with associated changes in the locus of entrepreneurial control. Farm owner-operatorship is declining, while ownership and managerial decisions are increasingly assumed by large firms in the input and output stages (Carter and Johnston 1978; Minden 1970; Vogeler 1982:71). This development is especially advanced in California, where many of the nation's largest farm credit, supply, processing, and marketing companies originated and are based, and where vertical integration between production and marketing is especially marked (Farrell 1987; Villarejo 1980; Fellmeth 1973; Friedland and Barton 1975; Zwerdling 1980).

Despite this increase in scale, concentration, and vertical integration, agricultural product markets remain essentially competitive. Producers are still much more numerous, and production and control are much more dispersed, than they are in the industrial sector of the economy. At the same time, the demand for agricultural products is relatively price- and income-inelastic, product differentiation is minimally available as a means of increasing demand, and producers are generally unable to control input prices or to raise product prices by restricting supply. These conditions are likely to continue because of inherent barriers to the concentration and centralization of capital in agriculture (Buttel 1983, 1987; Mann and Dickinson 1978). Growers' inability to leverage higher prices in competitive product markets or to lower input costs from powerful credit and supply companies increases their interest in productivity-enhancing and cost-reducing technologies.

The third significant change in U.S. agriculture is a growing dependence on technologies that increase productivity and capital intensivity while reducing the amount and requisite skill levels of hand labor (Carter and Johnston 1978). These changes have exerted conflicting pressures on profitability. On the one hand, costly innovations have contributed to indebtedness, farm liquidation, and the concentration of production (Friedland and Barton 1975; Leistritz and Murdock 1988:24–27). On the other hand, they have mitigated the impact of rising input costs by increasing productivity and have helped farmers solve their labor problems by eliminating unruly workers (Cochrane 1979:137, 157; Berardi and Geisler 1984; Friedland and Barton 1975; Runsten et al. 1987:52, 58). Nationally, the result has been a substantial decrease in the total number of agricultural workers, with a particular drop in the amount of family labor (Goss et al. 1979; Albrecht and Murdock 1988:41–43). The technification of agriculture is particularly advanced in California, owing largely to its highly developed and well-funded agricultural research and extension system (*California and* 1986:chap. 3; Carter 1986; Fiske 1979; Padfield and Greenleaf 1985, 1986). New technologies have displaced California farm workers and have changed the way that farm work is done. In processing tomatoes, wine grapes, and lettuce, for example, machine harvesters have eliminated a substantial portion of hand labor. New cultivars and cultural practices have reduced the amount of labor in harvesting, pruning, irrigating, weeding, thinning, and hoeing (Friedland and Barton 1975; Friedland, Barton, and Thomas 1981; Martin 1987; *Technological Change* 1978; Thompson and Scheuring 1978).

Although California follows the national pattern of the decrease in family workers and the elimination of some jobs, it diverges decisively in terms of the decline in hand labor. Whereas total farm employment in the nation has decreased steadily over the past fifty years, in California it has shot upward. Between 1940 and 1982, for example, the number of farm workers in the state increased by 233 percent, while it fell by 68 percent in the nation. California continues to employ more agricultural workers than any other state: about 52 percent of all hired U.S. farm workers are employed in California, and 78 percent of the state's farm work is performed by hired workers, as opposed to about 30 percent for the nation as a whole.[3]

Response to the Farm Crisis

California's relative economic stability during the farm crisis is related to the salience of hand labor. In fact, California's experience of continued vitality is much less unique than commonly thought. Diverse responses to the economic downturn of the 1980s have been masked by the tendency of most studies to use nationwide data and to focus on the Midwest or on producers of capital-intensive commodities that are internationally traded and receive direct federal subsidies (Hardesty 1986; Johnson et al. 1985; Johnson et al. 1986; Jolly et al. 1985; Jolly and Barkema 1985; Leholm et al. 1985; Salant et al. 1986; Watt et al. 1986). Producers of dairy products, wheat, rice, feed grains, cotton, peanuts, tobacco, and sugar beets, for ex-

[3]See, for example, Albrecht and Murdock 1988:42 and U.S. Bureau 1946:vol.1:pt.33:30, table 1; 1984a:vol.1:pt.5:199, table 9; 1984b:pt.5, table F.

Table 1. Change in California agricultural acreage, by use, 1950–82

Type of land	1950	1954	1982	Acreage change 1950–82	Percentage change 1950–82
Fruit and nut acreage	1,470,657	1,322,985	2,158,404	687,747	46.76
Vegetable acreage	537,681	560,116	894,573	356,892	66.38
Cropland	13,765,110	13,229,708	11,257,374	–2,507,736	–18.22
Pasture land	3,350,589	3,018,010	1,344,619	–2,005,970	–59.87
Irrigated cropland	6,438,324	7,048,049	8,460,508	2,022,184	31.41

Sources: U.S. Bureau of the Census, *U.S. Census of Agriculture, 1950* (Washington, D.C.: GPO, 1952), vol.1:pt.33:3, table 3; *1954* (1956), vol.1:pt.33:2, table 1, pp. 107–12, table 9; *1982* (1984), vol.1:pt.5:1, table 1, p. 324, table 28, p. 312, table 27.

ample, were particularly subject to the cost-price squeeze of the 1980s because of their high capital investments in machinery and land, their dependence on falling world prices, and their responsiveness to changes in government price and supply control programs (Gardner and Howitt 1986; Learn and King 1986). Other industries and regions fared differently, however. In fact, most financially stressed farmers in the 1980s were located in the Great Lake States and on the Northern Plains and were engaged in dairy or cash grain production (Leistritz and Murdock 1988). The contrast between their economic condition and that of fruit and vegetable producers is marked: one study found that 20.2 percent of dairy farmers and 13.3 percent of cash grain producers had high debt-to-asset ratios and negative cash flows in 1985, as opposed to only 9.8 percent of fruit and vegetable producers (Leistritz and Ekstrom 1988:88). This pattern is directly linked to the high value of their products. Fruit and vegetable crop farms are more highly leveraged, but they tend also to be financially healthy because they have such high per-acre incomes.

Not surprisingly, California's increasing focus on high-value, labor-intensive fruit and vegetable crops is largely responsible for the vitality of its agricultural sector. Although the state is a major producer of field crops, livestock, and dairy products—commodities sensitive to shifts in world economic conditions and in U.S. farm programs—over half of its gross agricultural income comes from fruits and vegetables (*California Agriculture* 1988; Carter 1986). This emphasis developed particularly after World War II, when it was paralleled and facilitated by the expansion of state and federal irrigation projects (Worster 1985) (see table 1). Some crop industries have expanded especially rapidly: since 1960, grape acreage has increased by 572 percent, broccoli acreage by 275 percent, and avocado acreage by 228 percent (U.S. Bureau 1961:vol.1:pt.4:224, 238, 250, table 11; U.S. Bureau 1989:vol.1:pt.5:342, 358, table 28). Much of the expansion has occurred in regions that previously had little labor-intensive agriculture, as in the case of the avocado trees planted in northern San Diego County and the citrus trees planted on the eastern edge of the San Joaquin Valley. In some instances, labor-intensive commodities have replaced capital-intensive ones: thus, vineyards have replaced wheat farms, and cattle ranches and vegetables have replaced sugar beets, in Santa Barbara, Kern, Ventura, and San Luis Obispo Counties (Haley 1987; Palerm 1984). In other instances, existing labor-intensive acreage has been expanded: Imperial Valley broccoli and cauliflower acreage increased from 500 acres in the early 1970s to 15,000 acres in 1987 (Martin 1987). In yet other instances, new production practices have increased labor needs in already labor-intensive crops, as in the case of vegetable growers who now use greenhouse preplanting and field transplanting to shorten the time that crops are in the field, thus reducing maintenance costs and permitting three annual harvests and a substantial increase in productivity (Palerm 1984:6).

The regional availability of cheap hand labor, along with productivity-enhancing technological changes and sharp increases in other costs, fostered this expansion of specialty crops and buffered the state from the national farm crisis. The rapid increase in nonlabor costs places a premium on crops that use the cheap and plentiful input of hand labor. So advantageous is labor intensivity in the current economic climate that some California growers have actually discontinued mechanical weeding, pruning, and tree harvesting and readopted traditional manual procedures (Palerm 1984:6). At the same time, the high value of fruit and vegetable crops accords their producers an additional edge over growers of field crops. The dimensions of this disparity can be substantial: in 1987, California vegetable farms generated $1,750 per acre in gross cash receipts, while midwestern grain farms only generated $125 (U.S. Bureau 1989:vol.1:pt.5:9, table 2).

Other economic blows of the 1980s fell more lightly on fruit and vegetable producers, as well. Because they do not receive direct government payments, they were minimally affected by decreases in the level of government support to farmers. Because most producers rely heavily on domestic sales, they were relatively protected from declines in world market prices (*California Agriculture* 1988; Farrell 1987:10). This is not to say that decreasing world demand for U.S. exports and increasing foreign competition for U.S. markets are irrelevant to California growers: international markets account for almost one-fourth of farm sales, and foreign imports have seriously eroded California's advantage in some specialty crop industries.[4] Nonetheless, in comparison with other farm commodities, the value of California's specialty crops remained relatively stable during the 1980s (Carter and Nuckton 1987:147–59; *California Agriculture* 1988; Farrell 1987).

Overall, then, the farm crisis was felt in California in a muted and uneven manner. Though financial stress according to some indicators and for some crop industries was severe, for others it was minimal (California Institute 1985; Villarejo 1989). As in the rest of the nation, the years between 1981 and 1986 were the worst: land prices plunged, agricultural lending institutions suffered hundreds of millions of dollars in losses, and between 15 and 25 percent of the state's 50,000 commercial growers went out of business (DePietro 1987; Hall 1989; Richardson 1990; Runsten et al. 1987). Still, farm incomes were much more substantial in California, and fruit and vegetable producers fared best. Between 1950 and 1985, real net farm income declined by 43 percent in the United States as a whole and by 46 percent in the Midwest, but only by 3 percent in California (see figure 2). In the farm crisis year of 1986, California's fruit and vegetable crops actually increased in value by 12.3 percent from the 1985 season, while the value of its field crops fell by 18 percent (*California Agriculture* 1987:4).

The Development of the Industry

The California strawberry industry has fared particularly well in the postwar period. Climatic, technological, and economic advantages have concentrated market power in the hands of California berry producers and have insulated the industry from world economic swings. The strawberry industry is exceptionally endowed with the features that have buffered the state from the national farm crisis—labor intensivity, high per-acre yields, and high crop value. It diverges from statewide structural trends, however, in terms of the smaller scale of its farms and the lesser extent to which off-farm entities directly control production. All in all, industry-specific economic and technological constraints increased berry producers' resilience during the farm crisis while restricting their means of enhancing the rate and stability of capital accumulation.

[4]During the 1980s, for example, California growers of grapes, processing tomatoes, broccoli, and peaches were swamped by inexpensive foreign imports. The passage of NAFTA has seriously alarmed California growers (DePietro 1987:370; Hall 1989; Runsten et al. 1987).

Figure 2. Decline in net farm income: California, the Midwest, and the United States, 1950–85 (in millions of 1967 dollars)

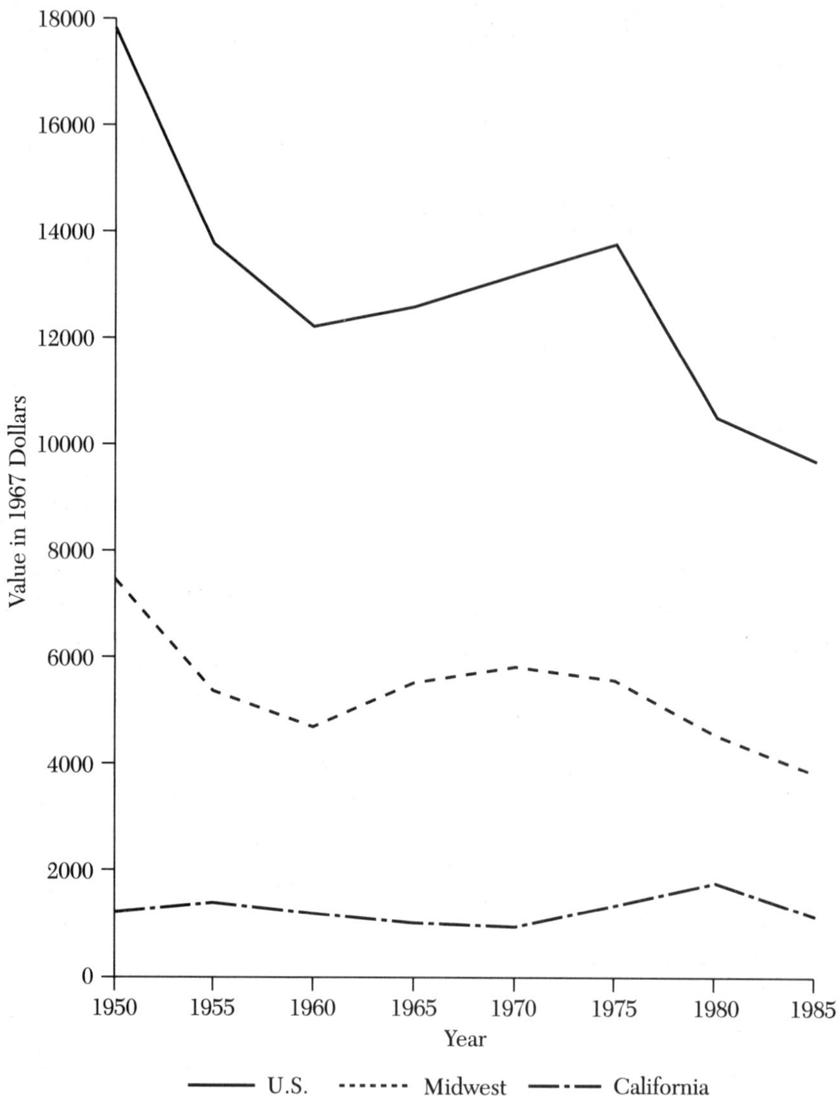

Sources: U.S. Department of Agriculture, *Economic Indicators of the Farm Sector: State Income and Balance Sheet Statistics, 1981* (Washington, D.C.: GPO, 1982), pp. 60–83, table 5; *1984* (1986), pp. 14–37, table 4; *1985* (1987), p. 8, table 1.

California Rises to the Top

The California strawberry industry rose rapidly to its position of national leadership after World War II. Before the war, acreage was spread across thirty-one states and methods of transport and preservation restricted most distribution to in-state markets. California was a minor participant at that time, producing only 4.2 percent of the U.S. crop on 3.4 percent of the acreage. Since the war, however, the Pacific Coast region and California in particular have come to dominate the U.S. industry (see figure 3). Although California, Oregon, and Washington produced only 17 percent of the national berry crop in 1946, by 1953 their proportion had increased to 61 percent, and by 1988, to 84 percent. Within this region, California was preeminent. New methods of cultivation, high-yielding, disease-free plant strains, improvements in transportation and handling, and the development of quick-freezing quickly transformed the California industry into a business with international distribution, tremendous costs and returns per acre, and large amounts of seasonal hired labor. As input costs rose and competition increased, the relative importance of the hot summer/cold winter states diminished, and that of California expanded. California's share of the national product expanded from 6 percent in 1946, to 36 percent in 1953, to 74 percent in 1988. Only thirteen states now produce a commercially significant fresh berry crop. Florida is currently California's nearest competitor, with only 11 percent of the national product (Bain and Hoos 1963:11, 26, 40, 128–29, 132–33; PSAB 1989; USDA 1989:222, table 323).

California's rise to preeminence was accomplished through a remarkable increase in productivity. Even before the war, California's climate supported per-acre yields over twice those of the nation as a whole. After the war, California's yield differential skyrocketed: between 1946 and 1988 the state's yields rose from 3.7 to 24.2 tons an acre—almost five times the five tons per acre averaged by the U.S. excluding California (see figure 4) (Bain and Hoos 1963:23, 141–43; PSAB 1989).

The state's productive edge was enhanced by the shift of acreage away from the hot interior and toward the temperate coast. This shift can be explained in terms of the growth requirements of the crop and the increasing rationalization of production. Strawberry plants produce best in temperate climates: high temperatures truncate blossom production and diminish fruit quality, and cold temperatures delay the harvest and stimulate excessive vegetative growth. Because strawberries are fragile, highly perishable, and susceptible to molds and moisture-generated pests and diseases, rain can be particularly damaging during the harvest season. Rich soils are unnecessary because nutrients can be added, but good drainage is essential

Figure 3. Change in proportions of U.S. strawberry production by state, 1946, 1953, and 1988

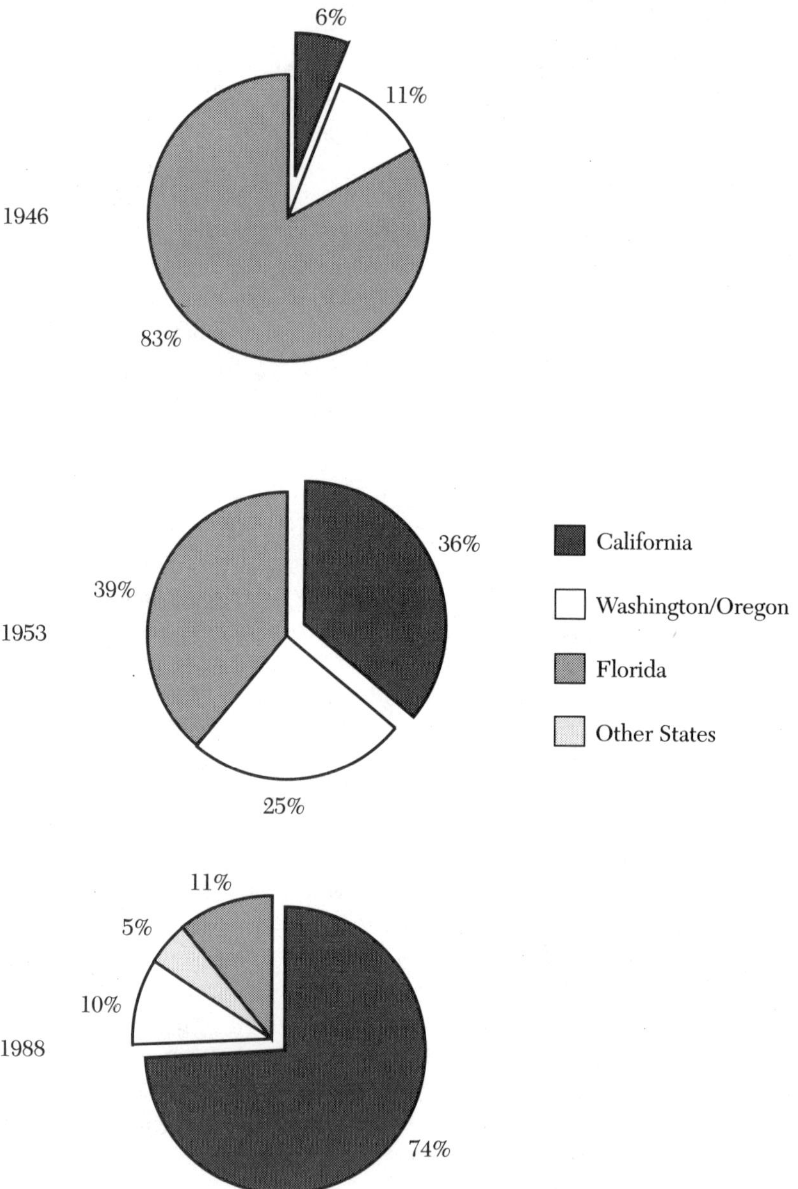

Sources: Beatrice Bain and Sidney Hoos, *The California Strawberry Industry,* Giannini Foundation Research Report no. 267 (Berkeley: University of California, 1963), p. 133; Processing Strawberry Advisory Board, *Annual Report* (Watsonville, Calif., 1989).

Figure 4. Change in per-acre strawberry yields, California and the United States, 1939–88

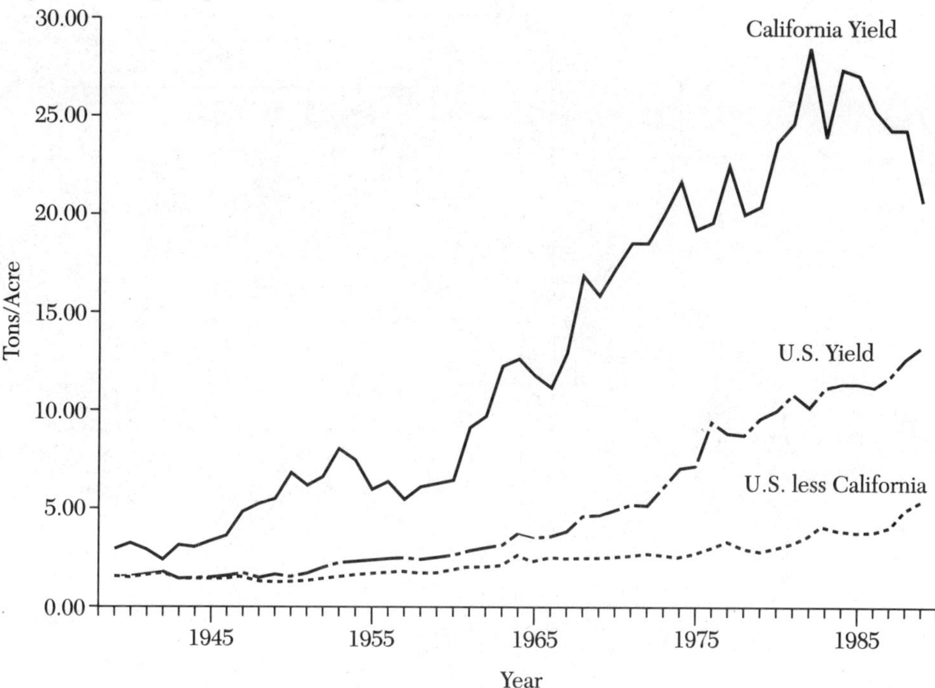

Sources: Bain and Hoos, *California Strawberry Industry,* p. 40, table 9, p. 26, table 3; U.S. Department of Agriculture, *Agricultural Statistics, 1962* (Washington, DC.: GPO, 1963), p. 238, table 292; *1964* (1965), p. 196, table 288; *1966* (1967), p. 299, table 369; *1968* (1969), p. 298, table 368; *1970* (1971), p. 249, table 363; *1972* (1973), p. 245, table 355; *1974* (1975), p. 242, table 343; *1976* (1977), p. 247, table 372; *1978* (1979), p. 246, table 369; *1980* (1981), p. 246, table 368; *1983* (1984), p. 230, table 333; *1984* (1985), p. 22, table 325; *1986* (1987), p. 223, table 325; *1988* (1989), p. 223, table 325; *1989* (1990), p. 223, table 324.

Note: The yield per acre for the United States less California is calculated by (1) subtracting California total strawberry production from U.S. total strawberry production, (2) subtracting California total acreage from U.S. total acreage, then (3) dividing (1) by (2) to get the average yield per acre for strawberries grown outside California.

to prevent the accumulation of moisture and salts. All in all, the temperate, sunny climates, the long, rain-free bearing seasons, and the sandy loam soils of California's coastal valleys promote possibly the heaviest harvests in the world (PSAB 1989). Whereas commercial berry acreage was spread throughout the state before the war, with 41 percent in the inland valleys, it is now concentrated in a three-mile-deep strip along the central and southern coasts, with about 56 percent on the north coast, 43 percent on the south coast, and only one percent in the interior (see figure 5). Santa

Figure 5. Counties producing 1 percent or more of total California strawberry crop, 1988

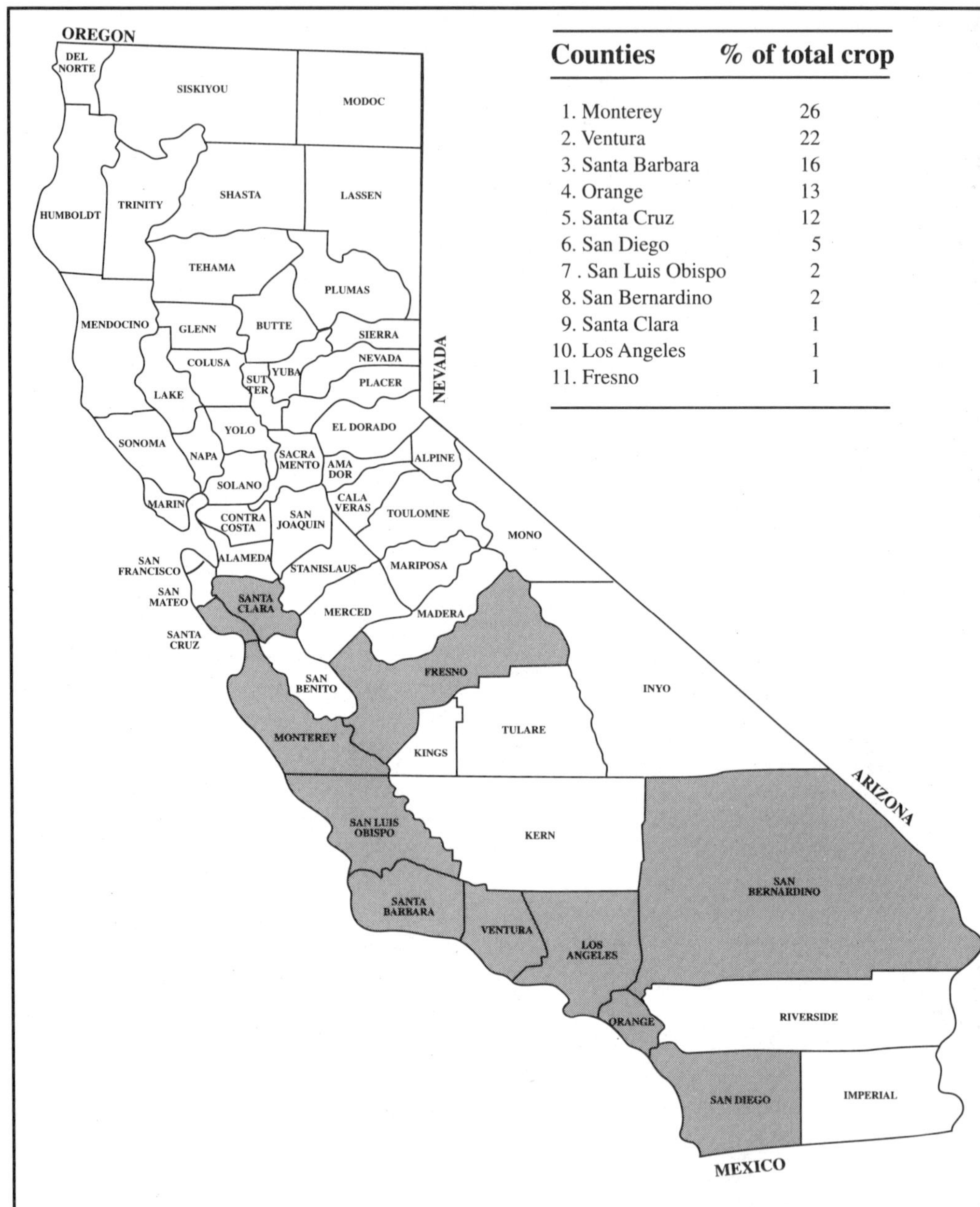

Counties	% of total crop
1. Monterey	26
2. Ventura	22
3. Santa Barbara	16
4. Orange	13
5. Santa Cruz	12
6. San Diego	5
7 . San Luis Obispo	2
8. San Bernardino	2
9. Santa Clara	1
10. Los Angeles	1
11. Fresno	1

Source: Agricultural Statistics Service, *1988 Agricultural Commissioners' Data* (Sacramento: California Department of Food and Agriculture, 1989), p. 246.

Table 2. Regional comparison of strawberry seasons

Location	Length of season	Months of season
Northeastern United States	3–4 weeks	June
Midwestern United States	3–4 weeks	June
Oregon-Washington	6–7 weeks	June–July
Florida	2–3 months	Dec.–Feb.
California	9–11 months	Feb.–Dec.

Source: U.S. Department of Agriculture, *Agricultural Statistics, 1988* (Washington, D.C.: GPO, 1989).

Cruz and Monterey Counties now constitute the largest single berry-producing region, with 38 percent of the state's acreage (McDowell and Tilden 1951; PSAB 1989).

Strawberries are a highly seasonal crop with harvest initiation, peak(s), and duration based almost exclusively on location and climate, but partially determined by plant variety and cultural practices. California occupies a unique position in the national calendar because of its unusually long bearing season, with an early spring peak in the south and a large midspring peak and smaller late summer–early fall peak in the north (see table 2). California now ships strawberries almost every month of the year. Its nearest competitor, Florida, ships for only two to three months. Most other states ship for one or two months.

The Stability of the Market

In addition to their astonishing yield differential, California strawberry growers benefit from an exceptionally stable market structure, based on the coexistence of fresh and processed production. Before the war, strawberries were primarily a fresh, locally sold commodity. Prices were more variable than for perhaps any other crop because of extreme supply fluctuations due to sharp seasonal production peaks, climatic changes, crop perishability, and disorderly market mechanisms (Bain and Hoos 1963:5). After the war, improvements in post-harvest handling and storage and in truck and air transport smoothed the distribution process, and the refinement of quick-freezing transformed strawberry supply, demand, and price (Kader et al. 1985; Mitchell, Maxie, and Greathead 1964; Thomas 1939; Welch et al. 1982). Between 1941 and 1957, national freezer capacity increased by 326 percent and the U.S. frozen strawberry pack exceeded that of any other frozen commodity except orange concentrate (Bain and Hoos 1963:5–6).

Freezing differentiated the strawberry crop and market into two commodities: fresh and processed (mostly frozen) berries. As freezer sales increased, they stabilized fresh market prices, smoothing out the extreme fluctuations of the pre-war period. Supply variations and marketing bottlenecks diminished in importance because the crop could be preserved and sold over an extended period. Demand also increased considerably: between 1946 and 1988 U.S. frozen berry consumption more than quadrupled and total demand increased 2.5 times (PSAB 1989). Enhanced demand heightened the advantage of California's seasonal length, and acreage in the state exploded (see figure 6). Long-time growers increased the size of their farms and new producers rushed to enter this lucrative market. From less than a thousand acres in 1945, state berry acreage soared to a high of 20,700 in 1957. About half of the crop marketed in this period was sold to freezers, which situated their plants in the growing regions because of the fragility and perishability of the crop. Large processing plants located in the central coast cities of Watsonville and Salinas and acreage in this area burgeoned.

In 1957, however, record acreage and large freezer carryovers from 1956 overwhelmed market capacity. Prices plummeted, driving many growers out of business. The industry responded to this landmark year in two ways. First, state acreage declined by over half and remained fairly stable for over two decades (see figure 6).[5] Second, growers began to direct an increasing proportion of their crop to the fresh market, aided by the development of dual-purpose plant strains suitable to fresh and processed use. By 1988, fresh market sales comprised 76 percent of the volume and 89 percent of the production value in California (PSAB 1989). Fresh market prices are generally higher, averaging 53 cents per pound as opposed to an average of 27 cents per pound for processing berries between 1980 and 1988 (PSAB 1989). As a result, California growers now sell to processors only when climatic difficulties such as sustained rains or heat make the quality too low for fresh shipping or when fresh market prices fall below those offered by processors. Because the fresh market demands higher quality, and hotter climates and older plants reduce quality, the fresh market emphasis has reinforced the shift to coastal production and annual planting. In essence, California's dual marketing system stabilizes prices by expanding producers' alternatives for disposing of their product. Although growers encounter some constraints on their free movement between markets,[6] the processed

[5]Acreage increases since the mid-1980s have raised fears of a repeat of 1957, but price fluctuations have remained relatively small.

[6]Different maturity and packing requirements prevent picking for both markets at once.

Figure 6. Changes in California strawberry acreage, 1939–88

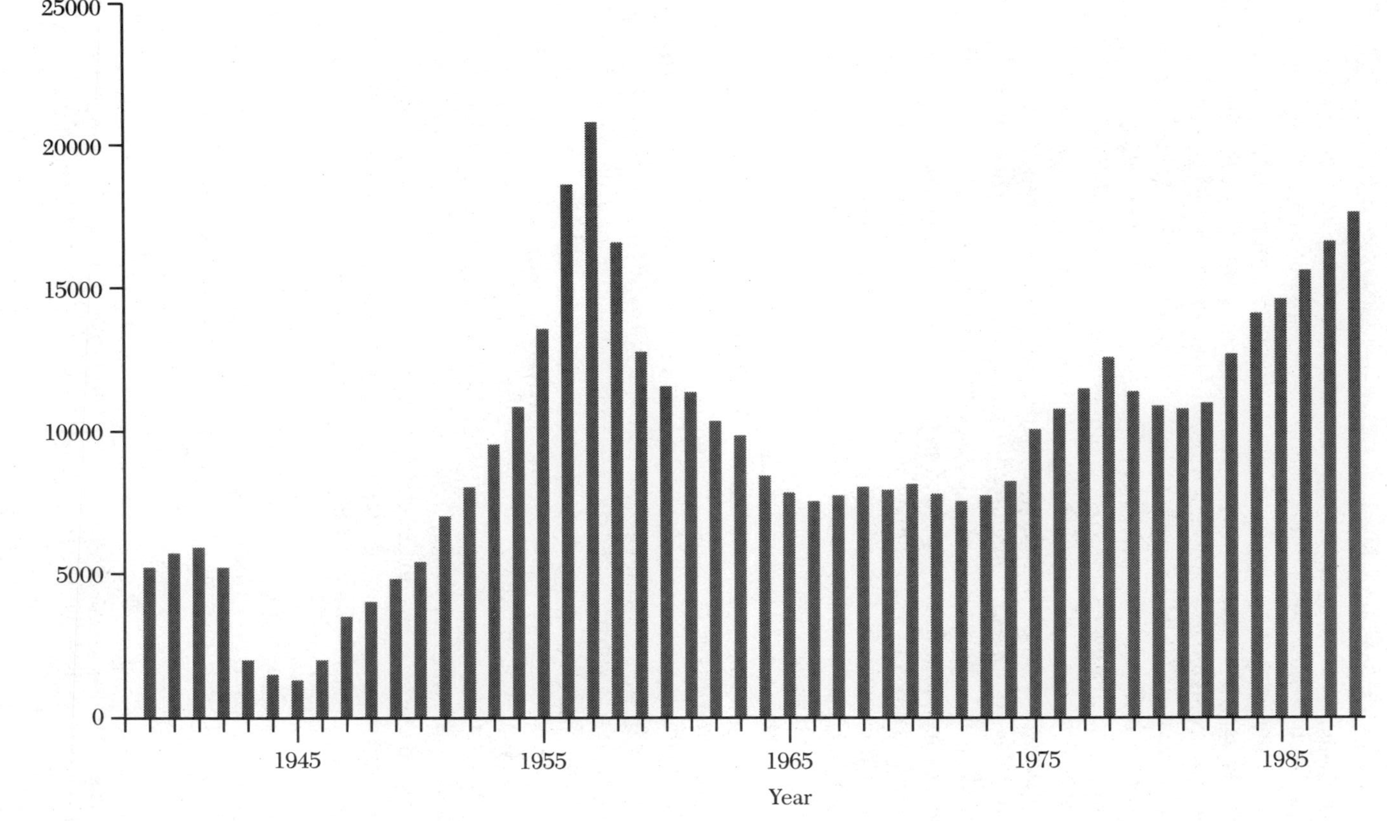

Sources: Bain and Hoos, *California Strawberry Industry,* p. 26, table 3; U.S. Department of Agriculture, *Agricultural Statistics, 1962* (1963), p. 238, table 292; *1964* (1965), p. 196, table 288; *1967* (1968), p. 299, table 369; *1970* (1971), p. 249, table 363; *1973* (1974), p. 245, table 355; *1976* (1977), p. 242, table 343; *1979* (1980), p. 247, table 372; *1981* (1982), p. 246, table 369; *1983* (1984), p. 230, table 333; *1986* (1987), p. 222, table 325; *1988* (1989), p. 223, table 325; *1989* (1990), p. 223, table 325.

market creates a floor beneath fresh market prices, preventing the extreme price swings characteristic of solely fresh crops such as lettuce, or strawberries before the war.

The fresh market concentration of the state helps buffer producers from domestic and foreign competition, as well. California strawberries are preferred by large U.S. fresh produce buyers because they have the highest quality over the longest period of time. Although there is always local demand for local fruit within each state, only Florida sells a significant volume of fresh strawberries across state lines. It provides late winter berries before the California harvests begin, but drops out of the market as its own temperatures rise and as the firmer California fruit enters the market. Because strawberries are so fragile and perishable, and because transport is so costly, fresh imports from abroad have not been able to compete with the California product. Over the last several years, however, Mexican and Californian producers have planted strawberries in Baja California, which enjoys the same temperate climate as San Diego without its restrictions on labor costs, production practices, and marketing. As a result, San Diego County berry acreage has shrunk substantially, and inexpensive fresh imports from Baja have cut into the market previously dominated by producers in southern California and Florida. To date, however, different market timing and inferior climate, technology, and market access have precluded competition with the central coast (Runsten 1987).

The fresh market emphasis of California berry growers also protects them from international fluctuations in frozen berry supply and price. Losing a share of the frozen market is less consequential for California producers than it is for those in the northwest and other cold winter–hot summer states who, in the face of competition from California, have relegated their fresh berries to U-pick or local markets. Thus, when Mexico's frozen strawberry industry ballooned between 1965 and 1974 and flooded the United States with low-priced frozen fruit, California growers intensified their fresh market focus. In Oregon, however, where over 90 percent of the berries are sold to freezers, growers suffered serious losses in market share (Padfield and Thaler 1984; Padfield and Greenleaf 1985).

Even though California growers depend less on processing sales, they dominate the U.S. processed market. Precisely because the state's climate promotes unparalleled fresh yields, it leads the nation in frozen sales as well, even though location would seem to be less of a boon for processing

Moreover, workers do not select, handle, and pack fresh market berries as carefully when picking regimes are changed. The longer ripening period for processing fruit also depletes the plants for fresh production, so that fresh production suffers thereafter.

berries because of their less demanding locational requirements. Over the course of the 1980s, California consistently gained market share at the expense of its competitors in the northwestern United States and Mexico. Currently, it supplies about 70 percent of the frozen strawberries produced in the nation (Carter and Nuckton 1987:49–67). This leadership is a result of the state's joint production system, in which the high prices received for fresh berries more than cover the overhead costs for berries sold to freezers. In California, freezer prices need only return a profit on the variable cost of harvesting, because the fresh market subsidizes the fixed costs. The magnitude of this subsidy is substantial: one study concluded that if processing berries had to cover their share of fixed production costs (one-third) in 1984–86, freezer prices would have averaged over 35 cents a pound, as opposed to their actual average of 21.6 cents (Runsten 1987:9–11). This subsidy gives California producers a distinct advantage over those in Washington and Oregon, where freezer prices must cover average total cost over the medium term to keep growers in business (Padfield and Thaler 1984; Padfield and Greenleaf 1985).

The fresh market demand profile has also favored California growers. Between 1980 and 1988, domestic fresh berry demand actually expanded by 59 percent (PSAB 1989), due both to the vigorous marketing efforts of the CSAB and to the enhanced interest of U.S. consumers in fresh fruits and vegetables. Although fresh, like frozen, berry demand may have reached the limits of its elasticity, its expansion to this point has benefited California producers. In addition, exports are still a small part of the state's berry business, a fact that is itself advantageous. According to the fresh and processing Strawberry Advisory Boards, over 90 percent of the state's fresh berries were sold domestically through the late 1980s: about three-fourths to retail outlets and one-fourth to food service buyers. Exports comprised only 7 to 8 percent of sales: about 6 percent went to Canada; the remaining 2 percent, to Europe and Asia, mostly Japan (PSAB 1989; California Agricultural 1989).[7] Some observers anticipate that the falling U.S. dollar may increase the demand for U.S. fresh imports in Europe, but in any event the domestic focus of the industry's fresh sales minimizes the significance of changes in international demand.

[7]Interviews with officials on the fresh and processing advisory boards and with berry exporters on the central coast provided the California figures. Most fresh exports to Japan come from California's central coast because of the timing of the Japanese demand. The Japanese American marketing cooperatives centered there are the major exporters. The Japan trade offers the advantage of high prices and extra market demand in August and September when domestic strawberry demand is often low.

The Structure of the Industry

In the California strawberry industry, crop characteristics and market organization have enhanced the economic viability and production control of relatively small-scale producers who specialize in strawberries and operate in a single region. Farms in this industry thus differ markedly from the large-scale, diversified, vertically integrated units of the southwestern vegetable industry, which stretch across several states and often several countries (Thomas 1985). California strawberry farms are much smaller than the statewide average, although in this they are not atypical.[8] Thus, in 1985–86, they averaged about 34 acres, as opposed to about 370 acres for all farms in the state.[9] Small (under 15 acres) and medium (15–49 acres) berry farms are especially characteristic of the central coast, where average berry farm size is about 27 acres, as opposed to an average of 49 acres for San Diego, Orange, Los Angeles, Ventura, Santa Barbara, San Luis Obispo Counties combined (PSAB 1986). Large nonfarming corporations are rare in strawberry production, especially on the central coast. Whereas some shippers provide production financing and limited technical support, most production decisions and operations are undertaken by farm owner-operators. Almost all of the few berry-farming corporations are family owned.

Small Farms, Big Yields

Commodity characteristics both permit and encourage smaller scale. Berry production requires a level of capital outlay and an intensivity of management that militate against large farm size, while high per-acre returns sustain small-scale operators. Although small size minimizes the con-

[8]The economic contribution of small farms in California is more significant than commonly recognized. Despite the overall concentration of farm production, 84 percent of California farms are under 500 acres, 71 percent are under 180 acres, and 47 percent are under 50 acres (Small Farm 1977:7). Farms with annual gross receipts of $250,000 or less produce about $2.1 billion in crop value each year, a greater value than all of the farms in each of twenty-six other states combined (California Institute 1985:1). Small size, then, especially in the context of high crop values, neither establishes the strawberry industry as unique nor indicates its economic marginality.

[9]The actual state average for all farms is probably higher, due to the Census Bureau's practice of identifying the geographically dispersed ranches of a single grower as separate "farms." My figures for the strawberry industry come from the manager of the California Strawberry Advisory Board and the farm advisors' and agricultural commissioners' offices in each of the berry-producing counties.

tribution of land to total costs,[10] the per-acre investment for strawberries is much greater than that for field and short-lived vegetable crops. This high level of investment creates particular incentives to maximize returns. Here small size is especially advantageous. Strawberries require much closer attention to the timing, performance, and coordination of tasks than do field and vegetable crops. Optimal times for planting, harvest, and pesticide applications are very precise, and their observance is crucial to yields and crop value. Strawberries are also much more fragile and perishable, so that harvest and postharvest handling must be heavily supervised. In addition, because strawberry plants are in the ground for from one to two years—as opposed to the several month cycle for vegetable crops—they must be protected from weeds, weather, disease, pests, and worker abuse for this extended period, creating yet another incentive for close supervision. Finally, experimentation and innovation are especially important in this industry: microclimatic variations are significant and require the active judgment and accumulated expertise of the grower, and the new plant strains developed every few years require the wholesale readjustment of cultural practices. The highest yields are achieved by growers who are closely in touch with their fields and who continually reassess, experiment, and refine their production practices. All these forms of managerial involvement engender diseconomies of scale.

In these senses, strawberries are less "produced," using an industrial analogy, than "gardened." The role of the grower as the initiator and coordinator of horticultural tasks is paramount. This is not to say that large berry farms are invariably unprofitable: historically, farm size has increased when external forces have substantially augmented managerial capacity, as in the case of the U.S. government's assistance in labor management during the bracero program.[11] Under present conditions, however, it is costly and difficult to achieve the necessary intensity and complexity of management on a large farm. Because per-acre costs are so high, the consequences of managerial neglect are sobering, and because per-acre returns are so great, well-managed small farms are profitable. Fresh shippers are therefore emphatic in their preference to leave the managerial complexities and risks of production to growers, rather than shouldering them directly as do the shippers of many other crops.

[10]Land-use patterns have reduced the impact of the farm crisis as well. Because farms are small and most growers rent at least some of their land, they have been less affected by falling land values. Moreover, those who rent have benefited from falling rents.

[11]During the bracero program, one Salinas Valley berry ranch grew to over 2,000 acres. When the program ended, the ranch was cut to a fraction of this size (see Chapter 3).

Market Access and Production Control

Market organization also supports the viability of small-scale producers. The stability of market prices engendered by the coexistence of fresh and processed production contributes importantly. Whereas the extreme volatility of prices for fresh crops such as lettuce fosters dispersed, diversified, well-capitalized, and vertically integrated companies that can withstand sustained losses (Thomas 1985), relatively stable strawberry prices support the operation of smaller-scale, less-endowed, single-crop producers. Moreover, although marketing is more aggregated than production, the market is still relatively open and competitive, and sales agents exert limited influence over production decisions.

Both fresh and processed wholesale markets are located close to producing farms because the fruit is so perishable and must be cooled and sold immediately. Three major categories of handlers provide access to fresh shipping-point wholesale markets: (a) grower-shippers, which involve the largest, best-financed growers; (b) marketing cooperatives, composed primarily of small and medium-sized growers; and (c) independent shippers, the major sales outlets for the smallest-scale, lowest-resource producers (see figure 7).[12] Only a fraction of growers work through produce brokers who simply mediate transactions between sellers and buyers. Procedurally, growers deliver their fruit to the handler or broker of their choice, who then sells the fruit on the terminal wholesale markets located in major cities across the country or directly to retailers or institutional outlets. Most agents sell to both sorts of buyers to balance the possibility of higher prices in the terminal market with the advantages of large size and stability of demand offered by large retail buyers. Most California berry sales involve such intermediaries: few growers sell directly to local retailers, terminal wholesale markets, or consumers. Market share information is confidential, but interviews with leading strawberry handlers and brokers indicate that the fresh market is relatively concentrated. Of the 48 million crates of fresh strawberries sold in California in 1986, for example, about 60 percent was shipped by seven handlers, including two grower-shippers, one marketing cooperative, and four independent shippers, two of which had freezing facilities as well. The top two handlers shipped almost 30 percent of the total volume.

Despite this considerable concentration, sales entities have not usurped

[12]Figure 7 was constructed from interviews with strawberry growers, handlers, and brokers, in conjunction with secondary sources dealing with fresh produce marketing systems (e.g., Finney 1981; Goldberg 1980, 1981).

Figure 7. The California strawberry market system

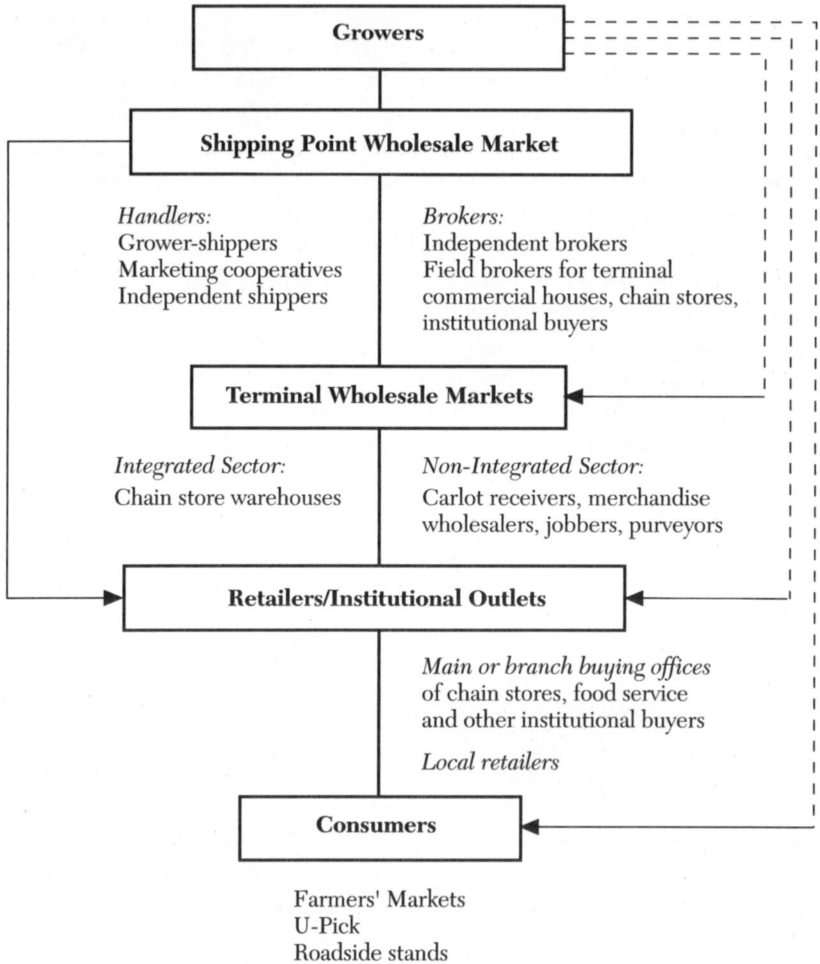

growers' control over production, both because grower-shipper organizations and marketing cooperatives are themselves controlled by growers, and because independent shippers and brokers are minimally involved in production. Nor has aggregation eliminated the market's competitive character: no firm monopolizes the market, although some leverage higher prices through their consistent adherence to strict quality standards. Market access is also widely dispersed. For the most part, growers have little difficulty securing an agent to market their berries. Expanding demand for fresh berries has ensured a niche for large growers who can finance their own shipping operations. Cooperatives have enabled small and medium-sized producers with adequate financing and connections to established growers to achieve sufficient scale and leverage in the market. Several fresh berry shipping companies have provided financing and market access to new, low-resource growers.

As is the case with other commodities, concentration is more marked in the processed market and has increased over the past forty years. According to the director of the Processing Strawberry Advisory Board, about thirty-four processing companies operated in California in the mid-1950s. By 1960, when the marketing order for processing strawberries was enacted, that number had fallen to twenty-six, due to the market glut of 1957 and to the marketing order's imposition of uniform quality standards and fair trade regulations. During the 1970s and early 1980s, low profits further reduced the number of processors, although an upturn in the freezer market during the second half of the 1980s drew in new firms. In 1987, there were twenty-one berry processors in California, four of which put up 80 percent of the state's freezer pack. The three largest produced 35–40 million pounds of frozen strawberries annually. All three are based in Watsonville. Two of the three are also fresh berry shippers who have processing plants and fresh sales operations in southern California as well. The third is one of the largest preservers in the nation and also has plants in several other states.

Despite greater concentration in the processed market, processors have even less influence over production decisions than do fresh market sales agents, because processing is the residual component of growers' production strategies. Decisions about what plant varieties to plant or the number of years plants will be kept in the ground are made with an eye to maximizing fresh rather than processed returns. Moreover, because the proportion of processed strawberries has declined consistently, processors are generally short of fruit and are in no position to dictate to growers.

The Role of the Advisory Boards

California berry growers have augmented their competitive edge through the activities of their marketing order associations. These organizations, the California Strawberry Advisory Board (CSAB) and the Processing Strawberry Advisory Board (PSAB), administer the provisions of the state fresh and processing marketing orders, respectively.[13] Both boards are based in Watsonville. They are the major industrywide vehicles for producer communication and collective action. They have played an important role in regulating market processes and in supporting the research and advertising that few growers can afford to undertake on their own.

The processing marketing order was established in 1960 after the sobering oversupply and market crash of 1957. It arose from processors' concerns about the uneven quality of California's frozen strawberries, which was losing them sales, and from the state's concern about the deceptive and collusive trade practices of some processors. This order authorizes the PSAB to set grade standards for the raw and finished product, inspect and certify the quality of the product, prevent unfair trade practices through price posting, and assess growers for research and advertising promotion. Like the fresh marketing order, the processing order includes no provision for control of berry supply. The PSAB affects growers primarily through the quality standards and orderly marketing mechanisms that it establishes. It has two full-time employees and hires seasonal inspectors and supervisors to administer the quality control program in different parts of the state. A committee on grading standards is composed of processors elected by district. The PSAB provides a forum for processors to address common problems. For example, California processors attempted through the PSAB to obtain trade restrictions on imports of Mexican strawberries in the 1970s, with only short-lived success. In practice, although the PSAB is authorized to do strawberry research, advertising, and promotion, it leaves the bulk of these activities to the CSAB. As a result, funded research on such topics as pesticides and plant strains attends to the needs of the fresh, rather than the processed market, another instance in which the needs of producers of fresh berries take precedence.

The fresh marketing order was established in 1955 when the industry was rapidly expanding. It grew out of the Strawberry Council, a voluntary association of growers and shippers that wanted to tithe the growers to promote the sale of California strawberries. Through its association, the CSAB, this marketing order is authorized to assess growers and handlers to promote advertising and trade, as well as research in production, processing, and marketing. The CSAB is much more substantial than the

[13]This section is based on Garoyan and Youde (1975:17–18), on interviews with two directors each of the fresh and processing advisory boards, and on interviews with four longstanding actors in central coast shipping organizations.

PSAB in its staffing, activities, and impact on growers. By the late 1980s, it had thirteen permanent full-time staff located in Watsonville, five field representatives located in major marketing regions across the country, and five standing subcommittees: research, food service, food safety, export, and consumer. Its twenty-three-member board includes twelve growers, five shippers, five processors, and a public member, all elected for a one-year term. The board meets five times a year and sponsors at least three additional meetings for growers, at which matters crucial to the industry are discussed. The CSAB publishes a weekly news bulletin listing strawberry shipments and three monthly newsletters dealing with sales and research.

The CSAB has played a pivotal role in fostering the competitive advantage of the industry. Initially, its assessments were low and its budget and activities were limited. In the late 1950s, however, small and medium-sized central coast growers, who lacked the resources themselves to promote sales and sponsor research, began to push for higher assessments and greater funding of research and advertising. After 1975, the budget and activities of the CSAB expanded substantially: assessments were raised, California berry volume ballooned, and the board's annual budget rose from an annual average of under $200,000 for the years before 1975 to $3.5 million in 1987 (Fujimoto and Kopper 1978; Runsten 1987:12–13). As a result, the CSAB's support for strawberry research and marketing far outstrips that of competing berry-producing states. The state of Washington, for example, has no marketing order board. Oregon's Strawberry Commission has an annual budget of about $90,000 (Padfield and Greenleaf 1985:127). California's annual research effort on strawberries in 1985 totalled about $1 million and ten scientist years, with two full-time plant breeders. Oregon and Washington each had an average annual strawberry research budget of about $200,000 and two scientist years, with no full-time breeders (Padfield and Greenleaf 1985:127). The CSAB has been the largest single supporter of the University of California's strawberry breeding program, which developed the larger fruit and higher yields that have accorded the state its productive edge.

Strawberry Returns and the Importance of Labor

Industry characteristics have shielded California strawberry producers from the recent world economic downturn, making control over labor the central determinant of profitability.

The Stability of Profits

Shrinking farm profits cannot account for postwar labor process changes in this industry, for California strawberry profits did not follow the national agricultural pattern of a gradual decline between the early 1950s and 1970s, a sudden rise, and then a precipitous drop in the early 1980s. In fact, real net returns to California berry growers have been remarkably stable and growing (see figure 8).[14] The conditions supporting their vitality are especially marked on the central coast, where lenders report that bankruptcies are particularly rare among established berry growers and did not increase during the national farm crisis.

Strawberry producers have, however, experienced some of the economic strains facing other industries. Production costs have risen dramatically as scientific experimentation and innovation have rationalized all aspects of production. Plant varieties and cultural practices are now highly refined and attuned to maximum productivity. These technological changes, along with rising input prices, have radically increased expenses in field labor, materials, and overhead. Between 1959 and 1985, for example, total per-acre costs in real 1967 dollars rose by 216 percent. Strawberries are now one of the most expensive of all crops to produce, requiring outlays of $18,000 to over $25,000 an acre.

At the same time, real strawberry prices have fallen considerably—by 41 percent between 1959 and 1985, the period for which full production cost data are available (see table 3). Taking a longer time span, we find that real berry prices declined by 48 percent between 1950 and 1988, and by 22 percent between 1980 and 1988. Thus growers have been squeezed in terms of the per-unit price of their product, although price declines have been less severe than for some commodities because of expanding domestic demand and the insignificance of international imports and exports. Falling world demand has had little impact, because most of the crop is sold within the United States. The centering of fresh berry supply sources within California further limits sources of price instability. As a result, California berry prices did not drop in 1982 with the contraction in the world economy as did the prices of many crops. In fact, prices actually rose because of the state's lower supply that year. On the whole, price fluctuations in the California strawberry industry tend to reflect variations in the state's production volume rather than changes in world supply (Valenzuela and Snyder 1987).

Falling prices and rising costs have been counterbalanced by increasing demand and productivity. The rise in yields is especially notable: between

[14]See Appendix, this chapter, for sources for figure 8 and tables 3 and 4.

Figure 8. California strawberry production costs versus income, 1956–85

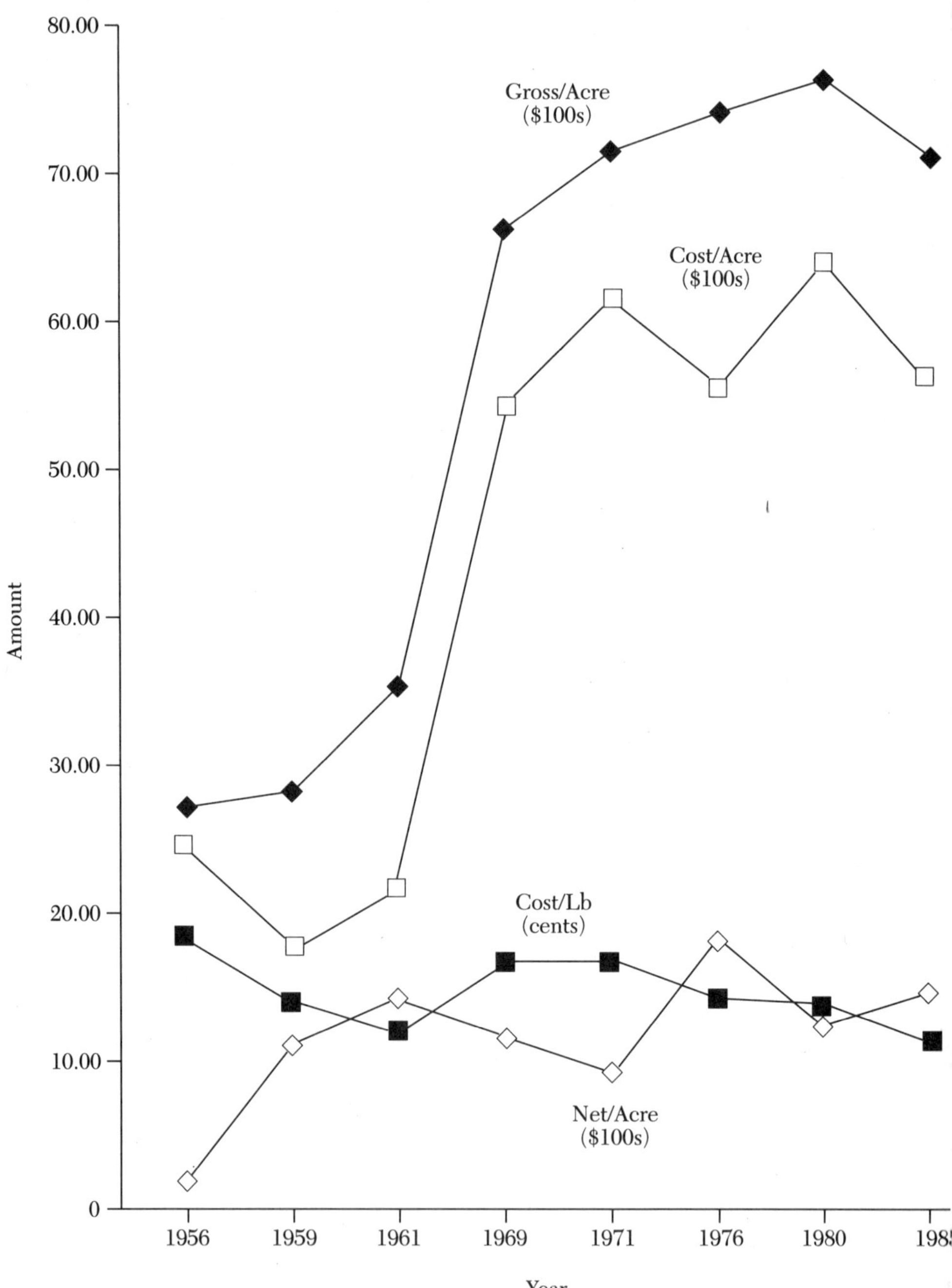

Table 3. Changes in strawberry production costs versus income, 1956–85 (in real 1967 dollars)

Year	1967 $ multiplier	Yield lbs/acre	Cost/acre	Labor cost/acre	Labor cost as % total cost	Cost/lb	Price/lb	Gross income/acre	Net income/acre
Real costs (in 1967 dollars)									
1956	1.229	12,800	$2,482	$1,675	67	$0.19	$0.21	$2,658	$176
1959	1.145	12,900	$1,786	$1,140	64	$0.14	$0.22	$2,821	$1,035
1961	1.116	17,800	$2,148	$1,401	65	$0.12	$0.20	$3,496	$1,348
1969	0.911	32,000	$5,431	$2,518	46	$0.17	$0.21	$6,588	$1,157
1971	0.824	36,500	$6,164	$3,155	51	$0.17	$0.20	$7,128	$964
1976	0.587	39,000	$5,568	$3,089	55	$0.14	$0.19	$7,372	$1,804
1980	0.406	47,505	$6,342	$3,250	51	$0.13	$0.16	$7,599	$1,257
1985	0.310	53,000	$5,644	$2,798	50	$0.11	$0.13	$7,098	$1,454
% change, 1959–85 (in real terms)									
		311%	216%	145%		–23%	–41%	152%	40%

1945 and 1988, California strawberry yields rose by a full 700 percent; in the period between 1959 and 1985, yields increased by 311 percent. As a result, the per-pound cost of strawberries actually dropped by 23 percent between 1959 and 1985 despite the substantial rise in costs, while increases in yield lifted gross returns by 152 percent and net returns by 40 percent.[15] In short, California strawberry farms continue to be profitable, despite unusually high input costs. Per-acre net returns in strawberries outstrip those for almost every other crop, with the exception of a few commodities such as nursery crops. On the central coast, for example, farm advisers' production cost studies projected that a competent and adequately financed (but not extraordinary) grower could gross almost $23,000 an acre in 1985 and net almost $4,700 profit (Welch, Greathead, and Beutel 1985). Thus a small-scale grower with 14 acres could gross almost $321,000 and net about $65,700; a medium-scale grower with 32 acres could gross about $733,000 and net about $150,000; and a large grower with 100 acres could gross almost $2,300,000 and net almost $470,000.

The Centrality of Harvest Labor

Overall, postwar technological developments have diminished the need for nonharvest labor, but increased the labor intensivity of the harvest. Whereas most berries were harvested by family workers before the war, by 1950 the harvest required substantial amounts of hired labor. By the mid-1990s, longer, flatter, and more bountiful harvests required pickers earlier, later, and more intensively during the season, making strawberries one of the most labor-intensive of all crops to produce. With a harvest labor requirement of 1.5 to 2 persons per acre, even small family farmers must hire extra workers at the peak. Up to twenty-eight pickers are necessary for a small (14-acre) farm at peak harvest, sixty-four pickers for a medium (32-acre) farm, and two hundred for a large (100-acre) farm.

Because pickers are generally paid on a piece-rate basis, yield-enhancing varieties and cultural practices have also raised harvest labor expenses. Labor is the largest single component of production costs and most is absorbed by the harvest (see table 4). Between 1959 and 1985, real labor costs increased by 145 percent, although even greater increases in the cost

[15]Many central coast growers received larger net returns than this figure indicates, because yield and return totals are depressed by the large number of low-resource growers whose berries are of lower quality and price. Southern California has relatively few such marginal producers.

Table 4. Changes in per-acre production costs for nonharvest, harvest, and total labor, 1956–85 (in nominal and real 1967 dollars)

	Nonharvest labor		Harvest labor		Total labor	
Year	Costs	% of total production costs	Costs	% of total production costs	Costs	% of total production costs
1956	$456 ($560)	23	$907 ($1,115)	45	$1,363 ($1,675)	67
1959	$369 ($423)	24	$626 ($717)	40	$995 ($1,140)	64
1961	$351 ($391)	18	$905 ($1,010)	47	$1,255 ($1,401)	65
1969	$721 ($657)	12	$2,042 ($1,860)	34	$2,763 ($2,518)	46
1971	$893 ($736)	12	$2,937 ($2,420)	39	$3,829 ($3,155)	51
1976	$847 ($497)	9	$4,416 ($2,592)	47	$5,263 ($3,089)	55
1980	$1,333 ($541)	9	$6,671 ($2,708)	43	$8,004 ($3,250)	51
1985	$1,516 ($470)	8	$7,509 ($2,328)	41	$9,025 ($2,798)	50
			% change, 1959–85 (in real terms)			
	11%		225%		145%	

of other inputs reduced labor's share of all costs from 67 to 50 percent. Thus within the general labor category, the cost of harvest labor increased by 225 percent in real terms, from $626 to $7,509 an acre, representing an increase in the harvest's proportion of all costs of only one percentage point. At the same time the cost of nonharvest labor only increased by 11 percent, from $369 to $1,516 an acre—a decrease in nonharvest labor's share of all costs by 16 percentage points. Currently, the harvest absorbs 83 percent of all labor costs. Rising wages have contributed to the absolute increase in labor expenses, and commodity characteristics preventing harvest mechanization account for the divergent tendencies of harvest and nonharvest labor. Wages increased by 620 percent in nominal dollars and by 112 percent in real dollars between 1963 and 1985.

Technological changes have not only increased the amount and cost of harvest labor, they have enhanced the importance of its quality and timing. The quality of harvest labor is crucial. According to university bulletins on strawberry handling, the care with which workers select, handle, and pack the fragile fruit is the greatest single determinant of market price. Careless picking can make over one-third of the fruit unmarketable, and "nullify all other attempts to maintain fruit quality" (Mitchell, Maxie, and Greathead 1964). The timing of harvest labor is also critical. Strawberries have a high rate of metabolism and decay rapidly. The fruit ripens sequentially over the seven- to nine-month harvest period, and it must be picked every few days. Fruit left on the vine for as little as a day too long is likely to be unsuitable for market. Plants that are picked too rarely stop producing blooms. Because the crop is so valuable and so costly to produce, and because farm profits derive entirely from the harvest, delays in harvest schedules can be disastrous.

All in all, then, labor is the largest single component of cost and its timely and careful execution is the main determinant of market returns. Growers' concern with the price and performance of labor is enhanced by the fact that locational advantages, commodity characteristics, and market factors restrict other means of increasing profits. Unlike growers in the lettuce, processing-tomato, and grape industries, California berry growers have not been able to reduce labor by mechanizing the harvest. The emphasis on the fresh market, the fragility of the fresh commodity, the sequential ripening of the fruit, the lengthy harvest season, and the difficulty of effectively removing the stem and leafy cap from freezer berries have discouraged the adoption of current plant-destroying mechanical harvesters. Despite industry investment in mechanization research in the embattled 1970s and hopeful forecasts of "Strawberry Harvesters Galore!" (1971) and "At Last! Strawberry Mechanization Is On Its Way" (Morris 1978), no strawberry harvesters have yet been developed that are reliable and cost-efficient for California. Even the yields of usable fruit achieved by the most promising experimental harvesters, employed in conjunction with new simultaneously ripening plant strains, have approached only a fraction of California's annual yields per acre. Moreover, the quality of machine-harvested fruit is inadequate for the lucrative fresh market on which the bulk of the California crop is sold. In short, though machines have saved some nonharvest labor, and though some experts expect that mechanical harvesters will be adopted by states that focus on the processed market, no forecaster expects harvest mechanization in California ("Berry Mechanization" 1977).

Nor are growers able to leverage higher prices in the market to offset increased costs. Producers have little control over the prices they receive for their fruit, and for the most part they enter the season without a fixed contract specifying the price and amount of fruit that buyers will purchase. As noted previously, access to the market is dispersed among the large grower-shipper firms, the marketing cooperatives, and the independent shippers. To be sure, an estimated 80–85 percent of the state's crop is sold through aggregated marketing mechanisms, and two such entities—Naturipe Berry Growers and Driscoll Strawberry Associates—account for the bulk of that crop, but neither of these organizations enjoys a market monopoly. Although some firms leverage somewhat higher market prices through their long-term adherence to strict quality standards, neither labeling nor market domination accords any fresh shipper consistently higher prices. The same case holds for processors, because most processing berries are frozen and most of the freezer pack is sold for remanufacturing (Runsten 1989: 15). Moreover, some important determinants of product price come from outside the industry, both from the supermarket chains to which the crop is preferentially sold and from the competition with other producing areas. Although the fresh/frozen differentiation of the commodity increased demand initially, most observers believe that demand will be relatively stagnant in the years to come. Thus, product differentiation is not the ongoing means of increasing demand that it is in manufacturing industries. Nor are producers allowed to restrict supply in order to raise prices through the CSAB or the PSAB, thus eliminating another potential means of market control. Although the former has invested heavily in promotion, market prices and consumer demand have risen more slowly than costs.

Finally, central coast growers cannot reduce their costs and increase the stability of their production environments by moving to another region. Their options for dealing with changes in the cost and malleability of labor are constrained by the competitive advantage accorded by location. Even if historical tradition, personal connections, and the accumulation of an industrial infrastructure did not bind central coast strawberry growers so closely to this region, the tremendous yields of the locality would still encourage them to remain. Because of these strong ties to the region, growers are especially subject to the sociopolitical pressures exerted upon it. In these regards strawberry growers exemplify one of the features thought to distinguish the agricultural and industrial sectors of the economy (Mann 1990; Mann and Dickenson 1978): that is, their profits are directly dependent on their relation to the natural environment—in this case an unparalleled climate. This dependence does not distinguish them diametrically from industry nor merge them with agriculture, since many agricultural industries are less particular in their locational requirements, and profits in extractive industries like mining derive directly from access to an immobile natural resource. Thus, though their link to the natural environment may generally distinguish agricultural producers, variation by industry is still consequential.

The Impact of Industry

In sum, industry characteristics have shaped the interests, resources, and alternatives of central coast California berry growers, rendering control over harvest labor the central determinant of profitability. Shrinking farm profits cannot account for changes in the labor processes of this industry, for not only have farm returns been relatively high and stable, but producers have enjoyed a preeminent competitive position in the nation and world. Since the war, changes in the commodity, technology, and market have accorded growers some formidable tools for dealing with macroeconomic challenges. Industrial constraints have also, however, restricted producers' strategic options and created significant areas of economic vulnerability. Most critical and problematic for their continued capital accumulation is their need to control the price and performance of harvest labor. As we have seen, the importance of labor control derives in part from industry-specific requirements as to its timing and quality, in part from the size and malleability of its cost, and in part from growers' inability to replace or offset it. Increases in productivity are slowing in this industry, although technological advances have decreased per-unit costs over the long run. Not only is labor the largest single expense and one of the only costs growers can influence in the short run, but they cannot leverage higher prices or lower the cost of other inputs.

Industry characteristics, then, importantly structure the interests and options of growers. They also shape the concerns and leverage of workers. Before turning to the experience of workers, however, and exploring the relations between them, let us step back and examine the overarching regional context within which both classes operate.

Appendix
Sources for Strawberry Production Costs and Returns

Figure 8 and tables 3 and 4 are based on the following sources and calculations. First, bulletins issued by central coast county farm advisers comprise the major sources for production costs (Koch et al. 1956; Koch et al. 1961; Burlingame et al. 1969; Greathead 1971; Welch and Greathead 1976; Welch et al. 1980; and Welch et al. 1985). Despite regional variance in prices, costs, and yields, the robust economic condition portrayed by these figures holds statewide as well. Second, *pounds per acre* were obtained from different sources, because the bulletins used (higher) anticipated, rather than actual, yields. Yields for 1956–62 were obtained from Bain and Hoos 1963:26, 40. Those for 1963–85 were obtained from the USDA's *Agricultural Statistics* bulletins (1971:249, table 363; 1974:245, table 355; 1980:247, table 372; 1982:246, table 369; 1987:222, table 325). This use of actual rather than anticipated yields resulted in a downward adjustment in harvest costs, since costs depend on the number of pounds picked. All other costs were included as they appear in the bulletins.

Third, *costs per acre* were calculated by totaling all costs and dividing by the number of acres and the number of years in a production cycle, as indicated in each production bulletin. The production cycle is the number of years over which plants are harvested. Over time, production cycles have become progressively shorter. Until the mid-1960s, plants were replaced every four years. Since the late 1970s, farm advisers have used a two-year production cycle in their calculations and some growers replace their plants annually. These practices increase costs significantly. Fourth, my treatment of depreciation differs from that in the bulletins. The bulletins count the establishment costs incurred in the first year as "expenses" and "depreciate" them over subsequent years. Thus these costs are counted twice in the "total cost." I consider it more accurate to count these costs as they occur in the first year and not to depreciate them at all. Thus my "total costs" are lower than those listed in the bulletins by the amount of this depreciation on the first year's expenses. All other depreciation is treated as in the cost bulletins.

Fifth, *price per pound* in the figures is the average price that a pound of berries brought in the market in that year, as indicated in the USDA's annual *Agricultural Statistics* bulletins. The price includes fresh and processed sales in the proportion of each sold in a particular year. Sixth, I measured change from the 1950s to 1985 starting with 1959 rather than 1956, because the 1956 bulletin lists an unrealistically high labor cost. Thus, though labor rates were higher in 1959 than in 1956, total labor costs are listed as 27 percent higher in 1956, despite the fact that average yields for the two years differ by less than one percent. This cost figure results in an improbably low income of $144 an acre for 1956. It is impossible to detect the source of a possible error given the data presented in the 1956 bulletin. Consequently, the 1959 bulletin was deemed a more accurate base for comparison. Finally, the 1956 bulletin did not show a breakdown of harvest costs into labor costs and miscellaneous costs. Typically, harvest labor consists of picking labor and supervision labor. Miscellaneous harvest costs include the costs of hauling and materials. Because 1959 and 1956 had similar yields, as well as similar data in other respects, I used the 1959 harvest cost breakdown to estimate a breakdown for 1956. For 1956, I used the same total harvest cost as in the 1956 bulletin, but the breakdown shown is from my calculations using 1959 proportions of harvest labor to total harvest expense (={$942.70 picking labor + $135.00 supervision labor}/$1113.70 total harvest expense) and harvest hauling to total harvest expense (=$36.00 hauling/$1113.70 total harvest expense).

[3]

The Political Construction of the Farm Labor Market

It is impossible to make sense of labor resistance and labor process change in this industry without understanding the impact of the labor market on class relations at work. The farm labor market is the overarching, determining environment in which strawberry workplace struggles unfold. It comprises the broader opportunity structure in which the buyers and sellers of labor come together to negotiate the terms of their contracts. It is also the reference point to which both refer in renegotiations. The interests, capacities, and alternatives of each party, even the extent to which either can negotiate or must simply accept the terms offered by the other, are shaped by the broad forces structuring the market.

There is a widespread tendency to assume that economic forces determine the intersection of labor supply and demand and thus the exchange value and bargaining power of labor in the market. In many contemporary labor markets, however, these balances are politically established. The salient feature of the strawberry labor market—indeed of southwestern agricultural labor markets generally—is the political mediation of labor supply. Despite the perception of California's farm labor market as archetypically unstructured and competitive, political forces have long constrained its operation and defined the options of its participants (Galarza 1964; McWilliams [1935] 1971). They include the ideologies, laws, and institutions that establish the legitimate entitlements of particular groups and the interest groups that try to improve their members' claims on public resources. Thus the political constraints on class relations in the labor market at any given time—the labor market regime—are part and parcel of class relations at work. They affect the status and options of both classes in the labor market, conditioning their leverage even before they engage about work. They help define the goals and tactics of each class, and they become the subjects of efforts to change the relations between them.

This chapter explores the changing political construction of the strawberry labor market. It focuses on the postwar era, when the industry matured as a capitalist enterprise and hand labor attained its present centrality to profits. Two regimes structured the labor market in the period of this study: the first reigned from 1942 to 1965, the second from 1965 to 1988.[1] Three political forces were most influential in composing these regimes: the changing stipulations of immigration policy, the expansion of protective labor legisl[illegible] nd the rise of agricultural unionization. Although political forces [illegible] rivileged those with economic power, they have also, in t[illegible] e interests of workers. The dismantling of the firs[illegible] trol over the cost and deployment of labor, [illegible] power away from capital and toward [illegible] ilted back toward capital, not by im[illegible] f political constraints—a new regi[illegible] existing constraints.

[illegible] Control

[illegible] nin which central coast berry growers and [illegible] ployment base in Monterey and Santa Cruz [illegible] e reproduction in the states of central Mex[illegible] are immigrants, U.S. immigration policies [illegible] ge in the local labor market. Between 1942 and 196[illegible], [illegible] directly shaped by and supportive of grower interests: the[illegible] age levels, undermined labor organizing, and even took on certain la[illegible] management functions. But toward the close of this era, other voices gained a say in the formulation of border policy, and the policy environment thereafter was less favorable to growers. Not only did subsequent policies end the state's direct role in labor management, but they fostered the differentiation of California's farm labor markets and increased their vulnerability to local struggles.

[1]Although the Immigration Reform and Control Act of 1986 formally initiated a new labor market regime, it was not seriously enforced in agriculture until 1988–89. As I note in the conclusion, many aspects of the preceding regime remained unchanged after the act as well.

The Bracero Program: 1942–65

From 1942 until 1965, border policy shaped the labor market through an agreement between the U.S. and Mexican governments providing for the importation of contract workers.[2] This program—called the bracero program after the Mexican word for its workers (*braceros:* those who work with their arms)—was due primarily to the efforts of California growers and the powerful American Farm Bureau Federation, in concert with growers from the American South (Jones 1970; Hawley 1966; McConnell 1953). When domestic workers left the fields in the early 1940s for the armed services and more profitable urban employment, these interests pressed explicitly for a federally supervised labor supply program. Representing their request as "in the national defense," they were aided in their campaign by the importance of food production to the regional and national economies (Galarza 1964:46–70). Although the agreement was represented at the outset as an emergency measure to deal with the wartime labor shortage, it proved so profitable that growers secured its continuation for a total of twenty-three years. It was terminated by the U.S. government in December 1964.

Over this period the bracero program imported almost five million workers, bringing in as many as 450,000 annually during its peak in the late 1950s (Briggs, Fogel, and Schmidt 1977:82; Galarza 1964:79). Most braceros worked in Texas, Arizona, or California. California was the major employer of braceros by far: 90 percent of the workers imported in 1945 worked in California (Craig 1971; Galarza 1964); by the late 1950s, braceros constituted one-third of California's peak harvest labor force, averaging 90,000 a year (Sosnick 1978:388). Strawberries, lettuce, grapes, and tomatoes were especially dependent on braceros. In 1962, for example, state records listed over 70 percent of peak harvest strawberry workers as braceros (*Seasonal Labor* 1963). A statewide survey of seventeen large berry growers conducted by the CSAB found that braceros accounted for 95 percent of the total picking hours in 1963 and 91 percent in 1964 (CSAB 1965). Braceros were even more heavily used on the central coast: growers claim that their workers were almost 100 percent braceros from 1950 until 1965.

The bracero program minimized growers' direct investment in labor recruitment, incentives, and control, and provided an unprecedentedly cheap, malleable, and diligent labor supply. It was no accident that unionization and intervening labor protections were practically nonexistent during its

[2]The Alien Land Laws were an important exception that will be discussed later. They structured the strawberry labor market regime before and immediately after World War II.

tenure. The program set minimal standards for the wages, working conditions, housing, and transportation of contract workers. To avoid adverse impacts on domestic workers, braceros were limited to positions thought to be unattractive to citizens, including all row crops and strawberries. They were not assigned to jobs such as apple thinning and pruning which were customarily done by domestic workers. In practice, however, braceros did adversely affect the conditions of domestic labor. They set the standards that domestic workers had to accept, depressing agricultural wages and insulating the farm labor market from competition with the higher wages and better working conditions in urban areas. The readily expandable bracero labor pool easily met—and often exceeded—the labor demands of employers, especially given the availability of domestic and nonbracero immigrant workers (Briggs, Fogel, and Schmidt 1977:82; Galarza 1964:94–115, 209–18; Jenkins 1978:526; McWilliams [1935] 1971:26).

The program also restricted workers' physical and socioeconomic mobility, thus limiting their ability to shape the terms of their employment. Braceros were certified to work in a particular region, industry, and job. Their contracts lasted from six weeks to two months. When their contracts expired, they were required to return to Mexico, although in practice some deserted their contracts to work in other U.S. industries. Braceros found employed outside their contracts were subject to immediate deportation. Those who engaged in labor organizing or who tried to negotiate wages or working conditions could be immediately decertified and deported. This threat alone was usually sufficient to squelch labor opposition (Galarza 1964:183–98). In fact, braceros were used heavily as strike breakers and effectively undercut attempts at unionization (Jenkins 1985:114–30; Majka and Majka 1982:136–66).

The bracero program involved the government directly in labor management, enabling growers to externalize most of the costs and headaches of labor recruitment. The program was closely responsive to employer needs. Formally, it was administered by the U.S. Department of Labor, in close cooperation with the Mexican consulate, the state department of employment, and local employers' labor associations whose formation was authorized under the law. Typically, growers in a region would form an association and fund the operation of a local office through their dues. These associations almost unilaterally established the numbers, employment periods, and wage rates of braceros to be hired in an area (Jenkins 1978:526). Although in theory the Department of Labor set contract wages according to prevailing wage rates in the region, in practice, it relied directly on the representations of employer associations as to what prevailing rates were. In California, these associations carried out the day-to-day administration of the program.

Central coast berry growers engaged actively in this process of co-management. The first association on the central coast, the Grower-Shippers Vegetable Association of Central California, was formed in 1942 by large vegetable growers in the Salinas Valley.[3] Berry growers channeled their requests for braceros through this association until 1952, when they formed the Central Coast Farm Labor Association in Watsonville to service the growing demand for berry workers in that area. In 1954, they formed another association in Watsonville, again to accommodate the burgeoning strawberry industry. All three organizations covered the counties of Santa Cruz, Monterey, San Benito, Santa Clara, and San Mateo. At the program's peak, the Salinas association brought in from 14,000 to 16,000 braceros annually; each of the two Watsonville associations brought in from 4,000 to 5,000. The offices were active for eight or nine months a year, with the most intense activity from April through September. Each local office had a manager who administered the program, a clerical staff person who handled paperwork, and a field person who checked local housing and employment conditions and helped resolve disputes between growers and braceros. Growers first submitted their requests to the state Department of Employment Development (EDD) for a certain number of workers, over a certain period of time, to perform certain tasks. Requests were usually submitted about thirty days in advance of the need. The EDD then certified that the request would not displace domestic workers, and growers presented their certified requests to their labor association, whose manager cleared them with the U.S. Department of Labor and the Mexican consulate. After approval, central coast requests were communicated to the El Centro office of the U.S. Immigration and Naturalization Service (INS), which then had workers bused to the region from the border. The associations monitored the growers' payrolls every two weeks to ensure that they paid the requisite amount for wages, housing, transportation to work, and association dues.

Central coast growers, farm advisers, and association managers agreed that this system worked remarkably well. Those who required more workers in midseason contacted their association manager. One Watsonville association manager said it was "very rare" that he and his colleagues could not fulfill a midseason order for workers. "This was a program that responded to need," he continued, "I know of no case where a grower suf-

[3]Information about the bracero program on the central coast was obtained from interviews with farmers, farm advisers, farm workers who worked as braceros or as illegals during the bracero program, and with an individual who managed one of the Watsonville labor associations.

fered loss of crop." When a grower submitted a midseason request for additional braceros, managers would first check within the locality to see if local growers anticipated extra workers by the date requested. They also received phone calls from other associations informing them of surplus workers. While braceros could only work in the counties and through the association that had initially engaged them,[4] their assignments could be amended by approval of the U.S. Department of Labor and they could be sent to labor-needy areas. Such approval was easily granted on evidence of employer need. If all else failed, managers could secure additional braceros from Mexico within a week.

This system admirably met central coast strawberry labor demands. Though the steep peaks of the harvest generated some supply problems at the start of each season, and though large farms were especially at risk because association managers tried to spread available workers among all growers, shortages were quickly eliminated by importing additional braceros. During the 1950s and early 1960s, the EDD's weekly *Farm Labor Report* identified areas of labor demand and helped channel workers toward them. It regularly reported labor shortfalls of from 6,000 to 9,000 workers on the central coast in April and May and their disappearance by June and July. Although some central coast berry growers hired illegals at the peak when braceros were in short supply, field workers were almost exclusively braceros. Growers considered braceros to be the most efficient and trouble-free source of labor they had ever experienced. They strongly preferred braceros to the contentious and unpredictable union-inspired immigrant workers of the 1970s and 1980s. One Watsonville grower aptly summed up the sentiments that many voiced:

> Braceros were here to make a living, not to make trouble. They were family men, not juvenile delinquents like you get today. We knew we could send them back if they complained, but we rarely had to. The bracero program helped everyone. Mexicans supported their families and Americans made money. It was the finest Peace Corps activity in reverse. Instead of us going to their country to teach them, they came up here to learn from us.

Growers particularly praised braceros' "motivation"—a quality that ex-braceros attributed to their political vulnerability and limited alternatives. Strict field supervision and small farm size further ensured care and dili-

[4]According to the Watsonville association manager interviewed, few braceros in his area deserted their contracts to work in noncertified positions. He estimated that the two Watsonville associations had from fourteen to fifteen desertions a year, out of the total of 4,500 braceros each hired.

gence, and the nature of the work permitted replacement at relatively little cost. Strawberry growers reported that they could usually train inexperienced pickers in a matter of days. If they could not, they were easily replaced. Moreover, although growers were not guaranteed a continuity of workers, many were able to secure the same workers year after year. If they liked a person's work, they would talk to him at the end of the season and ask him to return. Some wrote letters to their best workers in Mexico before the season started, reiterating their offers of employment. At the border, those individuals would then ask to be sent to Watsonville or Salinas, where they would ask to go to a certain grower. Because the associations were formed by and managed for growers, they—in the words of one manager—"made every effort to accommodate" such requests.

In their relatively unqualified enthusiasm for braceros, berry growers differed substantially from those in lettuce. Their difference underscores the importance of industrial variance. As both Galarza (1964) and Thomas (1985) note, southwestern lettuce growers turned to illegals during the bracero program because they could not be guaranteed return of the same braceros annually. Lettuce labor processes encouraged this resort: whereas strawberries can be harvested by individual workers who are minimally skilled, lettuce is harvested by crews whose performance depends on a high level of *group* skill, coordination, and trust. Continuity is therefore more important and replacement more costly for lettuce producers. Larger farm size also makes it harder for lettuce growers to monitor field performance and attend to the return of each worker. In short, the particular utility of the bracero program to strawberry growers was directly related to the commodity-constrained organization of production.

By the early 1960s, strawberry growers recognized that the future of the program was in jeopardy. An Anglo grower from Watsonville elaborated: "By 1963, we knew we were going to lose the program. It was killed by the bleeding hearts. It was those do-gooders like Mrs. Roosevelt that got rid of it." This assessment of the program's opposition had some basis in reality. Although California growers continued to favor it, some of its traditional supporters fell away and new opposition emerged. After the cotton harvest was mechanized in the late 1950s, farmers in the American South no longer needed braceros and withdrew their support from the program (Hawley 1966; Craig 1971). By the early 1960s a new alliance had emerged, linking the civil rights and antipoverty movements, organized urban labor, and the increasingly active agricultural union movement in California. This alliance attacked the bracero program for depressing domestic wages, displacing citizens, and using public funds to further private business (Bach 1978; Jenkins and Perrow 1977; Majka and Majka 1982).

The program's detrimental impact on unionization came under special fire. The Reverend Chris Hartmire, Jr., former director of the California Migrant Ministry, articulated its opponents' concerns: "It is not possible to describe adequately the demoralizing effect this program had on domestic workers. Many strikes were crushed in advance by this demoralization; others were beaten by the use of braceros as strikebreakers or by the threatened use of braceros" (Kushner 1975:115).

Owing mainly to the efforts of these interests, the United States terminated the bracero program in December 1964. With it ended an era in which agribusiness could secure favorable border policies with little public discussion or dissent, and the political constituencies shaping immigration legislation became increasingly diverse and vocal. Although subsequent policies have been attentive to agribusiness, their control over labor supply has been neither as complete nor as effective.

Stratification by Citizenship: 1965–88

When the bracero program ended, its supporters forecast agricultural disaster, and its opponents anticipated rising wages, improved working conditions, and the entry of domestic workers into the fields. Neither prediction proved entirely accurate. Farm wage levels did take a leap upward, and labor protections increased. Yet most farm industries survived and continued to employ immigrant workers. Some, such as the tomato, wine grape, and lettuce industries, were able to control and reduce their need for labor by mechanizing part or all of the harvest. In the strawberry industry, however, commodity characteristics prevented harvest mechanization. Growers responded with a concerted effort to rationalize production processes and eliminate labor wherever they could. Industry support for productivity-enhancing and labor-reducing scientific research ballooned in this period, and innovation adoption was particularly rapid. Nonetheless, the continued need for hand harvesting, combined with rising yields and labor demands, actually increased growers' vulnerability to the cost and performance of labor. Rising wage levels compounded this sensitivity. Regional harvest wages began to climb as soon as the bracero program ended. Whereas local wages for bracero berry pickers averaged $.95 an hour between 1950 and 1964, they had increased by 80 percent, to $1.80, by 1969 (Burlingame, Farnham, and Greathead 1969). By 1976, the hourly wage was $3.70 and by 1985 it was $7.20 (Welch and Greathead 1976; Welch, Greathead, and Beutel 1985). All in all, wages took their largest single upward leap in the five years after the bracero program ended.

Many observers predicted that the end of the program would drive California berry growers out of business or force them to move to Mexico where costs were lower (*Seasonal Labor* 1963). They envisioned a decimated state strawberry industry conducted by a small number of family and tenant farmers. In fact, although some berry growers from Texas and California border counties did move to Mexico (Feder 1977:11–41), central coast growers did not: they were situated in a climate that produced a more bountiful and higher-quality crop than did any Mexican alternative, and they were closely connected to local residents and institutions because many had lived in the region for generations. They were therefore highly motivated to develop solutions to their labor problems that would permit them to remain. Like other California growers, many found this solution in the form of documented and undocumented Mexican immigrants.

Ironically, the success of the civil rights and antipoverty movements in increasing the entitlements of U.S. citizens also enhanced the relative vulnerability of noncitizens and increased their utility to employers (Thomas 1985:70–73). From the mid-1960s through the 1980s, only a fraction of California farm workers were citizens. The California farm labor market became increasingly subdivided by region and industry, and the labor force became increasingly stratified along lines of citizenship. The government no longer managed farm labor directly, but its policies managed workers indirectly by creating different citizenship statuses that accorded unequal access to political and economic resources. The most important such statuses were those of citizen and documented and undocumented immigrant. In the strawberry labor market, as in California agriculture more broadly (Thomas 1985), the very existence of these categories undermined labor resistance and solidarity and augmented the workplace control of growers.

Documented immigrants, called "green carders" after the original color of the identification cards given them, were admitted as early as 1965 under the terms of the McCarran-Walter Act of 1952. Green carders are certified to live, travel, and work anywhere in the United States. They may visit extensively, even live abroad, and they may reenter the country as often as they like provided they are not absent for over one year. Currently, many green carders live in Mexico and commute across the border daily to work. Most work in agriculture, although manufacturing, sales, and service also employ many (Cornelius, Chavez, and Castro 1982; North 1970). The number of green carders rose sharply in the first years after the bracero program ended, because certification was made easy to soften the transition for growers. A grower's written promise of employment virtually guaranteed certification. With the subsequent imposition of immigration quotas for Mexico and other countries, it has become increasingly difficult to obtain legal immigrant status. Despite a thriving business in forged documents and various channels for circumventing the rules, the growth of this category had practically ceased by the mid-1970s and remained relatively static until the late 1980s (Sosnick 1978:124–53, 409–10, 417–21). Although the Immigration Reform and Control Act of 1986 (IRCA) again facilitated obtaining legal immigrant status, it was not significantly enforced during the period of this study.

Undocumented workers (in Spanish, *indocumentados* or *sinpapeles*—those without papers) comprised the largest group of new entries. They had been used throughout the bracero program to smooth out its inefficiencies and ensure the continuity of key employees, and when the program ended, illegal entry became the single major means of labor force replenishment (Bach 1978; Jenkins 1978:517–19). It is impossible, of course, to determine the exact number of undocumented immigrants working in California agriculture because they are so mobile, underprotected, and fearful of apprehension. Moreover, the prevalence of forged green cards, social security cards, and other evidence of legal status makes it difficult to trust apparent legality. Nonetheless, some approximations of their proportions are possible. In 1977, the California Department of Housing estimated conservatively that from 40 to 50 percent of California's farm workers were undocumented (1977:17). In some local, especially border, labor markets they may comprise from 80 to 90 percent of the workforce. Overall, based on my own research and on the informal assessments of other farm labor researchers, it seems reasonable to assume that as many as 80 percent of California's farm workers were noncitizen immigrants from the mid-1960s into the late 1980s. About half of the total workforce was undocumented, another 30 percent were green carders, and about 20 percent or fewer were citizens. Most of these were born in California; a small minority were born in Texas (Martin 1987:54; Mines and Martin 1986; U.S. Congress, Senate 1969:65). Of the noncitizens, over 90 percent were of Mexican birth or descent. About half were born and grew up in small towns in Mexico's south-central highlands, although many also came from border and inland cities. In both areas, low wages and high unemployment have long encouraged seasonal outmigration to the United States. They were exacerbated by the Mexican economic crises of the 1980s (Brannon et al. 1984; Dagodag 1975; Dinerman 1982; Grindle 1983; Jones 1984).

The lifting of the bracero program's institutional controls permitted the fragmentation of California's farm labor market. The citizenship composition of regional and industrial labor markets has become increasingly differentiated. Border areas tend to be heavily illegal because of the large number of undocumented residents and the ease of border crossing (Ericson 1970; Jones 1984; North 1970). Some border industries employ *sinpa-*

peles almost exclusively, as in the case of the strawberry and pole tomato industries of north San Diego County. Illegals are less prevalent farther from the border, comprising, for example, only about 40 percent of the mushroom pickers in Monterey County and less than one-third of the citrus workers in Ventura County and the grape workers in Tulare County in the mid-1980s. Based on my own and other research (Martin et al. 1984; Martin et al. 1985; Mines and Martin 1986), it seems likely that, from the 1970s to the late 1980s, about 70 percent of central coast berry workers were undocumented and over 95 percent were not citizens.

Wage rates in local labor markets have also become more varied. During the bracero program, wages rose little and contracts exerted a leveling effect on local markets. In 1963, for example, the average hourly wage in California agriculture was $1.28 and most workers received from $1.15 to $1.40 per hour. By 1983, the average hourly wage had risen to $4.66 and the regional and industrial variance was much greater. On the central coast the average hourly wage for all agricultural industries was $5.24, in the Sacramento Valley it was $3.97, in the San Joaquin Valley it was $4.46, and in southern California it was $4.86. The statewide averages for different industries also varied. Workers on large vegetable farms received an hourly wage of from $8.00 to $11.00, those harvesting mushrooms and citrus received from $6.00 to $8.00, those harvesting melons about $5.00, and those thinning and weeding a variety of crops from $3.35 to $4.00 (Martin 1987; Martin et al. 1984; Mines and Martin 1986). On the central coast, strawberry pickers averaged about $7.00 an hour by the mid-1980s.

The Advantage of Immigrant Workers

In California agriculture as in other nations and economic sectors, the use of immigrants helps employers maintain profit rates by increasing the flexibility of labor exploitation (Castles and Kosack [1973] 1985; Portes and Walton 1981). All producers benefit from the downward pressure on wages and working conditions that such a labor supply exerts, but many small, low-resource producers require it as a condition of survival. Noncitizen immigrants can be employed more flexibly than either braceros or citizens. Unlike braceros, work certifications do not restrict the duration and continuity of their employment. Growers therefore often hired undocumented workers during the bracero era in positions that required more skill, commitment, and longevity than could be expected from braceros (e.g., foreman, irrigator, truck driver, or lettuce crew member) (Galarza 1964:30, 57–62, 69–71, 79; Majka and Majka 1982:142–46; Thomas 1985). Immigrants are less affected by the constraints on the deployment of citizens that unions and government policies have imposed since the mid-1960s, in part because they are excluded from some benefits, in part because they are less likely to assert their rights. Illegal immigrants are, of course, especially manipulable, because their employment alternatives are more limited and because the potential of apprehension and deportation dampens their resistance to grower impositions. Immigration laws increase the fearfulness of illegals without seriously hampering their movements. Although, in theory, the INS is responsible for enforcing immigration laws and halting the illegal influx through its enforcement branch, the Border Patrol (*migra* in Spanish), in practice, the Border Patrol has never had the budget or staffing to enforce the law, largely because of pressures from agriculture (Greene 1969; Jenkins 1978:527). Moreover, until the IRCA, growers were not penalized for hiring illegals. In effect, the Border Patrol has operated to minimize its impact on employers, while ensuring that illegals remain fearful and are not a community burden in the off-season (Burawoy 1976; Thomas 1985).

On the central coast as elsewhere, the Border Patrol did not attempt complete enforcement. The agents in charge of its Salinas station, which is responsible for the central coast region, described their policy as "keeping a presence," and they considered themselves to be "extremely understaffed."[5] In 1986, they had only four agents to cover major portions of a four-county area and "could use another twelve agents easy." Their staffing had not increased since 1968, despite the significant growth of labor-intensive agriculture in their region. Although these patrol agents did some routine checking on large ranches situated near the road, mostly they responded to initiated complaints of illegal employment. Nor did these complaints necessarily indicate flagrant violations of the law: usually they came from neighbors who "had a gripe with" the employing grower or from documented workers who had been displaced by illegals. Even with a tip, apprehensions were difficult because of the prevalence of forged papers and the rule of solidarity among workers on many ranches requiring that both legals and illegals flee when the *migra* appeared. Certainly the hiring of illegals continued unabated through the period of this study. One patrol agent summarized the situation in 1987:

> Illegals are a fact of life in California agriculture. Growers depend on them. They work harder than legals and they stick with the work. If politicians were concerned about illegals, they would give us the staff to make a differ-

[5]Direct information sources on the operation of the Border Patrol on the central coast include interviews with growers, workers, and the agents in charge of the Salinas Border Patrol station, and my presence in the fields during six raids.

> ence. Right now all we do is harass a few workers and harass a few growers. We don't stop the use of illegals. Workers return in three to five days. They're gone on Friday and back on Monday. It's the norm. We scare them a little and cost them a lot. That's all.

Although many workers do return in such short order, the monetary and psychic costs of recrossing are substantial. Many cannot return that same season. In effect, illegals' constant fear of deportation increases their compliance and reduces their willingness to join unions or make requests of public institutions, even when their reception might be favorable. The fact that citizens and documented noncitizens often resent them as illegitimate competitors reduces their support in the wider society and undermines the solidarity of the workforce overall. Moreover, illegality has a significant impact on the earnings a worker can expect, in that *sinpapeles* are generally concentrated in the most arduous, lowest-paid, and least-protected positions. Illegals do not always make less than legals, though: they often work in skilled, stable, and better-paid positions where their vulnerability helps prevent the claims for higher wages that their skill and economic centrality might otherwise leverage (Thomas 1985). Generally, illegals are paid the same wage as other workers when they are distributed randomly, but their wages tend to be lower when they cluster in certain regions or with certain employers (Ericson 1970).

Documented immigrants also lack the full privileges and supports for resistance that are available to citizens. Legally, green carders must have an offer of employment before entering the country. They can work only in industries or positions in which the Department of Labor has declared a labor shortage, and they may be deported if they have been unemployed for a long period of time. Their presence in the United States and their access to benefits are thus directly contingent on active labor force participation. They are eligible for job-related benefits such as unemployment insurance and workers' compensation insurance, but they may not receive state or federal welfare assistance until they have lived in the country for five continuous years. Although green carders may legally join unions, their labor-contingent status weakens the base from which they can make claims. Because many are oriented toward Mexico for their long-term advancement and do not claim the entitlements of citizens, they are also less likely to speak out. Studies show that legal and illegal immigrants are harder to organize than are citizens and that border commuters of both categories are particularly difficult. Along the border, illegal and legal commuters are often used as strikebreakers, and the fear of losing their jobs to commuters stops many resident workers from striking (Ericson 1970; Sosnick 1978:425–27).

Administrative provisions limited wage levels and ensured a matching of labor supply to demand during the bracero era, and the immigrant-dominated labor market has ensured this fit since. For both legal and illegal Mexican immigrants, unemployment, underemployment, and low wages in their region of origin reduce their wage claims in the United States and the wage levels in the labor markets in which they predominate (Burawoy 1976; Cornelius, Chavez, and Castro 1982; Gonzales 1985). The urgency of immigrants' economic need and the proximity of the Mexican supplying regions have generated chronic labor surpluses in California agriculture (Ericson 1970; Fisher 1953; Fuller 1939; McWilliams [1935] 1971; Sosnick 1978). Surpluses have varied since the mid-1960s: they shrank temporarily when the bracero program ended until new recruitment mechanisms were developed, and they expanded after the early 1980s when the Mexican economic crisis enhanced incentives to work in U.S. agriculture (Brannon, Ibarreche, and English 1984; Dinerman 1982; Grindle 1983; Kearney and Stuart 1981). For the most part, however, surpluses have prevailed in post-1960s California farm labor markets, increasing the dispensability and the malleability of workers.

The impotence of immigrant workers should not be overestimated, however. Despite prevailing surpluses, local labor markets vary considerably. As noted, surpluses tend to be greatest along the border. Localities vary in the extent to which they have experienced an increase in labor supply since the early 1980s. Regions dominated by certain crop industries experience periods when demand is high and supply is low. In the central coast strawberry industry, labor is regularly scarce at two points in the season: in May and June, when the primary harvest peak coincides with expanding demand from other local farm industries; and in September, when the secondary harvest peak coincides with the return of many workers to Mexico. Labor shortages were severe in the region after the end of the bracero program, but surpluses were restored by the late 1960s and increased in the 1980s. The exact proportions of this increase are impossible to determine, but growers report a doubling in the number of workers who came unsolicited to their ranches for work between 1983 and 1986, an unprecedented number of whom begged for even a day's work so they could buy something to eat. Berry workers concurred, supplying accounts of their own days in the 1980s without food or a job and observing that they had never seen so many illegals in the region. All in all, these supply shifts affect workers' leverage in the labor market.

Because local labor markets are more fragmented, they are also more responsive to local class struggles. Moreover, immigrant workers are more able than braceros to organize and dissent. Immigrants are more manipulable than citizens, but they are decidedly less so than braceros. They lack the full privileges and sense of entitlement that come with citizenship, but they work alongside citizens in jobs that, since the mid-1960s, have become increasingly protected by state and federal laws. Whereas the wages and working conditions of braceros were set by government fiat, those of immigrants are set in local markets and shaped by the stipulations of protective legislation and the quantity and mobilization of local workers. Whereas the movements of braceros were orchestrated closely by the government and employer organizations, those of immigrants are often private, even clandestine, and are impossible to monitor or control entirely. Finally and most important, whereas braceros were indisputably foreigners and could be deported at the least sign of resistance, documented immigrants have some claim on public entitlements and cannot be expelled for labor organizing. Thus, the dismantling of the bracero program cleared the way for farm worker unionization and extended the impact of protective laws.

Protective Legislation and Farm Labor

In the mid-1960s, another aspect of the policy environment shifted, spurred by the same forces that ended the bracero program. State and federal protections already applicable to urban workers were extended to seasonal farm laborers, who had been explicitly excluded from most prior labor legislation. Labor protections were most extensive in California, because agricultural union activity was strongest there and had seriously destabilized agricultural production and marketing. In effect, protective laws compounded the attack on growers' labor market leverage by restricting their discretion in deploying and rewarding workers. Whether or not individual growers observed these laws, the formal hegemony of this legislation over labor market relations established the potential for enforcement. This potential could be actualized by government agencies or labor organizations and, thus, increased the leverage of workers.

To understand the current impact of protective laws in agriculture, it is useful to reflect on their historical intent and evolution. Their roots go back to the New Deal, when the U.S. government moved away from its mildly interventionist, business-dominated stance to become an active broker state that incorporated agricultural and industrial business interests into political bargaining at the national level (Skocpol 1980:156). Increasingly, the state intervened in production in two crucial ways: through social insurance legislation that guaranteed the reproduction of labor power at a minimal level, independent of workers' participation in production; and through regulatory legislation that limited managerial discretion in the deployment of labor. Both forms of intervention reduced workers' dependence on their performance at work (Burawoy 1985). The Fair Labor Standards Act (FLSA), which established minimum wage levels and overtime pay standards, and the Social Security Act (SSA), which provided relief for unemployed, disabled, widowed, and retired persons, were the most important representatives of the first type of law. The National Labor Relations (Wagner) Act (NLRA), which defined unfair labor practices and granted employees the right to organize and bargain collectively, was the most important exemplar of the second. Although enacted in large part to bolster the functioning of the competitive market,[6] these pieces of New Deal legislation instituted a new concept of citizenship that ensured equal social, political, and economic rights for all strata of society (Marshall 1965:v–xxii, 71–134). They acknowledged a particular obligation to protect wage laborers, a group whose security was viewed as especially precarious in the unregulated functioning of the market. These laws explicitly aimed to "extend the frontiers of social progress" by "ensuring to all our able-bodied working men and women a fair day's pay for a fair day's work" (Scher and Catz 1975:575). In fact, several important categories of workers were excluded, some initially and some as the acts were amended.

All three acts excluded agricultural laborers, in part because of growers' pressure, but also because farm workers were unorganized and because the general public and urban unions were largely indifferent to the problems of farm labor (Bernstein 1950; Gorman 1976:31; Millis and Brown 1965; Morris 1966; Skocpol 1980). In this setting, as Congress and the executive branch tried to accommodate the diverse interests petitioning for relief, seasonal farm workers were excluded with little opposition (Morris 1966:1956). Their exclusion was based on the argument, presented forcefully by organized grower interests, that labor protections were unfair and unnecessary in agriculture because labor relations were generally harmonious and farmers were already unduly vulnerable to workers' demands. That is, given the perishable nature of farm products, the dependence of farmers' incomes on the short harvest period, and their lack of control over

[6]As Scher and Catz show for the FLSA (1975:575), and as Congress's following rationale statement illustrates for the NLRA, Congress clearly intended that these laws would eliminate obstructions to the free flow of commerce: "(1) the denial by employers of the right of employees to organize and the refusal by employers to accept the procedure of collective bargaining [which] lead to strikes . . . obstructing commerce . . . (2) the inequality of bargaining power between 'employees' and 'employers' . . . [which] . . . burdens . . . commerce . . . by depressing wage rates and the purchasing power of wage earners in industry and by preventing the stabilization of competitive wage rates and working conditions within and between industries" ({{1, 49 Stat. 449 [1935], 29 U.S.C. {{151 [1964]).

weather, production, prices, and markets, the right to organize would give farm workers inordinate power over growers. Moreover, it was argued, legal protections were superfluous because labor relations on farms were already familylike. Deploying the image of the midwestern hired hand, farmers and farm workers were pictured kneeling together in prayer and eating from the same table, and unions were portrayed ominously manipulating the nation's food supply (Gorman 1976:31; Lee 1966; Morris 1966).

These arguments, promoted by agribusiness interests who were heavily represented in Congress and whose support was essential for the passage of urban labor protections, dominated labor legislation discussions in the 1930s and 1940s. They were raised again by growers during the 1961 hearings on farm labor before the Cobey Committee of the California State Senate (California State 1961:pt.1:202) and in 1965–1967 before the Senate Subcommittee on Migratory Labor (Majka and Majka 1982:172–75). Many articulate counterarguments were presented over the years (Morris 1966), and farm workers did receive limited coverage under the SSA in 1955. But it was not until they became more organized and militant in the mid-1960s and attracted allies from outside their ranks that legislative measures to protect them gathered force. The shift began in 1963, when the state of California set a minimum wage for farm workers. In 1966, farm workers were included under the FLSA; in 1974, a minimum age of twelve years was established for farm work under the FLSA. In 1976, California extended unemployment insurance and workers' compensation insurance to farm workers, and it established state overtime pay standards for adult males working in agriculture. All of these measures were supported and many were initiated by the growing alliance among civil rights interests and industrial and agricultural labor.

The California Agricultural Labor Relations Act (ALRA) was a particularly important victory for this alliance, particularly for the UFW, whose vigorous unionization campaign and direct lobbying with California legislators and the public were the major pressures behind its enactment. By the late 1960s, the exemption of farm workers from the NLRA had become a mixed blessing for California growers. Although it permitted them to avoid elections and recognition of the UFW, the California courts ruled that growers could not fire or otherwise discriminate against field workers because of their union activity. In addition, exemption from the NLRA freed the UFW from the act's restrictions on unfair labor practices, including the secondary boycott (Sosnick 1978:374). In 1969, a coalition of grower groups that included the American Farm Bureau began to press for bills to limit farm labor union activity ("Farm Bureau" 1973; Geyer 1970a, 1970b; Sosnick 1978:364–86). Between 1969 and 1975, grower-supported bills were initiated in Congress and in the legislatures of California and sixteen other states. These bills contained proposals that would help growers in their struggles with unions: they outlawed the secondary boycott, some required "cooling-off" periods encompassing the harvest to help growers avoid bargaining, others outlawed harvest strikes entirely, and many excluded certain issues from negotiation in collective bargaining, such as the union hiring hall and pesticide controls. The UFW mobilized against these bills. It sent staff to Washington, D.C., and to other states at substantial cost to union resources (Majka and Majka 1982:208–16). Before its 1973 convention, the UFW began to discuss legislative initiatives of its own. In 1974, it sponsored a bill to establish an agricultural labor relations commission which passed the state assembly but died in the senate, escaping the expected veto of Governor Ronald Reagan. Meanwhile, ten years of almost continuous strikes and consumer boycotts had increased growers' interest in a resolution. Citizens' groups, political leaders, churches, urban unions, and farm workers themselves all issued calls for farm labor reforms. Both sides focused on the state, as the guarantor of social order, to devise a solution.

The election of Jerry Brown as governor in 1974 loosened growers' hold on the state political apparatus and permitted the design of legislation that could mediate between the interests of growers and workers. Brown expressly viewed this as his task and set out to craft and secure agreement to the first farm labor relations bill in the country (Levy 1975:529–35). He met directly with union and grower representatives in an effort to incorporate the positions of all parties. The act itself was a compromise. Growers represented Brown as a UFW agent, but in fact the bill he proposed in April 1975 was more closely attuned to grower interests. The UFW immediately informed Brown that the bill was unacceptable and began a national lobbying and speaking tour against it. In response, Brown met with growers, the UFW, and the Teamsters and finally emerged with a bill that all three would endorse.

The ALRA was based on NLRA definitions and precedents. Its preamble expressed opinions also voiced by lawmakers in the 1930s—that unregulated labor relations had become intolerable for all parties and that all would benefit from restoring stable production conditions:

> In enacting this legislation the people of the State of California seek to ensure peace in the agricultural fields by guaranteeing justice for all agricultural workers and stability in labor relations. This enactment is intended to bring certainty and a sense of fair play to a presently unstable and potentially volatile condition in the state. . . . [I]t is the hope of the Legislature that farm

> laborers, farmers, and all the people of California will be served by the provisions of this act. ({1, CAL. LAB. CODE {{1140 [1975] rev. Mar. 26, 1982).

The opening paragraph of the ALRA identified protecting farm workers' right to organize and bargain collectively as crucial to reinstating peace in the fields:

> It is . . . the policy of the State of California to encourage and protect the right of agricultural employees to full freedom of association, self-organization, and designation of representatives of their own choosing, to negotiate the terms and conditions of their employment, and to be free from the interference, restrain, or coercion of employers. . . . [T]his part is adopted to provide for collective bargaining rights for agricultural employees. (ibid. {{1140.2 [1975] rev. Mar. 26, 1982)

The bill that was finally signed on June 5, 1975, gave farm workers the right to organize, hold harvest-time elections, and bargain collectively free from employer interference. It gave growers protection against picketing and boycotts, and it gave the Teamsters the right to keep their existing contracts until elections were held. Unions already representing workers covered under the NLRA were protected from infringement. Overall, the ALRA's provisions and procedures focused on two areas: union representation elections and the certification of union representatives, and the determination and prevention of unfair labor practices. It was administered by an appointed general counsel and a five-member board, which were located in Sacramento and assisted by regional directors and office staff.

After the mid-1960s, then, the political climate surrounding protective labor legislation began to tilt in the direction of workers. Protective laws took the treatment of workers out of the private domain of grower prerogative and into the public realm of legal stipulation. In the process, workers gained legal support for many of their claims against growers. True, the standards established for farm workers were still lower than those for urban workers, and stipulations regarding coverage excluded a substantial portion of the rural work force;[7] nonetheless, the new laws restricted growers' control over the cost and management of labor. Significantly, most of the new laws did not discriminate on the basis of citizenship but specified acceptable terms and labor practices for agricultural work, regardless of the citizenship status of those who performed it. Covered employers were required to pay the minimum wage and overtime pay and to refrain from

[7]Although the FLSA formally covered farm workers after 1966, it actually excluded 98 percent of the nation's farms (Scher and Catz 1975:577-79).

firing labor organizers, regardless of the immigration status of their workers. Immigrants were still less likely to assert their rights than were citizens, and illegals were ineligible for some benefits, but state intervention did reduce the dependence of workers on their performance at work and limit the ability of employers to arbitrarily impose the terms of employment. On the central coast, these limits were most potent when union mobilization was at its height.

The Rise of Agricultural Unionism

Also in the mid-1960s, the third political factor structuring power relations in the central coast strawberry labor market began to shift: unionization gathered force. Aided by the end of the bracero program, but still hindered by the prevalence of immigrant workers in the fields, the UFW dramatically altered the balance of power in California agriculture. Union pressure combined with the new immigration and protective legislation to generate a labor market regime more supportive of labor. Although few central coast berry farms experienced strikes or union contracts, UFW militancy augmented workers' political leverage and transformed labor supply and price conditions throughout the region.

Agricultural union activity was at a low ebb for most of the bracero period. It picked up in the early 1960s and increased markedly when the program ended: between 1964 and 1965 alone, the annual number of workers involved in agricultural work stoppages rose by 159 percent, from 2,190 to 5,660 (CDIR 1965, 1966). As table 5 shows, union activity was most intense during the 1970s.[8] By the end of the decade the annual number of farm workers involved in strikes had increased by 400 percent over the first year of record keeping in 1952, and the annual number of person-workdays idle in agriculture had increased by a remarkable 3,233 percent. Work stoppages decreased after 1980 but were still more frequent than in the 1950s. Overall, the unionization struggles of the 1970s demonstrated an unprecedented capacity for collective action among California farm workers and permanently transformed the public dialogue surrounding farm labor.

Union activity touched the central coast differently over the course of

[8]The California Department of Industrial Relations gathered data on work stoppages and person-workdays idle in agriculture only from 1952 through 1981 (CDIR 1953-82). These data aggregate agriculture, fishing, and mineral extraction into a single category, but agricultural field labor comprises the bulk of activity in this category. A person-workday (to them, man-workday), is the equivalent of one person working for one day.

Table 5. Work stoppages in California agriculture, 1952–82

Time span	Average number of workers per year	Average number of person-workdays idle per year
1952–59	1,420	18,023
1960–69	2,764	41,800
1970–79	5,792	140,050
1970–74	9,504	76,850
1975–79	2,080	106,740
1980–82	4,200	76,850

Source: California Department of Industrial Relations, *Work Stoppages in California* (San Francisco: State of California, Division of Labor Statistics and Research, 1953–83).

this period. Until 1970, its impact was primarily indirect: the example of the UFW's accomplishments in the San Joaquin Valley grape campaign stimulated the fears and hopes of central coast farmers and farm workers. After 1970, its impact was direct: the UFW turned its attention to the prosperous central coast lettuce and vegetable industry, initiating a paralyzing general strike in August–September of that year. Over the 1970s, it engaged in heated contract struggles with lettuce producers and bitter jurisdictional battles with the Western Conference of Teamsters. The union's focus on the central coast and the coexistence of lettuce and strawberry production within that region were of critical consequence for strawberry growers. They were never the UFW's primary target, mainly because larger farms in other segments of agriculture promised greater returns for organizers' efforts (Friedland, Barton, and Thomas 1981). Whereas it might appear that berry growers escaped the constraints of unionization because so few contracts were signed in the industry, in fact, the intense union campaign increased labor uncertainty and cost and reduced the managerial control of growers throughout the region.

The UFW's impact on the central coast can best be understood by examining three periods in its history: first, its ascent to power between 1962 and July 1970, when it organized and conducted a successful union campaign in the San Joaquin and Coachella Valley grape industry; second, its maturation in the 1970s, when it turned its attention to central coast vegetable growers and maintained a level of union pressure throughout the decade that transformed labor relations in all regional crop industries; and third, its decline after the early 1980s due to changes in its own tactics and to shifts in the wider political and economic environment (see Brown 1972; Jenkins 1985; Kushner 1975; Levy 1975; Majka and Majka 1982; Meister and Loftis 1977).

The Ascent of the United Farm Workers

Central coast growers' fears of the union, and workers' hopes for it, were engendered by its early methods and successes. The UFW began in 1962 as a service organization for seasonal farm workers. It was founded by Cesar Chavez, a Mexican American former farm laborer who quit his job as an organizer for the Community Service Organization to dedicate himself to building a union for agricultural workers. Basing his operation in the city of Delano in the heart of California's grape-producing San Joaquin Valley, Chavez first organized a mutual benefit association, which he called the Farm Workers Association. Soon the organization offered a credit union, a purchasing cooperative, group burial insurance, and help with problems ranging from immigration difficulties to unpaid wages, court appearances, and access to public services. In 1964, the association adopted the name of National Farm Workers Association (NFWA); by August its membership included 1,000 dues-paying Mexican American families in seven San Joaquin Valley counties (Brown 1972:121). In September 1965, Chavez joined the Agricultural Workers' Organizing Committee in its pathbreaking dispute with wine and table grape growers in the Delano area. In August 1966, AWOC and NFWA combined to form the United Farm Workers Organizing Committee, AFL-CIO. Although it did not formally establish itself as a union until 1972, when it assumed the name of the United Farm Workers of America, it was the major bargaining agent for California farm workers from 1965 on. For convenience, we will refer to Chavez's organization after 1965 as the UFW.

The Delano grape strikes spread, polarizing California's valley communities. Strikers picketed fields and packing sheds. They harassed strikebreakers and the contractors who brought them in, and blocked the entryways to farms. They were beaten by local police and were jailed in large numbers. In a consequential strategic decision, the UFW decided to broaden the arena of conflict from California's grower-dominated agricultural valleys to its urban centers and then to the nation, where public sentiment increasingly supportive of civil rights and the poor could make a difference. The grape campaign developed the tactics that were to prove so effective during the central coast lettuce encounters: the drawing in of new public allies, the effective use of the mass media, the augmentation of strikes in the fields with consumer boycotts, and the presentation of a public image combining Mexican religious and cultural symbolism.

In marches and rallies drawing over ten thousand people, Chavez enlisted the support of established unions, as well as liberals in the government and private foundations, civil rights sympathizers, clergy, youth, and the poor. Union organizers visited state and federal government centers, unions, campuses, and churches. Chavez focused the eyes of the nation on the struggle between grape growers and workers. A small man of humble demeanor and charismatic speaking style, he conveyed the ideals of nonviolence, hard work, self-sacrifice, piety, and respect for the dispossessed. In contrast to the well-publicized opulence in which established union leaders lived, the UFW leadership exhibited a monastic quality. Chavez's tactics conveyed his idealism, his Mexican Catholicism, and his dedication to Gandhi's tradition of nonviolence. He shunned suits, ate tortillas, and drew a subsistence salary. He affirmed his Mexican farm-worker roots in dress and life style. The union presented its marches as pilgrimages and timed them to coincide with Mexican religious occasions. Union leaders and volunteers alike lived in poverty.[9] Chavez repeatedly undertook fasts to add moral impetus to his pleas. In his speeches he emphasized that the UFW was engaged not simply in a campaign for agricultural unionization but in a moral cause—La Causa—a crusade to reclaim the dignity and civil rights of Mexican-origin farm laborers.

In late 1965, the UFW initiated a national consumer boycott of the products of certain wine grape growers. In June 1966, distressed by the publicity and financial impact of the boycott, Schenley Industries, a large Delano wine grape grower, signed a collective bargaining agreement with the UFW that secured higher wages, fringe benefits such as paid vacations, consultation with the union concerning health and safety, and guarantees of job security through a hiring hall and union shop. The elements of this agreement, along with limits on the use of labor contractors and pesticides, were repeated in later contracts. They set the basis for what growers anticipated—and feared—from capitulation to the union. Over the next several years, the union secured other contracts in wine grapes. In 1967, it began a nationwide boycott and organizing effort in the California and Arizona table grape industries. The organizational capacity demonstrated by this boycott was unsurpassed in the history of U.S. farm labor organizing: full-time boycott committees, most led by strikers with families, operated from churches and community organizations in thirty-one large American and Canadian cities and in some two hundred smaller communities as well (Brown 1972:137, 169). The boycott generated wide public sympathy. Estimates of its economic impact in 1969 alone ranged as high as $20 million (Sosnick 1978:322).

[9] In 1972, for example, union officers received room, board, medical costs, and $5 per week. Chavez received a total of $5,144, including $1,904 for medical bills incurred during his 24-day fast to protest Arizona's restrictive farm labor law (Sosnick 1978:344–45).

Faced with this pressure, grape growers began to capitulate. In March 1970, the largest table grape grower in the Coachella Valley signed a contract. Over the next several months other Coachella and San Joaquin Valley growers followed suit. On July 29, Giumarra Vineyards, the largest table grape grower in the United States, along with twenty-six other San Joaquin Valley grape growers, signed three-year contracts with the union. The UFW now had contracts covering 150 grape ranches in the two valleys, representing twenty thousand jobs in table grapes and over ten thousand members (Brown 1972:140–43; Jenkins 1985:162–74; Majka and Majka 1982:186–99).

The Central Coast Unionization Struggle

On the night that the UFW signed the table grape contracts, its negotiating team learned that about 40 percent of the vegetable growers in the Salinas and Santa Maria Valleys—65 out of 170 companies—had signed five-year sweetheart contracts with the Teamsters. Signers included all of the large central coast lettuce and vegetable producers and one strawberry company—Pic N Pac—the largest in the region and the only one owned by an out-of-state corporation. The contracts declared the Teamsters to be the exclusive bargaining agent for field workers and it left other conditions to be filled in later. Workers were not consulted in the negotiation of these contracts; they were told that they had to sign union authorization cards in ten days or lose their jobs and that dues would be deducted from their pay. The contracts instituted no grievance procedures or limits on hiring policies, the use of pesticides, or labor contractors, although they did ultimately increase wages.

The UFW was outraged, since it had a jurisdictional agreement with the Teamsters ceding to it the representation of field workers. The next day UFW leaders headed for Salinas. They set up a small storefront office in the city center and summoned their boycott teams from San Francisco and Los Angeles to help in the new campaign. They immediately demanded that growers void their Teamsters contracts and recognize the UFW. The conflict escalated rapidly. By August 24, the UFW had declared a general strike in the Salinas, Pajaro, and Santa Maria Valleys that involved as many as ten thousand workers in what may have been the largest strike in California's agricultural history. This strike showed central coast growers that they too were at risk, and it formed the reference point to which they responded over the rest of the decade.[10] In a 1987 interview, Marshall Ganz,

[10]No secondary sources describe the impact of union activity on the central coast strawberry industry. The following picture has been reconstructed primarily from interviews with

the former civil rights activist, UFW executive board member, and head of the international grape boycott who headed up the UFW's new Salinas office, described the unanticipated character of its unfolding:

> The 1970 strike was an explosion. We didn't make it happen. We had no intention of going to Salinas. We were pulled there by the force of events. We wanted to stay in the grapes and consolidate our wins there, but the growers precipitated things by signing on with the Teamsters. It was a classic self-fulfilling prophecy. We never would have had the success if they hadn't overreacted and brought the Teamsters in. The workers had been ready for a long time. We were totally unprepared for the level of organization among workers that we found there.

Origins of the 1970 Strike. To comprehend the origins and development of the 1970 strike, one must appreciate both the bases of union opposition among growers and the bases of union support among workers. Growers' responses to the UFW had been brewing for years. As early as 1961, Bud Antle, a large central coast lettuce producer, had signed a contract with the Western Conference of Teamsters in order to diffuse the pressure of AWOC organizing. Other lettuce growers were angered by this concession and expelled him from the Grower-Shippers Vegetable Association of Central California. In spring 1970, however, as one grape grower after another capitulated to the UFW, their attitude began to change. Their fears increased in May when the UFW sent a request for union recognition to some lettuce growers in the area. Finally, on July 12, the Grower-Shippers Association appointed a committee to discuss a collective bargaining agreement for its members with the Teamsters. In late July, the agreement was reached.

Central coast farm workers responded to the agreement with a militance that would have been unthinkable before Chavez. Their response had been building for years among lettuce workers in the Salinas and Santa Maria Valleys, and it was based in the distinctive structure of the lettuce labor system. These two valleys, situated one hundred miles apart on California's central coast, produced about one-third of all lettuce in the United States. The large lettuce companies located there had ranches in other areas as well, so they could harvest lettuce throughout the year. From April through October their harvest crews worked in the Santa Maria and Sali-

---

growers, workers, sales agents, and union organizers, and from perusal of union contracts in strawberries and vegetables, and of the *Salinas Californian* and the Watsonville *Register-Pajaronian* for the periods of intense union activity. This section has benefited particularly from the insightful comments of William H. Friedland.

nas Valleys. In November they moved to central Arizona. From November or December into March they worked in Yuma, Arizona, or in California's Imperial Valley. In March and April they moved back to central Arizona, and then they returned to California's central coast. The lettuce crews were composed of young Mexican men in their twenties, many of whom left their families in the Mexican border towns and traveled together throughout the season. Crews were paid relatively high piece rates, and the earnings of individuals were based on the output of the group. Lettuce crews were self-regulating, self-pacing, and self-reproducing (Friedland, Barton, and Thomas 1981; Thomas 1985). They tended therefore to be closely knit, and turnover was relatively low. In 1970, many were ex-braceros or sons of braceros.

Coincidentally, central coast lettuce workers *(lechugeros)* had early contact with the UFW. In 1967, in an effort to strengthen its hold in the wine grape industry, the union sent organizers to the central coast to sign up workers on the Paul Masson and Almaden ranches in Soledad and Hollister. In the course of this organizing, the union's reputation spread to nearby lettuce farms. In the same year, the UFW began organizing in the border town of Mexicali to interrupt the flow of strikebreakers that grape growers were recruiting from the area. Because its approach was to set up farm worker service centers, it soon drew in the families of *lechugeros.* When they returned home on weekends and between seasons, the family heads too encountered the union. Because their wages had been frozen since shortly after the end of the bracero program, they were receptive to the union. Soon the union began to organize wage strikes among lettuce and cantaloupe workers along the border, many of whom migrated to Salinas later in the season. In spring 1968, the UFW sent an organizer to the central coast to hold house meetings and build a grass-roots base similar to that established by the NFWA. Again, *lechugeros* were particularly responsive and sent a delegation to Delano that winter requesting support for a strike. Chavez asked them to wait, saying that the union had only enough resources for one campaign at a time. In spring 1970, Salinas lettuce crews again sent delegations to Delano requesting strike support. Again the UFW put them off, but it sent a request for recognition to some of their employers.

The lettuce delegations were just the tip of the iceberg. Workers throughout the region had been watching the UFW and were inspired by its victories. One strawberry worker described the mood of the period:

> We heard about Cesar Chavez. For years we didn't talk about much else. The first time I saw Chavez on television, I was surprised. I thought he

would be light-skinned and [six feet] tall, but he's small and dark just like me. My friend said, "That's Cesar." I said, "You're kidding. I don't believe it." And then I got very excited. The [UFW] was something different. It was an organization for Mexicans. It wanted to give us back our respect. We all wanted to be part.

Some berry workers learned of the UFW from friends and relatives in other crops:

I had a cousin in grapes and he told us about the strikes over there in Delano. He was on the ranch committee. They went to talk with the owner. That was unheard of. An Anglo *patrón* sitting down with Mexican *peones*. Things were bad in grapes, but they were pretty bad in strawberries too. "Why not here?" we thought.

It was only a matter of time until this tinder would ignite into a flame. Ironically, the growers themselves provided the spark by signing contracts with the Teamsters. Lettuce workers, their communication bolstered by the longevity and cohesion of harvest crews, were the first to respond. A steady stream of lettuce crew leaders began to pour into the UFW's Salinas office, declaring their interest in joining the union and asking for help in countering the Teamsters. Many were heads of the committees that had been formed in response to Chavez's call during the grape campaign to organize workers within their ranches and sign up members for the union. UFW leaders such as Marshall Ganz were taken aback by their reception:

It was so different from the grape deal. There, the workers were hopeless and terrified. The union was remote from their experience. The people who were first attracted to our meetings were the malcontents, the ones everyone thought were jerks. We had to work to get beyond them to the natural leaders and get them on our side. In Salinas, all of that was different. It was the community leaders, the heads of families, who were on our side from the start. We were lucky. There was no way we had the staff to go out and organize ranch committees ourselves. The workers did it for us . . . helped by the growers' Teamster contracts.

Ganz related this receptivity to the rising aspirations engendered by Chavez:

When we came to the central coast, the people were ready for us. People don't organize around problems, you know, they organize around solutions. Hope is usually the missing ingredient in terms of creating a really explosive situation. Well, the success of the union had planted a spirit of hope. With Chavez, farm workers finally had a hero, someone the growers had to listen to. After that, things were never the same.

Ganz also attributed the militance of Salinas Valley workers to the large number of ex-braceros in the leadership. In his view, the UFW was always strongest in regions like Salinas, the Imperial Valley, and Oxnard, which had been heavily bracero, because of the rigid stratification that had developed between domestic and contract workers. He contrasted these areas to the Santa Maria Valley, where large numbers of domestic workers were used during the bracero program and where farm laborers were more compliant. Ganz maintained that former braceros were always the most class-conscious, hostile to growers, and receptive to the union. They believed most strongly that power relations had to change before their situation would improve, and they were the most likely to go beyond wage issues in contract negotiations to demand control over hiring and work conditions. Ganz attributed their polarization to the harsh treatment and lower wages of braceros and to the fact that their contracts required them to return to Mexico. As a result, he said, "they had no illusion that they were going to be a boss or a foreman some day, or start a small business. The line between management and labor was always sharper for braceros."

Although this argument has merit, another factor came into play as well. The ex-bracero leaders whom Ganz and the UFW encountered in Salinas were *also* lettuce workers—individuals whose work experience had built a high degree of cohesion and trust. By contrast, the bracero experience was dispersed: braceros were sent to diverse and varying employers, and they came from and returned to many separate villages. Even in the case of strawberry workers, who had greater longevity with certain employers than customary, bracero employment alone did not create cohesion or lead to common action. In short, although the bracero program may have encouraged a more polarized world view among workers, the experience of working in lettuce crews most likely forged the solidarity and capacity for collective action that bore fruit in 1970.

Whereas lettuce workers took the lead in summoning the UFW and urging its rejection of the Teamsters contracts, they were soon joined by a second constituency: Mexican American men and women in their twenties and thirties who worked for large strawberry and, to a lesser extent, tomato companies. The largest and most militant part of this contingent worked for Pic N Pac, a subsidiary of the S. S. Pierce Company of Boston, the sole strawberry company to sign on with the Teamsters. These workers, too, gained solidarity from their employment context. Though forced to cut its size in half after the loss of braceros, Pic N Pac farmed over one thousand acres of berries in the Salinas Valley in 1970. At the harvest peak it employed almost two thousand workers. Many of them were large Mexican American families from the Rio Grande Valley in Texas who lived in a large housing camp next to the freeway in Salinas, called La Posada. Others came from a certain town in the Mexican state of Guanajuato and lived in a housing camp in Soledad. Solidarity was particularly strong among these workers because of their shared residence, work locale, and places of origin. They had no personal relationship with their employer, because the ranch was so large. In fact, as is common on larger farms, many did not even know the name of the company—only that of the foreman. Employment relations were tense at Pic N Pac because of long-standing disagreements about piece rates. Thus, when they heard of the Teamsters contract, Pic N Pac workers too organized ranch committees.

Given the high level of organization among workers and the intensity of antigrower and pro-UFW sentiment, events unfolded rapidly. On August 2, the UFW organized a big march in which over three thousand supporters converged on Salinas from surrounding towns. Within days of learning of the Teamsters contracts, a number of lettuce crews for Fresh Pict, a large vegetable-producing subsidiary of Purex farming 42,000 acres of land in Mexico and the Southwest, refused to sign union authorization cards and were fired. The next day, about five hundred workers walked off the job. One day later, one thousand strawberry workers from Pic N Pac joined them.[11] Organizing gained momentum throughout the region. Each night the ranch committee leaders met, packing as many as four hundred people into the UFW's small Salinas office. Again union organizers were astounded at the size of the meetings—comprised entirely of leaders. The lettuce leaders were young Mexican men in their late twenties; most strawberry leaders were women and men in their thirties. They came from the ends of the region: from small and medium-sized berry farms near Watsonville twenty miles to the north, and from large, corporate vegetable farms near King City forty-five miles to the south. Reviving the tactic that

[11]A humorous and telling misunderstanding led to Pic N Pac workers' involvement at that time. When the Fresh Pict strike began, the union sent sound trucks around Salinas and its periphery announcing in Spanish: "There's a strike at Fresh Pict. Don't go to work at Fresh Pict." Marshall Ganz relates receiving a puzzling phone call at eight the next morning from La Posada, saying, "We're out. What do we do now?" Upon querying the caller he found that Pic N Pac workers had heard the sound trucks and, already incensed at their employer and, like many workers on large ranches, uncertain of its exact name, they assumed the message was for them. Union leaders rushed out to La Posada, conferred with those gathered, then sent them out to bring workers from the fields and other camps. At midday, one thousand Pic N Pac workers voted to join the strike.

had proven so effective in the grape campaign, the UFW initiated boycotts against two companies: Fresh Pict, which was already on strike, and Inter Harvest, which was owned by United Fruit and was the nation's second largest head lettuce producer, growing one-fourth of Salinas Valley's lettuce. The UFW demanded that both companies annul their Teamsters contracts and recognize the UFW.

Faced with some fifteen hundred workers out on strike and the threat of consumer boycotts, on August 10, the Teamsters began meeting with the UFW to discuss voiding its contracts and reestablishing their jurisdictional agreement. With great difficulty, the UFW persuaded its ranch committees to observe a strike moratorium for three—and then ten—days. On Friday, August 21, the Grower-Shippers Vegetable Association announced that its members would hold the Teamsters to their contracts. That night, the union's ranch committee leaders met and voted unanimously to put the motion for a general strike before its members.[12] Union organizers scoured the city and countryside, spreading news of the vote and rally. Late Sunday, some four thousand workers gathered in Hartnell College field at the west edge of Salinas. The field bristled with hundreds of red and black UFW flags and with scores of smaller company banners. One by one, the representatives of each company came up to the front and announced their support for the strike.

Impact of the 1970 Strike. The next morning, August 24, some ten thousand farm workers walked off their jobs on the central coast. That night, the *Salinas Californian* announced that agriculture in the area was "virtually shut down" ("Salinas Valley" 1970:2). The strike was initially peaceful, but confrontations between growers, workers, and the UFW grew increasingly hostile, soon reaching a pitch of violence not encountered in the grape struggle (Sosnick 1978:33; Majka and Majka 1982:204). UFW leaders accused the Teamsters of importing "guards" armed with chains and shotguns to intimidate UFW supporters and disperse picketers. Three

[12]In the charged lull following the vote, a young *lechugero* stood up and entered a reservation that was to strengthen the bonds between the lettuce and strawberry leadership. Marshall Ganz described the exchange: " 'There's a problem,' the lettuce worker said. 'To have a legal strike [*huelga legal*] we need flags. But we *lechugeros* are just single men. We are here without our families. We don't know how to sew.' We were stunned. Into all that momentum he threw this roadblock. You see, a *huelga legal* has a special meaning in Mexico. It's a strike that the government approves and won't violently repress. The workers were very legalistic. They wanted to do it right. We didn't know what to do. Then a strawberry ranch committee head in her mid-thirties stood up and said: 'There's no problem. We are families at La Posada. We women will make your flags. Just bring us your designs and material.'" The next day and on through the night, a long line of young *lechugeros*, with hats, fabric, and hastily drawn designs in hand, filed into La Posada to have their banners sewn.

picketers were shot. Jerry Cohen, the UFW's attorney, was beaten unconscious and hospitalized for four days. Shots were fired at the UFW's headquarters, its Watsonville office was bombed, and bomb threats became a daily event. Strawberry workers joined the UFW's cause with a vengeance. Workers at Pic N Pac had reluctantly agreed to the strike moratorium. When it was lifted, husbands, wives, and children took to the picket lines, attended meetings, and lobbied friends and acquaintances to join the strike. Within a few days, walkouts and picketing spread from Pic N Pac's Salinas ranch to berry farms in the neighboring Pajaro Valley. Convoys of red-and-black banner–waving farm workers and union organizers walked and drove along the country roads throughout the two counties, calling to workers to leave the fields and join them. On larger berry farms the harvest virtually ceased, because UFW ranch committees had prepared their co-workers for the strike. Even on smaller berry farms, where workers generally had longer tenure and closer personal ties with employers, many workers walked out.

The strike decimated strawberry harvests. The Strawberry Advisory Board reported that central coast berry shipments shrank from about thirteen thousand crates the day before the strike, to about two thousand crates four days later ("Strike Tightens" 1970). Pic N Pac's directors acknowledged that they had "scarcely shipped a berry" since the onset of the strike and had been forced to "give up" on their $2 million crop for the year ("Inter Harvest Shut" 1970). With pickets surrounding many of their ranches, with a valuable crop yet to harvest, and with the incapacitation of Pic N Pac vividly in mind, some thirty Pajaro Valley members of the Naturipe strawberry marketing cooperative met to discuss a course of action. On September 2, they began negotiations with the UFW on behalf of the entire cooperative, with the understanding that picketing and strikes against negotiating growers would cease for thirty days. Soon members of the Watsonville Berry Cooperative and ten large independent berry growers joined Naturipe in their negotiations. Together these growers comprised most of the berry producers in northern California. On September 11, all agreed to recognize the UFW as their workers' collective bargaining agent.

The actual signing of contracts was not so easily concluded. On September 16, Superior Court Judge Anthony Brazil ended the strike by issuing a permanent injunction against picketing on the grounds that the strike was a jurisdictional dispute between the UFW and the Teamsters. Given this assurance, and as the harvest drew to a close, berry growers' willingness to compromise subsided. On October 9, Pic N Pac signed a contract that was much more stringent than the other growers were willing to accept. On

October 15, the group of growers "temporarily suspended" negotiations with the union on the grounds that the two parties were not progressing toward a compromise. The union tried to get the growers back to the bargaining table with accusations of bad faith, but to no avail. As the harvest resumed the following spring, the berry growers' spokesman assured the UFW that they would continue talks at some future date, but that as small and medium-sized producers, they were "a different animal than Pic N Pac" and could not agree to the wages and other terms that Pic N Pac had accepted ("Berry Growers" 1971). In the end, the talks were never resumed. Union mobilization never regained the momentum of 1970, and neither did growers' interest in negotiation. Growers ignored the scattered pickets and union accusations that persisted through that season. In effect, the "temporary" standoff of the previous fall permanently ended formal communication between the UFW and this group of northern Californian berry growers. When Pic N Pac went out of business two years later, its successor, Pic D Rite, also negotiated a contract with the UFW. Aside from these and several other contracts in the years since, however, the UFW has achieved no formal contractual power in the strawberry industry.

The strike's impact was nonetheless considerable. The strike cost central coast strawberry growers an estimated $2.2 million in crop loss (Federal-State 1972:9, 30). It crystallized a new sense of entitlement and possibility for workers. Both those who lived through the strike and those who referred to it afterwards said that something shifted for them in 1970: they came to believe that change was possible. For berry growers, the 1970 strike raised the specter of immobilizing and costly work stoppages. They came to realize that their workers were more sympathetic to the union and had stronger lines of communication among themselves than they had realized. They were also forced to recognize that small farm size and isolation could not prevent the ethnic and work-based solidarity that a union movement such as the UFW could generate, and that large farms such as Pic N Pac were especially at risk.

Pic N Pac's experience illustrated the burdens that negotiation could impose. Its workers emerged from the strike with great animosity toward their employer. In my interviews, growers, union organizers, and some of the workers themselves concurred that the process of contract negotiation and implementation became the forum in which this hostility was played out. The contract's terms were onerous for growers. It increased wages and set a guaranteed minimum hourly wage, unheard-of in the industry at that time. It established a graduated scale of piece rates with two step-increases over the season as the crop dwindled and as the difficulty of picking a crate of berries increased. It also raised wage levels for other categories of workers and established a set weight for a crate of freezer berries. All in all, these terms set a wage level for Pic N Pac that averaged fifty cents an hour higher than the prevailing wage in the industry that year (*Farm Labor* 1970). These provisions shifted the cost of worker inexperience and varying field yield from the worker to the grower, a consequence that was particularly burdensome for smaller growers. Perhaps more important, the contract introduced stipulations regarding hiring and firing, seniority, health and safety standards (including curbs on pesticides), overtime pay, record keeping, paid holidays and vacations, and an employee-financed medical plan. Berry growers regarded all of these terms as unwarranted intrusions into their managerial prerogatives. They particularly opposed the union hiring hall, not only because it was easier to recruit additional workers by word of mouth, but because the owner of Pic N Pac and subsequent union employers found hiring-hall workers to be less skilled and careful, and often unavailable.[13]

Aftermath: A Decade of Turmoil. Although the pitch of the 1970 general strike was never revisited, the UFW continued to focus on the central coast vegetable industry for the rest of the decade, thus increasing the uncertainty and cost of labor in the region and restricting growers' managerial latitude. The persistent salience of union struggle in the area is demonstrated by the records of the state Agricultural Labor Relations Board, which lists its Salinas office as first or second in the number of petitions for union election and unfair labor practice charges filed in all years from its establishment in 1975 through 1981, with the exception of 1976–77 when it was a close third (ALRB 1977–82). In 1970–71, 1973–74, and 1979–80, conflicts with the large lettuce companies flared up, resolved into contracts, and then flared again when the contracts expired. In 1979, the contract renewal struggle erupted in a lettuce strike that encompassed the Salinas and Imperial Valleys. Meanwhile, growers' counterattacks in the fields and legislative halls grew increasingly coordinated, the UFW engaged in largely unsuccessful attempts to renew and extend its contracts in the grape industry, and the jurisdictional dispute with the Teamsters continued (Majka and Majka 1982:chap.10). In 1977, the two unions finally reached a five-year agreement covering thirteen western states which granted the representation of field workers to the UFW.

Wage increases were closely associated with the periods of intense labor

[13]Growers' reasons for their opposition to UFW contracts were expressed often during my interviews, and were also articulated by their negotiating team in spring 1970 when they refused further talks with the UFW ("Berry Growers" 1971:1).

conflict.[14] On the central coast, as elsewhere, many nonunion employers also raised wages, provided fringe benefits, and improved working conditions in order to avoid unionization (Linden 1979a, 1979b; Martin et al. 1984:8; Perloff 1986). Although few contracts were signed in the strawberry industry, berry growers found that their workers kept close watch on lettuce negotiations and contract terms. Many strawberry workers walked picket lines and attended union rallies. When new lettuce contracts were signed, strawberry workers often approached their employers with direct or oblique requests for a wage hike. Growers who did not increase their wages ran the risk of unionization or of losing their workers to higher-paying crops or employers. Central coast berry growers formed two associations to help them respond to the union threat: the Salinas Valley Independent Growers Association, dominated by large vegetable growers, was founded in the summer of 1970, and the Pajaro Valley Strawberry Growers Association, comprised solely of strawberry growers, was organized in the spring of 1971.[15] Both organizations represented growers' pursuit of what the California Farm Bureau approvingly called the "third way" during the 1970 confrontations. That is, to prevent unionization, these organizations offered member growers fringe benefits for their workers equivalent to those won by union contracts. Both provided insurance plans with health, accident, and life insurance coverage for members' employees. They also offered labor relations advice and lobbied with state legislators and the courts to promote policies beneficial to agribusiness.

Several established organizations also helped berry growers deal with union pressure: the Western Growers and Shippers Association (WGA), the California Strawberry Advisory Board (CSAB), and three grower-shipper marketing associations. Berry growers regarded the WGA as their most powerful political representative on union issues. Dominated by large vegetable growers, the WGA had a history of opposition to unionization that stretched back into the 1930s (Friedland, Barton, and Thomas 1981:57–64), and it continued to play a major role in advising members on contract negotiations and labor practices. The WGA's substantial legislative budget and the numerous articles on labor relations in its journal, *Western Grower*

[14]The California Employment Development Department's *Farm Labor Report* (881-A) clearly shows the pattern of rises in central coast strawberry wages after the settlement of UFW's contracts with local lettuce producers (see Friedland 1984b on problems with use of 881-As).

[15]Information on the response of grower organizations to union pressure was obtained from interviews with seven different berry growers, two farm labor specialists in the Salinas and Watsonville offices of the state Employment Development Department, and four marketing cooperative staff members.

and Shipper, demonstrated the organization's powerful role as a lobbyist and strategist for grower interests. Throughout the 1970s and into the 1980s, the WGA lobbied actively to oppose legislative or contractual restrictions on growers' authority, while advising growers to offer wage increases and labor benefits privately in order to diffuse union pressure.

The UFW, meanwhile, also affected the formation and implementation of policy. First, as noted earlier, it directly lobbied for and secured passage of certain significant pieces of legislation: it was a major force behind the extension of the minimum wage, unemployment insurance, and workers' compensation insurance to farm workers, and its initiative was crucial to the passage of the ALRA. Second, the union increased the enforcement of existing laws, especially in the heat of labor conflict. Union representatives received frequent complaints of piece rates that resulted in less than minimum wages, and they helped workers bring these complaints to their employers, to government agencies, and in some cases to lawyers and the press. From the establishment of the ALRB in 1975 through the lettuce struggles of the late 1970s, union ranch committees supported farm workers in bringing petitions for union elections and charges of unfair labor practices before the board. Thus, the number of union elections held and of election petitions and unfair labor practice charges filed was greatest during the 1970s when union activity was at its height, especially before 1978, during the intense UFW-Teamsters rivalry.[16]

The UFW increased the enforcement of border policy, as well. Citizenship was a delicate issue for the union. Though it suffered from the organizing difficulties and the greater ease of replacement that a labor force augmented by illegals encountered, the UFW could not afford to exclude illegals or to oppose their presence in the fields, because so many workers were undocumented and most members had undocumented friends and relatives. The union therefore usually remained silent on the issue of citizenship and focused on drawing in all workers. In some periods, however, the citizenship divisions in the workforce so undermined union efforts that the UFW was forced to take a position. Thus, during the lettuce contract renewal struggles in 1974 and 1979, the UFW launched vigorous campaigns against undocumented workers on the central coast. The union's press statements emphasized the loss of jobs by legal immigrants and domestic workers, but its overriding concern was the use of illegals as strikebreakers. These campaigns caused wide-sweeping apprehensions of ille-

[16]Prior to 1978, the yearly average of election petitions filed was 328; from 1978–87, the average was 69. Prior to 1978, the yearly average of elections held was 244; from 1978 to 1982, the average was only 38 (ALRB 1975–88).

gals. In spring 1979, for example, the UFW instigated a public hearing at which Salinas Border Patrol agents acknowledged a "hands-off" policy toward illegal workers. As a result, a special detail of additional patrol agents was assigned to the Salinas patrol station and the arrests of illegals shot up. In the month of May, after the staffing had been augmented, the patrol reported 9,652 arrests on the central coast, almost double the 5,503 arrests made in April and many more than the usual handful ("Amplia" 1979).

The strawberry industry was strongly affected by this continuing union pressure. Berry growers viewed the risk of union organizing and contracts as a major threat. Even without contracts, union assistance for workers' complaints increased the friction surrounding employment relationships. Because berry growers relied so heavily on undocumented workers, the periodic round-ups of illegals significantly increased the uncertainty of the production environment.

The Balance Shifts Again

In the early 1980s, the balance of labor market power tilted back toward growers, for several reasons. First and particularly apparent to California observers, the transition to a more conservative state and federal political climate weakened labor's public clout and diminished the vigor with which labor protections were upheld. Second, the UFW cut back its organizing efforts, directing its attention instead to lobbying and consumer boycotts, thus effectively reducing union support for workers' initiatives in the fields. Third, Mexico's economic crisis increased labor surpluses and the number of illegals in California agriculture, making it easier to replace demanding workers and thus harder to organize and enforce labor protections.

To address the first cause: in 1982, the governorship of California passed from Jerry Brown, a liberal Democrat sympathetic to the interests of farm workers, to George Deukmejian, a Republican long supportive of the concerns of farmers. This change especially affected the implementation of the Agricultural Labor Relations Act (see Wells and West 1989). Because both the general counsel and the Agricultural Labor Relations Board (ALRB) are appointed by the governor, their interpretation and implementation of the act are highly sensitive to the ideologies and vested interests of the state administration. Almost all of Jerry Brown's appointees were Democrats whose prior involvements and public statements indicated a strong commitment to workers' rights (Bernstein 1975). Board member Jerome Waldie voiced a perspective common among Brown's board members when he stated: "I make no bones about my belief that the law was enacted to protect farm workers in their effort to organize for collective bargaining. . . . My belief—and it's a strong belief—is that this act is a pro-labor act that was designed to protect farm workers" ("Brown" 1985; Rodriguez 1985:A12). For their parts, growers felt betrayed by the composition of Brown's board and by the fact that, once created, it did not ask growers' concurrence with its decisions (Pollard 1983:443). The Farm Bureau accused Brown of stacking the board with pro-union members (Scholz 1987:375) and the chair of the Western Growers and Shippers Association, J. R. Norton III, declared: "Brown is unilaterally and absolutely totally dedicated to doing Chavez' will. He is without question the most venomous and vindictive politician toward agribusiness interests in all of the United States. At this time he is the most vicious enemy of agriculture in California" ("Norton" 1980:3AA).

George Deukmejian, by contrast, was the growers' candidate from the start. Generously financed by agribusiness (Sample 1987:A3), his campaign vigorously opposed the UFW's renewed grape boycott and promised to bring a new "balance" to the operation of the ALRA. After his election, Deukmejian immediately slashed the ALRB's budget, appointed a pro-grower general counsel, and began to replace Brown's appointees on the board with his own. Charging that the agency was overfunded, he cut about $2 million (28%) from the ALRB's FY 1983–84 budget, causing the loss of fifty staff positions. In July 1986, the legislature cut another $1.8 million (25%) from its FY 1986–87 budget, forcing the closing of the Oxnard regional office and the San Diego field office and the loss of thirty-three employees. To lead his transformation of the board, Deukmejian appointed strongly anti-union former Republican state assemblyman David Stirling as general counsel in January 1983 and reappointed him in March 1987. Stirling immediately launched a media attack against the UFW. He traveled around the state at taxpayers' expense speaking against the union and urging the public and government officials to ignore the grape boycott. This partisan behavior elicited sharp criticism from ALRB staff members, from the Northern California Ecumenical Council, from Archbishop Mahoney of Los Angeles (the first chair of the ALRB), from newspaper editors around the state, as well as from the UFW (Castaneda 1985:B12; "Caught . . . " 1985:4; "Keep . . . " 1987; Montana and Emshwiller 1986:25; Rodriguez 1986; Wagner 1987:26). One by one, as their terms expired, Deukmejian replaced Brown's board members with appointees of his own. His choices were applauded by grower interests and deplored by the union. They attained a majority of the board in January 1986.

David Stirling's anti-union stance was particularly consequential since the general counsel has the final authority to decide whether unfair labor practice charges have enough merit for a complaint to be issued and for compliance to be enforced. His perspective became even more important because he further centralized authority under himself by reducing the initiative to determine the legitimacy of complaints that had formerly inhered in the regional offices. The political sympathies of the board as a whole were of import as well, because it and its agents review and affirm, modify, or set aside decisions regarding unfair labor practices. They also receive petitions for elections and oversee their execution to assure fairness, and they receive and rule on objections to the conduct of the election or to the conduct of parties who may have affected the result of the election (ALRB regs. {1156.3(c)). Election challenges must be resolved before a union can be certified as the employees' representative. Because the duration of farm employment is so short, delays can seriously jeopardize labor's victories.

Under Deukmejian's administration, the number of unfair labor practice charges that were moved forward to complaint fell sharply. In May 1985, special reports to the California Legislative Joint Audit Committee by the auditor general and the executive secretary of the ALRB documented that the process of compliance had also slowed dramatically (Auditor General 1985:26, 42–44). They charged Stirling with wholesale dismissals of legitimate farm worker charges, with unconscionable delays in enforcing compliance, and with settlements that were biased in favor of growers. The resolution of election challenges also slowed substantially, fewer election petitions culminated in actual elections, and, as years passed, the number of election petitions presented diminished, as well. The UFW charged that fewer and fewer workers were willing to risk challenging their employers' conduct or pressing for an election because they did not expect fair treatment by the board and general counsel. At the end of 1985, after repeated efforts to ensure more sympathetic decisions, the UFW withdrew its participation from the ALRA entirely, turning its energies to its renewed grape boycott and direct-mail lobbying. In 1986, the UFW urged legislators to defund the board, and it brought a $100 million lawsuit against Stirling for failure to enforce the law. (Bernstein 1987; Lawrence 1985:20; Montana and Emshwiller 1986:1, 25; Wagner 1987:23; Sample 1987:A3).

The annual reports submitted by the ALRB to the legislature reveal a pattern after the early 1980s of fewer petitions for union elections, fewer union victories, and diminished support for workers' unfair labor practice charges. As table 6 illustrates, the reports show an especially sharp drop after Deukmejian was elected in 1982. Petitions for union elections peaked during the 1970s and fell most precipitously after 1982. They averaged 187 per year from the first year of record keeping in 1975 through 1981, but

Table 6. Union elections and unfair labor practice (ULP) charges under the ALRA, 1975–87

	1975–76	1976–77	1977–78	1978–79	1979–80	1980–81	1981–82	1982–83	1983–84	1984–85	1985–86	1986–87
Election petitions filed	604	221	148	97	63	140	38	69	53	68	62	31
Elections held	423	188	122	67	38	61	25	36	41	31	31	14
(as % of number filed)	(70%)	(85%)	(82%)	(69%)	(60%)	(44%)	(66%)	(52%)	(77%)	(46%)	(50%)	(45%)
Outcome determined	388	181	120	60	35	56	21	29	37	25	27	11
Unions won	355	167	105	47	25	53	15	17	20	14	10	3
(% won by unions)	(91%)	(92%)	(87.5%)	(78%)	(71%)	(95%)	(71%)	(59%)	(54%)	(56%)	(37%)	(27%)
Decertification elections held	–	–	–	7	3	4	10	4	7	10	6	11
(as % of all elections held)	–	–	–	(10%)	(8%)	(6.5%)	(40%)	(11%)	(17%)	(32%)	(19%)	(79%)
ULP charges filed	873	652	742	814	1302	938	930	1234	882	737	453	264
ULP charges included in complaint	250	–	–	345	438	426	366	192	162	133	86	46
(as % of charges filed)	(29%)	–	–	(42%)	(34%)	(45%)	(39%)	(16%)	(18%)	(18%)	(19%)	(17%)
ULP charges dismissed	364	199	–	215	258	–	–	–	–	674	332	207
Complaints issued	158	162	123	161	160	105	137	85	65	47	46	28

Source: California Agricultural Labor Relations Board, *Annual Reports* (Sacramento: State of California, 1977–87).

fell to an annual average of only 57 from 1982 through 1986 (ALRB 1977–87). Union success rates were highest under the Brown administration as well. An annual average of 109 of the elections held (86 percent) were won by unions (almost exclusively the UFW) from 1975 through 1981, whereas only an annual average of 13 elections (47 percent) were won by unions from 1982 through 1986. Union victories were especially great in 1975–78, when unions won 90 percent of all elections, and in 1980 when they won 95 percent. Even more indicative of the decline in union vigor was the increasing proportion of decertification elections after 1982. Whereas an annual average of only 9 percent of the elections from 1975 through 1981 were decertification elections, from 1982 through 1986 that average rose to 31 percent, peaking at 79 percent in 1986.

This pattern of delay, pro-grower bias, and under- and non-enforcement undoubtedly contributed to the decline in union membership and contracts. It is impossible to ascertain the exact proportions of this decline, however, or indeed the proportions of the earlier expansion, because the mobility and high turnover of farm workers make it difficult to count membership directly and because growers are interested in minimizing union influence, whereas the UFW is interested in maximizing it. It nonetheless seems likely that, although only about 10 percent of California farm workers were under union contract even during the 1970s, as many as 90 percent may have been union-influenced—by strikes and picketing, by the pro-union ALRB, and by nonunion employers' reactive improvement of wages and working conditions (Linden 1979a, b; Martin, Vaupel, and Egan 1986). Union contracts affected workplace relations not only by improving wages and working conditions directly for workers on the farms with contracts, but also by setting a baseline of entitlement for workers in the labor market, especially in the areas where union pressure was strong. In addition, by reducing turnover and protecting workers against arbitrary dismissal, contracts made it easier for them to organize and push for further change.

By the late 1980s, both participants and observers agreed that union membership and the number of farm labor union contracts had declined dramatically (Boitano 1987; Del Vecchio 1987; "Farm Workers" 1986; Hubner 1984:14; Lindsey 1984; Lloyd et al. 1987; Martin, Vaupel, and Egan 1986; Montana and Emshwiller 1986). The UFW had lost most of its base in the table grape industry, and even its strongholds in the Monterey County vegetable industry and the Ventura County citrus industry were being eroded. The few new contracts being signed eliminated prior protections and provided for no wage increases or dismissal of workers who were not members in good standing with the union. The UFW regarded its agreement to such weak contracts as necessary, because it could win so few legal battles through the ALRB. It hoped through these contracts to increase dues-paying membership and to establish contract protections that could be expanded in later negotiations (Bernstein 1986). In fact, however, these contracts themselves indicated the great reduction in union and worker power.

The UFW attributed its diminution to the pro-grower sympathies of Deukmejian's ALRB and general counsel. Other forces were also at work, however, one of which was the organizational reconfiguring of the UFW and its reduced involvement in organizing. In practice, most election petitions and unfair labor practice charges were initiated or assisted by union representatives; therefore, they were most frequent during the hotly contested union campaigns of the 1970s, and they fell sharply when the UFW withdrew its participation from the ALRA after 1985. In addition, the union's withdrawal from forwarding election petitions and unfair labor practice charges was part of its more general retreat from organizing. In the early 1980s, the union's leadership split on the question of whether to focus its energies on direct organizing and worker advocacy or on lobbying with politicians and consumers. Chavez emphasized the latter as most suited to the challenges of the 1980s and 1990s, and he cast dissenters as disloyal to the cause. As a result, most of the original leadership, with the exception of Chavez, his family members, and Dolores Huerta, left the union voluntarily or were forced out.

As documented by my interviews and confirmed by other sources (Bernstein 1987; Del Vecchio 1987), these individuals, who believed in the UFW's traditional, in-the-fields organizing approach, attribute the UFW's decline to its own intentional withdrawal from organizing after 1980. Some analysts also attribute contract and organizing setbacks to the movement of the union headquarters in the mid-1970s from Delano to La Paz, in Kern County's desert Tehachapi Mountains, a move that placed the leadership far from the terrain of workplace struggles (Hubner 1984:28). In articulating this perspective, Marshall Ganz, who left the union in 1981, pointed out that it was the UFW's reduced commitment to organizing, not the unsupportive political administration, that was new: "I don't want to minimize the problems of Deukmejian, but the fact is, we did build this union when Reagan was governor and Nixon was president" (Montana and Emshwiller 1986:25).

It is virtually impossible to determine the extent to which the decline in union influence was due to the shifting priorities of the UFW or to the reduced political support for labor. Furthermore, another factor must be considered: the increase in labor surpluses due to Mexico's economic crisis. As surpluses increased, growers found it easier to replace demanding workers who had lived through the empowering conflicts of the 1970s with illegals who were less willing to organize and bring charges. In this context, berry workers' support for the UFW dwindled. Whereas in the 1970s many expressed to me their support for Chavez and the UFW and their optimism about its prospects, by the late 1980s most were disheartened. They spoke anxiously about the number of illegals in the labor market and the lack of support for workers' petitions before the ALRB. They felt that Chavez had abandoned them and was pursuing a path they considered characteristic of Mexican labor leaders—that of promoting his own family members. They mistrusted his commitment to worker democracy, pointing to his expulsion of the powerful central coast ranch committee leaders from the union convention in 1981 and their subsequent firing. In the late 1980s, they saw the union as powerless and uninterested in their problems.

Despite this decline in the UFW's influence, its campaigns had transformed berry growers' expectations of potential challenges to their authority. Even as they expressed relief at the union's diminished presence, they feared a return to the volatile 1970s. Moreover, although such indicators of union activity as petitions for union elections and unfair labor practice charges declined after 1981, the Salinas office of the ALRB continued to be among the top four in the state in terms of petitions and charges filed (ALRB 1982–88).

Thus, political forces have shaped and reshaped class power in the regional labor market. They have helped mold its structure and operation, and the interests, capacities, and price of labor within it. From World War II until the mid-1960s, the labor market regime bolstered the position of growers and reinforced the relative dependency of workers. In the mid-1960s, changes in border policy, protective legislation, and union mobilization instituted a new regime that shifted the balance of power away from capital and toward labor. Although the balance tilted back toward growers in the early 1980s, it was by no means as advantageous for growers: protective laws restricted managerial discretion, border policies had to satisfy a range of political claimants, and the precedent for labor solidarity and disruption was evident to all.

[4]

The Local Organization of Production

The local organization of production introduces the third and most particular and differentiated set of constraints on class relations at work: those that arise from the patterned ways certain portions of class populations organize their social and economic relations within certain parts of the central coast region. This level of constraint encompasses the dimension of location—the climate, soils, hydrology, topography, and history of a certain locality—and the dimension of social organization—the localized character of class composition, economic organization, and social relationships. The historical conjuncture of contingent processes has generated different microregional production subsystems within the broader central coast region. These systems are important because growers and workers tend to concentrate their activities within a particular locality, so that their economic challenges and solutions are largely local.

This chapter and those that follow explore these daily contexts of work. They cluster into two groupings. Chapters 4 and 5 set the stage for understanding the local farming system, describing the prevalent dynamics of the labor process—wage labor—that has been dominant since World War II. Chapters 6 through 8 explore the variance in labor resistance and labor processes that characterizes the course of each season, the three production microregions, and the postwar period itself, showing how the constraints of the industry, labor market, and local organization of production combine to construct a differentiated pattern of workplace relations.

First, then, in this chapter I lay out the physical contours of the central coast as a production region, paying special attention to the three microregions within which strawberry farming has evolved; I discuss the historical development of the local economy, and of the strawberry industry within it; and, finally, I describe the class formation of growers, showing how differences in the structural opportunities and historical experiences confronted by members of the three ethnic producer groups have engendered ethnically differentiated farming subsystems with distinct modal patterns of farm management.

The Central Coast Region

From the city of San Francisco south for two hundred miles, California's coastal mountains drop almost directly into the sea. With its crashing surf, fog-shrouded cliffs, and wind-bent cypress, this rugged coastline is one of the most spectacular in the world. It is also one of the least conducive to extensive human settlement. For only one substantial stretch does the Coast Range give way, cut through by two river valleys that open out to the Pacific Ocean. Here, in the protected arc of Monterey Bay, the fortuitous conjuncture of topography, soil, water, and climate supported thriving Indian communities. Here, in 1770, the Spanish established the provincial capital of Alta California. And here, too, in the Salinas and Pajaro River Valleys and in the coastal highlands between them, the central coast strawberry industry took form.

Two major north-south highways carry travelers through the region: the narrow recreational route, Highway 1, winds along the coast from Oregon to the Mexican border; and the broad utilitarian route, Highway 101, exits the Bay Area urban complex at the tip of the San Francisco Bay, angles west, then cuts down the center of the Salinas Valley (see figure 1). A network of smaller roads crisscrosses the terrain between these two arterials, linking the three berry-growing microregions and the two major agricultural service centers: the cities of Watsonville (about 30,000 inhabitants) and Salinas (about 72,000 inhabitants). A handful of small settlements straggle along these minor roads, their residents comprised of farm workers, less prosperous farmers, and retirees.

The Pajaro Valley

Highway 1 is the front stage of the central coast. Its tourist towns of Santa Cruz, Monterey, and Carmel are wealthy and precious; its rugged natural beauty is extolled by travel agencies and chambers of commerce. Traffic moves haltingly along this route, as travelers swerve and pause to take in breathtaking views of the sea. The air is charged with salt spray, and the coastal bluffs are splashed with the gold of poppies and broom, the violet-blue of lupine and ceanothus. Above all, it is the ocean that draws the eye, and most travelers pass by with little sense of the rich and gritty agricultural hinterland that lies just to the east (see plate 1).

Only if the traveler turns inland—perhaps through the gateway of Watsonville and up the Pajaro Valley on Route 129—does the economic dominance of agriculture become apparent. Farms blanket the valley floor and brightly clothed workers can be seen from the road. Assorted tractors join and leave the flow of traffic. Produce trucks tumble strawberries, cauliflower, lettuce, and sugar beets into the ditches as they jostle toward processing and shipping facilities in Watsonville and Salinas. The Pajaro Valley is the northernmost of the three berry-growing microregions. It is 1.5 miles wide at its mouth, 10 miles long, and 120 square miles in area. High benches rise up from the river delta and reach north and south above the ocean's rocky cliffs. The protected oval valley stretches inland northeast from the river's mouth, turns eastward, then narrows and slopes slightly uphill until it disappears into the canyon created by the San Andreas Fault. To the north, the foothills of the Santa Cruz Mountains mound down to the valley floor, their grass-covered slopes carpeted green in the winter and spring, gold in the summer and fall. A series of lesser valleys reach like fingers into these mountains. As in the nearby Salinas Valley, soils are richest on the alluvial plain and river terraces, becoming less fertile near the foothills.[1] Strawberries currently dominate the Pajaro Valley agricultural economy, although tree fruits and vegetables contribute important income as well. Most berry farms are medium-sized here, averaging about forty acres. The enclosing hills shelter a relatively prosperous, long-standing, highly cohesive berry grower population.

The North Monterey Hills

Our traveler could continue east up the Pajaro Valley to Highway 101, but a more informative tour of strawberry terrain would lead her to the valley's southern periphery. Here the road angles up into the North Monterey Hills, winding through narrow valleys shaded by oak and eucalyptus, and

[1]Soils in the Pajaro and Salinas Valleys range from sandy to clay loams, depending on the amount of silt contained. The Salinas Valley is a former ocean inlet, so its soils are more sandy than those of the Pajaro Valley. My characterization of the history, economy, climate, soils, and topography of the area was informed by Allen (1934), Durrenberger (1972), Hartman (1964), Lantis (1962), Lydon (1985), Russell (1938), Seivertson (1969), and Wallick (1969), as well as by documents from the Santa Cruz, Watsonville, and Salinas Chambers of Commerce and the county agricultural commissioners' offices.

Plate 1. Watsonville, Santa Cruz, and the mouth of the Pajaro Valley. Photo © David Sievert

climbing steep granitic hillsides matted with thickets of manzanita, pampas grass, and poison oak. Occasionally, berry fields interrupt the thick undergrowth. Here and there, dirt tracks wander off the paved roadways, leading to ranches in interior hollows. The North Monterey Hills is the smallest of the three microregions, a rugged, eighty-nine-square-mile area that drains into the Elkhorn Slough estuary. Rock layers here are tilted, cracked, and deformed by the enormous geological forces that generate the area's earthquakes. Built on ancient sand dunes, topsoil overlays are thin and winter rains carve deep gullies into the sandy hillsides.[2] Though unfriendly to land passage, this barrier of hills is relatively narrow and low enough to permit the passage of ocean air. Only eleven miles to the south it falls off into the expansive Salinas River delta, which stretches uninterrupted to the Monterey Peninsula. Strawberries provide almost the only farm employment in the North Monterey Hills, with the minor exception of nursery crops. Strawberry growers here are relatively recent, poorly capitalized, and separated from each other by topography and social practice. Most growers farm fewer than fifteen acres.

The Salinas Valley

As our traveler winds inland along the serpentine arterials of the North Monterey Hills, she descends finally into the briskly moving current of Highway 101, which traverses the backstage of the central coast. Refrigerated vans careen toward terminal produce markets in San Francisco, Los Angeles, and a variety of eastern cities. Heading south, they pass processing, packing, and shipping sheds on the outskirts of Salinas, and continue into the agricultural heartland of the Salinas Valley. They enter, then quickly leave, a series of dusty farming towns that are familiar destinations to Mexican migrants: Chualar, Gonzales, Soledad, Greenfield, King City, San Ardo.

The Salinas Valley is the largest of the three microregions, although strawberries are only grown in its ocean-tempered northern twenty miles (see plate 2). About eleven miles wide at its mouth, the valley angles inland from the ocean in a southeasterly direction along the San Andreas fault system, following the winding course of the Salinas River to its terminus some

[2]The USDA's Soil Conservation Service claims that this 61,000-acre hilly region they call the Strawberry Hills Target Area has the highest rate of soil erosion west of the Rocky Mountains. Up to 145 tons of soil per acre are lost from it each year (SCS 1984). Daniel Mountjoy's excellent study of soil conservation practices in this microregion reveals a pattern of farm management practices and values adapting to circumstances that is consonant with the findings of the present study (1995).

Plate 2. Salinas and the Salinas Valley. Photo © Richard Wilson/Wilson's Photography.

one hundred miles from the sea. The valley itself encompasses about eight hundred square miles, including the low-lying flood plain and its proximate benches (Wallick 1969:10). Two mountain ranges rim the horizons: to the east, the light brown crests of the Gabilans; to the west, the dark, ragged peaks of the Santa Lucias. Vast fields of vegetables, grapes, and strawberries blanket the valley floor, stretching to the oak-studded foothills in the hazy distance. This is the home of California's famous "factories in the field"—huge agricultural estates with absent proprietors and reputedly interchangeable workers. This is the domain of agribusiness and the heartland of agricultural unionization. Large corporate vegetable farms dominate the local economy. The scale of production is largest here, in strawberries as in other crops. Salinas Valley berry farms average over seventy acres, and some even exceed several hundred. Berry growers in this microregion are generally well-capitalized. Collectively, they are neither as cohesive as those in the Pajaro Valley nor as dispersed and fragmented as those in the North Monterey Hills.

These three microregions enjoy the climate of a subtropical garden, its extremes tempered by the influence of the sea. The Pajaro Valley is the most protected and temperate, but all lie within the coastal fog belt. In the summer, billows of fog blanket the coast, reaching twenty miles down the Salinas Valley. By late morning, the sun breaks through and the sea breezes pick up, their cool, moist air keeping temperatures relatively low and the humidity relatively high. Temperatures average around fifty degrees in the winter and in the upper sixties in the summer. Frosts are rare, and the growing season is about three hundred days long. The region has two seasons: a dry, temperate summer lasting from May to October, and a wet, cool winter lasting from November to April. Most of the fifteen to twenty annual inches of rain fall in the cool season, although it does sometimes rain in May and October. The Pajaro and Salinas Rivers, which often overflow their banks in the winter, are virtually dry in the summer. Despite the absence of surface water during the warmer months, well-supplied aquifers underlie the entire Pajaro Valley and the northern reaches of the Salinas Valley. This coastal fog belt is ideal for growing strawberries. Its sandy loam soils, moist air, moderate temperatures, ample ground water, and absence of rains during the bearing season engender some of the most extended, bountiful, and high-quality harvests in the world. Farther inland, temperatures are too high, winds are too strong, and the humidity is too low, eroding fruit quality and ending the harvest.[3]

[3]The Pajaro Valley has the most temperate climate, but the range of winter lows and summer highs is narrow in all three microregions. In the Pajaro Valley, temperatures average

The Development of the Central Coast Strawberry Industry

Although the central coast strawberry industry did not mature until after World War II, its roots go back to the late nineteenth century. Central coast agriculture evolved from the pattern of large-scale land holding and extensive grain and cattle ranching begun by the Spanish missions. The Spaniards recognized early the potential of the fertile Monterey Basin. Between 1770 and 1800, they established missions in Monterey, Santa Cruz, Carmel, Soledad, San Antonio, and San Juan Bautista. Each was surrounded by rain-fed fields of grain, unfenced herds of livestock, and often a vineyard and an orchard for the use of the mission population. This subsistence economy persisted virtually unchanged for eighty years, until the demand generated by the 1849 gold rush stimulated the shift to market production. Between 1850 and 1900, intensive cattle ranching and commercial agriculture developed in the Salinas and Pajaro Valleys. Cattle ranching peaked first, but by 1870 it had declined, and wheat became the dominant export crop for the region.[4] That same decade, a new pattern of diversification began in the Pajaro Valley: the failure of orchards close to San Francisco stimulated the planting of plum, apricot, and apple orchards on the valley floor. By 1900, Watsonville led the nation in apple production (Seivertson 1969:47–48). Because of the time lag between tree planting and harvest, growers often interplanted strawberries, bush berries, and potatoes with their fruit trees, harvesting them for the first six to ten years while the orchards became established. Encouraged by consumer demand in the San Francisco Bay urban nexus, some growers even began to plant berries as their sole crop. By the turn of the century, almost five million pounds of

---

about 49 degrees in the winter and about 62 degrees in the summer. In Salinas, some ten miles from the coast, winter temperatures average 46 degrees and summer temperatures, 68 degrees. As one continues south down the Salinas Valley, highs and lows are more extreme. Rainfall is also greater in the Pajaro Valley, averaging twenty-one inches annually as opposed to only fourteen inches for the area around the city of Salinas.

[4]The hegemony of cattle and grain was short-lived in the 1800s. Within a decade after the gold rush, new settlers brought better breeds of beef cattle, slashing the demand for the tougher Spanish range beef. The droughts of 1862–64 clinched the demise of the Spanish and Mexican cattle ranchers, leading to the death or slaughter of almost all cattle and sheep in central and southern California. Without this economic base, most of the *rancheros* were forced off the land, and their land grants were taken over by European settlers who concentrated on raising grain for shipment to the gold camps (Allen 1934:12; Wallick 1969:10). By the early 1870s, wheat had become the major export crop for the region. In the late 1800s, however, high transport costs and tariffs protecting Commonwealth countries closed the English market to California wheat, undermining the market for wheat and turning growers' interests to new crops.

strawberries were being shipped each year by train to San Francisco (Mackie 1910:16; Seivertson 1969:46).

These early forays into berry production notwithstanding, the lack of irrigation prevented the expansion of commercial fruit and vegetable acreage. Finally, in 1888, sugar beet magnate Claus Spreckles built a processing plant in Watsonville, thereby stimulating the development of irrigation facilities and the planting of thousands of acres of sugar beets in the region. Thus was launched the agricultural pattern of the twentieth century: increasingly intensive, irrigated agriculture.[5] Over the next sixty years, sugar beets, alfalfa, dry beans, orchards, and dairy farms progressively pushed the less lucrative rain-fed wheat, barley, and grain hay to the hot, dry southern reaches of the Salinas Valley and to the hillsides and arroyos ringing both valley floors.

The shift to intensive strawberry and vegetable production awaited the development of transportation, storage methods, and markets after World War II (Cochrane 1979; FitzSimmons 1983; Seivertson 1969). With these changes, the importance of field crops in Santa Cruz and Monterey Counties dwindled, and strawberries and vegetables came to dominate (see figures 9, 10). Currently, fruit and vegetable crops have completely displaced grains and dry beans on the Salinas Valley floor and at its margins. Permanent plantings of artichokes occupy the immediate coastal region. Strawberry fields now extend into the North Monterey Hills and twenty miles down the Salinas Valley, to the southern edge of the fog belt at the Chualar River. Since the 1960s, a thriving nursery industry has developed in these same zones, and vineyards have been planted in the upper reaches of the valley and on its alluvial fans.[6] In Santa Cruz County, strawberries are grown on the high, rolling benches that flank the ocean and on the floor and adjoining benches of the Pajaro Valley. Tree fruit acreage has declined sharply, largely due to competition from other regions. In recent years, much vegetable acreage has been replaced by more profitable and reliable strawberries. As in Monterey County, nurseries have increased in impor-

[5]In 1889, the year after the completion of the beet sugar factory, 2,759 acres of sugar beets were grown in the Pajaro Valley. The Corralitos Water Company, already begun in 1884, expanded and improved its gravity-fed and pumping facilities. Beet acreage expanded more slowly in the Salinas Valley, where canals, direct pumping, and wells did not irrigate local fields until the late 1890s (Allen 1934:29–31; Seivertson 1969:53; Watsonville Chamber 1952:33).

[6]After the late 1960s, urban expansion elsewhere and structural change in the wine industry encouraged major California vintners to plant new vineyards in Monterey County (Dorel 1977; Haley 1987). In the same period, rising land costs and other factors led nurseries to relocate from the San Francisco Bay region to the fog belts of both Santa Cruz and Monterey Counties.

Figure 9. Monterey County: Change in real value of strawberries, vegetables, and field crops, 1945–88 (in 1982–84 dollars)

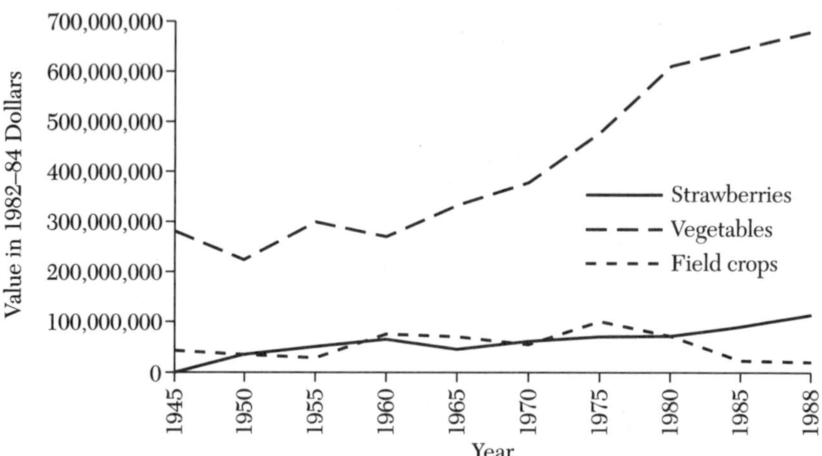

Sources: Agricultural Commissioners' Offices: Santa Cruz and Monterey Counties, *Annual Reports, 1945–88*; *Economic Report of the President, 1975* (Washington, D.C.: GPO, 1976):300, table C-44; *1990* (1991):359, table C-58; *Statistical Abstract of the United States, 1989* (Washington, D.C.: U.S. Bureau of the Census, 1990):462, table 748.

tance since the 1960s. Currently, strawberries contribute a major portion of the agricultural income in both counties. According to the county agricultural commissioners' *Annual Crop Reports,* strawberries are the largest single crop in Santa Cruz County, generating about 35 percent of the total agricultural income of almost 168 million dollars in 1988, followed by nursery crops with 23 percent and vegetable crops with 22 percent. Vegetables are the leading crop in Monterey County, contributing 68 percent of the total agricultural production value of 1,159 million dollars in 1988, followed by strawberries with 12 percent and nursery crops with 8 percent.

The expansion of central coast strawberry production was fostered by the region's privileged niche in the state strawberry market. California berry harvests begin on the south coast in February, with San Diego and then Orange, Los Angeles, and Ventura Counties dominating the early season, high-priced market. In April, Santa Barbara, San Luis Obispo, Santa Cruz, and Monterey Counties come in, saturating the market just as temperatures heat up in the south and begin to truncate production and erode fruit quality. By July 1, the south is out of the picture entirely. From May through November or into December in a mild year, the central coast dominates the market, exceeding all other regions in harvest length. The

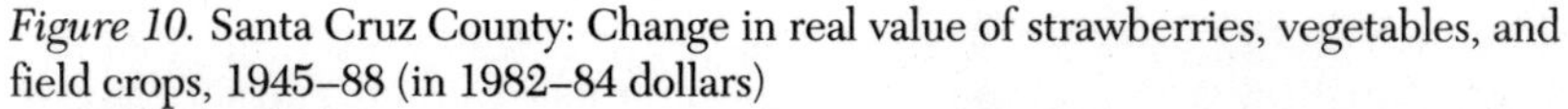

Figure 10. Santa Cruz County: Change in real value of strawberries, vegetables, and field crops, 1945–88 (in 1982–84 dollars)

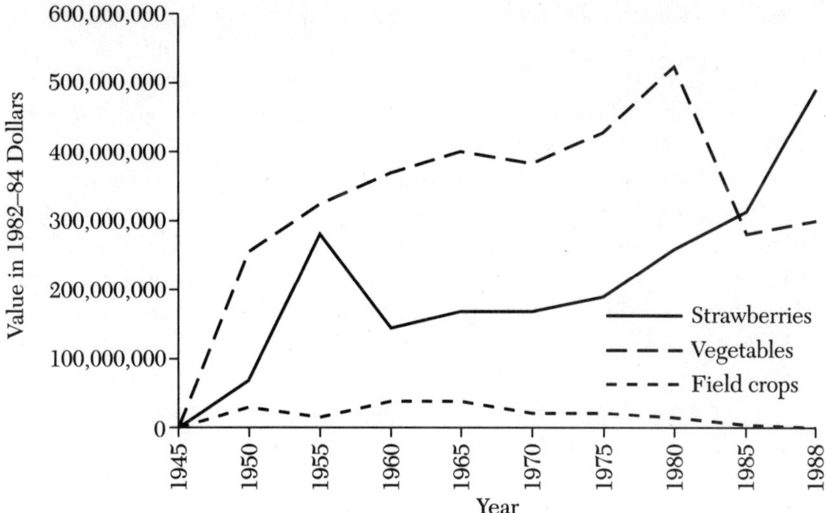

Sources: Agricultural Commissioners' Offices, Santa Cruz and Monterey Counties, *Annual Reports, 1945–88*; *Economic Report of the President, 1975* (Washington, D.C.: GPO, 1976), p. 300, table C-44; *1990* (1991), p. 359, table C-58; *Statistical Abstract of the United States, 1989* (Washington, D.C.: Bureau of the Census, 1990), p. 462, table 748.

interior counties contribute only a small amount of product in April and May and quickly fade as temperatures rise. Currently, the central coast is the largest and most productive berry-growing region in the state, with about 38 percent of the state's berry acreage and average yields of well over 30 tons an acre (PSAB 1989).

California's increasing emphasis on fresh berry sales has also reinforced the market position of the central coast. When southern California growers begin harvesting in February, they direct all of their crop to the fresh market. Prices are exceptionally high in this early season fresh market because of the lack of competition from other areas. In April, however, the central coast begins to produce, increasing supply and depressing fresh market prices. At the same time, fruit quality in the south declines as the hot weather sets in, so that buyers pay a premium for the firmer northern California fruit. Southern growers then shift to the processed market. By mid-May, the south is picking almost exclusively for the freezers. They continue in this vein until July, when the heat terminates production for good.

Thus, southern producers have two months of strong freezer production, which constitutes an economically important part of their market returns. Overall, they have a shorter bearing season, a shorter period in which they can deliver to the fresh market, and a relatively greater reliance on the processed portion of their harvest. On the central coast, temperatures remain moderate, berry quality remains high, and growers can ship fresh berries from April into November.

As a result of these locational advantages, most central coast growers now treat the processed market as a "safety valve" or emergency market. Because of its hegemony in the mid- and late-season market, the central coast enjoys high demand for its fresh market fruit. Demand for its processed fruit is also high, since the central coast is virtually the only source of berries in the nation after early summer. Market trends for the northern and southern regions reflect these location-imposed sales emphases (see figure 11). According to the records of the Processing Strawberry Advisory Board, Santa Cruz and Monterey Counties produced 54 percent of the state's processing berries in 1967, but less than 17 percent in 1986. By contrast, the more southerly coastal counties produced 44 percent of the state's processing berries in 1967, but produced fully 81 percent by 1986. On the central coast, only 13 percent of all strawberries were sold for processing in 1986.

The Class Formation of Growers

Within this privileged geographical and economic context, the class of central coast strawberry producers has evolved over more than a century. Producers, in this case, are highly stratified according to ethnic background. Over the years, individuals of Japanese, Mexican, and European descent have been drawn into berry farming. The history of class formation in this case is one of ethnic stratification and upward mobility. Growers with these backgrounds entered the local economy at varying times and started from varying positions. They varied in the individual and group resources they brought with them and in the aids and barriers to becoming farmers they encountered. To deepen our understanding of the current grower class, let us look at the historical evolution of their positions in the local economy.

Strawberry Farmers before World War II

When berry growing began in the 1870s, most farm workers were Chinese. Farm owners were Americans of northern European, primarily

Figure 11. Change in production of processing strawberries in southern California and Salinas-Watsonville, 1966–88

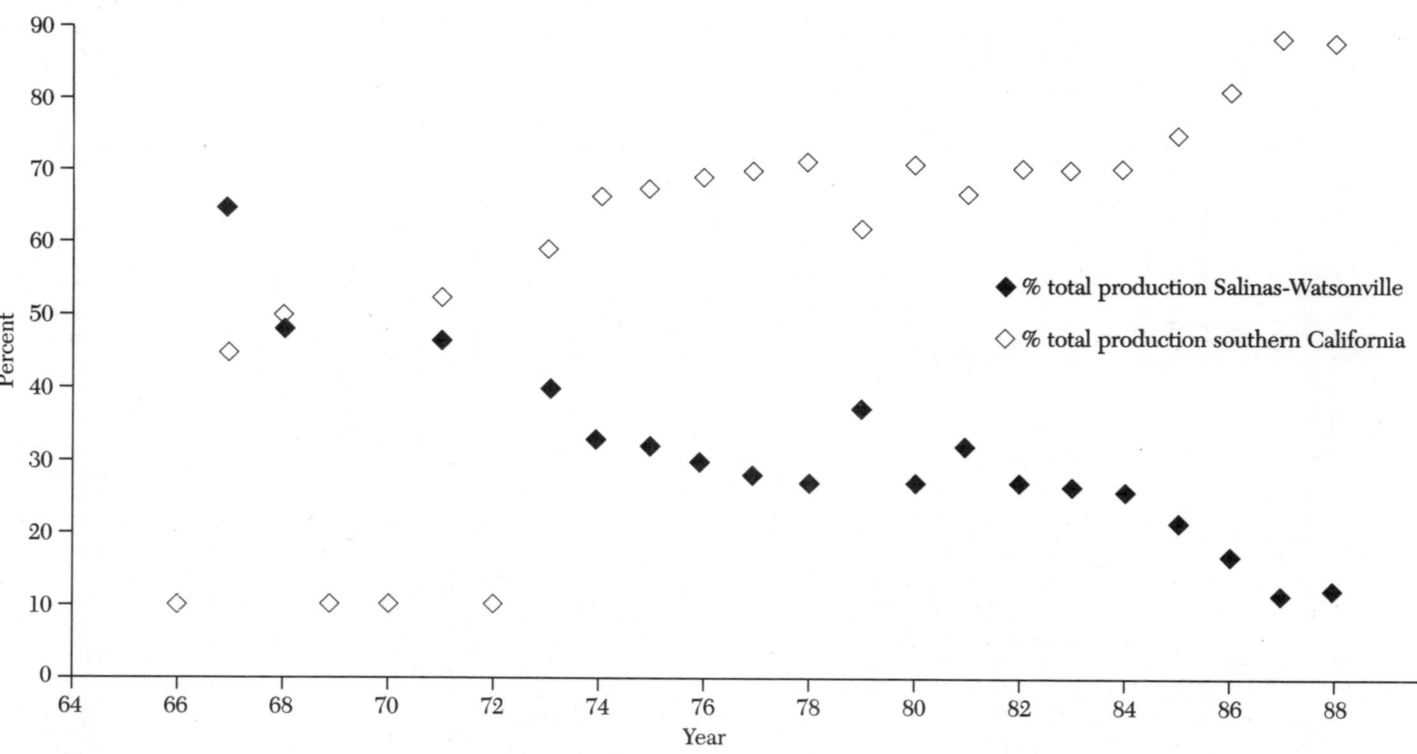

Source: Files, Processing Strawberry Advisory Board, Watsonville, Calif., 1966–88.

British and German, descent. Following the usage of many local residents, I refer to this established European American grower population as "Anglo" (see Appendix, this chapter). By the turn of the century, exclusionary legislation had decimated the number of Chinese available for seasonal farm labor, and Japanese immigrants had begun to take their place (Lydon 1985:75–77, 215–27; McWilliams [1935] 1971:65–77). Originating primarily in Yamaguchi and Hiroshima prefectures, many local Japanese farm workers came from families that had farmed labor-intensive crops in Japan. Although they started out as laborers, they hoped to become farmers on their own. Here, as elsewhere in the United States and Japan (Bonacich and Modell 1980; Light 1972), group solidarity and organization helped the Japanese prosper. Rotating credit associations based on Japanese village and prefectural ties supplied money for household purchases, land, and small businesses. As in other parts of California, local Japanese farm organizations assisted Japanese tenants, farmers, and farm workers in their relations with landowners, helping them find land, setting maximum rent levels and minimum wage levels that Japanese should accept, and mediating disputes between them and landlords (U.S. Immigration 1911:23:85–86; 24:341–45, 396–97). Thus, in this industry as in others, the Japanese moved quickly into positions of tenancy and farm ownership at a rate that startled and threatened Anglo growers.[7]

Largely in response to Japanese competition, grower-supported Alien Land Laws were passed in California in 1913 and 1920 and in other western states about the same time. This legislation prohibited foreign-born Japanese from leasing or owning land in the United States (Bonacich and Modell 1980:64–82; Bunje [1957] 1971; Coryn 1909; Iwata 1962; Parker 1921). On the central coast, however, a small core of Japanese berry growers had already become established. Some latecomers circumvented the laws by securing land in the names of their native-born children, who could legally own land after they reached the age of majority (see also Iwata 1962:29). Some paid American citizens to buy land for them. Before World War II, Japanese growers in the Salinas Valley directed their crop to the Los Angeles city market and wholesale produce terminal, where Japanese market dominance facilitated their access (Iwata 1962:34). Pajaro Valley growers sold through the San Francisco produce market and formed an organization to facilitate that process. In 1917, five Japanese and six Anglo

[7]Thus, in 1913, the U.S. Census and Immigration Commission reported that of 155,682 acres of land worked by Japanese in California, 2,442 acres (10.6%) were owned, 80,682 acres (51.5%) were held through cash rent, and 59,001 acres (37.9%) were farmed on shares (Iwata 1962:29).

Pajaro Valley berry growers founded Central California Berry Growers' Association (later Naturipe), a marketing cooperative aimed to give them leverage with the large San Francisco commission houses that were their main sales outlets and sources of credit before the war.[8]

Despite the various attempts to evade the Alien Land Laws, the legislation did impede Japanese farm ownership. Most Japanese immigrants to the central coast became sharecroppers in the interwar period. Share cropping became—in the words of one second-generation Anglo grower—"just the way we grew strawberries. Nobody thought it could be done any other way." With the exception of a few Filipinos, virtually all of the sharecroppers were Japanese. Most farm owners were Anglos. As I discuss in Chapter 7, this early sharecropping, in which sharecroppers had substantial control over the process of production, was quite different from the form that surfaced in the mid-1960s. Sharecroppers and their descendants are emphatic about the reasons they turned to sharecropping: they attribute its initial attraction to the limited resources of Japanese immigrants and its persistence to the barriers posed by the Alien Land Laws. As one Japanese grower put it: "Sharecropping was a good way to get a start in farming, but most Japanese wanted to farm on their own. We'd have stopped sharecropping in a couple of years if it hadn't been for the Alien Land Laws."

Growers emphasize a different part of the picture: they attribute the pre-war prevalence of sharecropping to the lack of an alternative labor supply. The strawberry labor market was, in fact, poorly developed at that time, and wage laborers became even more scarce after the immigration restrictions of the 1920s. Many growers tried to recruit the Mexicans, Japanese, Filipinos, and Dust Bowl migrants who harvested other California crops but found they were not available in the manner and at the times required. These groups were mostly itinerant, moving from region to region to work in the crops that offered them the longest and most substantial income possibilities. On both counts, they found strawberries unattractive. Berry growers found it hard to secure wage workers for the small

[8]According to a 1979 interview with Tad Tomita, former president of Naturipe Berry Growers, this cooperative gave members daily reports of prices and sales, collected money due growers, and used the threat of withdrawing business to secure better prices. It established enduring relationships with certain commission houses, thus helping growers in their need for credit. Both Japanese and—in the usage of that time—"Caucasian" growers were firmly ensconced in the organization's founding charter: its bylaws called for ten directors, five of whom were to be Japanese and five "Caucasian" (see also Wilhelm and Sagen 1974:206–13). My own interviews with berry growers and the life histories I collected from an additional fifteen Japanese growers and marketing organization officials have helped me reconstruct the pre-war system.

but essential amounts of weeding, watering, spraying, and pruning in the winter. Some jobs, like tractor work and furrow irrigating, required a degree of skill that most migrants did not have. The heavy late-spring harvest posed an especially difficult recruitment challenge, requiring a large number of workers for less than two months.

In contrast to these other labor sources, the Japanese had experience and interest in labor-intensive farming. They expressly preferred sharecropping to wage labor. Given this context, it is a moot question as to whether or not other sources of labor could have been developed. Because sharecropping functioned so smoothly, alternative workers were rarely sought. Locally based sharecroppers who could draw workers from an extended network of family, friends, and ethnic group members, and who benefited directly from the quality of their care, solved growers' labor problems admirably. Many local growers were convinced that only Japanese families could provide the quality and intensity of care that strawberries required. Sharecroppers had great—in some cases lifelong—longevity in their positions. Although not without friction, bonds between landowners and share tenants were often personal and enduring. Even before the war, some landowners loaned the sons of long-time tenants money to start farming on their own. On the eve of World War II, berry growers and sharecroppers estimate that 90 percent of central coast berry farm owners were Anglos and 10 percent were Japanese and Japanese Americans. Most of the direct labor was performed by Japanese sharecroppers.[9]

In essence, then, the Alien Land Laws formed the basis of the pre-war strawberry labor market regime—a regime that engendered ethnic stratification between farm owners and laborers and fostered sharecropping as a labor process. Moreover, the Alien Land Laws dampened the development of the strawberry labor market by encouraging a labor system in which most work was done by unpaid family members. This system was disrupted in 1942, when the Japanese were forcibly relocated to detention camps. California strawberry production came to a virtual standstill during the war (Bain and Hoos 1963:12, 18–19). When the Japanese were released, a new technological, economic, and political climate spurred the expansion of the industry and discouraged the resumption of sharecropping.

[9]Sources for these estimates include interviews with individuals who were farm owners or sharecroppers before the war and with the descendants of such individuals. Written sources estimate that about 90 percent of the strawberries in California as a whole were grown by Japanese prior to World War II, including sharecroppers, fixed tenants, and farm owners.

Strawberry Farmers and Farms after the War

A new pattern of ethnic stratification among growers emerged after World War II. The Japanese moved out of sharecropping and into independent farming, Mexican-origin farm laborers moved up the agricultural ladder to become producers, and new Anglo growers entered the rapidly expanding market. When the Japanese were released from the camps in 1945, most returned to the Pajaro rather than the Salinas Valley, because the pre-war anti-Japanese sentiment had been milder there. Although many returned briefly to sharecropping to get their bearings and earn some money, most were waiting for a chance to farm on their own. Some left sharecropping after the first four-year crop cycle, purchasing land in the names of friends or native-born relatives. The real exodus came after 1952, when the California Supreme Court overturned the state's Alien Land Laws. Some sharecroppers received loans of money, equipment, and land from their former employers. In some cases, this aid was solely an expression of the patronal relations generated by pre-war sharecropping. In others, large grower-shippers coupled their assistance with a mutually advantageous agreement to sell the fruit from the "spin-offs" they sponsored.

Industry characteristics—the high per-acre profits, the improvement of yields with intensive farm management, the high labor costs reducible by family labor, and the amenability of plants to low-quality land—helped the Japanese start small and build slowly. Japanese growers generally began farming in the available and inexpensive hilly portions of the region: the coastal bluffs and the North Monterey Hills. Many of these new growers formed partnerships with relatives or friends who had also been sharecroppers, renting or buying a larger piece of land and subdividing it into family-sized parcels. They used family members for nonharvest and some harvest labor and as supervisors of hired workers, thus lowering high labor costs and ensuring careful and reliable work. To secure production capital, Japanese growers used their savings from sharecropping and their legitimacy with local credit sources and established farmers developed through years of residence in the area. They initially sold their fruit through Naturipe Berry Growers, the marketing cooperative organized by Japanese and Anglo growers in 1917. By the mid-1950s, Naturipe was an almost exclusively Japanese organization, for most of its Anglo members had left to form their own grower-shipper company, Driscoll Strawberry Associates. In 1957, as Naturipe expanded to other production regions to increase its volume and market clout, a group of Japanese growers—some calling themselves "traditionalists"—split off to form Watsonville Berry Cooperative, a smaller, more locally based and ethnically and socially cohesive organization. These cooperatives were invaluable to small and medium-sized Japanese producers trying to enter and compete in the market.

The end of the Alien Land Laws thus transfigured the demography of the industry. By the late 1950s, growers of Japanese origin and descent had increased to about three-fourths of the total grower population. Anglos had decreased to one-fourth. Some of the latter were descended from families that had owned berry farms in the area since the turn of the century. Others were corporate producers or newer agricultural businessmen attracted by the profits of growing strawberries. In the mid-1970s, a new ethnic group joined this established population: individuals of Mexican origin or descent who had acquired management skills and integration into farming networks through their experience as sharecroppers and production cooperative members. Mexicans had become sharecroppers after the mid-1960s, when some central coast berry growers returned to sharecropping and recruited skilled Mexican pickers as sharecroppers. Although, as we will see, this new share tenancy permitted tenants less independence and decision-making latitude than did the old, it still represented a step up from simple weeding and picking. The production cooperatives came on the local scene through a different avenue: between the late 1960s and the mid-1980s, over seventy such cooperatives were sponsored in the state by public agencies and private charitable organizations as a means of fighting rural poverty. Most grew strawberries and were located on the central coast. Their members were former strawberry workers and sharecroppers (see Wells 1982).

Both institutions served as stepping-stones for Mexican farm workers to become strawberry farmers. Through their work as sharecroppers and cooperative members, Mexicans gained management skills, access to land, and contacts with established growers, plant salesmen, marketing agents, farm supply companies, and farm advisers (Wells 1990). Through political lobbying at the state level, the cooperatives secured the translation of Cooperative Extension berry-growing publications and meetings into Spanish. They also pressed to have sharecroppers accorded a vote in CSAB decisions. As sharecroppers began to "go independent," some of their former employers provided equipment loans, recommendations for land rental, and advice on growing berries. The motivation here was much the same as with the Japanese: a special favor to a long-time employee. Some former sharecroppers and cooperative members from the same ranch still consult each other about farming. Some rent in groups to use large parcels that landlords will not subdivide. Some use land that was formerly farmed by their cooperative or owned by the same landlord. All in all, sharecropping and production cooperative membership were the most significant prior occupations of the Mexican berry growers interviewed in 1987: about 82 percent had been either sharecroppers, cooperative members, or both. According to organizers of two of the largest cooperatives, 75 percent of their former members are now, or have been, independent strawberry growers.

Like the Japanese, Mexican growers have benefited from the industry characteristics that encourage small scale. They, too, use family workers for most nonharvest and much harvest labor. They, too, started with a few acres of marginal, hilly land, primarily in the North Monterey Hills. Such plots were readily available in the mid-1970s, because by then most Japanese growers had moved down to richer, more easily farmed parcels on the Pajaro Valley floor and coastal headlands. Unlike the Japanese, Mexicans had neither the accumulated savings, the farming experience, nor the legitimacy in the eyes of local lenders and community leaders to leverage the large amounts of capital necessary to farm strawberries. They also lacked access to markets. They were too small and poorly capitalized to pursue the tack of Anglo growers of becoming grower-shippers themselves. Only a few had strong enough ties with the Japanese community to gain membership in the marketing cooperatives. Some who had such connections chose not to join, because the cooperatives could not provide the credit that they needed.

In the mid-1970s, a unique conjuncture in the history of the industry gave Mexican growers access to capital and markets. Shortages in fresh and processed berry supply prompted some local processors and fresh shippers to finance Mexicans. For processors, the trend toward annual planting and fresh market sales had severely constricted supply on the central coast. Because of their large fixed investments in facilities and the crucial role of late-season fruit from the central coast, processors were unwilling to leave the area in the face of shrinking supply. At the same time, new fresh shippers were drawn to the area by increasing consumer demand and by the unparalleled duration of the central coast shipping season. Between 1970 and 1987, the demand for fresh berries rose by over 50 percent, and the number of local fresh shippers more than doubled. Whereas in 1976 produce publications listed twenty-five (14.3 percent) shipping point sales agents in the region with strawberries as one of their top four products, that number had risen to sixty-four (27 percent) by 1986 (*Blue Book* 1986; *Packer* 1976; PSAB 1987). When these new shippers arrived, they too had difficulty obtaining fruit, because most growers sold through established companies.

To solve their supply problems, both processors and the new shippers sought out and financed new growers. Mexicans were the obvious candidates, because some production cooperatives were disbanding and some sharecropping ranches were converting back to wage labor at the time, releasing a pool of individuals with the motivation and some of the skills to farm berries on their own. Both processors and new shippers began aggressively to recruit Mexican sharecroppers and cooperative members, sending their agents out to the fields, querying growers for recommendations, and taking prospective candidates out to lunch. They offered production financing and market outlets in return for growers' agreements to sell their fruit through them. Some shippers funded up to 75 percent of preharvest costs and offered winter subsistence loans. Processors generally offered less, from $2,000 for smaller growers, up to $30,000 for larger ones. At the start, some shippers and processors were so eager for product that they financed individuals with little screening or communication regarding the risks and responsibilities of farming. Some report having lost "tens of thousands of dollars" in past years on delinquent loans. Currently, they mitigate their risks by charging above-prime interest rates, giving fewer loans, and dealing with more experienced growers.[10]

With this assistance, the number of Mexican growers increased rapidly after the mid-1970s. Before 1975, local observers estimate that fewer than six independent Mexican berry growers operated on the central coast. By 1985, the county agricultural commissioners' pesticide enforcement records show that their numbers had increased to seventy-eight, or almost 48 percent of the total number of berry growers in the two-county region. These records also show that fifty-two (32 percent) of the independent berry growers were of Japanese descent and most of the rest (34 or 21 percent), were Anglos (see figure 12).

The Contemporary Farming System

Together, these ethnic groups form a distinctive farming system with common, cohesive elements and group-specific, segmenting elements. The cohesion of this system has to do with participation in a common in-

[10]Interviews with the major processors in 1987 indicate that they have evolved toward giving fewer loans and securing a larger volume of their product from fewer growers. Thus, one processor said that in 1982, 5 growers averaging 100 acres each supplied 60 percent of his berry volume, and 200 growers with from 1 to 2 acres each supplied the other 40 percent. Seventy-five percent of these growers had loans of from $5,000 to $10,000. By 1986, 10 growers with an average of 100 acres each supplied 90 percent of this processor's fruit volume, whereas 100 growers with from 1 to 3 acres supplied only 10 percent. Only 5 percent of the small growers received loans, and these ranged from $2,000 to $6,000. Ninety percent of the large growers received loans of from $20,000 to $30,000. All of this company's growers were Mexican.

Figure 12. Ethnic backgrounds of strawberry growers, Santa Cruz and Monterey Counties

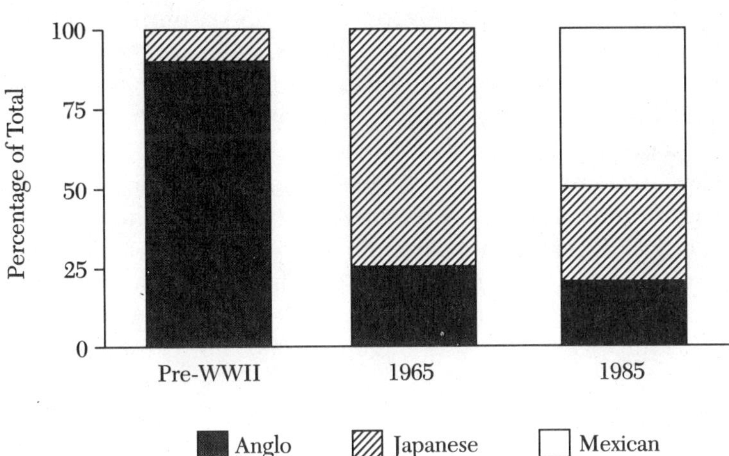

Sources: Interviews, 1986–87; Offices of the Agricultural Commissioners, Santa Cruz and Monterey Counties, *Pesticide Use Reports*, 1985.

stitutional and physical environment. Its segmentation has to do with the ethnic differentiation of the local opportunity structure.

Two commonalities—shared geography and shared institutions—bind central coast berry growers into a single system. Geographically, this system revolves around the two urban service centers—Salinas and Watsonville—and around the three berry-growing microregions—the Pajaro Valley, the North Monterey Hills, and the Salinas Valley. All berry growers are oriented toward the towns of Watsonville and Salinas to some extent, because they are the regional hubs of agricultural service, sales, and processing. They also house the county farm advisers', agricultural commissioners', and state Department of Employment Development offices. The regional Border Patrol and various agencies that enforce labor protections are based in Salinas. Watsonville is the social and economic focus for central coast berry growers. Although buyers of fresh and processing berries are located in both cities, most operate out of Watsonville, as do both the fresh and processing Strawberry Advisory Boards. Whereas berry growers tend to be community leaders in Watsonville, they play less substantial roles in the city of Salinas, which is larger, more industrial, and more dominated by absentee-owned vegetable companies. At different points in the day small groups of berry growers meet in designated Watsonville coffee shops to share news and camaraderie. Such gatherings are less frequent and less institutionalized in Salinas and the North Monterey Hills.

The California Strawberry Advisory Board (CSAB) provides the most inclusive local component of grower organization and communication. Growers from all parts of the state sit on its subcommittees and board of directors, but central coast producers are especially involved because the office is located in Watsonville. The meetings of standing subcommittees are open, and local growers often attend. They also comprise the majority of attendees at the board's three annual meetings and at the special meetings it calls to discuss unanticipated industry problems. At these gatherings, growers help shape the board's research and marketing agendas, develop collective responses to industry challenges, and interact with the university researchers to discuss the results of board-sponsored research.

Farming Resources and Ethnic Knowledge Systems

Although growers are linked by shared participation in the region and common interest and membership in the CSAB, the social system of strawberry farming is by no means homogeneous. Beneath its superficial sources of integration, one finds ethnically differentiated farming subsystems, or "knowledge systems" (Wells 1991). These systems have a certain structure (social networks), a certain content (farm management styles), and a certain pattern of dispersal across the three berry-growing microregions. They are highly correlated with another important ethnic contrast: varying patterns of farming practices and farming success. These latter differences are usually attributed to the economic endowments and the cognitive, often culturally based orientations of decision makers. Thus the innovation diffusion and rational choice literatures argue that differential tendencies to innovate or pursue optimal production strategies are explained by the attitudes and the human and material capital complements of individuals (see Wells 1991:739–41). From this perspective, it is the lack of economic resources that keeps motivated individuals from advancing. Many studies of the poor and of non-poor ethnic groups take a different tack, attributing economic success and failure to the values of the group. They argue that certain groups, especially those with a history of poverty, have developed self-defeating attitudes that now independently foster their marginal status (Banfield 1951; Erasmus 1968; Foster 1965; Lewis 1965; Sowell 1981). Hence groups "cause" economic outcomes through their cultural values: the less prosperous reproduce their own failures, and the successes of the more prosperous are idiosyncratic and not replicable.

I would suggest that the first approach leads analysts to neglect the social systemic factors that shape farming practices, while the second one posits a vision of culture that is unresponsive to environment and mistakes expedient adaptations to circumstances for value-driven behavior. Drawing on the 1986–87 grower interviews (see Appendix, this chapter) and building on more aggregated decision-making models which portray culture as a means through which groups adapt to environmental circumstances (Bennett 1969; Liebow 1967), I argue that differences in farm management approaches in this case are the result neither of inherent cultural values, nor of individual skills and resource endowments. They are, rather, adaptive responses to the social-organizational and economic opportunity structures confronted by members of the different groups. Here, varying initial endowments and opportunities have involved group members in different farming networks, which purvey distinctive farming outlooks, shape farming decisions, and reinforce resource differentials within the producer population. These knowledge systems are themselves a productive resource—a social form of capital. Thus Japanese, Mexican, and Anglo growers entered the local economy with varying background experiences and endowments, in varying roles, at varying points in time. Over the years, these differences and subsequent experiences have generated cumulative contrasts in the pools of human and material resources contained within each ethnic group. These contrasts encourage and permit their involvement in particular knowledge systems. Let us examine these processes more closely.

Human Capital. First, ethnic contrasts in human capital—the individual skills, abilities, and experiences which can be brought to bear on farming—are marked. Interviews reveal that Mexicans are the least endowed in all regards. They are the closest to their immigrant roots and the least established in and familiar with the local community. Almost all of their parents and over 90 percent of the growers themselves were born in Mexico. Though about half speak some (usually halting) English, Spanish is their language of choice. Most confine their social contacts to persons of Mexican birth or descent. By contrast, three-fourths of Japanese growers' parents were born in Japan, but three-fourths of the growers themselves were born in California, and one-third were born on the central coast. The older growers speak both Japanese and English. The older generation socializes most within the Japanese community, in family networks or ethnic organizations such as the Japanese American Citizens' League and the Buddhist Church. Although their children are more active in non-Japanese organizations, their intimates are still more likely to be Japanese. Anglos are the most firmly embedded in the local community: only one-fifth of their parents were born abroad, and these are the oldest growers. Eighty percent of the growers and their parents were born in the state, and 60 percent of the growers were born on the central coast.

Educational endowments also distinguish the three groups, including their formal schooling and training in farm management, as well as the informal education of experience. Here again, Mexicans are the least endowed: they have the least experience as independent berry growers (ten years), most of their prior agricultural experience has been as peasant farmers in Mexico and farm laborers in the United States, and they have the fewest years of formal education (under six). They average forty-eight years in age. On the average, the Japanese are the oldest (fifty-five years), fall in the middle in terms of formal education (fourteen years), and have the longest and most intensive direct experience farming strawberries (twenty-seven years)—as independent operators and as sharecroppers before the war, when sharecroppers had virtual charge of their farms. These averages disguise disparities within the group, however, which includes a majority of growers in their sixties who have farmed berries all their lives and have little more than a grade school education, and a minority in their thirties and forties (their sons), many of whom have postgraduate professional degrees and work experience, and who have returned to take over their family farms. Anglos are the youngest (forty-two years), have the most formal education (sixteen years), and fall in the middle in terms of farming experience (eleven years). As a group, they have the greatest longevity and social status in the local system: about one-third of the older growers are second-generation strawberry producers. The group also incorporates the largest amount of professional training in agriculture: about one-third entered farming as a business, either as owner-operators or as professional farm managers.

Their former occupations provide varying amounts of farming expertise as well. In most cases, the grandparents of Japanese growers had small-scale commercial farms in Japan. Over two-thirds of their parents were central coast berry farmers and one-third were sharecroppers. The parents of most Mexican growers were, or still are, subsistence farmers in the states of Michoacán, Guanajuato, and Jalisco. Almost half also worked as strawberry pickers on the central coast, over one-fourth were sharecroppers, and only one-sixth were independent growers. Most Anglo growers' parents were in business or the professions (30 percent) or in central coast berry farming (30 percent), reflecting the division in the group between those who inherited a family berry farm and those who entered farming as a business (or profession in the case of professional managers). Growers' own previous occupations echo this general pattern. Anglos are most likely to have held a job in business or the professions (one-fifth), or in another sector of agriculture (one-half), before farming strawberries. One-fourth of the Japanese and almost two-thirds of the Mexicans interviewed have been sharecroppers. An additional one-fourth of Mexican growers were members of a production cooperative. Over three-fourths of Mexican growers worked as farm laborers into their adult years, almost all in the strawberry industry. The few Japanese and Anglos who worked as farm laborers did so as youths on their parents' or friends' farms.

Material Capital: Credit, Investment, and Capitalization. The grower categories also diverge in their command over material resources. One measure of this command is their ability to obtain credit, which is highly correlated with economic and educational histories. Most berry growers rely heavily on credit to cover such production expenses as fuel, plants, chemicals, and labor. Three sources provide most operating capital: commercial banks, the Production Credit Association (PCA), and strawberry sales agents (fresh shippers or brokers and processors). Commercial banks and the PCA are preferred, both because they lend—in growers' words—"enough money to do a good job," and because they do not tie a grower to a particular sales agent. To qualify for such loans, however, growers must have attributes that most Mexicans lack: collateral, extensive farm management experience, a sound cash-flow history, and current evidence of a stable farming operation. The recommendations of established growers also help. Over 90 percent of the Anglos and 67 percent of the Japanese interviewed received loans from these sources, as opposed to only 29 percent of the Mexicans—a proportion that is undoubtedly lower in the group as a whole.[11] Mexicans rarely even apply to these institutions, believing they could not qualify or even complete the required projections of costs and expenses.

As could be expected, independent shippers and processors are the main credit sources for Mexican growers. Of those interviewed, 57 percent of the Mexicans, but none of the Anglos or Japanese, received credit from strawberry processors or shippers. Loan quantities from shippers and

[11]The few Mexicans who get PCA or commercial bank credit tend to be those who belong to the predominantly Japanese marketing cooperatives or who have worked through a Salinas-based loan guarantee program for low-resource growers. My interviews included relatively more individuals with these connections than does the overall Mexican grower population. In the case of the cooperative members, their colleagues informed them of credit opportunities, bolstered their confidence about applying, helped them fill out forms, and in some cases even cosigned bank notes. Both Mexican growers and finance officers in lending institutions speak to the importance of such aid.

Table 7. Number of growers and size of acreage by ethnic group, Santa Cruz and Monterey Counties, 1985

Category	Mexican	Japanese	Anglo	Total[a]
Number	78	52	34	164
% of all growers	48%	32%	21%	100%
Acreage	1730	2782	2878	7391
% of all acreage	23%	38%	39%	100%
Average farm size in acres	22	54	85	45
Farms with less than 6 acres	22%	6%	15%	15%
Farms with less than 15 acres	64%	29%	32%	46%
Farms with 15–49 acres	25%	46%	21%	31%
Farms with 50 or more acres	12%	25%	47%	23%
Acreage on marginal hilly land[b]	68%	21%	15%	29%

[a]Totals sometimes exceed 100 percent because of rounding off.

[b]Includes 10 growers with acreage on both marginal hilly and flat land (2 Mexican, 5 Japanese, and 3 Anglo).

Source: Offices of the Agricultural Commissioners, Santa Cruz and Monterey Counties, *Pesticide Use Reports*, 1985.

processors vary: when strawberry supply is plentiful, loans are small and difficult to obtain; when supply is scarce, some companies pay all production expenses. In general, shippers and processors pay operating credit directly to plant, fumigation, pesticide, fertilizer, and drip irrigation companies, to increase the likelihood of its being used for farming. They charge above-prime interest rates and their loans are small, so that growers relying on them must continually cut costs. Overall, most Japanese and Anglos are adequately financed, although the Japanese provide a higher proportion of their own financing, and Anglos rely more heavily on credit. Mexican growers depend almost entirely on credit and are chronically undercapitalized. Because they lack collateral of their own, they are the most vulnerable grower group.

The groups also exhibit substantial differences in investment and capitalization, which are reflected in the resource levels or "quality" of their farms, measured in terms of land quality, equipment, size, yields, market prices, and wages and benefits paid. In the mid-1990s, the Japanese are concentrated on the rich river bottoms and proximate slopes of the Pajaro region, the Anglos on the vast expanses of the Salinas Valley floor, and Mexicans in the steep, sandy, erosion-prone North Monterey Hills. As the agricultural commissioners' records show (see table 7), Anglos are particularly concentrated in the large farm category: almost half have fifty or more acres. The Japanese are concentrated in the medium farm category: almost half have from fifteen to forty-nine acres. Mexicans are concen-

Table 8. Indicators of grower resource level by ethnic group

Indicator	Japanese	Mexican	Anglo
Average rent per acre	$436	$428	$627
Total value of land and buildings	$1,166,550	$728,350	$3,328,000
Value of strawberry sales	$1,079,200	$368,600	$2,706,000
Average number of fresh crates per acre, 1985	5,081	2,787	4,842
Average income per fresh crate, 1985	$5.43	$4.53	$5.59
Percentage of group supplying worker benefits	58%	10%	51%
Average hourly wage for pickers	$6.24	$4.88	$6.03

trated in the small farm category: almost two-thirds have under fifteen acres and over one-fifth have fewer than six acres. Anglo farms are almost four times as large as those of Mexicans on the average, and they are much larger if one excludes a couple of very large Mexican farms. The grower interviews confirm this pattern. They also show that Japanese midsize farms sometimes outrank larger Anglo farms in terms of investment and performance on a per-acre basis.

Japanese growers generally have the highest per-acre investment in land and exhibit the highest rate of self-financing. Over three-fourths of the Japanese growers interviewed owned from half to all of their land, as opposed to half of the Anglos and only one-third of the Mexicans. To put it another way, 60 percent of the Mexicans own no land, as opposed to 17 percent of the Japanese and 30 percent of the Anglos. The Japanese also own the highest proportion of their own machinery, and it tends to be of high quality and in good repair. Anglos own half as many tractors as do the Japanese and are much more likely to contract out expensive jobs like preplanting ground work. Mexicans own almost as many tractors as the Japanese, but they are small, old, and frequently out of commission. As table 8 shows, Anglos pay the highest rents, occupy the best land, and have the highest total value of land, buildings, and strawberry sales. In 1985, the average yields per acre on Mexican farms were 44 percent lower than those on the farms of Japanese and Anglos combined. Mexicans' market prices were almost 20 percent lower. The capital scarcity of Mexicans is reflected in their greater use of family workers and the lower pay rates and benefit levels of their hired workers.[12]

Social Capital: Farming Information and Social Networks. Not only have common immigrant histories, education, and economic experiences

[12]The hourly pay rate is calculated here by applying a season average of four crates per hour to the pay method used by a particular grower. See Chapter 5.

Table 9. Most important source of production information by ethnic group

Source	Japanese (% of group interviewed)	Mexican (% of group interviewed)	Anglo (% of group interviewed)
Marketing company	50	14	60
Field men	8	36	0
University of California	25	23	20
Researchers	8	9	10
Extension (farm advisers)	17	14	10
Experience	17	28	20
Other growers'	17	5	10
Own	0	23	10

led to comparable human and material resource endowments within each ethnic group, but these endowments have encouraged and permitted group-specific patterns of involvement with the social networks through which farming information is generated, transmitted, evaluated, and applied. These networks, or "knowledge systems," exhibit distinctive contents, consisting of shared approaches to farm management, and they exhibit distinctive structures, consisting of sustained patterns of connection among certain institutions, organizations, and individuals. Network participation is largely bounded by ethnicity: each group tends to obtain information from certain preferred sources and to evaluate and apply it with reference to certain sets of significant others. Farm management styles in this sense are socially constructed through participation in particular knowledge systems. Moreover, engagement in these systems is conditioned by, and in turn reinforces, resource differentials among producers.

Answers to the question, "What is your most important source of production information?" suggest the character of local knowledge systems.[13] As table 9 indicates, growers obtain their production information from five major sources: marketing companies, University of California researchers and extension agents, the CSAB, agricultural "field men" (the representatives of companies who sell agricultural services and supplies), and their own experience. Marketing companies are the primary information source for 50 percent of the Japanese growers and for 60 percent of the Anglos,

[13]Table 9 represents growers' spontaneous answers to the question. None of the groups spontaneously mentioned the CSAB as one of their top sources of production information. Probing disclosed that this omission was partly due to the CSAB's being especially associated with its initiatives in the realm of marketing and promotion and partly because contacts with university researchers that came through the CSAB were attributed to the researchers.

but for fewer than 14 percent of the Mexicans. These differences arise largely from the varying roles that sales organizations play for each group.

Anglo knowledge systems focus on the grower-shipper organizations through which most Anglo producers market their fruit. Growers must be relatively large-scale and economically well-endowed to form, or to be asked to join, a grower-shipper company. In the latter case, they must also have social connections to member growers. Grower-shipper companies present a number of advantages. First, evidence of membership in a prominent grower-shipper organization facilitates credit from commercial banks and the PCA, because the ability to obtain credit depends not only on a grower's own collateral and performance record, but also on the social stature, information, assets, and recommendations of his or her network of associates. Second, these organizations foster an especially high density of farming information exchange, both horizontally among member growers and vertically between the organizations and their members, and between the organizations and outside sources such as the CSAB, university researchers and farm advisers, field men, and credit suppliers. Grower-shippers are the most active participants in political interest groups such as the Farm Bureau and the Western Growers and Shippers. They also offer the widest range of immediate farming services. They have their own labels, cooling facilities, and sales personnel. They maintain strict quality control operations that involve precise grading standards and one or more daily visits to members' fields to assess fruit quality and quantity, to evaluate and suggest treatment for pests and diseases, and to monitor fruit packing. Because the companies' own field agents provide such extensive advice, and because many purchase supplies in bulk, member growers turn to commercial field men only for the actual provision of a small range of services and supplies.

Grower-shipper companies have marketing advantages as well. Most have members in both northern and southern California, so they can offer buyers an extended shipping season. Most companies aim primarily or exclusively for the top end of the fresh market, which requires the highest uniformity and quality of fruit and secures the highest prices. The interviewees who sold through grower-shipper companies averaged $7.00 a crate for their fresh berries in 1985. Because grower-shipper organizations are highly cohesive, and because members can afford recommended production practices, they are the most able to achieve the standards required by the top segment of the market. Overall, their high volume, quality, consistency, and lengthy shipping seasons secure them the highest proportion of coveted and less risky chain store contracts and cash purchase sales.

Growers who sell through grower-shipper companies rely on research that their organizations conduct, as well as on University of California (UC) research. The companies hire research staff to fine-tune university recommendations to suit the microclimates and soils of their members. The relatively high educational levels and professional agricultural training of members lend them comfort with technical inputs. Although their organizations have been less aggressive in developing ongoing relations with university researchers than the Japanese cooperatives, as individuals they are the most likely to seek out farm advisers, initiate contact with researchers, and offer their farms for test plots. One company, Driscoll Strawberry Associates (DSA), is unique in the extent to which it has invested directly in research. This Watsonville-based company is the largest grower-shipper company in the state, with growers in both the north and south. It developed from a core of relatives and friends whose families have grown berries on the central coast since the late 1800s. Most members are related by blood or marriage, and those in the Salinas-Watsonville area often come into contact daily. In 1944, DSA set up a private research organization and hired UC plant breeder Harold Thomas to direct it (Wilhelm and Sagen 1974:230–31). Observers estimate that over the years DSA's extensive research on pests, diseases, and cultural practices, and its patented plant varieties that have historically peaked when yields from university varieties were subsiding, have given the company a seven- to eight-year advantage over the UC research program (Runsten 1987:14). Dialogue between growers and researchers is unusually close in this company: growers sit on committees that parallel and provide input into the staff departments; research agents monitor each grower's fields once or twice a week for blossom production, pests, diseases, and nutrition; most growers have test plots on which researchers conduct experiments and then discuss their results with host growers. Overall, DSA researchers do more intensive field testing and get more input from growers than do university scientists.

Japanese knowledge systems revolve around the two marketing cooperatives through which almost all sell their fruit: Naturipe Berry Growers and Watsonville Berry Cooperative. Both are based in Watsonville, although the larger, Naturipe, now has members in Anaheim and Oxnard as well. Most local members are small and medium-sized Japanese growers; a few are Anglos and Mexicans. Neither cooperative offers loans to members, but both are well-reputed among agricultural lenders, so that membership facilitates the credit applications of smaller-scale producers. It is no accident that most of the few Mexicans who have PCA or commercial bank loans belong to one of these cooperatives. Both cooperatives have their own labels, coolers, and sales departments. Both purchase supplies in bulk. Naturipe has processing facilities whose profits bolster fresh market returns, thus guaranteeing members a market for their lower-quality fruit and enabling them to respond more easily to the relative advantage of the fresh and processed markets than can growers who must negotiate separately with a processor. The cooperatives tap the middle price and quality range of the strawberry market: interviewees who sold through them averaged $5.00 per fresh crate in 1985.

The cooperatives exhibit a high density of vertical and horizontal information exchange and a high level of internal cohesion. Both have quality control personnel who visit members' fields twice a day to check the volume and grade of fruit coming to market. In general, cooperative members adhere less closely than do grower-shippers to the company's recommendations for quality standards and cultural practices—in part because lower resource levels prevent some growers from meticulously following technical advice, and in part because, as we will see, members have a different perspective on the element of experience. In the case of Naturipe, the fact that the company is large makes for less cohesion. Like grower-shippers, members choose their farming peers from within the organization. Although levels of trust and intimacy vary, members constitute a community for purposes of information exchange. One fifty-five-year-old Japanese grower described the clustering of his farming communication around Naturipe:

> I talk a lot to growers in the cooperative. If I lived in Salinas, I wouldn't see people so often. Here I see them in the barber shop, at [the Buddhist] church, at the JACL [Japanese American Citizens' League] lodge, even on the street because it's a small town. I sometimes visit other growers' fields if they are doing exceptionally well . . . that is, if they are within our co-op. Within the co-op most growers feel you're welcome to take a look any time. For growers outside, not so much.

In practice, Japanese growers are less likely than Anglos to approach university researchers and farm advisers directly. They turn mainly to friends and associates within the cooperatives for farming information. The cooperatives have taken special initiative to build organizational links with university researchers and advisers and to convey their advice through meetings and field staff. In addition, certain members have developed decades-long relationships with university researchers, helping them shape research directions and test new varieties and cultural practices. These individuals serve as information conduits to their farming peers, who speak proudly of them and seek their advice. Though the cooperatives do not undertake research themselves, they are distinguished by the extent to which they have supported and utilized the University of California's research program. Beginning in the 1950s, they led the campaign to expand the CSAB's research budget, an effort opposed by the Anglo grower-shippers who had started their own research program. The Naturipe president was instrumental in recruiting plant breeder Royce Bringhurst in 1954 to reestablish the strawberry research program disrupted by Harold Thomas's departure. It was no accident that the big leap in the CSAB's research budget came in the mid-1970s, when a Naturipe member became president. Over the years, the cooperatives have cultivated close relationships with university researchers and extension personnel and have made a special effort to transmit their findings to members. Both cooperatives hold weekly membership meetings and monthly board of directors' meetings at which production practices, varieties, and disease and pest problems are discussed. University of California personnel are often invited to answer questions and discuss new developments. All in all, the cooperatives have been remarkably effective at enabling small-scale producers to utilize a public institution to perform research functions that only large, well-financed growers can undertake on their own.

As table 9 indicates, Mexican growers' knowledge systems are less focused around a single information source. Field men are their major source of information, experience is a relatively close second, and marketing companies and farm advisers tie for third. Their knowledge systems have less internal cohesion and density of information exchange than those of Anglos or Japanese, and they foster farming practices that reinforce growers' subordinate position in the industry. Mexicans' limited human and material resource endowments account for the shape of their knowledge systems. A look at the few Mexicans who belong to a marketing cooperative is instructive in this regard: all gained admission through the recommendation of an existing member, which could only be secured if the aspirant had a facility in English, an opportunity for extended contact so as to develop a personal relationship, a sufficiently sound economic situation to dispense with the loans that shippers offer, and an impressive farming track record. Few Mexicans have these requisites, suggesting that they do not so much choose their marketing organizations as qualify for them.

Capital scarcity forces most Mexican growers to sell their crops to agents who can provide credit, mostly independent shippers and processors. Engagement with such agents has a number of disadvantages. Both types of agents require loan recipients to sell all of their fresh or processing fruit to the lending company, thus binding them to lower market returns. In the 1970s and 1980s, processors offered prices an average of ten cents a pound lower than those in the fresh market. Some processors establish a set field price and require delivery of a certain minimum volume. Others require that processing deliveries start by a particular date, regardless of the relative prices in the fresh and processed markets. Some contracts involve agreements to keep second-year plants and to plant varieties especially suited to freezing. These practices are attractive to processors because they generate more processing fruit, and they may also be attractive to low-resource growers because annual replanting is costly, but on the whole they reduce market returns. Independent shippers tap the lower-quality, lower-price segment of the fresh market: interviewees who sold through them received an average of four dollars per fresh crate in 1985. Few shippers take title to the fruit upon its delivery, so that market and transport risks rest with the growers. The differential between the prices quoted at the time of delivery and those returned to growers is greatest in these companies. Whether the disparity is caused by changing market conditions, transportation damage, the downward pressure on pooled prices exerted by the low-quality deliveries of some growers, or shippers' chicanery, most Mexicans are convinced of the latter. Many refer to themselves as the shippers' "slaves." This perception of dishonesty and exploitation undermines growers' identification with their marketing organizations and reduces their willingness to seek their advice.

Although shippers and processors offer loans, in most other ways their services are inferior to those of cooperatives and grower-shippers. Both accept, grade, and cool the fruit, either in their own or in rented coolers. Here the input of processors ceases. One fresh shipper has a processing plant, thus according clients some of the dual-market benefits enjoyed by Naturipe growers. Independent shippers play a limited role in purveying farming information. Although their clients share commonalities that could conceivably increase cohesion—language, national background, problems of resource limitation, and, often, kinship and prior acquaintance—shippers provide no context for collective decisions. Growers are dispersed on their farms and they interact with shippers individually. Shippers establish standards and procedures unilaterally and do not hold grower meetings. Because shippers aim for quantity rather than quality, they invest little in conveying production information. They neither conduct research themselves nor link growers to university personnel. Their few field agents lack the formal agricultural training characteristic of cooperative and grower-shipper agents. For the most part, their agents concentrate on conveying the daily market prices to growers and the number of crates coming into the cooler to shippers.

Mexicans get most of their farming information from a small number of field men who visit growers' ranches in order to generate business. Although they help growers identify and solve pest, nutrition, and disease problems, they are a restricted and potentially biased source of information. Not only do they lack technical training, but both their expertise and their solutions tend to revolve around their products, which many observers think they overprescribe. Moreover, their efforts dwell on the curative rather than the preventative, so that growers who rely on them must continually work against handicaps. Overall, field men, like independent shippers, neither link Mexican growers among themselves nor connect them with outside sources of expertise. Although not clearly revealed by the responses reported in table 9, the linkages of Mexican growers among themselves and to UC researchers and extension agents are much more limited than are those of the other two groups. They verbally accord researchers about the same importance as do Japanese and Anglos, but in fact, few visit the university test plots, read extension bulletins, or attend the CSAB's informational meetings in English or in Spanish. Nor do they directly approach researchers. The handful of Mexicans who belong to a marketing cooperative have attended meetings with researchers. A few link up to the university through the farm adviser, with whom they built a relationship as production cooperative members. In general, though, Mexicans' expressed valuation of university research is not backed up by actual contact.

The three ethnic groups also vary in the roles they accord experience, both verbally and in practice. Mexicans identify it as most important, with 28 percent identifying it as their main information source, second only to field men. Anglos and Japanese rank it somewhat lower (20 and 17 percent, respectively), although in practice they enjoy a great deal of input from experience, both from their own years farming and their frequent consultations within their marketing companies. They interact almost daily with these peers, and they report initiating contacts with other growers almost four times more often each year than do Mexicans. Mexicans are the least likely to seek out peers for production advice, and they lack the natural social contexts for such exchanges. Paradoxically, although Mexicans have the least experience and training, they are the most likely to identify themselves as their major source of information. Japanese and Anglo growers do not verbally accord their own experience such salience, in part because they have other information inputs, and also because Japanese cultural values discourage direct praise of oneself. Mexicans' community of trust is usually confined to friends and relatives, who may or may not belong to their marketing company. These individuals usually lack experience, financial resources, and integration into the farming community. Thus Mexicans are not only the most physically isolated on their small farms in remote hollows of the North Monterey Hills, they are also the most socially isolated and receive the least input into their farming decisions.

Ethnic Approaches to Farm Management

Farm management styles vary significantly among the three ethnic groups.[14] The approach most characteristic of Mexicans can be characterized as "maintaining," that of the Japanese as "micromanaging," and that of Anglos as "building a business." Whereas scholars might—and local residents do—attribute these differences to inherent cultural predilections, I argue that they are adaptive responses to the structural conditions faced by members of each group. In practice, the structure and content of local knowledge systems are mutually reinforcing: confinement to a certain set of farming networks encourages and permits a particular management style, and pursuing that style reinforces socioeconomic divisions among the ethnic groups. Answers to the open-ended interview question "What is the most important determinant of success in growing strawberries?" help clarify ethnic differences in farm management style. As table 10 shows, the first three factors that growers identified have to do with information: the first, with knowledge and observation of the precise technical requirements to maximize yields; the second, with the wisdom gained through experience; and the third with forward-looking experimentation and change.

Whereas all three groups recognize that market returns are affected by the precise timing and performance of certain procedures, they vary in the importance they accord attention to detail and in the ways they approach it. Japanese growers regard attention to technical detail as the single most important determinant of success. Listening to their responses, one is struck by the frequency with which they refer to the challenge of a grower as "learning the rules" of strawberry growing. These rules are to be learned in part through attention to the findings of university researchers, to which their English speaking and reading ability, their special connection to UC researchers through their cooperatives, and the high educational levels of the younger generation all facilitate access. The rules are also to be learned by refining technical recommendations through their own farming experience. Although most Japanese lack formal training in the agricultural sciences, as a group they have the greatest depth of direct experience as farming practitioners and the longest tenure on particular plots of land. Thus they are especially able to deploy experience. Many are highly systematic

[14] John Bennett uses "management style" to refer to a farmer's level of entrepreneurial activity and stage of enterprise development (1982:315–448).

Table 10. Most important determinant of success in growing strawberries by ethnic group

	Ethnic Group									
	Japanese			Mexican			Anglo			Total
Determinant	Number of respondents	%g[a]	%t[b]	Number of respondents	%g[a]	%t[b]	Number of respondents	%g[a]	%t[b]	Number of respondents
Attention to detail	9	75	20	5	23	11	4	40	9	18
Experience	2	17	5	4	18	9	1	10	2	7
Innovation	0	0	0	0	0	0	3	30	7	3
Labor control	0	0	0	1	5	2	2	20	5	3
Money	0	0	0	5	23	11	0	0	0	5
Hard work	1	8	2	7	32	16	0	0	0	8
Total	12			22			10			44

Note: [a] %g = percentage of ethnic group
[b] %t = percentage of total farmer population

in their experimentation, comparing their own yields with certain practices against UC predictions as to grams per plant and crates per acre and contrasting their own actual returns with the market prices and net profits projected for each variety. One individual, who described himself as an "analytical grower," expressed this perspective:

> The farming part isn't doing the work, it's making sure it's done right. Each variety has its potential and every region presents a grower with certain things he can or should exploit. What distinguishes a good grower from a bad grower is recognizing the areas of exploitation. I try to learn the rules for each variety, so I can realize its potential on my land. It takes careful observation, but when you learn the rules, it's easy. But you have to do everything exactly right. It's a straight and narrow path. Anything a grower does that deviates from those rules costs him.

As they work to adjust researchers' prescriptions to conform with the soil, terrain, and climatic conditions on their own ranches, Japanese growers take a cautious approach to experimentation. They set its parameters narrowly: modifying practices, refining them, but not casting off in uncharted directions. Their approach reflects the risk aversion that guides their farm management style generally. They attribute this caution directly to their loss of most possessions during the war and to the market crash of 1957, in which many lost their farms and had to start anew. Most of the Japanese interviewees stated their preference to remain at a medium farm size, even when they had the resources to expand. They also preferred to provide as much of their own financing and to own as much of their own machinery and land as possible, so as to buffer themselves from fluctuations in the external economy. They are not quick to adopt new plant varieties: most wait until a new cultivar has proven its worth before adopting it.

Anglos also attend to the recommendations of researchers and modify them to suit their microregions, but their attention has a different tenor. In general, their management style focuses on innovation and risk taking as the keys to building a business. About one-third of the Anglo growers assert that innovation is the key to success (see table 10). They are much more likely than the other groups to launch a large planting of an experimental variety, to increase their acreage substantially, or to incur indebtedness if they anticipate economic advantage. The independent research facilities contained in their knowledge systems and their high levels of material resources support such practices. Anglos emphasize managing the farm as a business and anticipating future challenges, rather than doing or overseeing the work. Their approach reflects their considerable education, the training of many as farm managers, and their social and linguistic comfort and involvement in the local, state, and national political economies.

Anglo growers' experimentation is the most wide-ranging and takes the broadest view of production challenges. Some have pioneered new means of pest control, anticipating increased public opposition to pesticides. Only Anglo grower-shippers have undertaken varietal research, an endeavor made possible by the substantial resources of their organizations. Many Anglos speak to the importance of grower initiative in responding to the threats of labor organizing, immigration laws, and pesticide regulations. They are also more active than the other groups in political interest groups that deal with such challenges, such as the Farm Bureau and the Western Growers and Shippers. One grower articulated this multifaceted, forward-looking approach:

> Research gives a grower ideas, not answers. Above all, you have to look ahead. You have to experiment constantly with plant spacing, bed size, fertilization, planting dates, and plant digging dates. You have to think about the market—when the demand is greatest and the supply least—and then you have to develop plant varieties that will give you an edge over other growers. Nowadays you have to think about the public too and its opposition to chemicals. The strawberry industry will be in real trouble if it doesn't find new ways to control pests. Growers have to get off the ranch and pay attention to politics. We growers have to speak up for ourselves. A guy can do a good job farming and get destroyed by politics.

To Mexicans, hard work and money are the major determinants of farming success (see table 10). The first is the resource they have in most abundance; the second is the one they lack most painfully. It is interesting to note how few members of the other groups identify either of these factors as important—possibly because financial resources are not a major problem for them and because their own labor is not their major solution. Mexican management styles emphasize deploying their own and their families' labor and reducing their need for money in every way possible. Repeatedly, interviewees used the phrase *mantener la vida* (to maintain life) to characterize their main goal in farming. This phrase has the connotation of providing the essentials, of not going under. Many Mexicans operate on the brink of survival. Some even leave farming for a season or two to accumulate money as farm laborers, then start up again. Although they verbally acknowledge the importance of technical detail, they accord it the least weight of any of the three groups, and their observance of it is the most variable.

Local observers identify two aspects of Mexicans' management styles as evidence of self-defeating and irrational farming values and behavior: their apparent disregard for technical advice and their mistrust of, and failure to consult, information sources outside themselves. Their lack of concern for technical precision is construed first from their farming practices: they are much less likely than members of the other groups to observe university recommendations regarding ground preparation, plant densities, planting dates, harvest frequency, weeding, and fertilizer and pesticide application. They may plant too early, too late, with too few or too many plants. Their strawberry beds often lack the height and soil aeration necessary for optimal root growth and drainage. They may apply too much or too little fertilizer, and they tend to harvest and weed too infrequently. Their alleged disregard for technical expertise is also construed from the way they appear to "bargain" with technical advice. For example, I was present during a conversation among six growers discussing the farm adviser's plant density recommendations. "Who is he to tell us how to run our ranches?" demanded one. "We're the ones in charge here," agreed another. "He suggests [a certain number of] plants per acre. I'm going to plant [two-thirds that many]." In the end, each of the growers opted for a different plant density: three planted fewer than advised, one planted slightly more, and two planted significantly more. According to farm advisers, those who plant fewer reduce their per-acre yields, while those who plant significantly more are likely to crowd the plants and reduce fruit size and quality. Such technical "bargaining" also occurs with field men. Thus, on one of several similar occasions a grower told me, "When [the field man] tells me to put on one pint of something, I put on three. I don't trust him. Besides, I'm the boss here. It's cheaper than having him come back again and again—and more effective." Again farm advisers disagree, pointing out that too much fertilizer weakens the plants and elicits vegetative growth rather than fruit.

Mexicans' mistrust of outsiders, especially experts, and their tendency to self-isolate, are also construed from their lack of attendance at farm advisers' and CSAB informational meetings. As one farm adviser put it: "They are at home fixing their tractors when they should be at our meetings." In practice, Mexican growers' social isolation is even more extreme than non-Mexicans recognize, extending far beyond their relations with outside experts. As we saw in our discussion of their knowledge systems, their information sources do not connect them among themselves, as do those of Japanese and Anglos. Moreover, they explicitly dismiss their peers as an information source, citing their lack of experience, unreliability, and "egoism." They see self-sufficiency as the hallmark of a good grower and seeking advice as a sign of weakness. One grower's comments convey the tenor of this perspective:

> Those people [farm advisers and university researchers] are from the schools. They don't know what it's like in the *campo.* All they have is book learning. I've spent all my life taking care of strawberry plants [mostly in his case as a farm worker]. I don't ask advice from anybody, even my neighbors. They won't tell me the truth anyway. The best thing is to work hard and don't pay for anything you can do yourself. If I don't know how to do something, I teach myself. I do all the welding, all the mechanical work, all the building here. I build my own furniture. My kids don't go into town for a haircut. I cut their hair. I cut my own hair. I've been cutting my own hair since I was twelve.

How are we to explain these different farming attitudes and practices? Are they, as local non-Mexicans sometimes claim, evidence of the inherent "sloppiness" and "suspiciousness" of Mexican culture? Or, as some scholars allege, do they reflect a cultural predilection to confine trust to the nuclear family and to compete with and undermine others (Foster 1965; Rubel 1966)? I think the evidence contradicts both explanations. First, let us note that Mexican growers' limited human capital endowments—the inability of many to speak or read English, their lack of formal education or training in farming, and their lack of farming experience—hinder them from taking advantage of, understanding, or evaluating much of the technical information available. As newcomers to strawberry growing, few recognize the severe yield consequences of not adhering to recommended practices. The farming experience of some in Mexico is no help, since the crops they grew—corn, beans, and squash—were by no means as temperamental as strawberries. Their assertion that turning to peers would not help them has some basis in fact, in that their peers have the least to offer in terms of technical expertise and experience—not to mention social connections, time, money, and the things that money can buy.

Mexicans' lack of material resources also diminishes their ability to observe recommended practices and consult outside experts. Thus some disadvantageous practices are not value-driven at all, but are forced by their resource scarcity. Many cannot afford to monitor and spray regularly for pests. Some delay ordering plants because they cannot pay the deposit, and delay planting because they cannot pay the balance, causing serious reductions in yields. In the case of the aforementioned conversation about plant densities, the three growers who planted fewer plants than advised in fact lacked the money to plant at the advised density, even though their bravado in announcing their decision suggested a voluntary choice. Because the cheap North Monterey Hills land on which Mexicans farm is also more physically isolating, and because so much of their time is spent doing the work on their farms, they are less able to engage with others. Few can afford to rent twice as much land as is bearing in order to plant at the ideal time. They must choose between plowing under a still-bearing field, or delaying planting until the harvest subsides. Because they lack the large tractors and expensive bed-shaping implements necessary for optimal land preparation, they are generally unable to achieve the height and regularity of Anglo and Japanese strawberry beds. Even their reluctance to seek out university researchers and instead to get advice from self-interested supply and service salesmen has in part a material base: because they have less time to seek information, they tend to rely on those who seek them out. Moreover, university advice often requires more tractor attachments, land, and capital than Mexicans command. In some cases, the solutions of field men are less expensive and technical. One dealer taught his customers to apply pesticides with backpack applicators and fertilizers by hand, eliminating the need for costly tractor attachments.

Their experience as peasant farmers in Mexico and as farm laborers in the United States further contributes to this management style, engendering expectations and attitudes appropriate to those former circumstances which they carry into the present. Thus, Mexicans' belief that the family is the reliable circle of trust and that outside authorities are out to subordinate them is rooted in past experience. When they were farm laborers, job acquisition was indeed competitive, and the extended family was the source of job recommendations and subsistence between jobs. Their relations with the government and bank representatives who dealt with peasant farmers in Mexico, and with the growers and their agents who supervised them in the United States, were indeed hierarchical and dominating. Consequently, their step up to farm operatorship is a matter of great moment to them. More than anything, they see farming as a chance to escape domination. They speak proudly of no longer being a person whom "everyone can push around," of becoming a person who is "his own boss," who "doesn't have to take orders from anyone." Yet the reality is much different: as recent, undercapitalized farmers, whom many locals still consider appropriately farm laborers, the status and independence they hope for is not yet within their grasp. It is in their contacts with outsiders that this becomes most apparent, and therefore individuals take a stance that supports their self-respect. One often hears references to farm advisers and field men as "just another *norteamericano* telling us what to do."

Thus, whereas Japanese and Anglo growers, with greater resource endowments and legitimacy in the local system, can view researchers' advice as the neutral, factual discoveries of scientific observation, Mexicans tend to see it—and it is sometimes extended—as the stuff of potential domination. The view that the adoption of technical advice signals acceptance of subordinate status polarizes discussions of farming practices and shapes production strategies. When Mexicans bargain with technical specifications, they frame it as supporting their personal dignity, as asserting their independence and authority in a context where, in fact, they still have little. As noted by one of the individuals who planted many more plants per acre than advised: "What would be left to me if I didn't take charge here? I can't control the rains, I can't control the [market] prices, [my shipping company] cheats me, and my income is less safe than if I were a farm worker." Some growers who applied too much fertilizer expressed similar sentiments. Because such attitudes and behaviors are adaptive to context, they are likely to continue until their initiating conditions have changed sufficiently, and for a long enough period, that they are no longer necessary (Liebow 1967). They are maintained by the ways that the present echoes the past: by the continued tendency of some local residents and experts to patronize them, and by the lack of supportive networks outside the family. Most important, they are maintained by the structure of their knowledge system.

Mexicans' knowledge system is the fourth factor shaping their management styles. Because their farming networks place them in individual asymmetrical relationships with information providers, link them minimally among themselves, and convey only a limited amount of farming information, they in fact perpetuate their historically adaptive attitudes. Moreover, in this context, Mexicans' high valuation of their own experience may express their lack of reliable connection to other sources of support. A closer look at the matter of farming advice is instructive. In fact, Mexicans' tailoring of technical advice is not unique: most growers do some of that. However they do so with the help of their own education and experience in a social context that compensates for individual shortcomings. Anglo and Japanese growers receive and evaluate technical advice in the context of their knowledge systems, which provide frequent opportunities for interaction and information input, and a peer group that is cohesive and respected in the local community. In other words, the kinds of linkages their knowledge systems have created among peers and the kinds of relationships they have developed as a group with outside authorities counteract perceptions of extrafamilial unreliability and expert domination and provide a depth of experience for evaluating farming information. It is no accident that the Mexican in the above example who planted only slightly more plants than advised was a member of one of the marketing co-ops. He consulted his peers, saw that the advice was extended to legitimate local residents as well, heard the pluses and minuses of adhering to it, and arrived at a density well within the range of variation of his cooperative peers.

Environment, Values, and Farming Success

In sum, the local organization of central coast strawberry production is much more heterogeneous than apparent from the outside, for both the farming terrain and the farmer population are internally segmented. This evidence challenges the representations of microeconomic commodity systems, and farming systems analyses that portray individual decision makers as operating in structurally homogeneous systems. As we have seen, growers engage with the local economy through ethnically differentiated "knowledge systems," which link them to farming resources and foster certain farming attitudes and practices. Ethnic distinctions in farm management practices in this case are not the result of inherent cultural values or of individual skills and resource endowments. Nor are they the ultimate cause of differential farming success. Rather, they are adaptive responses to the social organizational and economic opportunity structures engaged in by members of the different groups. Here, local knowledge systems derive from, and in turn reinforce, historically generated resource differentials within the producer population. The evidence suggests that a certain baseline of human and material capital—especially facility in English and the ability to do without shippers' loans—is necessary for individuals to break free from isolating and economically disadvantageous information sources and to engage in social networks that could challenge and obviate disadvantageous attitudes and behaviors.

This analysis of ethnic farming orientations reveals an adaptation of values and behavior to environment. Though some observers might attribute the Anglos' expansive risk-taking, business-oriented approach to an entrepreneurial cultural predilection suggested by studies of European American farmers elsewhere (Raney [1940] 1963; Salamon 1992), in this case growers' educational and economic endowments and their social systemic supports permit and encourage such a tack. Similarly, it is not necessary to appeal to a cultural reserve, respect for education, or attention to detail to explain Japanese growers' management style: the special links their organizations have established with UC researchers, their generations of farming, and their historical experiences on the central coast support such an orientation. Finally, though some might criticize Mexicans' out-in-the-fields, do-it-yourself approach as shortsighted and self-defeating, it makes sense given their historical and—to a large extent—present environment. In fact, it may be precisely their exceptional self-reliance and dogged labor that have enabled them to "maintain" without the experience, capital, or social connections that the other groups have found essential to success. Notably, the dynamics of this local system depict a pattern of farming success which diverges sharply from the familiar image of the yeoman farmer braving the elements and markets on his own. Not only are the management styles of successful farmers in this case highly social, but one could argue that their success is predicated precisely upon their social interconnectedness.

Appendix
Methodology for Grower Interviews

A few words are in order regarding my methodology in the 1986–1987 grower interviews. To develop the pool of interviewees, as I noted in the preface, I obtained a list of all berry growers who had registered with the county agricultural commissioners' offices in Monterey and Santa Cruz Counties to apply restricted chemicals in 1985, a list that local farm advisers and farmers thought included about 98 percent of the grower population. These pesticide use reports provided names, addresses, telephone numbers, and ranch locations and acreages by crop. Thus armed, I stratified the population according to primary production locale, ethnicity, and farm size. These designations were modified as my interviews proceeded. "Primary production locale" was the microregion in which a grower farmed the greatest number of acres, situated his (all were men) headquarters, and was the most involved in social relationships and institutions. I assessed grower ethnicity initially from surnames, categorizing them as Japanese, Mexican, or "Other." The small size of the population, my familiarity with the industry, and the help of my principal informants helped me identify the few ambiguous cases. In the interviews, I asked growers how they would categorize themselves and others ethnically. "Japanese" and "Mexican" were clearly the local terms of self and other ascription for Japanese Americans and Mexicans and Mexican Americans. Almost all "others," in fact, were European Americans, with a couple of outliers such as a Chinese American investor. The "self" and "other" designations of European Americans were more varied. They most often called themselves and were identified by others as "Anglos" or "whites." A few older Japanese used "Caucasian." Mexicans used "Anglos," "whites," *norteamericanos,* or (pejoratively) *gringos,* but were on the whole less likely to refer generically to the other two groups and more likely to speak individually of *el patrón* (the patron, boss) or *el dueño* (the farm owner). The term "Anglo" refers generally to the dominant society's European American population, as contrasted with the large Latino, particularly Mexican, population. It does not assume English ancestry. In the present case, the terms "Anglo" and "white" were used interchangeably, with "white" being slightly more prevalent. I chose to use "Anglo" as my term of reference here, however, because "white" includes Mexicans in census designations and implies a racial rather than a social categorization.

Size categories were established in consultation with the local farm advisers, using their designations of small (1–14 acres of berries), medium (15–49 acres), and large (over 50 acres) strawberry farms. Since most berry growers here grow only strawberries, and since land for crop rotation was frequently rented in the year it was needed and thus not associated with a particular grower in the prior production year, berry acreage in production was the best measure of farm size. Through my own knowledge and principal informant verification, I categorized all farms according to labor process (sharecropping or wage labor). This designation was checked in the course of the interviews. In some cases the county agricultural commissioners' pesticide use reports listed the plots of berries grown in different microregions separately, creating confusion about whether these were different farming entities or subparts of a single entity. I consolidated such separate ranches under the name of the umbrella farm to get a more accurate reading of the number of growers and their distribution by ethnicity, region, and size. Thus, for this study, a "farm" is the sum of all separate ranches operated by a single grower or farming "company." The grower is the operator of this overall entity. He may be an owner-operator or the hired manager of a farming corporation. The total number of 160 here is

Table 11. Distribution of growers by ethnic group, region, and farm size, Santa Cruz and Monterey Counties

	Population[a]		Sample[b]	
	Number	%	Number	%
Ethnic group				
Japanese	51	32	12	27
Mexican	79	49	22	49
Anglo	30	19	11	24
Region				
Pajaro	65	41	18	40
N. Monterey County	62	39	18	40
Salinas Valley	33	21	9	20
Farm size				
Small (1–14 ac.)	74	46	16	36
Medium (15–49 ac.)	51	32	15	33
Large (50+ ac.)	35	22	14	31

[a]Population total of 160 growers.
[b]Sample total of 45 growers.
Source: Offices of the Agricultural Commissioners, Santa Cruz and Monterey Counties, *Pesticide Use Reports,* 1985.

less by 4 than published in some earlier reports on this project. The discrepancy is the result of information gained since those reports were published.

From this list of 160 growers, a sample of 45 growers (28 percent) was selected for interviewing. Interviewees were chosen initially to reflect the regional proportions of small, medium, and large berry farms. Within these categories, I tried to achieve proportions of the different ethnic groups and primary production locales that were characteristic of that size category in the population as a whole. Personal and reputational acquaintance with many growers made it possible to include a mix of growers who were active in industry organizations, as well as those who were more isolated. Similarly, the sample included long-time growers who could describe the industry's historical development, as well as recent arrivals who could speak to its constraints on newcomers. I made a particular effort to interview as many of the largest producers, and of those who used sharecroppers, as possible, because of their disproportional impacts on labor processes in the industry.

The resulting sample was substantially representative of the distribution of the population along the three key axes of differentiation (see table 11). The dominant tendencies among the ethnic categories of growers in the population were reflected in the sample as well. That is, Mexican growers in the sample (64 percent) and region (65 percent) are heavily clustered in the small-size category; Japanese growers in the sample (58 percent) and region (49 percent) are clustered in the medium-size category, and Anglo growers in the sample (73 percent) and region (47 percent) are clustered in the large-size category. Similarly, North Monterey County is the primary production region for 68 percent of the Mexican growers in the sample and for 60 percent of those in the region. The Pajaro region is the primary production locale for 67 percent of the Japanese growers in the sample and for 59 percent of those in the region. Anglo growers are less concentrated in a single production locale: 64 percent in the sample and region produce berries primarily in the Pajaro Valley, but another 27 percent of Anglo growers in the sample and 30 percent of those in the region emphasize the Salinas Valley. Because the latter are larger farms, Anglos account for the major component of berry acreage in the Salinas Valley. My understanding of the Japanese portion of the grower population was aided by ten in-depth interviews I conducted with such growers during the cooperative research.

The grower interviews included 275 items. They posed basic demographic questions about the interviewee, his family, and his farm and included questions about farm and work history, farming input sources and problems, labor recruitment methods, the numbers, pay levels, and benefits of employees, production practices, work organization and management practices, marketing arrangements, the roles of producer organizations and the union, and labor market conditions. The schedules included both closed and open-ended questions to allow respondents to elaborate on important items.

[5]

Wage Labor and Workplace Control: The Complementarity of Labor Supply and Demand

Workers' characteristics—their human, material, and social resources and aspirations—also shape the relations of production, generating a labor supply that is especially willing to fulfill the labor demands of the industry and relatively less willing and able to challenge them. This chapter explores the complementarity between labor supply and demand, showing how it reduces the necessity for direct control within the wage labor process. The social processes through which labor demand is met and workplace conflict is dissipated depend crucially on the nature of labor supply. In this case, however, supply characteristics do not derive from workers' inherent qualities, but are conditioned by the political forces that limit and channel their options. As a result, the aspirations of workers and the attributes of jobs are not as spontaneously congruent and the choices of workers are not as freely made as they might otherwise appear.[1]

I develop this argument in three steps. First, I show how industrial constraints have generated a particular annual cycle of labor demand whose fulfillment is crucial to producers' profits. Second, I demonstrate that workers' distinctive backgrounds and social patterns, which are embedded in the local organization of production, combine with politically established constraints on their options in the labor market to produce a particularly willing and compliant labor force. Finally, I show how labor supply and demand characteristics converge in the wage labor process, at once generating and dispelling the potential for labor resistance.

[1]In this analysis I concur with Charles Sabel's ([1982] 1985) claim that workers' experience and consciousness help shape patterns of collective action at work. I differ, however, in my emphasis on the ways that workers' resources and interests are politically constructed.

Industrial Constraints and the Demand for Labor

As noted earlier, industrial constraints establish a crucial role for hand labor from the point of view of growers: its cost is the largest and most malleable component of expenses, and its timely and careful performance is the major determinant of crop value and returns. With this broad characterization of growers' interests in mind, I would like to move to a more fine-grained analysis of the production process, to reveal exactly how and when labor demand shapes class interests and class leverage. Though its labor intensiveness might suggest that strawberry production is relatively "backward" or inefficient, in point of fact, its procedures and technologies have been finely tuned for maximum profitability. The California strawberry industry is remarkable in the sheer volume of scientific research that has gone into raising yields, reducing disease, and improving handling.[2] Most of this has been carried out by University of California researchers, with the cooperation and financial assistance of the strawberry industry. Over the years, technological experimentation has reduced labor demand and raised capital intensivity outside the harvest while raising labor intensivity within it. A review of the annual cycle demonstrates the precision of production procedures and the crucial involvement of labor.

Strawberry production tasks fall into four categories: land preparation, planting, maintenance, and harvesting. The annual cycle begins with land preparation, which includes cultivation and leveling, soil fumigation, and bed formation. It is initiated in late summer and in late fall, a few weeks in advance of planting (see figure 13). Currently, it involves no seasonal hand labor: some tasks are performed by the grower's own year-round employees, primarily tractor drivers; others are contracted out to surveyors or to laser leveling, fumigation, and ground preparation companies. The procedures of land preparation are exacting. (See Appendix 1, this chapter.) First, the soil is ripped, disked, and cultivated; then the desired slope is determined, either by visual surveying or with recently perfected computerized laser levelers; finally, the land is leveled with a tractor-pulled implement. Next, the ground is fumigated by injecting methyl bromide and chloropicrin under a plastic sheet that is spread over the field, to control a variety of soil-borne diseases that had decimated harvests and seriously

[2]To illustrate the extraordinary investment in the rationalization of production in this industry—and for those inherently interested—I detail the historical development of farming practices in Appendix 1, this chapter. Here, I have profited from interviews with growers, farm advisers, fumigation applicators, nurserymen, supply dealers, and researchers, including Harold Thomas, Stephen Wilhelm, Victor Voth, Royce Bringhurst, as well as from historical documents, university bulletins, and other written sources.

Figure 13. The annual cycle

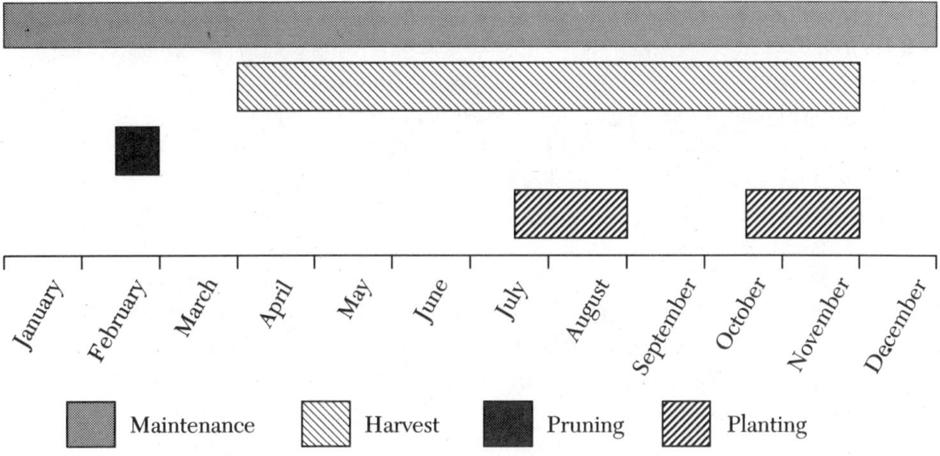

constrained land availability and farm size before its adoption in the mid-1960s. Coming upon one of these plastic-shrouded fields in the slanting light of late day can be startling, for it conveys the illusion of a shimmering lake where before there was land. Next, the soil is listed up by tractor into long peaked mounds and a tractor pulling a specialized bed-shaping attachment squeezes in the sides of the mounds and flattens their tops, creating raised beds with alleys between. The dimensions of these beds are matters of much deliberation. On the central coast they currently range from 48 to 52 inches in width and from 8 to 10 inches in height. Tractors then cut from two to four parallel slots in the pre-formed beds, leaving markings at regular intervals to indicate where the plants are to be placed.

Planting is carried out almost entirely by hand, because yields are so dependent on the correct placement of the plants in the ground. Irregular spacing reduces yields by overcrowding or underutilizing available space. Insufficient root-soil contact or placement too high or too low also lowers yields and may even kill the plants. Planting is undertaken by pairs of workers who move in tandem down the shaped beds. One person carries a burlap shoulder bag containing plants and tosses a plant at each marking along the slot; the other inserts the plant in the slot to the proper depth and tamps the soil down around it with a trowel. A tractor driver follows them, pulling a drum over the beds to further firm the soil around the roots and crowns of the plants (Welch et al. 1982:7). The timing of planting is as important as its careful execution, for the window for planting is relatively narrow. Planting too early reduces plant vigor with too many fruit buds, resulting in lower yields and small, soft fruit—especially when early planting is followed by a warm winter. Planting too late causes excessive vegetative growth, reduced and delayed fruit production, and excessive foliar and runner development. As little as a week's delay beyond the advised planting date can seriously cut yields (Welch 1989:7).

The scientific fine-tuning of cultural practices is particularly marked in the blend of planting dates and cultivar selection. Most central coast growers plant both in July-August (summer) and in October-November (winter), using a combination of short-day and day-neutral cultivars. This mix maximizes yields and market returns while minimizing costs and fluctuations in labor demand. Winter plantings cost less to maintain and peak early in the season, when the prices are high and the supply low. Their yields decline sharply after the peak, however, and the overall volume of fruit is lower. Summer plantings, meanwhile, start bearing later, but they produce throughout the summer and into the fall, giving a higher volume of fruit overall and tapping the low-supply, high-priced late season market. The choice of planting season is linked to varietal selection, since each variety has its optimal planting date. Both short-day and day-neutral varieties are important in growers' production strategies. Short-day varieties set fruit when the days are short, resulting in a heavy early harvest peak, a midsummer slump, and a smaller early fall peak. Day-neutral varieties produce flowers cyclically regardless of day length, giving a longer, more even harvest without heavy peaks but with a higher total yield than many short-day varieties. By combining the two types of varieties and planting seasons, growers extend and flatten the fruit-bearing curve, optimize market returns, and make more efficient use of costly inputs.

Production activities in the third category—maintenance—are undertaken throughout the year. They include irrigating, weeding, removing blossoms, pruning and cutting runners, manicuring, fertilizing, and controlling pests and diseases. Currently, with the exception of manicuring, which is carried out in conjunction with picking, little seasonal labor is used in maintenance. Irrigation begins with overhead sprinkling after planting, which continues until the plants are established. Growers use their year-round employees to set the sprinklers up and take them down. After that, the plants are watered using drip irrigation, which has almost entirely replaced the hand-built, hand-operated furrow system. Because drip systems are regulated by automatic timers and tensiometers that monitor the soil's humidity, a single year-round employee can irrigate an entire ranch. Labor requirements for blossom removal have been greatly reduced as well.

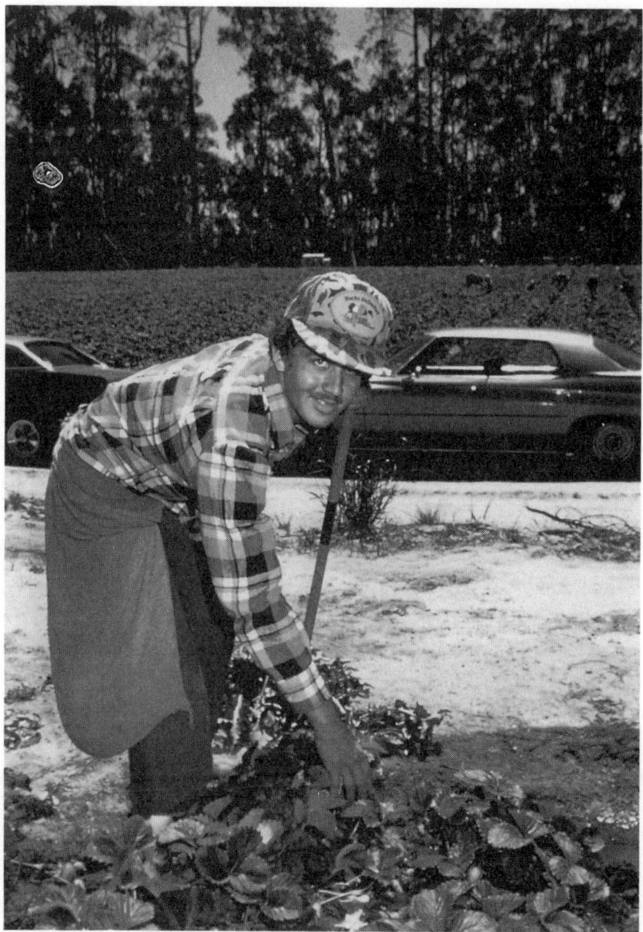

Plate 3. Weeding. Photo Jack Kelly Clark, courtesy University of California

Whereas the first round of blossoms is removed from summer plantings to divert the plants' energy to root formation, blossoms are allowed to develop on winter plantings, generating their valuable early season crop. Weeding begins shortly after bed establishment, and it continues as needed throughout the life of the planting. Weeders uproot weeds from the beds by hand and with hoes and discard them in the furrows for later removal, or they place weeds in a burlap bag slung from the waist or shoulder (see plate 3). The amount of weeding labor has diminished greatly in recent years, because drip irrigation and fumigation retard weed growth, and because some growers use herbicides to kill weeds in the furrows.

In late winter, before the spring growth spurt, old leaves are pruned to conserve the plants' vitality and prevent the spread of pests and diseases. Currently, this operation requires little hand labor, for the new cultivars produce less foliage, winter-planted varieties do not require pruning, and many growers have adopted small rotobeaters to replace the small, curved pruning knives that have been employed for a century. To foster fruit production, runners are also removed from the plants as they appear in the course of the season. Although some growers use rotobeaters or simple tractor-pulled attachments to accomplish this task, these methods can damage the fruiting plants, so most growers employ crews of workers to remove runners with pruning knives. Runner removal requires little labor, however, because winter planting suppresses runner production and the new cultivars have been bred not to runner. Pest and disease control and fertilization are carried out throughout the production cycle, but they utilize almost no hand labor. Fertilizer is broadcast over the fields and inserted into the beds by tractors prior to planting. Liquid fertilizers are injected into the drip irrigation system during the bearing season. Herbicides and pesticides are generally sprayed over the beds with tractor-pulled attachments about five times during establishment and ten times during the harvest.[3]

At no point are the quantity of labor demanded and the importance of its quality and timing greater than in the harvest. Although technological changes have reduced the need for labor outside the harvest, they have actually increased labor demand overall and within the harvest. Labor is currently the largest single source of production cost, and the harvest is by far its greatest component (see figure 14).[4] The growth patterns, high value, fragility, and perishability of the crop all shape the contours of harvest labor demand. Over the years, improved varieties and production practices have increased the demand for pickers earlier, later, and more consistently during the season. The harvest now starts in early April on the central coast, builds toward a heavy May-June peak, subsides in midsummer, revives for a smaller peak in September, and then declines until harvest volume and market prices no longer merit the investment of picking costs. In cold years, growers may stop picking in October; in mild years, they may

[3]The extensive use of chemical pest and disease controls, along with political contestation of such methods and price premiums paid for residue-free products, have encouraged experimentation with organic practices (Gliessman et al. 1990). Nonetheless, chemical controls still predominate (Haley 1982:44–52; Razee 1979:9–10; Welch et al. 1982:12–13).

[4]See Appendix to Chapter 2.

Figure 14. Changes in harvest, nonharvest, and total labor costs per acre, 1956–85

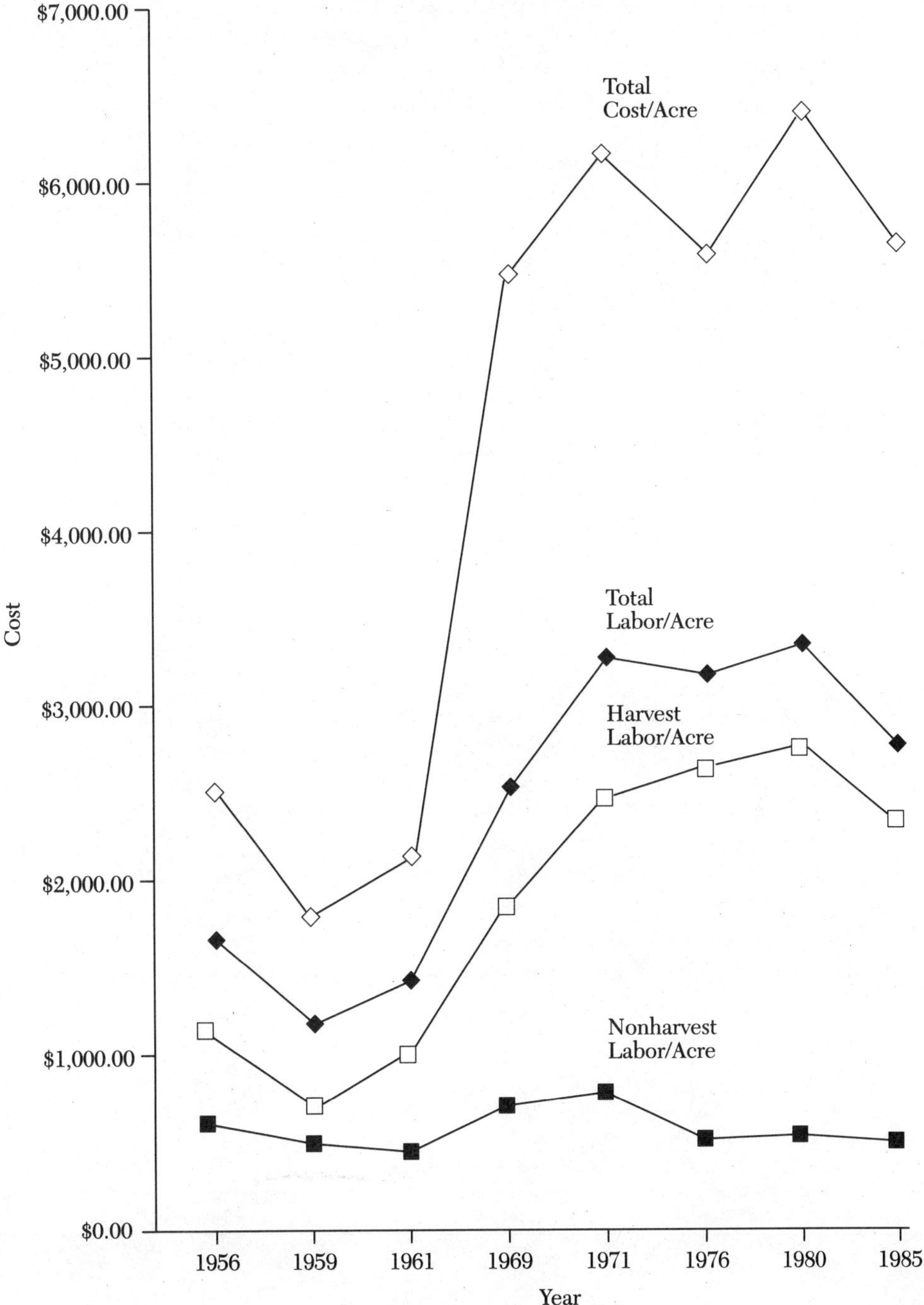

continue into December. Currently, labor demand is heavily concentrated between April and October (see figure 15).[5]

The overall procedures and equipment for the harvest have changed little since the war. The crop is still harvested entirely by hand and deposited into crates that rest on small, metal, front-wheeled carts that have been in use for over a century (see plate 4). Yet the importance of workers' care, judgment, and skill have increased, as overall costs and quality standards for fresh and processed fruit have risen. Current market treatment standards are exacting. Berries destined for the processed market must be picked fully ripe, the stem and calyx (cap) removed in the field, and the berries deposited in wooden crates that hold from fifteen to eighteen pounds of fruit. Some growers have workers toss the lowest marketable grade of berries into gallon cans that are fastened to their carts to be delivered to the processor for juice. Fresh market berries must be picked slightly pink with the calyx and one to two inches of stem still attached. To avoid bruising, they are picked and packed directly in the field into twelve one-pint plastic baskets contained in a cardboard shipping crate. Because these baskets are the final retail product, and because their quality and appearance are the major determinants of market price, their contents must be uniform, unblemished, and attractively arranged. This necessity involves placing good but less attractive berries on the bottom and the best sides of the most attractive berries on the top and sides. This process requires a level of skill informally understood by those in the industry but rarely given explicit recognition. The strawberry harvest is more skilled than acknowledged, though no more so than the work of many other putatively "unskilled" workers in agriculture, and much less than that of such historically familiar rebels as the nineteenth-century craftsmen studied by Montgomery (1979).

It is not simply workers' skill that is crucial to growers' profits: the fragility and the variable quality and quantity of the crop place a particular premium on their effort and reliability. The extreme perishability of the fruit and the concentration of growers' returns in the relatively short har-

[5]The Employment Development Department's *Farm Labor Report* (881-A) is the major data source on the number of people working in California crops over time. It provides data by county and types of activities. However, the numbers it lists as working are not based on an actual count of workers on a given day, nor on an inventory of workers by name, but rather on estimates derived from the number of acres harvested and on estimates of labor requirements per acre (or other unit) which have been developed by economic studies of labor inputs. The "numbers working" figures are also inconsistent over the years as to the types of activities they record, posing additional problems for the consistent categorizing of demand. These caveats notwithstanding, the 881-As are what we have to work with. See Friedland (1984b) for a valuable discussion of their use.

Figure 15. Fluctuation in monthly demand for pickers, Santa Cruz and Monterey Counties, combined average for 1985–87

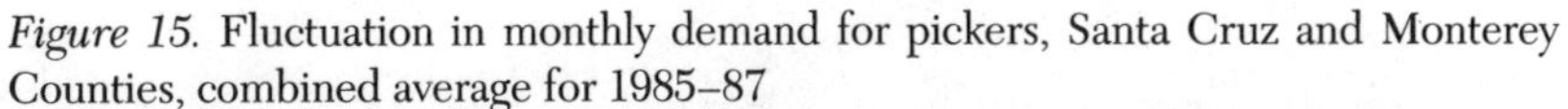

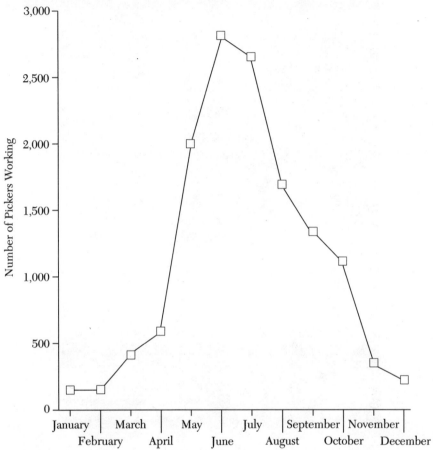

vest peaks increase the costliness of harvest delays and interruptions. Whereas the skills of harvest workers are not difficult to replace, the accumulated capital of their care and commitment is harder to lose. Moreover, replacement can be costly if it involves a large portion of the workforce at once, or if it is required during periods of labor scarcity. In addition, the timing of labor availability is crucial, and its requisite amount fluctuates widely over the season. In short, in the strawberry industry—as, I would argue, in the production of other labor-intensive fresh commodities such as citrus, table grapes, lettuce, and tomatoes—production processes accord workers minimal leverage on the basis of skill and more substantial leverage on the basis of their care and commitment. This fact motivates

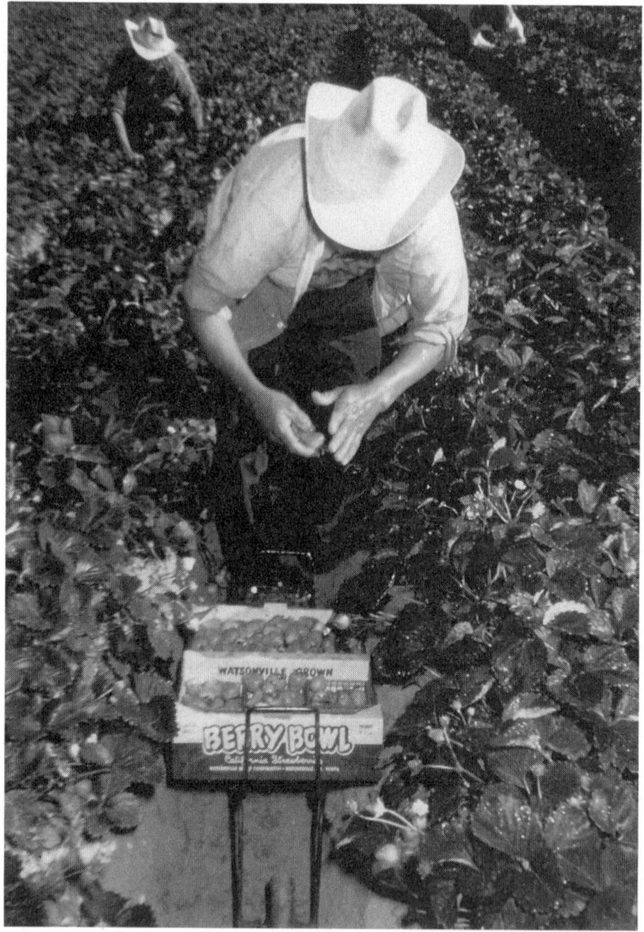

Plate 4. Tools of the trade: (Hat), cart, crate, baskets. Photo Jack Kelly Clark, courtesy University of California

strawberry growers to try to preserve their relationships with long-term employees and to control the performance of their work. Such concerns have led employers in core sector industries to raise wages, increase formal guarantees of job security, and expand workers' autonomy (Edwards 1979; Friedman 1977). Strawberry producers have not pursued this tack, however, in part because, during most years and at most points in the annual cycle, workers' backgrounds and labor market conditions accomplish the same ends by easing replacement, enhancing job commitment, and dispelling resistance.

Locality, Labor Market, and the Supply of Labor

One cannot explain on-the-job configurations of labor compliance and resistance without discussing the impact of labor supply—of the human, material, and social goals and resources of workers, as these are shaped by political constraints on the labor market. In practice, characteristics of labor supply augment growers' control over the labor process by encouraging workers to comply with the rules and reducing their ability to challenge them. On the one hand, workers' world views, aspirations, resources, and social commitments incline them to accept, even prefer, the conditions of strawberry labor. Moreover, their social organization off the job reinforces their kin-based organization on the job in a way that limits broader alliances and prepares them to accept the terms of their work. On the other hand, labor market conditions—especially chronic labor surpluses and the lack of citizenship and legal immigration status—contribute to this process by limiting workers' job choices and shaping their ideas of what is worth fighting for and against. Here, as in other California crop industries (Thomas 1985), labor market conditions exert a constant pressure toward compliance, intensifying workers' job commitment as well as growers' ease of replacement. But the way in which this pressure is felt and its impact on the relations of production are particular to the strawberry industry. Let us draw out this interweaving of labor force and labor market.

The Specificity of the Workforce

Workers' national, regional, and family backgrounds, the interpersonal networks that have evolved historically within their communities and between them and central coast berry growers, and their demographic characteristics and life cycle goals, incline them positively toward strawberry work.

Regional and Family Origins. Not surprisingly, most strawberry workers are of Mexican birth or descent. They come from regions where economic pressures for out-migration have long been significant and where most job seekers lack the personal attributes that would grant them access to other employment. The 1986–87 interviews illustrate the impact of workers' origins (see Appendix 2, this chapter). As table 12 demonstrates, the vast majority of central coast berry workers were themselves born in Mexico, mostly in its southwestern and central states. Almost 75 percent of the wage workers interviewed came from the states of Jalisco and Michoacán. Two sorts of sending locales predominate: small rural communities and larger urban neighborhoods comprised primarily of rural-to-urban migrants.

Table 12. Background similarities of wage laborers interviewed

Characteristic	Percentage of/mean among interviewees
Male	71%
Age	28 years
Married	56%
Number of children	1.8
Born in Mexico	95%
Born in Jalisco or Michoacán	74%
Parents were peasant farmers	66%
Grandparents were peasant farmers	93%
Size of birth family	9.5[a]
Year first came to U.S.	1976
Undocumented immigration status	44%
Number of years of school	6 years
Cannot speak English	95%

[a]Average

About 66 percent of the interviewees had parents who were peasant farmers in Mexico; about 90 percent had grandparents who were. The interviewees averaged only six years of formal education. None had training in or linkages to nonagricultural employment, although over 80 percent said they would prefer to work "indoors," and over 95 percent said that they hoped their children would not have to work in the fields. Only 5 percent spoke English, a capacity that is required in many nonagricultural jobs.

Family and regional origins involve strawberry workers in particular patterns of economic distress and in particular possibilities for economic advancement. As studies attest, conditions in southwestern and south-central Mexico have long encouraged seasonal out-migration to the United States (Jones 1984; Dagodag 1975; Dinerman 1982; Rouse 1989). Most interviewees came from communities that traditionally relied on small-plot, rain-fed agriculture, and where sustained droughts and the lack of irrigation facilities made it hard to survive on the land. Even in the 1950s and 1960s, rural households in this area had to supplement subsistence production with earnings from wage labor on nearby large farms, from street vending or craft production, or from periodic migration to the United States. Conditions have worsened in subsequent years: rapid population growth has accelerated the subdivision of already-small plots and increased the number of landless families. The lack of irrigation has kept productivity low, while rampant inflation has raised the cost of farm inputs, decreased real incomes, and exacerbated economic inequality. At the same time, large-scale, irrigated agriculture has pushed out smallholders, and many families have become wage workers on the new agricultural estates. Others have joined the flood of migrants to the cities, where low wages, a surplus of unskilled job seekers, and an underdeveloped economy preclude the generation of an adequate household income. In this region, as in others, unemployment and underemployment have neared or exceeded 50 percent in recent decades, and peasants have borne a disproportionate share of the burden (Baird and McCaughan 1979; de Janvry 1981). Not surprisingly, interviewees report that their communities of origin have long-standing traditions of seasonal employment in California agriculture. Interviewees from both rural and urban areas estimate that from half to two-thirds of the households in their home communities supplement Mexican incomes and subsistence production with money earned in the United States.

In short, workers' positive assessment of strawberry employment is encouraged by the long-standing and increasing economic distress of their nation, regions, and communities of origin, by the prevalence of out-migration as a solution to that distress, and by the fact that they lack explicit job training, education, and links to nonagricultural work.

Strawberry Linkages. Workers are also inclined toward strawberry jobs by the interpersonal networks that have grown up over time between their communities and extended families and certain strawberry employers. In the Mexican communities from which most workers come, employment in this regional industry has become a common solution to local economic problems. Beginning during the bracero program and intensifying thereafter, certain communities and family groupings developed connections to jobs on central coast strawberry farms. As in other cases of U.S.-Mexican migration (Dinerman 1982; Kearney and Stuart 1981; Martin 1988; Rouse 1989), interpersonal networks are a crucial support resource for immigrant workers. In fact, they provide the primary access channels to strawberry employment, fragmenting the regional labor market and restricting job access for unconnected workers. Over 90 percent of the interviewees in my sample said that they got their jobs through friends or family (see table 13). Almost two-thirds had parents who were strawberry pickers; about 40 percent had wives or other nuclear family members who currently worked in the industry. Many heard stories of what to expect from strawberry employers for years before heading north.

Workers value these employment networks highly, because low individual earnings in seasonal agriculture mean that several household members must work to support the group. Most families hope to develop a long-term relationship with a single grower. Some family networks have been sending workers to the same ranch for nearly twenty years. The individuals in-

Table 13. Characteristics of wage workers' employment in the industry

Characteristic	Percentage of/mean among interviewees
Worked previously in strawberries	100%
Year first worked in strawberries	1978
Number of seasons in strawberries	8[a]
Got job through family, friends	93%
Parents worked in strawberries	61%
Nuclear family works in strawberries	40%
Number of months per year in strawberry work, last five years	6[a]
Mean annual income of individual, 1985	$6,290
Mean annual income of household, 1985	$14,233

[a]Average

volved have changed over that period—fathers passed the torch to sons, daughters, nieces, and sons-in-law. In some cases, the locale of primary residence had shifted from Mexico to the United States. These changes notwithstanding, the pattern of linkage between a certain extended family and a particular central coast employer has remained constant. As a result of these family-based employment networks, workers speak of their involvement in a "tradition" of strawberry work. Many call themselves "strawberry specialists." Interviewees averaged eight seasons working in the industry and most of their income came from that work. Over the five years prior to the interviews, they worked an average of six months a year in the strawberry industry. Though this average is comparable to the statewide average for farm workers, the extent of its concentration in a single industry is unusual. Interviewees earned 80 percent of their individual income and 71 percent of their household income from strawberry employment alone. Their incomes are also higher than customary for California farm workers: the mean annual income in 1985 for berry workers interviewed was $6,290, whereas the state average was $4,200. Their mean annual household earnings are also higher: annual incomes of berry workers' households of four averaged $14,233 in 1985, whereas farm worker families of four statewide averaged $8,277, and those on the central coast averaged $7,472 (Mines and Martin 1986).

These means gloss over great variation within the group and over the years. Workers' individual incomes vary according to whether they are part of an employer's core labor force, and thus work more months of the year, or are peripheral workers employed only at the peak of the harvest. They also vary according to the wages and other benefits offered by their employers, which range widely enough to justify categorizing workers into lower, middle, and upper tiers. If one calculates a base wage using the pay method and rate (hourly, piece, hourly-plus-piece) received by the particular worker and figuring that workers estimate that an "ordinary" individual can average four boxes an hour over the course of the season (energetic workers in fact average more), "upper-tier workers" had a wage base of at least $6.30 an hour in 1985, with health insurance, and with an hourly or an hourly-plus-piece payment method that provided a floor to their earnings. "Middle-tier workers" had insurance and a wage base between $5.50 and $6.30 an hour or no insurance and a wage base of $6.30 an hour. "Lower-tier workers" had a wage base of less than $5.50 an hour with insurance or less than $6.30 without insurance. Most were paid by the piece, so their earnings had no floor. Workers' well-being is also affected by the ability of other household members to find work. Periods of unemployment are frequent, given customary labor surpluses, and workers try to reduce such jobless periods and maximize the employment of all household members. The impact of variations in employee pay level, number of months worked, and success in employing household members can be considerable. For example, one typical upper-tier core worker made $12,000 in 1985 as an individual, and his household earned $36,000, because his wife and teenaged son worked. Lower-tier and middle-tier workers generally earn less, but may augment their berry income with work in other crops. Thus one typical peripheral lower-tier worker made only $4,000 from strawberries in 1985, but made $9,500 including other agricultural work. He and his wife combined earned $17,500.

In sum, the interpersonal networks among strawberry workers, and between them and central coast strawberry employers, constitute a valuable economic resource for individuals with limited options. These networks provide access to work that is not only far better than they could expect in Mexico but is also more desirable than many U.S. alternatives. These historical connections also prepare workers to anticipate and accept the terms of strawberry work.

Demographic Characteristics and Employment Strategies. Strawberry income plays an important role in workers' wider lives: it enjoys a centrality that derives from workers' gender, stage in life, marital status, and household structure. The individuals who come to work in the industry are under great pressure to generate a stable income for themselves and their families. Their demographic characteristics incline many to prefer seasonal employment, in which remuneration is directly tied to labor effort, to year-round jobs with more stable, but lower, income streams. Workers fall into two social categories: individuals and families. The individuals are mostly young men in their early teens to their early twenties, not accompanied by spouses or children. Some are unmarried; many have families who remain in Mexico. Berry-picking families include a husband, a wife, and usually one or more children who work in the local farm economy. They range in age from their mid-twenties through their thirties. By their forties, most workers leave the industry. The fortunate find less strenuous work or are supported by relatives. The less fortunate are pushed out involuntarily by younger, more energetic workers. Interviews and my own observations suggest that about two-thirds of the workers are resident or migratory families and one-third are single men. About two-thirds of the workforce overall is male and one-third is female. My interviewees averaged about twenty-eight years in age, which is probably a few years older than the industry's actual average.[6]

Berry workers vary in terms of orientation toward Mexico or toward the United States for primary residence and long-term economic advancement. For any individual, these orientations may shift with changes in life stage and opportunities. Virtually all of the single men are based in Mexico. Most come in the spring at the start of the season and stay for six to nine months, depending on their income aspirations, their luck in evading the Border Patrol, and their commitments in Mexico. Some come on their own to build a nest egg for their own futures; others come as "adventurers" *(aventureros)* to see what the United States has to offer. Yet others are sent by their Mexican households as an investment in their own sustenance. Such households often raise the substantial (in Mexican terms) $250–$300, U.S., which is required to pay a *coyote* to smuggle an undocumented worker across the border. Households frequently gather this sum through a series of small loans from friends and relatives in the community, thus creating a debt that encourages future reciprocity and puts strong pressure on the migrant to make good on his family's investment. The earnings of such migrants help support parents, siblings, wives, and children south of the border. Most such workers prefer the piece-rate pay methods that prevail in the industry, because they reward workers directly for strenuous labor and enable them to make as much money as possible before the season's end or apprehension by the *migra.* They also appreciate the cash payment methods of some growers, because they are less likely to lose earnings if they are apprehended.

[6]My sample underrepresented young, single, recently arrived illegals. Thus, age, marital status, years in the United States and related characteristics are all higher in the sample than in the population as a whole. My descriptive understanding of this portion of the workforce came from illegals and from documented workers who started out without papers.

In the case of family workers, some are based on the central coast; others in Mexico. Most are part of households in which a number of individuals contribute to the support of the unit. Many Mexico-based workers are part of an extended family in which some household members work in Mexico and others work in the United States. Like individual workers, young and middle-aged couples who are part of a larger household often go north to work during the harvest season. They return to Mexico for three to four months in the winter, where their relatives may have been tending a small farm, taking care of younger children, hawking goods on the street, or even operating a small business. Families based on the central coast tend to have smaller residential household units than those based in Mexico, but they still rely on the income of more than one wage earner. They tend to develop networks of communication and mutual support among the households of relatives in the locality. Most retain ongoing contact with their home communities in Mexico as well, returning around Christmas for two weeks to two months, and providing information, hospitality, small cash loans, and job recommendations to migrants from their home towns.

In sum, the demographic characteristics of the worker population render strawberry income crucial to workers' personal mobility and family support. They also engender a preference within the workforce for seasonal jobs in which individuals can earn a relatively large amount of money in a short period of time. These factors increase workers' commitment to their jobs and dampen their tendency to resist.

The Political Construction of Workers' Options

Granted that workers' interest in and compliance with the terms of strawberry employment derive in part from their regional origins, employment networks, and personal goals, these characteristics do not exist in a vacuum. In fact, workers' world views, goals, and employment strategies, as well as their difficulties in improving their human capital endowments and acquiring other work, are shaped by the ways that political forces constrain their options. One cannot fully account for the importance to their lives of personal job-access networks, commitment to their immediate employers, and the relative continuities of their employment arrangements (Rouse 1989) without speaking of their political disempowerment in the labor market. Conditions of surplus labor supply and the noncitizen status of most workers are the two chief forms of this disempowerment. As noted in Chapter 3, the chronic labor surpluses and the definition and consequences of citizenship status are politically established. Immigration policies and protective labor legislation have shaped the criteria, benefits, and costs of different citizenship statuses, as well as the flow of workers into and out of California agriculture. Whatever strawberry workers may do as individuals to improve their circumstances, they always operate in an environment in which they are politically disadvantaged. They do indeed share this disadvantagedness with other farm workers in the state, but its impacts are distinctively shaped by the strawberry industry.

Citizenship status is of serious import for central coast strawberry workers. The vast majority are noncitizen immigrants, and an exceptionally high proportion—as compared with California farm workers as a whole—are in the country illegally. Of the wage workers interviewed, 44 percent were themselves undocumented (see Appendix 2, this chapter). Although one cannot determine the exact proportion of undocumented workers in the regional industry, some close approximations are possible. Workers themselves estimate that from 75 to 100 percent are illegals, with the "100 percent" response coming from Mexico-based undocumented workers who were employed on farms that hired only illegals. Interestingly enough, some of these had been working in the area for two or more seasons, but because of the isolation of their employment circuits, they were poorly informed about conditions on other ranches. Growers voice a more conservative estimate of 50 to 75 percent. Based on these assessments, my own observations, and the experience of significant actors such as employment and immigration officials, farm advisers, and farm supply dealers, it seems likely that about 75 percent of central coast strawberry workers were undocumented from the early 1970s into the late 1980s. The distribution of citizenship status is uneven across employing farms, however, in that some hire only illegals and others hire mostly documented workers. Of the latter group, it is unlikely that more than 15 percent are citizens. Labor surpluses mean that a person can look for weeks—sometimes an entire season—without securing employment. Such periods without work are costly for Mexico-based workers because survival in the United States is so expensive in Mexican currency; they are also consequential for noncitizen workers because their alternative avenues to employment are so limited; they are literally dangerous for undocumented workers because job seeking increases their exposure to the *migra.*

The interviews reveal several important differences between documented and undocumented workers. First, undocumented workers are much more likely to aspire to return to Mexico for their long-term economic advancement. While in the United States, they do not aspire to move up the agricultural ladder into positions of more responsibility and job security, but rather hope to work in piece-rate field labor, where their wages are directly responsive to the level of their effort, and where the length of employment enables them to return to Mexico for at least one-third of the year. Documented workers are more interested in movement up the agricultural hierarchy, although many share with undocumented workers a preference for seasonal employment that they supplement with unemployment insurance in the winter months. Undocumented workers are more likely to prefer cash wage payments on a daily or at most weekly basis, so as to capture as much of their income as possible in the eventuality of being apprehended by the *migra*. This preference tends to constrict their income stream, because it leads them to the lower-resource, lower-paying employers who pay cash. Growers agree that illegals—to use their oft-repeated phrase—work "hard and fast." They tend to push themselves more than documented workers and they pick more crates per hour. Virtually all of the unaccompanied men in the sample were undocumented.[7] Contrary to what one might expect, undocumented status does not signal any lesser job commitment or longevity. *Sinpapeles* are if anything more eager to find a reliable patron who will employ them and their relatives year after year, so they can reduce their periods of job search and thus their exposure to apprehension. They tend therefore to aim not for the highest-paying, largest ranches, but for the medium and smaller ranches in more secluded locations, where they are more likely to develop a personal relationship with the grower or foreman and to have access to a barn, a shed, or even a protected gully, for shelter. The undocumented workers interviewed had fully as many seasons of employment in the industry as did documented workers. If anything, they looked around less for better options.

In sum, the political construction of workers' status in the labor market strongly conditions their job alternatives, preferences, and evaluations, and contributes to the fit between labor supply and demand.

The Wage Labor Process and Workplace Control

Workplace control in the wage labor process relies on this mutual reinforcement of labor supply and demand. To demonstrate how control is effected and how supply characteristics contribute to it, I look now at the organization and social relations of wage labor. As we will see, the wage

[7]This greater orientation toward Mexico and lesser interest in stable, high-status jobs is not characteristic of all undocumented workers: witness the lettuce crew members that Thomas studied (1985) and Galarza's observation (1964) that illegals were often hired during the bracero program in positions requiring continuity and responsibility.

labor process captures the initiative and compliance of workers, while simultaneously eliciting and dispelling resistance.

The Organizational Hierarchy

Farms that use crews of wage workers to plant, maintain, and harvest strawberries are called "commercial," as opposed to sharecropping, ranches. The organizational hierarchy on commercial ranches is topped by the grower or his hired manager. The ranch's permanent employees—who may include bookkeepers and sales staff, ranch managers, field and ranch foremen, truck and tractor drivers, and irrigators, depending on the size of the ranch and the degree of involvement of the grower—comprise the second echelon. Next come the harvest season supervisory workers (called subforemen, or crew or row bosses), and the quality-control workers (checkers, sorters, and loaders). At the bottom are the field laborers: the wage workers who plant, maintain, and harvest the crop. Permanent employees are sometimes salaried, but those other than farm managers are usually paid by the hour. Their pay rates usually exceed those of field workers. Foremen often receive a piece-rate "kicker" to their hourly rate that ties their wages to the performance of their crews. What permanent employees enjoy most over field workers is their authority and the length and security of their employment. Most can expect to work from nine to eleven months a year and are virtually guaranteed renewed employment—both important privileges in the chronically surplus labor market.

Job types and responsibilities vary somewhat, but farm managers generally operate the farm in the stead of the owner—an arrangement rare in this regional industry where about 95 percent of the farms are run by owner-operators. Bookkeepers and sales personnel provide administrative support. Ranch managers administer the operation of the dispersed subunits (ranches) of larger farms. Ranch foremen supervise the production tasks aside from picking, and they oversee the truck and tractor drivers, as well as the irrigators, who perform most of the machinery-intensive tasks, such as ground preparation, irrigation, fertilization, and pest and disease control. Field foremen head up labor recruitment and management. Except for the bookkeeping and secretarial staff, permanent employees tend to be male. Perhaps 80 percent are of Mexican origin or descent.

Labor Recruitment

Wide seasonal swings in labor demand and the sensitivity of profits to the careful and timely performance of tasks create major recruitment challenges. One has to do with the magnitude and fluctuation of harvest labor demand; another, with obtaining enough conscientious workers to do the critical, but shorter and lower-paying, tasks of planting and maintenance. Such challenges are greater for central coast growers than for those in the south, because it is harder for them to recruit and replace workers since they are farther from the border, and because their lengthy harvests require sustaining a harvest workforce over a much longer period. Planting is also problematic. Whereas summer planting usually coincides with the late summer harvest lull, thus freeing up pickers to plant, the weather can create considerable variability in harvest timing, so that growers may be forced to hire planting crews from outside their usual workforces, drawing in workers whose performance quality and reliability are lesser. Summer planting also involves considerable hand labor for preharvest maintenance and may require hiring supplemental crews. If winter planting takes place just as the harvest subsides, it can extend the employment of a harvest crew. In a good year, however, picking may occupy all available regular workers in October and November and force growers to hire temporary planting crews. If planting takes place long after picking has ended, the growers' need for planters may conflict with pickers' desire to return to Mexico or to draw unemployment checks. Although growers try to use their pickers to do the maintenance work of weeding, pruning, runner cutting, and blossom removal, these tasks often conflict with the prior claim of the harvest, again necessitating the engagement of temporary workers.

Most growers respond to these labor deployment challenges by developing enduring relationships with a core of wage workers and by tapping into their personal networks to recruit and motivate a supplemental workforce. Core workers provide the bulk of harvest labor and as much as possible of nonharvest labor. They are valued not only for the constancy and diligence of their own labor, but for their ability to mobilize and demobilize family members in response to fluctuating labor demand. In effect, commercial growers externalize and thereby reduce their own investments in labor recruitment and control by ceding some of it to core workers. In this way, they develop an interest in sustained employment relationships that matches that of workers. Although growers' recruitment methods achieve an admirable fit between variable labor demand and supply, they also unintentionally generate workforce solidarity. How does this come about?

Recruitment processes in the central coast strawberry industry are overwhelmingly informal, based in the interpersonal connections among workers. Use of the local employment office for the harvest is unheard-of; its use for other tasks is virtually so. The vast majority of workers—probably over 90 percent in the late 1980s—are hired directly by the grower or his foreman. On small farms, growers may handle recruitment themselves; on medium and large farms, the foremen make hiring decisions. A small proportion of wage workers are hired by farm labor contractors who contract with growers to recruit and employ workers. A third and minor contingent of seasonal employees are "walk-ons," who appear at the ranch gate and ask for work without prior connections to that farm or farmer. In hiring new workers, growers view experience as desirable but not imperative, because they can train motivated recruits in about a week. Their primary concerns are diligence and reliability, which they believe to be furthered by the process of personal sponsorship. Growers and foremen do not actively recruit workers. Rather, in the surplus farm labor market, job seekers come to them. Sometimes the foreman has a circuit of personal connection to his home village in Mexico or to an extended family network in the United States or Mexico. In such cases, job seekers come directly to the foreman, regarding him as their personal patron and benefactor. More often, job seekers approach a relative or friend who is already employed at a particular ranch, asking him or her to recommend them.

Workers have a personal stake in securing jobs for relatives. Being a successful intermediary accords them the esteemed status of patron among their peers. Moreover, providing jobs to friends and relatives increases the likelihood of reciprocity and contributes ongoing support to their households. There are potential costs to their recommendations as well: a recommendee who is dismissed for misbehavior may threaten his sponsor's relationship with the foreman and ultimately his job security. Recommendations are therefore not given lightly. Employed workers carefully assess the attributes of those who seek their sponsorship, including their prior experience and motivation to perform. Relatives candidly discuss the work qualifications of unemployed family members, evaluating the advisability of sponsoring them for a job. Workers with the choicest jobs—those working for high-resource growers who pay the highest wages but are also the most exacting—are particularly chary of lending their support. They commonly ask inexperienced petitioners to get a season of experience with a less-demanding employer before they will provide a recommendation. Once an employed worker has decided to recommend an individual, he or she approaches the labor supervisor—the grower or more often the foreman—and presents the petitioner's case. If the individual is hired, the recommender keeps pressure on him or her to perform well, often working alongside to help train the newcomer. Because recommendees frequently live in the apartment, house, or trailer of their recommenders, pressure to perform extends to off hours as well.

In essence, then, strawberry growers cede to workers important aspects of labor recruitment and management. This practice not only reduces growers' costs, but it achieves a labor supply that is especially—and inexpensively—responsive to fluctuating demand. Though it involves workers in one version of what Burawoy (1979) aptly dubbed "manufacturing (their own) consent," it also offers them social and economic benefits: it raises their standing among their peers, and it increases the security and level of their incomes. So substantial is workers' contribution to labor recruitment that growers call their workforces "self-recruiting." Both core workers who come for the full course of the season and peripheral workers who fill in at the harvest peak are recruited primarily through the networks of existing employees. One Anglo manager of a large corporate farm described the (to him) unexpected advantage of this situation:

> The year I started in strawberries I used to lie awake nights, wondering if the workers would be here on time and how I'd get rid of them. I called a friend—another grower—and he said: "When the little brown guys show up, you put the berries in the box. When they leave, you stack up the crates and call it a season." That's about how it works. The workers call a friend or relative who lives here and find out down to the day when my crop is coming on. They call two days in advance and they're at the ranch on the appointed day. They don't want to be too early, because it's expensive to live up here. And it's the same at the end of the season. They can look at the crop and read the blossoms. They know how long it takes for the next crop to come on, how much they'll be able to earn, given how heavy it is. They know the difference between a temporary harvest slump and when it's declining for good. When they aren't earning enough and there's not enough to look forward to, they just disappear. They are supposed to ask me first, but they never do. Only two or three times out of two hundred do I ever have any problems with the time they leave. They know how many workers I need as well as I do.

A Watsonville-based Japanese grower with a medium-sized berry farm described his use of worker networks to adjust labor needs over the season:

> When I need more workers, I always ask them [my core workers] first. They would be hurt if I didn't. I ask them if they know any experienced pickers who could help out for the next stretch of time. I expect them to bring whoever they can. They always do. I remind them that there are a million guys out there who would like the work, but I ask them first because we're all one big family. Family members take care of each other. I need them and they need me. Sometimes we have to work overtime, but I tell them that it's

either that or give the work to someone else. I say, "We'll have to run for awhile, but pretty soon we'll be able to walk again." They are glad for the chance to do it. The new workers understand they'll have to leave when the crop lets up.

Despite the benefits these recruitment methods offer growers, they exact some costs as well. Because growers rely on workers' personal networks to secure a workforce, most employ from one to three "family groupings"—clusters of kin, fictive kin, and close friends. Most come from the same town in Mexico. Some individuals live in nuclear households; others, in multigenerational, extended households. Some are based in the United States, others in Mexico. In practice, most core workers on a given ranch belong to such clusters of prior connection. These groupings have no formal decision-making structure, but one or more senior men usually emerge as spokespersons and reputational leaders. Workers acknowledge the social interconnectedness of the workforce with an oft-repeated phrase: "You can't get a job in strawberries unless you know someone." Whereas these networks augment growers' formal management inputs, they also increase workers' ability to respond in concert to differences with their employers. Some growers explicitly try to avoid this eventuality by hiring at least three groupings. Many ranches employ only one or two, however. In most years and at most points in the season, this practice poses no serious problems, because work organization and labor market conditions counteract the potential for labor resistance.

The Harvest

On most ranches, berry pickers begin to gather at 6:30 a.m. When the crop is heavy, the day may begin earlier. It rarely begins later. Workers arrive in battered cars and trucks, sometimes in vans that the grower or an independent entrepreneur has engaged to transport them for a fee. Most are bundled against the morning chill in multicolored layers of short- and long-sleeved shirts, jackets, and sweatshirts. A motley assortment of sombreros and long-billed caps anticipates the sun's glare, which will burn through the fog in late morning. Women knot cotton kerchiefs around their necks to be pulled up over mouth and nose against the onslaught of sun, dust, and pesticides (see plate 5). As they straggle in, individuals join the small groups of acquaintances who cluster in the parking lot or along the dirt road. Women and men usually gather separately, bantering and exchanging news until almost 7:00, when they press around the foreman to receive his assignment of starting rows. A scattering of subdued groans and cheers greets the fore-

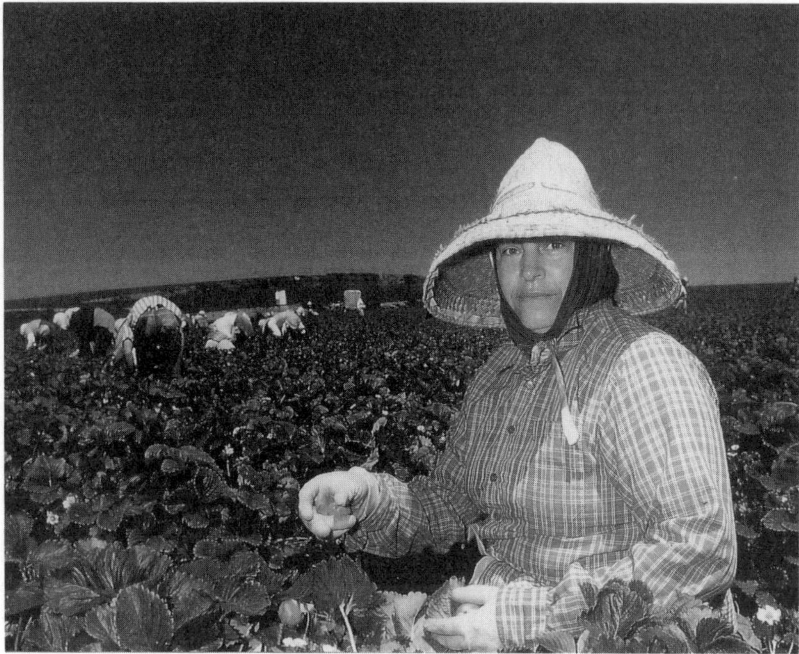

Plate 5. Protection against sun, dirt, and pesticides. Photo Jack Kelly Clark, courtesy University of California

man's announcements: all hope to avoid the rows near the road, where the dust encourages pest infestations and fruit deformity and pickers cannot fill their baskets as fast. Each picker then seizes a crate and a cart and moves to his or her assigned row. When the foreman gives the signal—a shout, the honk of a horn, or a whistle—the work day begins.

In a matter of minutes the colorful line of pickers' backs begins to curve and billow as the younger, more energetic (often undocumented) workers forge out ahead (see plate 6). On ranches that pay a straight piece rate, workers may literally run down the rows to deliver filled crates. Work is brisk, too, on ranches that use the combination of an hourly base to encourage careful work, plus a piece-rate kicker to encourage speed. Work proceeds most slowly on the few ranches that pay a straight hourly rate, although job commitment and the fear of job loss still ensure speed and care. Pickers squat or bend from the waist, leaning out over the beds as they pick. They push their carts down the furrows, their eyes and swollen, berry-stained hands moving constantly. Deftly pushing the leaves aside to disclose the fruit, they evaluate and select those of appropriate size and

Plate 6. Berry pickers spread out. Photo Jack Kelly Clark, courtesy University of California

form. Grasping each berry gently between thumb and the first two fingers, they pick it with an upward twist of the wrist, and deposit it neatly into a plastic basket. One by one they fill their crates of twelve baskets, rise, and hurry down the furrows to place their crates on the flatbed truck or other receiving station where the fruit is stacked for delivery to the cooler (see plate 7). They present their tally cards to the checker to punch (see plate 8), then grab an empty crate and hurry back down the row to resume. With two-row beds, one individual picks both from a single side. With four-row beds, each person picks two rows on either side. In the latter case, arguments often arise over the theft of choice fruit from the other person's side.

Pickers are required to pick all berries of the proper size, ripeness, shape, and regularity. They are also required to remove and discard all old leaves and misshapen, overripe, rotting, sunburned, or insect-damaged fruit as they go, in order to sustain blossom production and prevent the spread of pests and diseases. This operation, called manicuring, relies on workers' job commitment, since it is not rewarded by piece-rate pay methods. Picking requires judgment as well as physical stamina. Pickers refer to

Plate 7. Delivering the filled crates. Photo Jack Kelly Clark, courtesy University of California

strawberries as "the fruit of the devil," because of the toll the harvest takes on their backs and lungs. Whereas growers tend to regard the job as "easy," in contrast with jobs such as the lettuce ground pack, in which workers must lift heavy boxes, interviews with workers attest to the physical strain of bending over the rows for eight to ten hours a day. Many suffer back strain and back injuries, as well as respiratory problems from the cold, damp morning air, the dust, and the pesticide residues.

Pickers generally concentrate on their work. Some individuals banter; some talk quietly as they go—about family, friends, their escapades the night before, their home communities in Mexico. From time to time a lone voice rises in plaintive song, snatches of Mexican music escape from the taco truck that jostles down the dirt road at midmorning and midday, and bantering challenges of "*Hola,* Francisco, are you sleeping over there?" drift across the shimmering fields. Here, as in some other work contexts (Burawoy 1979), some workers compete with each other, thereby increasing their own earnings and those of their employers. Young illegals boast of picking as many as twelve to fifteen crates an hour during the peak, far

Plate 8. Picker gets his crate tally card punched. Photo Jack Kelly Clark, courtesy University of California

more than the seasonal average of four for all workers. Not all compete in such games, however, and quality-conscious growers often discourage them. Some pickers pace themselves as individuals; others work with one or two other people at a pace they establish as a group. Whatever an individual's personal pace decision, each ranch also has an explicit or implicit minimum that pickers are expected to achieve at that point in the season. Those who consistently fail to achieve at least that minimum risk being replaced.

On most ranches, pickers pause for a midmorning break of ten to fifteen minutes, during which they may rest in the fields, use the field toilets, or eat a small snack. At midday they take a half-hour lunch break, during which they stand in groups or sit in small clusters at the ends of the rows or on embankments to eat and talk. Those who live in apartments or houses and who have kitchen facilities and easy access to stores generally bring bag lunches. Those who live in the fields or in farm outbuildings are often forced to buy drinks, chips, and tacos from the mobile lunch trucks that visit most large ranches over the noon hour, cutting significantly into their already meager incomes. Women tend to eat with each other or close relatives. Men keep an eye on the women they consider to be "under their care." Checkers, sorters, and subforemen sometimes eat with the pickers. The foreman eats in his truck or the office. Work resumes at 12:30 until another short break around 2:30. It then continues until 4:30 or 5:00 p.m. when the last truck leaves for the cooler. It may continue until dark if the crop is heavy.

Sociopolitical Status and Labor Process Role

It is instructive to consider the roles of women and undocumented workers in the process of production. On the whole, although strawberry work occupies distinctive places in the lives of women and illegals, they do not occupy structurally distinctive positions within the wage labor process. In this, the strawberry industry differs significantly from such industries as the southwestern lettuce industry (Thomas 1985), in which employers use gender and documentation to differentiate their labor forces and wage labor processes, thereby improving their direct control over labor. This contrast in the economic deployment of sociopolitical status is encouraged by biologically based differences in the technical constraints of these industries. That is, lettuce producers have been able to mechanize part of the harvest, differentiating it into two labor processes: skilled ground crew production, into which they preferentially hire undocumented men; and unskilled machine-wrap crew production, into which they preferentially hire documented women. They then use women's disadvantaged labor market status, legal citizenship status, and dual roles as wives and wage earners to depress wages and ensure that wrap-crew positions are filled regularly. They use the political vulnerability of undocumented workers to undercut wage demands and prevent the consolidation of power that ground crew members' skill and cohesion would otherwise accord them. Overall, employers' assignment of different social categories of workers to different types of jobs undermines the solidarity of the workforce. Berry growers, by contrast, have been unable to mechanize the harvest. There is only one wage labor process in strawberry production and one situs for harvest workers within it. It is accomplished by crews of individual piece-rate wage workers who are not differentiated systematically along lines of gender or citizenship. Although these statuses play supportive roles in sharecropping, they do not form the basis for systematically subdividing or controlling the wage labor force or labor process. Thus, wage labor processes in this industry do not accord a special advantage to employers' direct manipulation of gender and citizenship to control labor, indicating that industrial constraints shape the meaning and utility of sociopolitical status.

Strawberry work does, however, play different roles in the lives of women and men, and of documented and undocumented workers. In the strawberry industry, as in many others, women are fully responsible for the home. As one husband unapologetically put it: "Women just have a bigger job than we do. Our job stops at the ranch gate. They have to keep working all evening until the dinner and wash and children are taken care of." As a result, some women prefer to stay at home or work as little as possible. Some husbands concur, in part because it supports their social status as the providers and protectors of women's honor. In a culture strongly concerned with female purity, sending a woman into a public workplace is dangerous: not only is she exposed to the rough language and sexual advances of other men, but when the offender is a workplace superior, her protector may find it hard to prevent or avenge the offense. In practice, however, most berry-picker families cannot afford to, or do not want to, do without the income that women could bring in. Most women try to get a job—out of the fields, if they can. Many work in strawberries. They mitigate the difficulties of this choice by socializing almost exclusively with women on the job, and by using locally resident young, unemployed, or retired female relatives (daughters, nieces, mothers-in-law, mothers, grandmothers) to care for home-bound children. Oldest daughters are often kept home from school to care for siblings.

In practice, women and illegals have somewhat different employment patterns, although they occupy the same positions in the wage labor process. Most women with children prefer to work only for the peak season (May through August), because it enables them to spend the least time away from home when older children who could care for younger ones are at school. As noted, illegals also tend to prefer peak season employment, because harvests are heaviest and earnings are highest then, and they can get the greatest return for their risks of apprehension. As a result, women and illegals are somewhat more highly represented in peak season employment than in full season employment, although not because of growers' selection processes. Moreover, women and men, and documented and undocumented workers, are distributed in both patterns of employment. Nor do differences in pay reflect gender or citizenship status: rather, pay rates are attached to the production region and resource level of the employer. Women are somewhat more highly represented in the peak season mobilization of supplemental workers, again not because of growers' selection criteria but because men are more likely to have full-time work that precludes such temporary employment.

The Personalization of Direct Control

Whereas workers are controlled indirectly by recruitment processes that engage them in their own management, they are also controlled directly and painstakingly by an overlapping mesh of supervisorial agents. This control does elicit tensions and animosities, but the personalism of its implementation undermines collective opposition. Harvest supervision is headed up by the field foreman or, on small ranches, by the grower. Because most growers employ foremen, I refer to this primary labor supervisor as the foreman in the following discussion. Field foremen are assisted by subforemen, checkers, sorters, and loaders. The intensity of supervision and the manner of its implementation vary. Most growers hire about one supervisory employee for every thirty to thirty-five pickers, depending on the market niche to which they aspire and the number of other supervisory and quality control personnel they employ. Growers who aim for the high-quality fresh market have a higher ratio of supervisory personnel to pickers. Some hire foremen without subforemen and give each one a thirty-person crew; others hire a field foreman for every one hundred pickers, but then hire two or three subforemen to work beneath him. Subforemen, like field foremen, are almost always men of Mexican background.

In the course of the picking day, foremen and subforemen walk up and down the rows constantly, scrutinizing the quality and rate of the harvest. They look over workers' shoulders to examine rows already picked. They check to see that pickers are removing all marketable fruit, that they are manicuring the plants thoroughly, that they are packing neatly and cleanly, and that they are meeting the expected rate of production. Checkers, sorters, and loaders help ensure observance of quality standards. The former two are usually women; the latter are usually men, again of Mexican background. Checkers punch workers' cards to record crates delivered. The checkers and sorters periodically dump out market baskets and take samples from freezer crates, sorting through them to determine the quality of the pick. When they find debris or unsellable fruit, they notify the picker and either reject the crate summarily, or ask the picker to sort and resubmit it. Loaders help with quality control by taking random samples from stacks of crates to evaluate the quality of the pick and the pack. Repeat offenders are reported to the foreman, who issues warnings. If these warnings are not heeded immediately, the foreman may fire the picker that very day. Foremen keep an overview of the pace, work quality, promptness, and reliability of each worker. Foremen can and do fire workers on the spot for repeated tardiness and absence, for slow or sloppy picking and packing, and for insubordination. They are strict with poor quality, but some are somewhat lenient with slow pace, giving pickers a week or so to improve their rates.

Control relationships are highly personal. There is no mystification on strawberry ranches about how work standards are enforced and who is enforcing them. The foremen and growers who head up supervision are the primary targets of grievances arising from coercive management practices. Such grievances rarely erupt into open or collective opposition, however, in part because of the aforementioned dependence of family groupings on their connection with their employer, in part because of the divergent pulls of the worker-foreman relationship. At base, the foreman's authority is arbitrary. There are no formal guarantees of due process, job security, or advancement. Nor are there sources of appeal from the foreman's decisions regarding punishments or privileges. The very arbitrariness of the foreman's authority generates personalism in his relationships with workers. The foreman is not only the direct and ultimate enforcer of labor control, but also the major source of differential personal advantage on the job. Consequently, his role engenders animosity and the urge to resist, as well as gratitude and the desire to please.

Each worker has a personal connection of accrued debt and anticipated reciprocity with the foreman, which begins with his "gift" of a job. After this initial debt, the foreman has many opportunities to increase a worker's indebtedness and to respond to reciprocal gifts. At the same time, the foreman has personal relationships with other members of the worker's family grouping, so that individual dyadic relationships are nested within a wider structure of family groupings. The social embeddedness of these control relationships significantly affects the outcomes of individual grievances. Although workers constantly evaluate their relationships with and treatment by the foreman, they also assess the pattern of treatment that their friends and kin experience. The tenor of this pattern may either reinforce or transform the meaning of individual experience. This dynamic blunts the impact of the three most common categories of resentment.

The first important set of tensions involves the differential enforcement of rules. Infractions of work rules regarding tardiness, absence, slow picking rate, and poor picking quality can be the basis for dismissal. Instances of each, however, can be overlooked if a worker has a good relationship with the foreman. It is virtually impossible for a person to work for long without breaking at least some of these rules. In fact, foremen often seek out occasions to "overlook" an infraction, explicitly pointing out their generosity and reminding the offending worker of his or her consequent obligation. In return, workers told me, they are expected to work especially hard so that the foreman will "forgive" violations of the rules. Such exchanges of careful work in return for the "forgiveness" of rule infractions are part of an implicit social contract, a vision of workplace justice. In it, workers accept the foreman's arbitrary authority, as long as they or their families receive a generally positive balance of dispensations. In the fields, in cars on the way to work, in bars after work, and at home, workers compare their own experiences with those of their cohorts. While they seek to accrue personal favor in the eyes of the foreman, they usually overlook personal affronts in order to preserve a favorable group standing.

The dynamic is essentially the same with regard to the second common set of resentments: those that revolve around the differential granting of privileges. Foremen can dispense such privileges as overtime work, jobs for family members and friends, approved lay-offs for workers who want to receive unemployment insurance payments, and recommendations for valued positions such as core worker, checker, loader, sorter, and subforeman. In the absence of formal means of earning privileges, and in the context of low individual earnings and a surplus labor market, these privileges are eagerly sought. Again, workers vie with each other, parlaying hard work and the provision of conscientious auxiliary workers into a good relationship with the foreman. Some bring him offerings of food and service. Their colleagues watch closely to see which gifts the foreman accepts, what favors he dispenses, and how privileges balance out among individuals and family groupings.

The third frequent source of resentment has to do with treatment that breaches a worker's "honor." Such tensions arise in relation to men as well as women. Growers and foremen speak openly of how "sensitive" farm workers are to slurs on their honor and how the tenor of reprimands is a delicate matter. One long-time grower expressed this awareness to me as follows:

> You can't just order Mexicans to do things a certain way. I'm the boss and it has to be done my way in the end. But if I don't speak to them with respect, they just might quit. Many of these people would rather quit and run the risk of not having the job they need to support their families in Mexico than compromise personal dignity. That's something you have to understand. Lots of times the things they will fight or quit over I don't think are worth it, but I've got to pay attention that it's worth it to them. I've had people quit over my putting them on the weeding crew because they regarded it as a demotion. You've got to take care how you treat them.

Workers are in fact less likely to take the extreme measure of quitting than this cautious grower implies. Affronts to personal honor do, however, increase the friction of the working relationship. They give rise to petty forms of sabotage, such as the intentional packing of hollow-centered market baskets (called *haciendo puentes,* "building bridges") or the placing of damaged fruit or debris in them. Affronts also provoke intentional "misunderstandings" of instructions, hostile demeanors, and tacit refusals to carry out tasks at peak efficiency. Because the harvest requires constant effort and because procedures such as manicuring are not reimbursed by piece-rate pay methods, supervision alone cannot ensure their optimal performance. Labor quality thus depends heavily on self- and peer-motivation. Breakdowns in these incentives can reduce the quality of the harvest, and thus the profits of the farm.

As a result, labor supervisors attempt to avoid personal offense. Most accord workers the latitude of isolated "mistakes." They are likely to simply "call workers' attention to" *(llamar la atención)* single infractions such as unexcused absences or tardies, or slow or sloppy picking. Several instances, however, could evoke termination. Whenever possible, supervisors let the "natural consequences" of infractions effect the reprimand, rather than delivering it personally. For example, they may save the worst rows for workers who are a minute or two late, assign them for the morning to the lower-paying weeding crew, or keep them out of the fields for fifteen minutes so that they forego the income of that period. Foremen and growers insist that supervising Mexicans requires a managerial tenor that is quite different from that required with Anglos. One professional manager who had worked in a variety of industries described this contrast graphically:

> Managing Mexicans is very different from managing white workers. You can't yell at them or joke with them. They're likely to take offense. If I had a crew of white guys and they made a big mistake, I'd yell and say, "Come on and get over there and make that right or I'll knock your eyes out." For a Mexican, I'd go over there and say, "Good afternoon, Juan. Nice day isn't it? How's the family? I've been meaning to talk with you about your work. I know you're trying but you'll have to do better. I want you to fix that mistake, okay?" These two are equivalent.

Respect and disrespect are also signaled by the terms of discourse. For example, labor supervisors generally preserve their connections to family groupings by addressing its senior men with the Spanish title of esteem, "Don." This term of address—also used by workers to refer to their supervisors and reputational leaders—acknowledges the personal dignity and the authority of patriarchs in their familial realms, while leaving untouched the superior job authority of the supervisor. Similarly, an entire etiquette of indirect reprimands has built up to prevent affront. Although the authority hierarchy requires admonishments, labor supervisors signal respect by phrasing reprimands in the Spanish passive-voice terminology of happenstance. Thus, a tactful foreman might say, "Take care, Señor Rodriguez, sticks are getting into your boxes on you," or, "Watch out, please, your picking is getting slow on you." One particularly flamboyant grower described the way he tempered his naturally direct response to secure compliance without affront.

> All of us growers have problems getting our workers not to drive over the pipes with the tractor. It happened to me a couple of times. The third time I grabbed the pipe, swelled up and got red, and went charging down the hill waving the pipe and bellowing at the top of my lungs. I was careful not to direct it at anyone, though I knew just who did it. It really had an impact. I haven't had anyone run over a pipe since. The poor guy who did it still goes rigid when I go past, afraid I guess that I'll discover he did it.

Most supervisors attend to these conventions of discourse and treatment, but examples of violations abound, and coercive management practices not framed in this convention are bitterly resented. Workers' accounts are full of the small and large humiliations they have suffered at the hands of their supervisors. Yet here again, their grievances rarely surface. As in the other two most common areas of friction, some are drained off through individual efforts at advancement, others are dispelled by the evidence of equitable family treatment. Bitter feelings are acted out in petty forms of sabotage and vented through gossip and the heated retelling of injustices. Far from leading to changes in power relationships, such actions and conversations in effect reinforce the terms of the social contract between workers and their superiors. Here, as in James Scott's account of power relations in the Malaysian countryside (1985), workers reemphasize their notions of workplace justice and the terms of their implicit contracts with their superiors by decrying unfair treatment to their peers and disparaging its perpetrators. Berry workers' unstated contract involves accepting their supervisors' arbitrary authority—both their right to overlook rule infractions and their right to dispense special privileges—as long as the balance of dispensations to them or their family grouping feels, on the whole, equitable. In return, workers labor hard and conscientiously, and they regulate their peers. It is the treatment of family groupings that is decisive: individuals are generally willing to overlook personal affronts in the interest of preserving their family's standing on the job. Thus here, as elsewhere (Granovetter 1990), the social context of individual economic behavior—that is, their personal relations as well as the structure of the overall network of relations—affects not only individual actions, but economic outcomes and institutions.

The three sorts of tensions discussed here, then, generally elicit open resistance only when one family grouping is thought to be favored or disfavored over others. In such cases, the spokesperson for the family grouping generally approaches the foreman with the family's grievance. Most complaints are resolved at this point, because growers and foremen are well aware that feelings must be very inflamed for them to have reached the point of open protest. If the issue is not resolved, collective action could result. Most commonly, the entire family grouping might walk off the job for several hours or a day. Family-specific disputes rarely reach this point, however. They are contained in part by the careful dispersal of favors among groups and by the fragmentation of grievances and resistance along family lines.

The overarching reference point of the labor market keeps this system in bounds. As workers contemplate responses to perceived injustice, they confront the facts that they are easily replaced, that they have few or no economic alternatives and little or no political clout, and that the impact on their families were they to lose their jobs would be severe. Foremen constantly remind workers of their redundancy, telling them how lucky they are, how a hundred others would be glad to take their jobs. And for most years and at most times in the season, they are correct. The wandering workers who come daily to the ranch gate to ask for work and the presence in every extended family of individuals without work reinforce this awareness. More than any other factor, it is workers' consciousness of their limited options and dispensability in the labor market that elicits their commitment to strawberry jobs, their engagement in their own recruitment and control, and their management of perceived personal affronts to secure family advantage. Thus, in strawberries, as in other California crop industries (Friedland and Barton 1975; Friedland, Barton, and Thomas 1981; Thomas 1985), workers are constantly managed and their discontents are dampened by the citizenship stratification of the labor market.

The Intersection of Labor Supply and Demand

In sum, labor supply and demand are mutually reinforcing in this industry, and their complementarity reduces the need for direct control. As we have seen, the social processes through which labor demand is met and workplace conflict is dissipated depend crucially on the character of labor supply. Yet the apparently personal attributes that incline workers to comply with and even prefer strawberry employment do not arise solely from their inherent proclivities and abilities. Instead, they have been importantly structured by the political construction of the labor market. Most important are the policies and government agencies that foster the maintenance of labor surpluses and the distinctions between citizen and noncitizen workers. Because workers evaluate advisable responses in light of their broader economic alternatives, the processes that structure their options and value in the labor market shape their interests and power at the point of production. In short, the overarching constraints of the labor market regime are the most intractable and consequential determinants of workplace compliance. Furthermore, sociopolitical status does not have a predictable significance for control relations or work organization. Rather, its economic utility is highly contingent and is shaped by the constraints of the industry and locality. Disadvantaged social status does not translate directly or uniformly into disadvantaged economic status, and such status will not necessarily be used by employers to directly control and cheapen particular types of work.

Finally, we have seen that growers capitalize on workers' social organizational resources and on their interest in stabilizing their sources of employment to reduce their own direct investment in labor management. Even as this delegation ensures a finely tuned and low-cost fit between labor supply and fluctuating demand, it also increases workers' family-based solidarity and their potential for resistance. For the most part, however, personal relations with supervisors and the employment of several family groupings individualize responses to grievances, reinforce kin-based divisions in the workforce, and dispel resistance to the coercive management of work. Overall, this system enhances the commitment of growers as well as workers to the longevity of the employment relationship. Over the course of each season, however, labor supply conditions and labor control challenges shift importantly. At two points, labor surpluses diminish and the relative leverage of workers increases. Simultaneously, an issue that bridges kin-based divisions in the workforce surfaces to challenge the legitimacy of the employment relationship. At these times and over this issue, wage workers are more likely and able to resist. The next chapter explores this dynamic, addressing seasonal and geographical variation in worker resistance within the wage labor process.

Appendix 1
History of Production Practices

Until the early 1960s, fields were leveled by surveying and then moving the soil with a tractor-pulled implement. When furrow irrigation was used (through the 1970s for many growers), the land had to be leveled completely so the water would flow evenly (Thomas 1939:32–35, 81). Since the advent of drip irrigation, the land is leveled to a 1- or 2-percent slope to allow winter rains to run off. Though the attachments used for tractor leveling have been improved, the process has changed little. In the early 1960s, computerized laser levelers that program the desired slope into the tractor-pulled leveling implement were developed. By the late 1970s, they began to replace the earlier method because of their greater accuracy, consistency, and speed. They are most effective on flat land, however, and cannot be used on steep slopes, so that from one- to two-thirds of central coast growers continue to use surveying and grading. Lasers reduce the need for farmers' leveling skills and the cost of surveying and tractor labor (Welch et al. 1982). They may increase the cost of land leveling, depending on soil type, topography, and previous leveling. The cost increase is hard to assess because many growers survey and level themselves and do not calculate the cost of their own labor. Growers report that the cost of hiring out surveying and grading averaged $150 an acre in 1987, and the cost of laser leveling ranged from $40 to $150 an acre for previously leveled land and from $250 to $900 an acre for new land.

Soil fumigation has had a revolutionary impact on the industry. Current (1995) threats to ban its chemicals seriously alarm growers. Previously, the fungus verticillium wilt, and, secondarily, xanthosis, black root and crown rot, red stele, and nematodes decimated California berry harvests. The main means of disease control was to avoid soil previously cropped to verticillium-prone crops such as strawberries, tomatoes, potatoes, peppers, or cotton. As a result, growers were forced to relocate their operations every few years, often moving great distances and finding only small parcels of disease-free land. Since 1965, virtually all California berry growers have fumigated. On the central coast, they contract out this expensive service for $950 to $1,500 an acre. The soil is moistened after leveling and a tractor spreads plastic over the field in strips, while simultaneously injecting the liquid chemicals into the soil, where they volatilize and diffuse. The tractor also seals the strips of plastic together and firms the soil over them at the edges so the gas cannot escape. After 48 hours the plastic is removed; fifteen days later planting can commence (Thomas 1939:27, 81; Wilhelm and Paulus 1980:266–69; Wilhelm and Sagen 1974:266–67). Researchers estimate that fumigation has increased yields from 30 to 50 percent, reduced fertilizer use because of concomitant weed control and because the organisms killed by the fungicide provide natural fertilization, and permitted the expansion of farm size and the adoption of annual replanting.

Methods of bed formation have changed little since the war, although bed height and width have changed considerably. Raised beds have been standard in the industry since the 1890s because of the plant's sensitivity to soil salinity, root compaction, and various diseases and pests fostered by excessive moisture. Before World War II, California strawberries were grown on slightly raised two-row beds that were 40 inches wide. In the late 1960s, however, experimentation began with wider beds containing two or four rows of plants, to increase plant density and yields per acre. Currently, about 85 percent of central coast growers use beds between 48 and 52 inches wide; less than 15 percent use the 64- to 68-inch beds prevalent in southern California, which are more costly to install and maintain. The minimum bed width advised for the region is 44 inches, but some low resource growers still use 40-inch beds. Bed height has also increased since the mid-1960s, improving root development and drainage and allowing workers to pick and manicure the plants more quickly and easily. It now ranges from 8 inches for 40- to 44-inch beds, to from 12 to 18 inches for beds over 52 inches wide. Overall, researchers estimate that the increased density from wider, higher beds has raised per acre yields by about 30 percent for winter plantings and by 10 to 15 percent for summer plantings. The costs of plants, planting and harvest labor, bed-shaping equipment, and two drip irrigation lines for four-row beds have also risen (Lydon 1985:76–77; "Strawberry Growers" 1977:13; Voth and Bringhurst 1978; Welch, Greathead, and Beutel 1985).

Although the preparation of planting slots and the final firming of the soil around the plants have been mechanized, the plants are still set in the ground by hand, as they were before the war (Thomas 1939:37–38). Planting dates have changed considerably. Shorter spans between planting and harvest have reduced the time from the investment of capital to the realization of profit, lowered the cost of pre-harvest plant maintenance, and diminished vulnerability to risks associated with over-wintering the plants. The manipulation of planting dates has extended the harvest earlier into the spring and later into the fall, both periods of low berry supply and high market price. Plant breeders have tried to develop varieties suitable to longer harvests and shorter waiting periods. However, since varieties are developed with other goals in mind as well, growers are limited in their planting dates by the optimal requirements of the strains they have chosen.

Before the war, strawberries were planted February through April on the central coast (Voth and Bringhurst 1958:186; Wilhelm and Sagen 1974:226). To develop sturdy plants, the blossoms were removed the first year. The plants were harvested the second year and for several years thereafter with progressively declining yields. In the mid-1940s experimentation began with winter planting, using the Shasta and Lassen varieties. In the 1950s and early 1960s, winter planting predominated in the state (Childers 1980:69; Voth and Bringhurst 1958:1; Wilhelm and Sagen 1974:222–26). By the mid-1960s, summer planting began to increase, as Lassen was found to yield better with summer planting in the south, and as new varieties such as Tufts and Tioga were developed that could be planted in either winter or summer in either region (California Crop 1964, 1967; Childers 1980:15–16; Welch et al. 1982:5). A mixture of summer and winter plantings was used throughout the state until the early 1980s, when southern growers began to switch to Douglas, which was introduced in 1979 and performed especially well under winter planting in the south (Welch et al. 1982:5). By 1987, almost all of the southern acreage was winter planted as the use of Douglas spread and as Chandler, another productive winter-planted variety, was adopted (California Crop 1980–87). Winter planting enables southern growers to start the harvest early, when supply from elsewhere is low and temperatures are cool.

Central coast growers continue to combine summer and winter planting, because their varieties perform well with either planting season and because a mix of planting times maximizes yields and market returns there. Winter planting takes place in October or November, and harvest commences from four to six months later, in late March to early April. Summer planting takes place in late July and August, and the harvest begins in mid-April. Winter planting offers a number of advantages. Since the plants are in the ground for a shorter period, they require less field labor, supervision, and materials for weeding, fertilizing, irrigating, pruning, removing runners and blossoms, and controlling diseases and pests prior to harvest. Winter plantings also yield larger, higher-quality berries, and the plants are smaller, thus making the berries easier to locate and pick and reducing per-unit harvest labor costs (Welch et al. 1982:9). Winter planting also has some disadvantages. Unexpected winter rains can delay the timing of planting, a variable critical to plant performance. The cost of bed establishment is also greater, since more plants are planted per acre because the plants stay smaller, and since the plants themselves are more expensive. Finally, winter plantings yield a lower volume of fruit.

Frequency of replanting has also changed since the war. Before 1960, most California growers retained their strawberry plants for at least two years, and often for three, four, or more. Since then, growers have shifted toward annual replanting, thus capturing the almost twice-as-large harvests that are obtained in the first production year. The shift to annual planting came earlier and more completely in the south, where high land and water costs and high grower resource level make per-acre yields more consequential and possible. By 1987, 99 percent of the southern acreage was annually planted, as opposed to about 80 percent on the central coast. Farm advisers and my interviews suggest that the large number of low-resource Mexican growers on the central coast account for most of this disparity. Currently, few growers in either region keep plants past the second year (Welch, Greathead, and Beutel 1985:4). This change has contributed importantly to increased yields and capital and labor requirements. A shift from a two- to a one-year crop cycle doubles the outlay for land preparation, plants, and planting. Shifts in planting times increase the complexity of labor management.

Strawberry varieties have improved greatly since the war. California plant breeders have focused their attention on disease and insect resistance, harvest timing (starting date, length, peak or even production), yield volume, regional adaptation, fruit quality (size, appearance, flavor), suitability for fresh and processed markets (ability to hold form, ease of calyx removal), plant size, sturdiness, and shape, fruit visibility (how it is held on the plant, stem length and position), runner production, and storage and shipability. The concerns of breeders have changed over time, as market demand, resource availability and cost, and production practices have shifted. Thus, while genetic resistance to pests and diseases was a primary concern before the war, it has since decreased in importance because of cleaner nursery practices, the development of fumigation, and other chemical means of controlling diseases and pests. Similarly, market-related concerns such as berry yield, size, shipability, and amenability to fresh and processed use were given less weight before the war when most berries were sold locally. Because labor needs have burgeoned, special attention has been directed to varietal characteristics that affect per-unit labor cost, such as runner and foliage production and fruit size, visibility, and ease of removal from the plant. Because berries are now picked over an eight- to nine-month period, researchers have also selected for sturdier plants that can withstand repeated harvests (Childers 1980:135–48, 156–63; Haley 1982; Thomas 1939; Thomas and Goldsmith 1945; Welch and Beutel 1987; Welch, Greathead, and Beutel 1985; Wilhelm and Sagen 1974). The 1945 release of the high-yielding Shasta, Lassen, Sierra, Tahoe, and Donner varieties catapulted California into world strawberry leadership (Thomas 1939:65–67; Thomas and Goldsmith 1945). Within ten years, 95 percent of California acreage was planted to these cultivars, which bore fruit well into

September and provided yields of up to twenty tons an acre (Wilhelm and Sagen 1974:213–32). Beginning in the early 1960s, a new generation of cultivars began to emerge. Some bore from April through November on the central coast and one, the Tioga, gave up to sixty tons an acre ("Cultural Practices" 1978). Subsequent varieties have been less prolific, but more profitable.

In recent years plant breeders have experimented with the manipulation of photo periodicity (fruiting response to day length) to produce a more stable supply that extends into the high-price, low-supply periods of early spring and late fall and that makes more efficient use of costly inputs. Special attention has been devoted to improving the short-day varieties that have heretofore dominated the industry and to developing new day-neutral varieties. Short-day varieties set fruit when the day length is shorter. They fruit early, exhibit a heavy harvest peak, and subside toward the end of the season. Day-neutral varieties produce flowers cyclically, both during the long days of summer and the short days of spring or winter, resulting in a longer, more even harvest and a higher total yield than many short-day varieties. They begin to produce three months after planting and have greater flexibility in planting time. In the late 1980s, day-neutral varieties produced lower-quality fruit but promised greater flexibility, productivity, and profitability. On the central coast, the main variety in use was Pajaro, a short-day variety that begins to ripen in mid-April and has a heavy May-June peak. It may cease production as early as July if the weather is too hot, but will continue bearing at a reduced level and even revive in September if temperatures stay cool. The day-neutral variety, Selva, has achieved widespread use as a means of increasing production in late summer and early fall (Haley 1982:32–35; Childers 1980: 13–19, 156–63; Welch and Beutel 1987; Welch, Greathead, and Beutel 1985:2).

Varietal development has had a huge impact on costs, labor demand and market returns. Varietal choice affects almost every phase of production. Cultivars vary in susceptibility to pests and diseases and in the desirable amounts and application methods of fertilizer. Because they vary in vegetative growth and runner production, they affect maintenance labor. Most important, however, is their impact on yields and harvest labor. Because they vary in the size, timing, and duration of yields, the optimal size of beds, the number of rows per bed, and the density of planting, they affect harvest labor demand. Improved berry size, firmness, visibility, stem length, and ease of removal from the plant increase the efficiency and speed of the harvest. Characteristics such as suitability for fresh and processed use and variations in the rate of decay affect methods of harvest and post-harvest handling. The longer and more even bearing season increases workers' strawberry-related income, thus enhancing their job commitment and reducing the labor management problems associated with a large, brief labor demand.

The procedures for maintaining plantings now involve less labor and more capital. Until the 1970s, California strawberry growers used furrow irrigation, which required the installation of a permanent pipe system and a powerful pump, as well as the painstaking leveling of the field to a zero degree slope so that the water would spread evenly. The furrows were flooded after each picking and the next picking could not take place until the furrows had dried, usually four to five days later (Wilhelm and Sagen 1974:164; Thomas 1939:39–41). Considerable hand labor was involved in land leveling, in furrow construction and maintenance, and in diverting the water to the different sections of the field. Over the course of the 1970s and 1980s, this system has been almost entirely replaced by drip irrigation (California Crop 1986:7:6); 95 percent of the state's strawberry acreage was under drip irrigation by 1986. Drip lowers the possibility of harmful salt deposits, reduces water requirements by as much as half, and thus reduces growers' exposure to the increasing political contestation of water supply. Drip can be used in very heavy or very light soils that would not moisten evenly with furrows. Because it can be installed on a slope, it permits the use of hilly land. Drip systems deliver the water directly to the plants and do not moisten the soil around them, thus reducing fruit rot and weed growth and enabling workers to pick as often as the crop requires (Thomas 1939:40–41; Welch et al. 1982:6; Childers 1980:67; Voth and Bringhurst 1978:12). The drip equipment itself is more costly than the simple pipes and pumps used previously, and its smaller tubing must be replaced with each planting. Electricity costs are also higher, but labor costs are lower. Drip eliminates the installation costs of furrows and replaces a hand-tended system with one that is mechanically regulated. Overall, it increases yields, reduces hand labor somewhat, and increases capital costs.

Prior to World War II, runner production was encouraged to increase the plant population (Thomas 1939:39). Runners from the sparsely planted mother plants were removed and laboriously set in the ground by hand to reach the desired plant density. This method fostered the spread of pests and diseases and resulted in lighter crops. Since the war, it has been superseded by nursery-based plant production. Because the strongest and most disease-free plants have been found to develop at higher altitudes away from the growing regions, the California strawberry nursery industry now centers in Shasta County in northern California (Wilhelm and Sagen 1974: 199, 218–26).

Appendix 2
Methodology for Worker Interviews

A few words are in order regarding the sample of labor-suppliers in the 1986–87 interviews. Overall, the sample interviewed mirrored the dominant characteristics of the regional strawberry labor force. All were of Mexican origin or descent, as were about 99 percent of the strawberry workers in the region at that time, with perhaps 1 percent of Central American or Southeast Asian derivation. Similarly, 77 percent of the interviewees were male and 23 percent were female, a proportion that my observations and interview responses indicate was roughly characteristic of the industry as a whole. Although an estimated 50 to 75 percent of the workers in the industry were undocumented in 1986 and 1987, only 44 percent of the wage workers I interviewed were. This shortfall is not surprising, given the mobile, hidden, and fearful nature of this population. I made a special effort to ascertain immigration status in the interviews. As other researchers have found as well (Cornelius 1981), the use of networks of interpersonal recommendation was especially valuable in developing the environment of trust necessary for this population. Following the advice of sharecroppers, workers, and labor organizers, I did not ask workers directly whether they "had papers" or not. I often knew the answer from other workers or from my intermediaries. In most cases, interviewees volunteered the information when they responded to questions about their work histories, the Border Patrol, and labor market conditions in general. Even without such direct acknowledgment, the nature of their responses often made immigration status obvious. In less than 5 percent of the cases, I judged immigration status myself on the basis of the content and tone of answers to the immigration status questions. I would be surprised if my judgment were incorrect in those instances. My understanding of this portion of the workforce was enhanced by the fact that almost every worker interviewed started out without papers. Narrative data on their experiences were gathered in every case.

In terms of the size of the employing farm, 45 (64 percent) of the interviewees worked on large farms at the time of the interview, 10 (14 percent) worked on medium-sized farms, and 15 (22 percent) worked on small farms. In terms of employer ethnicity, 25 (36 percent) worked for Japanese growers, 22 (31 percent) worked for Mexican growers, and 23 (33 percent) worked for Anglo growers. In terms of the location of the employing ranch, 14 (20 percent) worked in North Monterey County, 35 (50 percent) worked in the Pajaro region, and 21 (30 percent) worked in the Salinas Valley. In terms of labor process position, 20 (29 percent) were sharecroppers,

41 (59 percent) were wage laborers (encompassing 31 percent who were lower tier, including the employees of sharecroppers, farm labor contractors, and independent growers; 13 percent who were middle tier; and 14 percent who were upper tier workers), and 9 (13 percent) were supervisory or other workers. In general, the greater numerical representation of the Pajaro region among labor-suppliers was a result of the fact that more sharecropping farms were based in that area, and an effort was made to interview sharecroppers and their employees in as many different operations as possible. Small imbalances in the distribution of interviewees along some of these axes were minimized by the multiple involvements of most workers. Whereas detailed labor process data was gathered for the farm on which an individual worked in the 1986 harvest year, most workers had previously worked for farms of other sizes, production locations, and grower ethnicities. Many had been sharecroppers as well as wage laborers. In such cases, data on production relations and working conditions were probed in the course of the interview. Work history questions uncovered patterns of mobility among tiers.

Drawing on my prior understanding of the system, two variants of the interview schedule were constructed: one for sharecroppers and one for the rest. This interview involved 463 items, including some that were relevant only to certain categories of workers. Questions provided basic demographic information about the worker and his/her family and current employing farm. They explored work history by crop and company, migration and residence patterns, the task organization and management practices on the main employing farm for the 1985 crop season, a description of a typical working day, the intersection between family and work, the role of the union, and labor market organization and change. In addition, many open-ended questions were included to allow interviewees to elaborate on such matters as their views of sharecropping versus wage labor, class structure and class relations, management practices, the union, and their employment alternatives.

[6]

The Place of Justice and the Justice of Place

Early in 1979, United Farm Workers' (UFW) contracts with Imperial Valley vegetable growers expired, and strikes spilled over into the lettuce and broccoli fields of the Salinas Valley. Red and black union flags sprouted along the country roads in Santa Cruz and Monterey Counties, borne by caravans of picketers who marched from ranch to ranch, singing, chanting, and urging workers in the fields to join them. As the months wore on, the conflict grew increasingly violent. Growers accused picketers of blocking fields, throwing rocks, trespassing on private property, and heckling strikebreakers. Striking workers charged growers with hiring security guards who bullied strikers and bore loaded weapons, in violation of a court order.[1]

News of the struggle spread like wildfire. Cesar Chavez launched a national media campaign indicting President Carter, law enforcement officials, and growers. He graphically described the contest in the fields and urged consumers to boycott all lettuce not grown under union contract. These charges stimulated widely publicized legislative hearings, in which the U.S. Border Patrol was charged with harassing strikers and ignoring growers' use of undocumented strikebreakers. In response to these charges, the Immigration and Naturalization Service more than doubled its staff in the Salinas Valley and arrests of illegal aliens during the 1979 lettuce harvest were twice their usual number. Sympathy for the strikers burgeoned. On July 31, church leaders, civil rights activists, college students, and legislators joined Chavez on a nationally televised twelve-day march

[1]The violence of the 1970 strike was widely reported in the newspapers and in books chronicling the struggle (e.g., Jenkins 1985; Levy 1975; Majka and Majka 1982).

from San Francisco to Salinas. One by one, in the face of this public criticism, the growers began to renew their contracts. On August 31, the dam broke: the giant Sun Harvest, a subsidiary of United Brands, signed a three-year contract that increased the minimum wage of 1,200 lettuce workers to an unprecedented $5 an hour and guaranteed them health insurance, a seniority system, and a union hiring hall. By the season's end, the UFW had won contracts with most of the firms whose contracts were in dispute.

Behind this well-documented public saga, a curious and less-visible drama unfolded. Tucked between the vast, geometrical lettuce estates on the valley floors and contoured up steep hillsides unsuited to other crops, carefully manicured strawberry fields flourished. Day after day, Mexican men and women pushed their three-wheeled carts up and down the deep furrows, their shirts and long-billed caps splashing curved lines of primary colors across the deep green fields. To the public eye, this industry had escaped the turmoil in the central coast fields. With few exceptions, no picketing or sustained strikes interrupted the rhythms of the harvest, and no union contracts restricted growers' ability to set the terms of work. Yet the apparent tranquillity of this scene was deceptive. The lack of public strife and union contracts notwithstanding, labor relations in this industry were neither calm nor untouched by union mobilization.

Spatial Variance and Workplace Struggles

As I conducted my fieldwork that season and over the course of previous and subsequent years, I unearthed a substratum of labor-management struggles—some erupting into work stoppages—that persisted without the help of union organization. I learned that such small-scale protests and negotiations had existed in the early 1970s as well but had been overshadowed by more public union-management disputes. I discovered also that the pattern of these engagements was uneven: they varied in form and extent across the three microregions. Three vignettes drawn from my field notes help delineate their differences.[2]

The evening after the Sun Harvest agreement, forty-five berry pickers for a one hundred-acre corporate ranch on the Salinas Valley floor met to discuss the lettuce contract. Gathered in the dusty parking lot of the trailer

[2]These vignettes are composites constructed from the variety of informants (growers, foremen, workers) who provided overlapping accounts of the same events. The contrasts expressed by the vignettes run true to life, though some details of the events have been altered to preserve anonymity.

camp that had been home to migrants from their Mexican village since the mid-1950s, they weighed the wisdom of demanding higher wages themselves. The meeting wore on into the evening. Dogs quieted and men settled into comfortable positions on doorsteps and against battered cars. Women disappeared to put drowsing children to bed. After three hours, a committee of four older men was selected to approach the ranch manager. The following morning they presented their demand for an increase in the piece rate. When a response was not forthcoming after two days, ninety workers deposited their carts by the truck at noon and did not return. A few days later their demand was met.

Less than fifteen miles away, on a thirty-acre farm in the protected emerald amphitheater of the Pajaro Valley, the patriarch of a family network of berry pickers approached his Japanese employer at the end of the day. They greeted each other respectfully and the worker leaned against the truck, watching his employer rapidly check random berry baskets for inferior fruit. In a broken mixture of English and Spanish the men exchanged their customary inquiries about the health of relatives. Then the worker, gazing off toward the line of eucalyptus that stood between the valley and the ocean, observed obliquely that lettuce wages had risen. The grower understood that this comment was a threat. He realized that, although this group of workers had been with him for over a decade, their loyalty was not assured. Conditions had changed since the arrival of the union. The next day he summoned the patriarch and asked whether he and his relatives would wait until the season's end for a raise. The grower could not, he apologized, increase wages immediately, because he lacked the resources of the big companies.

Meanwhile, in the eucalyptus-ridged hills of North Monterey County, workers on an eleven-acre berry ranch did not mention the lettuce victory to their Mexican employer. None of them joined the union marches. Instead, most retired after each day's grueling work to the wheelless van, small shed, and dirt caves that comprised their shelter on the ranch. There, warming beans and tortillas over small cook fires, they exchanged reminiscences about their villages of origin, and recounted tales of close escapes from the *migra.* News of the Sun Harvest contract did reach them, through two men returning from a bar in Salinas. Quietly and excitedly they speculated about a new era in farm labor, when Mexican farm workers could force powerful Anglo growers to listen. They knew well, however, that this vision was distant from the reality of their own daily lives. These workers continued to labor without complaint until the end of the season. Some newcomers even worked the last two months without pay, in return for the privilege of being given a job. By the next spring, average hourly strawberry wages in the two valleys had increased from $4.15 to $5.00, while those in the north Monterey County hills remained unchanged at the previous year's rate of $3.30.

These vignettes typify the microregional dynamics of class relations on central coast strawberry farms. They highlight an important paradox in the link between labor processes and labor resistance. If skill and labor organizations are the major sources of wage worker control and opposition, how, then, was I to explain the existence, efficacy, and unevenness of resistance among minimally skilled, nonunionized workers? How and why did wage laborers who were neither union members nor covered by union contracts, whose skill gave them little influence over the production process, and who held a disadvantaged position in the labor market, stage these moments of collective protest? Even more curious, why was this opposition more frequent in some parts of the region than in others? From the late 1970s through the late 1980s, these questions became central to my research.

This chapter explores the microregional specificity and variance of class relations and labor resistance. It demonstrates that localized production contexts vary in ways that in some cases permit or foster, and in others discourage and dispel, class conflict at work. This chapter details the events, locations, and timing of labor mobilization, showing how seasonal swings in labor supply and demand and microregional contrasts in the local organization of production affect workers' abilities and inclinations to challenge the terms of their work.

Temporal Variance and the Negotiation of Justice

There is a distinctive justice associated with place and a distinctive place for the notion of justice on the central coast. That is, notions of workplace justice here are firmly grounded in place, in that different standards and etiquettes of justice have evolved within the three microregions. Justice controversies also occupy a distinctive "place" in time: they tend to surface at certain points in the annual cycle. To this point, I have emphasized divisive sources of workers' discontent—the differential enforcement of rules, granting of privileges, and according of respect. Such tensions tend to divide workers along family lines in their responses to perceived injustice. Thus, the social relations of production, in concert with labor market conditions, effectively keep most resistance in check. At two points in each season, however, the balance of class power shifts and the perceived legitimacy of employment relationships is called into question. At these junctures, another sort of discord surfaces—one that binds workers together and increases their ability to generate common cause around grievances.

When workers apply for and accept their jobs, they enter into implicit contracts regarding the just returns to their labor. These agreements involve a rate of pay expressed in terms of a starting hourly wage and a peak season piece rate. They may also include benefits, such as health insurance or housing. The agreements are not negotiated, but are rather handed down by the employer as a condition of employment. Nor are they uniform: there is no single standard of a "just" return to labor in the industry. Regardless of the locality in which workers operate, however, their acceptance of work on a particular ranch signals agreement to a certain reward for their labor. Both their evaluations of present employment practices and their expectations for future rewards are geared to this standard. But the strawberry production curve disrupts the implementation of this standard. Yields start low in April and early May, rise quickly to a May-June peak, subside to a fluctuating plateau in late July and August, then pick up for a smaller peak in September. Because of these swings, neither growers nor workers want to set a single method of pay: hourly wages do not reward workers for—or stimulate them to—greater productivity at the peak, and piece rates do not pay pickers enough at the start or end of the season to satisfy minimum wage laws or motivate their staying on the job. Most growers begin the season, therefore, with an hourly wage, which sets a floor to workers' earnings. As the harvest picks up, workers pick more crates per hour and growers' earnings increase proportionately. At this point, most growers switch to a piece rate—either a straight piece or an hourly base plus a piece-rate "kicker"—to reward workers for their productivity. As the harvest subsides in late summer or early fall, growers shift back to an hourly rate. Peak-season piece rates give pickers hourly earnings twice or three times those of the early- and late-season hourly wage. Although pickers vary in their speed, and thus in their earnings, they accept the early- and late-season terms with an eye to what they plan to earn in the middle.

In the transitions to and from piece rate, the fairness of the rate of pay is called into question. Both parties actively assess the balance of returns between them. Growers and foremen watch yields closely, correlate them with market prices, and decide when they can make the shift without sacrificing rates of profit. Workers also watch the harvests, calculating how many crates they can pick per hour and how much they would be earning if the grower switched to his last year's piece rate. Rumors regarding the market price of a crate of berries circulate regularly through the fields at such times. Albeit the rumors are often inaccurate, and workers do not know growers' expenses, they nonetheless use this information to judge how much growers are earning from their effort. So familiar are pickers with the signs of seasonal fluctuation that they anticipate the midseason slump and the early fall renewal with some accuracy. They pride themselves on their ability to "read the plants" by looking at the number of green berries and blossoms, and they use this reading to decide when to keep working in anticipation of future earnings and when to move on to other crops, claim unemployment insurance, or return to Mexico. Workers who are part of a grower's core workforce factor the promise of future work into their calculations. When the crop starts its final decline, pickers anticipate when their piece-rate earnings will fall below what they would earn with an hourly wage and hope for the switch to hourly before that point. As might be expected, the days and weeks approaching a pay method shift are uneasy, because the automatic implementation of justice is derailed and its reestablishment must be negotiated. In general, employees push for early transitions and employers try to hold out for late ones. The two parties are surprisingly close, however, in their views of when the shift should happen.

Workers' leverage also increases during these periods. Shifts in market prices and in the availability of jobs and workers help explain this increase. At the start of the season, growers are eager to placate workers because they want to stabilize their workforces in anticipation of the heavy peak. There are many workers in the area, but many growers are competing for their services. As the peak arrives, job openings are fewer because growers have already comprised their workforces. Latecomers and unconnected workers roam from ranch to ranch, providing ready replacements for the difficult. In the fall, fewer pickers are needed because of the dwindling harvest, but there are also fewer of them, because many have left to work in other crops or return to Mexico. Harvest disruptions are especially costly at this time because market prices are at their seasonal highs, and late-season income can mean the difference between profit or loss.

Growers' vulnerability and motivation to resolve labor disputes, and workers' alternatives and potential discomfort with employment relationships, are thus especially great in the ascent and descent of production. Not surprisingly, these are also the points at which labor resistance is most common. When the pay method is not shifted within the time range workers consider just, the wave of discontent can override regional and familial divisions. In such moments, workers share a sense of legitimate expectations thwarted and moral contract breached. The natural ties of trust and acquaintance created by their kin-based recruitment networks increase their ability to join in this frustration. As we saw in the initial vignettes, workers vary in their responses to a grower's protracted failure to shift the method of pay. Some meet among themselves without confronting the grower directly. Some send a delegate to their supervisor to request a pay method shift. Some walk out for a few hours to several days. Whatever form workers' initiatives take, their challenges do not disrupt the basic structure of capitalist property relations. This essential conservatism is, in part, because the challenges originate as efforts to restore a reputedly legitimate status quo; in part, because they are contained by the labor market.

First, the dialogues between growers and workers during the seasonal destabilizations of workplace justice are fundamentally conservative. Here as elsewhere (Moore 1987; Scott 1985), workers' protests aim to heal perceived breaches of the social contract. They protest that they should not work so hard for so little at a time when growers' returns are skyrocketing. Growers seem to share their implicit notion of a "just" return to labor, in that they openly discuss whether it is "fair" for workers to ask for the pay method shift at a particular time, given the balance between market returns to them and wages to workers. All in all, instead of attacking the established hierarchy of rewards and power—such things as the disparity of returns or the allocation of control over the production process—workers ask in these transitional periods for a return to a supposedly shared vision of justice. Thus, their requests tinker with the level of the reward to their labor, not with the structure of the labor-capital relationship. At the most, they stimulate minor increases in the distribution of benefits to themselves.

It is not only the normatively restorative character of workers' claims that prevents them from altering power relations; it is also the disempowering impact of the labor market regime. As history abundantly demonstrates, even initially restorative protests can snowball into challenges of capitalist control (Gordon, Edwards, and Reich 1982; Montgomery 1979). Moreover, in this industry, some nonrestorative claims originate from the daily process of work and from the regional context of labor struggle. Yet none of these claims seriously disrupts established authority relations. The main reason for their containment is the political construction of the labor market, especially chronic labor surpluses, and the immigrant and undocumented status of most workers.

The Microregional Contexts of Labor Resistance

Whereas the conditions engendering such seasonal frictions in work relationships cut across the production localities, the form and extent of open resistance vary decidedly. This variation results from crucial contrasts in the local organization of production, which alternately reinforce or undermine workers' abilities and inclinations to resist. As table 14 shows, the

Table 14. Microregional contrasts in the local organization of production

	Salinas Valley	North Monterey Hills	Pajaro Valley
ECONOMIC ORGANIZATION			
Average farm size	71 acres	27 acres	40 acres
Job alternatives	many	few	some
Job access structures	open	mixed	closed
Hourly strawberry wages	$5.11	$4.93	$6.29
Pay methods	piece rate	piece rate	hourly-plus-piece
CLASS COMPOSITION			
Growers			
dominant ethnicity	Anglo (Japanese)	Mexican	Japanese (Anglo)
capital availability	high/medium	low	high/medium
investment per acre	medium	low	high
Workers			
citizenship status	legal/illegal	illegal	legal/illegal
experience	medium	low	high
PRODUCTION RELATIONS			
Social distance	high	low	medium
Grower-worker ties	weak/impersonal	strong/personal	average/personal
Workplace norms	U.S.-based	Mexico-based	U.S.-based
Tenor of relations	oppositional/ class-based	deferential/ patronal	accommodating/ patronal
Terms of dialogue	"entitlement"	"privilege"	"fairness"
Workers' solidarity	high	low	medium
Growers' solidarity	medium	low	high
Investment in labor quality	medium	low	high
Workers' job commitment	medium	low	high
Proximity to union pressure	close	far	somewhat removed

microregions differ in terms of their structures of economic opportunity, the compositions of their grower and worker populations, and the norms and structures of their production relations. Each microregion exhibits a certain array of employment alternatives and a characteristic structure of job access and reward. They vary in the ethnic composition and resource level of growers and in the citizenship status and experience/recency of workers. Finally, they vary in the national reference points of norms of justice, in growers' and workers' commitment to employment relationships, in the level of solidarity within each class, and in the extent of polarization and social distance between them.

In all three areas, off-the-job community structure is pivotal: the degree of social distance between employees and employers strongly affects the tenor of their relations. The localities exhibit a continuum in community structure, stretching from autonomous to encapsulated. There is a corresponding continuum in class relations, ranging from oppositional to deferential. Overall, the Salinas Valley stands out for the historical depth and autonomy of its residential enclaves of workers and for the extent to which they have become independent carriers of a UFW-inspired vision of workplace justice. The North Monterey Hills are remarkable for the extent to which the social and work worlds of growers and workers are merged, and for the Mexico-based norms that guide employment relations. The Pajaro Valley stands out for the interweaving of relative autonomy and personalism in a U.S. context and for the extent to which growers actively invest in labor compliance and commitment.

These localized differences have emerged gradually, as geographical advantages and historical circumstances have drawn certain industries and class populations into subsections of the central coast region. Personalized recruitment processes have built sustained links between certain Mexican-origin families and communities and certain central coast employers and localities. These processes have fostered relatively distinct traditions of production relations and norms, and class resources and interests, within each microregion. Recruitment methods also segment the central coast strawberry labor market, hampering the free joining of jobs and job seekers, constricting the alternatives of both parties, and increasing their commitment to their current employment relationships. This subdivision of the regional labor market is not total. Workers move somewhat across microregional boundaries, although this movement is uneven because of localized differences in job access. Nonetheless, because growers recruit most workers through existing employees, they do not have access to the full range of job seekers. Because workers secure jobs through personal links, they are most familiar with and have greatest access to opportunities in their own locality.

The Salinas Valley

Salinas Valley strawberry workers are the most likely to openly challenge the terms of employment. The economic organization, class composition, and production relations of this locality all contribute to this pattern.[3]

[3]Some growers have ranches in more than one microregion. In such cases, their production practices tend to reflect the pattern in the locality in which they are primarily based. Thus growers based in the Pajaro Valley who also have acreage in the Salinas Valley—the most common kind of crossover—tend to aim for the high-priced, high-quality fresh market and to pay with an hourly-plus-piece method.

Economic Organization and Class Composition

The Salinas Valley boasts the largest strawberry farms on the central coast. The average berry farm size was seventy-one acres in 1985, and 88 percent of the acreage was on farms with over fifty acres. Berry farms here are most likely to be absentee-owned and manager-operated, although most are owner-operated. If one excludes one large manager-operated Japanese-owned company, which skews the statistics for Japanese farms in the locality, most workers are employed by large estates that are owned or operated by Anglos. All in all, berry farms here are well-financed, although their per-acre investments are lower than those in the similarly prosperous Pajaro Valley. This pattern of resource allocation is associated with production strategy: growers here aim for a higher volume of somewhat lower quality fruit than do those in the Pajaro Valley.

The Salinas Valley has relatively more employment opportunities and more open job access structures than the other two areas. Strawberry farms share the valley floor with a large and diverse population of vegetable farms that offer employment before, during, and after the strawberry harvest. In general, jobs on vegetable and strawberry farms are the most readily available here, because labor contractors are also most common. While vegetable companies rely on personal recruitment mechanisms to some extent, many use contractors rather than hiring their employees directly. Tasks such as weeding and thinning are almost invariably done by contracted crews. Some large berry farms even use contractors for the harvest, a practice that is virtually unknown in the other two microregions. Employment relations between contractors and their crews are relatively fluid. Contractors do not maintain permanent crews because their job contracts—and thus their labor needs—may change daily. Instead, they hire from one of several shape-up points where unemployed workers gather to get a job. In one large supermarket parking lot on the periphery of Salinas, as many as two thousand workers—mostly young Mexican men—gather before dawn every morning six days a week for about ten months of the year. Contractors compose their crews from this assemblage. Employment may last for a day or a week or more. Pay rates are lower than for comparable direct-hire jobs, personal bonds between contractors and their employees tend to be weaker, and job security is almost nonexistent.[4] Despite these disadvantages to the worker, contractors

[4]Although labor contractors convey to growers that their relationships with their employees and their employees' motivation to do good work are strong, I did not find this to be the case. A few contractors do maintain a pool of repeat hires with whom they have a relatively close relationship, these pools are relatively small and personal ties are generally weaker than

also offer a distinct advantage: they increase job mobility and thus reduce the dependency of displaced or unconnected workers.

As noted earlier, agricultural wage levels in the Salinas Valley are among the highest in the state, largely because of the intensity of union pressure. Most berry and vegetable farms provide the legal entitlements of a minimum wage, overtime pay, workers' compensation, and unemployment insurance. During the years of greatest union pressure, some berry growers also offered the exceptional benefits of health insurance and paid vacations, to match those offered by the large unionized vegetable companies. Strawberry wages are also relatively high here, although on the average they fall between those of the other two microregions. Thus, in 1985 the Salinas Valley farms studied paid pickers an average of $5.11 an hour, the North Monterey County farms paid an average of $4.93 an hour, and the Pajaro Valley farms paid an average of $6.29 an hour. Salinas growers pay by the piece for each crate of berries picked to encourage high volume, and they rely on labor surpluses and relatively good pay to motivate above-average quality.

Employment Strategies

The employment strategies of Salinas Valley workers generate household incomes that are comparable to those in the Pajaro Valley and higher than those in North Monterey County, although the proportion of strawberry-related income is lower than in either. These strategies reflect the opportunity structure of the microregion. Because most berry farms here, like local vegetable farms, use a straight piece-rate pay method, berry pickers often earn more per hour at the height of the season than do those in either of the other areas. Because many families combine peak-season piece-rate work in the strawberry harvest with peak-season work in one or more vegetable harvests, workers here are less dependent on strawberry work. Typically, some family members pick strawberries for the entire season, while others move on to another crop after the peak. Their access to regular work in these crops has evolved from years in the local system, during which many have forged connections with workers in other industries. Thus, some husbands work in the highly paid lettuce ground crews, while their wives work in strawberries. In other cases, wives or older children pick asparagus before, or tomatoes after, the strawberry peak, while the

on direct-hire farms. This situation is largely due to the high turnover, substandard wages and benefit packages, and the lack of job security.

husband stays in strawberries for the entire season. Such crossovers create an opening for the employment of a relative or friend, further elaborating inter-industry links.

Production Relations

Production relations on Salinas Valley berry farms involve a high degree of social distance between growers and workers and a U.S.-based reference point for workplace justice. These characteristics help workers coalesce common interests counter to their employers, eliciting class polarities rather than dyadic dependencies between them. This pattern is reinforced by the scale and structure of farming; by the ethnic identity and resource level of farmers; by workers' citizenship status, experience, and off-the-job community structure; and by the local intensity of union mobilization.

The large scale of farms reduces the opportunity for social exchange between growers and workers. Whereas workers on a given ranch tend to be highly interconnected because of personalized recruitment processes, class relations here are relatively less personal. Few growers are Mexican, and they lack the glue of ethnic commonality with workers that binds the classes in North Monterey County. Workers here rarely have face-to-face acquaintance with their employers. Patron-client relations are weak or nonexistent. Most workers have a personal tie to their foreman, but it does not tie them as closely to the interests of their employers as in the other two regions, since they do not know their employers personally. Community structure reinforces workers' solidarity and their physical and psychological distance from growers.

Salinas Valley growers rarely provide housing for their workers and workers rarely live on the grounds of their employers' ranches. Rather, most find housing themselves in apartment complexes, run-down houses, trailer camps, or housing camps in Salinas or the small towns that dot Highway 101 to the south (see plate 9). Their neighbors are friends and relatives who come from the same region in Mexico. Typically, a core of residents in a complex are legal immigrants, and a continually replenishing fringe are undocumented. Legal immigrants usually rent a unit for the year, and during the harvest peak they are joined by friends and extended family from Mexico. Neighboring units tend eventually to be absorbed into the family network and passed down to subsequent generations. To be sure, tensions exist in these residential communities, but the density of acquaintance, face-to-face interaction, and trust within them is relatively high. Here, the events of the working day are rehashed, and the norms of workplace justice are communicated and reinforced. Here, too, strategies of resistance take shape.

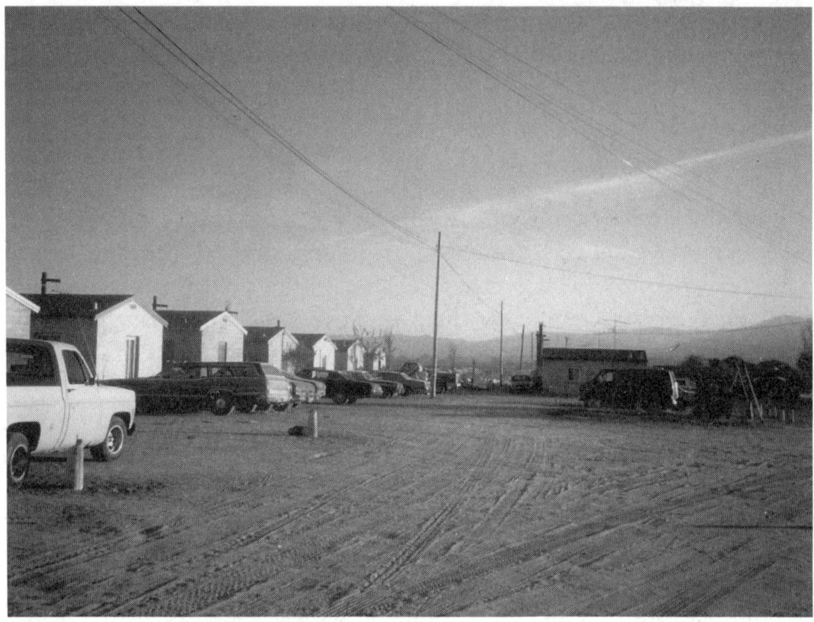

Plate 9. Strawberry workers' housing camp, Salinas Valley. Photo author

The norms that legitimate and stimulate challenges to growers' practices have been strongly conditioned by the local intensity of union struggle. Because the Salinas Valley was the center of union mobilization from 1970 into the early 1980s, and because many workers worked for the large companies that were the union's targets, workers here have been particularly exposed to the UFW's vision of justice. Theirs is a U.S.-based vision of entitlement: it claims for farm workers many of the rights granted workers in other sectors of the U.S. economy. It emphasizes the right to a minimum wage and limited hours of work, the right to safety-net protections like workers' compensation and unemployment insurance, and the right to organize and bargain collectively. Although wage and benefit levels expected do not equal those of non-farm workers, the standard of justice in this area encompasses the crucial notion that the conditions and returns of labor should be governed by external standards set by the government, not by the whims of individual farmers. In comparison with the other two microregions, workers here are the most informed about the legal entitlements of farm labor and the most insistent on obtaining them.

Labor Resistance

Not surprisingly, collective resistance is the most frequent and sustained on Salinas Valley berry farms. Workers inform their foremen of wage increases on neighboring farms with dispatch. Foremen are well aware that these farms might be employment alternatives for their workers, and they carefully tread the line between protecting the interests of the owner and maintaining the allegiance of workers. The negotiation of differences tends to be more protracted here, as foremen and ranch managers communicate with their superiors. At the same time, workers tend to be comparatively impatient, for they are strengthened by the presence of economic alternatives and by the militance of their peers. Strawberry walkouts occur most frequently and last longest here. A few walkouts have evolved into full-blown strikes and union contracts.

To show how the structure of economic opportunity and the norms and social relations of production combine to shape patterns of labor resistance, let us take the case of a large corporate farm that had over two hundred acres of strawberries on the Salinas Valley floor in 1986–87, which I will call "Johnson Berry Farm." The history of class relations on this farm challenges prevailing views of the stability of the agricultural labor force and the causes of union mobilization. As I discovered in short order during my interviews, most of the core workers and foremen on Johnson Berry Farm came from the same town in the state of Guanajuato, which I will call San Pedro. They also lived in the same housing camp in a small town south of Salinas. This pattern has persisted since the early 1960s, when the camp housed the employees of a labor contractor who served the bracero program. Paradoxically, although accounts usually portray farm workers as transients on the agricultural scene and farm owners as the permanent residents, the opposite was the case here. As on other large Salinas Valley berry farms, the workforce had remained relatively constant over the previous twenty years, while the owners had changed several times. Not only had many of the same workers passed on from one company to its successors, but the recruitment networks that replenished the labor supply were still based in the same familial and communal cores.

One Sunday afternoon in October, I arrived in this camp for the first of four interviews with resident workers. Children were playing in the dusty parking lot around which three rows of concrete bungalows and one row of trailers were clustered. My interviewee, a small, wiry man of thirty-two with bright brown eyes and curly black hair who had been coming to the camp since he was fifteen, stopped his project of fixing his trailer's roof. After we introduced ourselves, he took me on a brief walking tour up one dirt road of the camp, then down the other, while he described its history and residents. The picture he sketched was filled in by the rest of a four-hour interview with him, and by three subsequent interviews with other workers. Some workers lived in this camp year-round. Most returned to Mexico for one or two months around Christmas. From April through September, the camp's population ballooned, as most of the adult males and many of the women and children of San Pedro arrived for the harvest. A jumble of ramshackle cars, trucks, and vans nudged up against the trailers and bungalows of the permanent residents. My first interviewee pointed to these vehicles and said:

> You see those cars? Each one of them has three or four people sleeping inside. Most of them are related to those of us who live here all year. Many do not have papers. But they are much better off than the illegals without connections. They sleep in the cars but they also have a house where they can eat and be with their families. Their families help them find work and help them if anything happens. We are fortunate. The worst thing is to be alone in a foreign country. Most of the town is here in the summer. We like it here. Here, we are almost in Mexico [*Aquí, casi estamos en México*].

The history of this farm challenges notions of farm workers' impermanence and lack of commitment to their jobs, and it forces us to reassess causal relationships in union mobilization. Scholarly analyses of union movements, as well as popular discussions of the UFW, tend to view the union as the active party and workers as its targets and beneficiaries. Victories are attributed to the efficacy of union strategies and openings in the wider political-economic structure (cf. Majka and Majka 1982; Jenkins 1983, 1985). But in this case, and in others I encountered, the vectors of initiative were reversed. Workers on Johnson Berry Farm were strongly affected by union mobilization: they or their relatives had lived through the heady early years when the UFW swept in with its transformative vision of ethnic power and workplace justice. Many participated in union rallies and marches, some worked for unionized farms, and all shared the mood of raised expectations that accompanied the union's arrival. Over the years, these workers developed a tradition of workplace justice that was informed by the union experience but incubated in local communities on both sides of the border. Long before their first trip north, young people from San Pedro heard discussions about what they could and should expect picking strawberries in the Salinas Valley. All of the workers interviewed knew the minimum wage rate and were aware that they should be paid for overtime. All knew the difference between workers' compensation insurance, which is legally mandated, and the health insurance that some employers provide, which is not. All saw their employers as having interests that differed from their own.

As a result, these workers responded quickly to degradations of pay levels and working conditions, even without the stimulus of direct union organizing. One of my most interesting discoveries was that *all three* of the intense strawberry union struggles that gave the UFW its reputation for effective outreach in this industry were waged on this same parcel of land with the same communal core of workers. The Johnson company was simply the most recent occupant of this conflict-ridden terrain, whose crop was harvested by workers who were, by then, independent carriers of a community tradition of resistance. Johnson farms a portion of Pic N Pac—the huge berry ranch whose workers struck in 1970. Its two predecessors suffered union organizing campaigns and strikes, as well. In none of these cases did the union initiate the walkouts. Rather, workers formulated the grievances, initiated the confrontations, and then brought the union in for support. Although these struggles erupted initially over wages, they progressed into struggles for union representation. To outside observers, they appeared an example of effective union organizing; in fact, workers were their own organizers and initiators.

An extended walkout on this ranch the year before my interview illustrates the processes of resistance in this locality. That year, in order to improve the quality of its product and its market returns, Johnson Berry Farm changed its pay method from a straight piece method of $1.30 per crate to an hourly base of $4.00 plus $0.50 per crate. Although this change provided a floor to the earnings of full-season employees, it promised to depress the earnings of many (primarily men) who stayed only for the peak and then moved on to vegetable work. Even if their wives continued in strawberries for the entire season, workers figured that family earnings would suffer with the new pay method, given how hard they would drive themselves and how many crates they could pick at the peak. After discussing the pay method shift in the housing camp, the San Pedro workers asked one of their foremen to request a return to the previous method. When the manager of the company refused, most of these core workers walked out. "It wasn't fair," one explained to me heatedly. "We fought for that wage. It's less than what my uncle makes at Sun Harvest. They just wanted to make more off of us. They didn't think of us and our families." As the days stretched into weeks and the company persisted with its new pay policy, the striking workers sought work elsewhere. Most secured employment with a labor contractor who paid $1.27 per crate of berries. After the strawberry peak, many moved on to vegetable crops. Those I interviewed figured that they came out better with the lower piece rate than they would have with the hourly-plus-piece, because they picked so many crates when the crop was plentiful.

Meanwhile, Johnson Berry Company replaced most of its core workers with newcomers whom the long-time pickers, the foremen, and even the ranch manager characterized as inexperienced and slow. The company continued the new pay method for the entire season. When the next season started, it shifted the pay method again, a move workers interpreted as an effort to bring back the experienced pickers by rewarding their speed at a higher level, while still achieving a higher-quality pack by rewarding care. This pay method offered a \$3.35 base, \$0.65 per crate for the first three crates, then \$1.00 for each additional crate, with the requirement that pickers meet the average picking rate. With this shift, core pickers returned to the ranch, satisfied they had won their demands.

As this encounter shows, workers' long experience in the Salinas Valley has created a sense of entitlement to pay levels like those on nearby vegetable ranches. Their residential and communal cohesion helps them crystallize rapid responses to perceived infractions of justice. In contrast to workers in other areas, they have little empathy with owners. In fact they tend to think of management as an impersonal "they" or "it," rather than an individual "he." Because job alternatives are more plentiful, and structures of job access more open, workers depend less on strawberry jobs and can sustain resistance for an extended period of time. This pattern contrasts sharply with those in the other two areas.

The North Monterey Hills

Berry workers in the North Monterey Hills are the least likely to challenge the terms of work. This tendency, too, is based in the economic organization, class composition, and production relations of the locality.

Economic Organization and Class Composition

In comparison with the other two microregions, berry farms are the smallest and most poorly financed in hilly North Monterey County: the average berry farm size was twenty-seven acres in 1985 and 55 percent of the growers had fewer than fifteen acres. Almost 75 percent of the growers are of Mexican origin. Most lack capital, farming experience, facility in English, and social connections to the local farming system. Not surprisingly, growers here invest the least per acre in their crops, regulate workers least for the quality of their work, and direct their crops to the processed market and to the lower end of the fresh market.

Employment opportunities are limited here. Berry farms are virtually the only agricultural employers, with the recent and limited exception of nurseries. Farms are especially isolated, situated far from each other in remote valleys and at the end of winding dirt roads, and screened from paved roadways by live oak, pampas grass, and underbrush. Workers here interact little with individuals off their employing farms. They have the fewest social links to other jobs and are the least informed about other wages and working conditions. Job access structures here are mixed: both open and closed. Most core workers are recruited through networks of personal acquaintance, usually via the links of growers to their Mexican villages of origin. Most peripheral workers are unconnected "walk-ons." Overall, berry farms here employ the highest proportion of walk-ons and illegals. Growers' unpaid household members (daughters, sons, wives) work on small farms, and the vast majority of employees are young men in their mid-teens to early twenties. Growers and workers agree—and my experience confirms—that virtually all are illegal.[5]

North Monterey County is the major central coast entry point for unconnected illegals, in part because of the physical protection the area offers, and in part because of its less desirable jobs. New undocumented immigrants value the plentiful cost-free shelter of these sparsely populated hills and the rarity of Border Patrol raids on its secluded ranches (see plate 10). Beyond the advantage of sanctuary, however, illegals are more able to obtain work here because growers are more likely to employ walk-ons and because documented workers disdain the area's low, unstable wages and poor working conditions. Not only are growers lax in providing the legal entitlements of a minimum wage, overtime pay, and workers' compensation and unemployment insurance here, but health insurance and paid vacations are unheard of. In this locality, growers pay by the piece, encouraging workers to place speed above care. Many growers pay in cash, thus eliminating costly payroll taxes as well as records of employment. Average hourly wages and piece rates are lowest here and pay methods reduce the size and stability of incomes. Consequently, workers with experience, connections, or legal immigration status try to get work elsewhere. Growers are well aware of this pattern. "Legals," they say, "cannot be trusted to stay in the hills," and, indeed, many growers explicitly recruit illegals.

[5]Although I use the present tense in this discussion, let me remind the reader that conditions such as the proportion of undocumented workers may have changed with the enforcement of the Immigration Reform and Control Act after the late 1980s.

Plate 10. Approach to a strawberry ranch in the North Monterey Hills. Photo author

Employment Strategies

Workers' employment strategies reflect the opportunity structure of the microregion. Workers are highly dependent on strawberry jobs, because their alternatives are so limited. Core workers tend to stay in berries for the entire season. Some even stay for the winter because the return to Mexico is so costly and dangerous. Walk-ons remain until they hear of something better: perhaps in the middle of that season, perhaps two years hence. All in all, employment relationships are shortest here and the proportion of transitory workers is greatest. Although a few workers (mostly relatives of the grower) have stayed with the same grower for as much as a decade, most move down to the valley floors after several years. Salinas Valley labor contractors are the most common conduits out of the hills.

Production Relations

The paucity of resistance in this area reflects the social context. North Monterey County is a world apart from the valley floors. Here, growers' and workers' lives are intimately intertwined in a pattern of social exchange and expectation that is firmly based in the experience of Mexico. What makes the pattern here so distinct is the Mexican ethnic commonality of growers and workers, the economic and political marginality of both, and the relative isolation of the area from the central coast region as a whole. The vast majority of workers are inexperienced and undocumented, and most growers lack capital, experience, and integration into the established farming community. These factors generate a highly personalized pattern of production relations characterized by a low degree of social distance between growers and workers and a Mexico-based reference point for workplace justice. This pattern undermines workers' willingness and ability to challenge the mandates of their employers, creating dyadic dependencies rather than class-based opposition between them.

The limited resources of growers lead to smaller ranch size and the extensive involvement of growers in daily farming operations. Growers and workers therefore often have face-to-face relationships, a personalism that is enhanced by common linguistic, cultural, geographic, and even family backgrounds. All growers began as immigrants and many as illegals. As immigrant ethnics in a foreign country, they are part of the same enclave. Work relationships are paternalistic, couched in the patron-client conventions so central to Mexican culture (Wolf 1966). As a result, the structure and content of the social relations of production contrast sharply with those on the Salinas Valley floor. Their structure is one of generalized status asymmetry. Whereas authority hierarchies on Salinas Valley berry farms are focused narrowly around the employment context, the status asymmetry between North Monterey County growers and their workers extends far beyond the world of work. Mexican growers demand a personal deference not expected by Anglo employers. Its protocols mirror those found in Mexican employment relationships on the large agricultural estates where many berry pickers worked previously. Workers express their deference by calling their employer *el patrón* (the patron). The grower's status often extends to his village of origin, where he maintains the status of a patron in Mexico by employing villagers in the United States. This status is particularly important to growers because deference and authority, rather than significant economic gain, is the major benefit of their positions. In the Salinas Valley, by contrast, workers are more likely to refer to their employer as *el dueño* (the farm owner) or *la companía* (the company). Similarly, many North Monterey County growers and workers refer collectively to field workers as *peones* (peons). In Salinas, *trabajadores del campo* (farm workers) is the term of choice, and workers scorn the term *peón* as a degrading feudal relic.

The content of production relations is distinct, as well. In the Salinas

Valley, the implied obligation of employers and the evaluation of employment relationships are based narrowly on the terms of work—mostly on wages and legally mandated benefits. In North Monterey County, grower-patrons are more diffusely obliged to care for their worker-clients, and legal entitlements rarely enter into assessments of workplace justice. Growers here present the very act of employment as the gift of a gracious benefactor. For workers, this perception has some basis in reality, given their scarce alternatives and the high local influxes of illegal immigrants. In return for the "favor" of employment, workers are expected to work hard and without complaint. In some instances, repayment of their obligation approaches the status of debt servitude: in one case, eight first-time border crossers were hired and given a shed to sleep in at the start of the strawberry season. In return, they were expected to work without pay for the months of April and September.

Workplace norms in this microregion explicitly reject wages and legally mandated protections as standards of workplace justice. They do so, first, by framing the employment relationship as one of apprenticeship. This representation justifies low wages and accords growers credit for providing experience. It is reinforced by workers' knowledge that higher-paying employers require experience, and by the evidence that some of their colleagues move on to better jobs after working in the hills. Workers express this perspective through comments such as "I owe a lot to Don José. He taught me how to pick berries when I didn't know anything." Second, comparison with the alternative of Mexican employment dismisses U.S. entitlements as measures of workplace justice. Growers are familiar with economic conditions in Mexico, and they contrast their own jobs with those workers could get at home. A number of times, for example, growers pointed out to me and to workers in my presence that their employees were lucky to have their jobs, because they would be making $3.00 a day in Mexico. Such comments diverted attention from the fact that these growers paid a constant $3.00 to $3.50 an hour throughout the season, in a year when the minimum hourly wage in agriculture was $3.35, the average hourly wage on central coast berry farms was $4.21, and the average hourly wage incorporating the customary peak season piece-rate incentive was $5.53. Growers' familiarity with workers' communal and family backgrounds also helps them direct attention away from the rate of pay relative to regional practices and toward workers' paychecks as lifelines for their families in Mexico. Growers admonish workers not to complain, because many people depend on them. They may refer specifically to dependents whom they know. Such admonitions heighten workers' fear of dismissal and shift the reference point for assessing workplace justice away from

U.S. wage standards and toward workers' economic obligations and purchasing power in Mexico.

North Monterey County growers may not provide the labor entitlements that are legal and customary in the region, but many do provide an unusually wide range of other benefits that are seen as privileges of the patronal relationship. Workers focus on these privileges in their positive evaluations of their jobs. Here, again, their reference point is Mexico. For example, growers here are the most likely in the region to loan workers part or all of the *coyote's* fee of about $350. Such loans are usually made only to returning workers or to workers from families with whom the grower is closely connected. Usually growers deduct loan repayments from workers' paychecks over the course of the season. The hope of future employment and social pressure from the worker's extended family help ensure loan repayment and performance. Growers here are also the most likely to provide shelter, either in existing structures or vehicles on the ranch, or through explicit or implicit permission to camp out on the ranch property. Many provide transportation to town or to work, and the wives of some prepare food for their workers. All of these benefits are phrased as favors. The permission to camp is usually free, but charges for other services are deducted from workers' wages. The granting of such privileges sets up a dynamic of indebtedness and dependency that dampens the emergence of labor resistance. It also increases the isolation of these workers from workers on other farms.

The case of Zenón Sanchez illustrates this isolation and the socioeconomic motivations that support it. Sanchez first came to North Monterey County in February 1980 as a fourteen-year-old undocumented worker. He came from Michoacán, where his family had eight unirrigated hectares of land on which they planted maize for self-consumption. The only monetary income for the two parents and their seven children came from the erratic earnings of the eldest son, who worked as a taxi driver in a nearby town. To help the family survive, Zenón traveled north with a friend who had worked for two seasons with a North Monterey grower. He was accepted for a job immediately. Zenón lived and worked on this ranch for six years, picking berries in the summers and helping with ranch maintenance in the winters. He lived in a shed on the ranch and cooked his meals over a campfire with other workers. Constantly aware of the importance of his income to his family in Mexico, he did not leave the ranch at all for the first two years, to avoid getting caught by the *migra.* After the second year he began to make occasional trips off the ranch, but he still avoided bars and spent most evenings and weekends there. He returned home "to see [his] mother" in Mexico only once over the six years. Zenón was able to stretch his meager earnings to a remarkable extent. In 1980, he made $5,000 and sent $4,500 back to Mexico. In 1981, he made $4,000 and sent $3,000 back. From 1982 through 1985, he made $3,000 and sent about $2,000 back. Not only did he survive in the United States on $500 to $1,000 a year, but his remittances almost entirely supported eight individuals in Mexico.

In short, workers' off-the-job community structures here are highly intertwined with those of their employers, and connections to their peers on other farms are minimal. In effect, growers and workers occupy the same social world. Most workers live on or near their employing ranch, and many see their employers before and after work. The two share language, ethnic and national background, often relatives and acquaintances, and a Mexico-based perspective on workplace justice. Although their relations are often close, they are also hierarchical: growers are firmly the patrons, and they call the shots. Thus, personalism and paternalism predominate over polarity in class relations. Common backgrounds and dependency increase the closeness of employment relationships. The strongest social ties tend to be vertical rather than horizontal: workers are often more closely connected to their employers than they are to their peers. Because almost all daily life is incorporated into the patron-client relationship, workers have little physical or psychological latitude in which to develop perspectives independent from those of their employers. Much less can they mobilize acts of collective resistance.

Labor Resistance

To illustrate how the social and material conditions of work in this area undermine workers' perceptions and expressions of resistance, I offer the case of José Ballín, a North Monterey County berry grower charged with a wide range of health, housing, and labor code violations in 1985. These charges were initiated by the Salinas office of California Rural Legal Assistance (CRLA), a legal services law firm funded to protect the rights of migrant farm workers. The case came to CRLA's attention through one of its community workers—individuals, most with a Mexican and farm labor background, who are well-reputed in the worker community and help bring potential cases to the firm. In this case, the community worker heard through his networks that living and working conditions on Ballín's ranch were deplorable. He visited the ranch, talked with the workers and finally convinced four of them to come into the CRLA office to discuss their situation. It took lengthy conversations with these four workers and guarantees against retaliation to convince eight others to support the suit.

Their reluctance to speak up was based in the social relations of production. Ballín was an exceptionally large-scale producer for the area, with over three hundred acres of berries in 1985. About two-thirds of his land was sharecropped; the rest was worked by wage laborers. Despite the size of his operation, Ballín directly hired and helped manage his workers. According to workers interviewed by CRLA staff, most of his wage workers were in their middle teens. The oldest were in their mid-twenties. Many had worked for Ballín for several years. Virtually all were undocumented. According to workers, this composition was no accident: Ballín regularly asked new recruits whether they had papers, and he refused to hire those that did. During the peak, they worked from seven in the morning to ten or eleven at night, without overtime. They were paid $3.00 an hour throughout the season, in a year when the minimum wage for farm workers was $3.35 an hour. Most made from $2,000 to $3,000 annually, on which they supported a variety of dependents in Mexico. In a 1986 interview, Lydia Villareal, the CRLA lawyer who initiated the court suit, told me about her first visit to Ballín's ranch:

> I was devastated, physically ill, when I first went to the ranch. They [the workers] were living in holes in the ground, like rabbits. The workers said that when they arrived, Ballín handed them a shovel and told them to dig themselves a home. The caves were about five feet long, five feet wide, and two-and-a-half feet high. In some cases three or four workers slept in the same cave. The insides of the caves broke your heart. There were toothbrushes hanging on a nail and a few blankets. Inside one was a suitcase with a letter saying, "Be sure not to spend too much money up there. You know how much we depend on your income." Later the workers were checked by doctors and found to have dysentery and maybe tuberculosis because of the health conditions.

The Monterey County Health Department confirmed this desolate picture of workers' living conditions. On one ranch it found

> 50 to 60 farm workers living in storage sheds, pick-ups, campers, makeshift cardboard and tin shacks, outhouses and truck bodies; not adequate or approved toilet facilities; no potable water from an approved water system; all food preparation areas were sub-standard; an accumulation of garbage, trash and refuse scattered throughout the complex; no proper facilities for the disposal of garbage and trash; sleeping and living areas did not conform with the Uniform Housing Code, California Health and Safety Code and California Administrative Code; human waste was present inside and outside of the various living areas; pesticides, fertilizers and poison baits were stored within the living, sleeping, and cooking areas; open pesticide containers and spilled poison baits were within the living, cooking and sleeping

> areas; occupants ate their meals while sitting on and around pesticide containers; and hazardous materials, including pesticides, were stored on the premises and not registered with the Monterey County Health Department.[6]

The health department found similar violations on Ballín's other two ranches, affecting an annual total of about two hundred workers. The case drew national attention. Workers' name for the ranch—Rancho de Cuevas (the ranch of caves)—captured the imagination of the press. Photographs of a farm worker crawling out of a cave were sent out over the national news networks. The bishop of the Monterey County Roman Catholic Diocese visited the ranch and reported "subhuman conditions." Local editorials decried the contradiction between California's agricultural abundance and the squalor in which its producers lived. Governor George Deukmejian proclaimed it "totally inexcusable" for farm workers to live in cardboard shelters and holes in the ground, and he urged prosecution of growers who permitted such conditions.[7]

As shocking as outsiders found these conditions, neither the grower nor his workers found them particularly unusual. First, Ballín's own background and living conditions did not differ greatly from those of his employees. Far from being a member of the agricultural elite, he was a fifty-nine-year-old former farm worker who had been born in Mexico and had completed a sixth grade education there. He first came to the United States in 1952 as an illegal immigrant. He worked as a farm worker until he saved enough money to buy his first piece of property in 1960: a small berry farm six-and-a-half acres in size. He and his wife continued to work for other farmers to support their small farm. Gradually, they increased their acreage, until the farm reached its current size. At the time of the suit, he and his wife ran the farm themselves and said it took most of their time. They lived on one of the properties investigated, in conditions that were far below local standards. The court record summarized its report on Ballín's personal residence:

> The investigation revealed a travel trailer occupied without approved sewer or water connections; a pit privy being used for sewage disposal; an accu-

[6]Action No. 31891, Municipal Court of California, County of Monterey, Salinas Judicial District, State of California, December 16, 1985, p. 7.

[7]See " 'Inexcusable,' Governor Says of Some Farm Workers' Plight," *Los Angeles Times,* 4 October 1985, p. 1; "Suit Claims Grower Kept Farmworkers in Slave-Like Conditions," *Davis Enterprise,* 24 September 1985, p. 7; "Border Patrol Finds Some Aliens Anxious to Go Home," *Daily Californian* (El Cajon, Calif.), 9 November 1985, p. 2; "Workers Live in Caves, Suit against Farmer Says," *Sacramento Bee,* 24 September 1985, p. 1; "Sub-Human," *Salinas Californian,* 24 September 1985, p. 2.

> mulation of trash and debree [sic] scattered about the west portion of the property; a gas fired water heater in a bedroom; no ventilation in the bedroom; no openable windows in the bedrooms; improperly installed wood burning stove; unvented gas stove in the bedroom; no electrical outlets in the bedroom; a leaking sink trap which was taped; a travel trailer attached to a stationary dwelling; a building not designed for occupancy was currently occupied; and sewage was running on the ground. The defendant and his family were occupying the units in violation. (note 6, p. 8)

Not only did Ballín himself live in circumstances that many U.S.-born growers would have found unacceptable, but he saw his workers' shelter as evidence of his generosity. Ballín saw himself as his workers' *patrón,* and he offered many benefits in addition to wages. He let workers live on his land without charge, he made small loans to sustain some between paychecks, and—in response to phone calls from the border—he paid the *coyote* for several reliable returning workers and deducted it from their first paychecks. The court's summary of Ballín's statement reveals his perspective (pp. 9–10).

> The defendant stated that it was his opinion they liked it there because there was no charge. They were not on his property permanently, only during the strawberry season. . . . The defendant was asked how he felt about the conditions under which the individuals lived. He indicated that they lived that way by choice. He pointed out that some of the people lived under worse conditions in Mexico. While on his property, these individuals never complained. They received their salaries, the areas were relatively clean, and they were out of the weather. . . . He indicated that (with regard to the matter of their using the hillside as a toilet) in Mexico it is very common in the poor neighborhoods for individuals to go outside and away from their residence to go to the bathroom. . . . He went on to state that he feels somewhat betrayed by the individuals who have testified against him. He gave them the opportunity to save their money and to move to a place of their own. However, they refused, staying voluntarily.

According to CRLA lawyers and community workers, most of Ballín's workers would have confirmed his representation of their situation and sentiments, before the court case gathered steam. It took weeks of favorable local and national publicity, the personal visits and support of church and community leaders, assurances from the Border Patrol that illegals would not be deported, and the provision of alternative shelter to eventually draw a remarkable total of fifty workers into the suit. The rest remained silent.

The social dynamics of this case are by no means unique. Many of the North Monterey workers I interviewed described similar circumstances on their ranches. "It's what *sinpapeles* can expect," one commented with a shrug. Growers on the valley floors often refer to the hills as "little Mexico," thus acknowledging (but also exaggerating) the uniqueness of the locality by placing it symbolically in a different country. Health, employment, and housing authorities express frustration at the repetitive citations they have issued here over the years: the reoccupying of condemned living quarters and the resumption of illegal employment practices shortly after reprimands have been issued and fines paid. In fact, the public testimony of Ballín's workers and the extent of their public support were unprecedented in the locality. Other cases have surfaced briefly since that time. In one, local officials initiated the investigation. In the other two, workers who had recently gained legal immigration status through the Immigration Reform and Control Act of 1986 brought unlawful conditions to public attention.

In short, social and economic conditions in the North Monterey Hills discourage the expression, and even the experience, of a sense of injustice at the conditions of work. Workers here are generally ignorant of U.S. labor entitlements and unlikely to challenge the practices of their employers. To my knowledge and that of my informants, strikes and walkouts are unheard of here. Minimum wage rates and overtime pay, which are seen as contractual and impersonal entitlements in the Salinas Valley, are viewed as the employer's personal dispensations here—appropriately contingent on the tenor of his relations with his employees. None of the workers I interviewed here knew that workers' compensation insurance was legally required. They thought it was grower-provided health insurance—evidence of their patron's magnanimity. Workers in North Monterey County accept employment conditions which would galvanize resistance in the other two microregions, and growers appeal to the personal relationships between them to secure tolerance of substandard conditions. Growers protest with some justification that they cannot afford Salinas Valley wages. They represent their farms as family and Mexican businesses—as stepping-stones for kin and compatriots to the opportunities of the north. In return, they expect their workers to help the family farm prosper. Although most hire enough workers to fall under protective laws, many ignore them in practice. Some growers pay a low hourly rate throughout the season, relying on personal obligation and threats of replacement to ensure the speed of labor. Most pay a low piece rate throughout the season, using the same pressures to ensure labor's care. Even those who shift from hourly to piece and back, as the yields fluctuate, tend to delay their seasonal switches longer than growers on the valley floors and thus lower workers' earnings. In the context of North Monterey County, however, the practice elicits no open protest.

The Pajaro Valley

The Pajaro Valley falls between the other two localities in the form and extent of workers' resistance. This pattern, too, has roots at the local level.

Economic Organization and Class Composition

Pajaro Valley berry farms tend to be well financed and intermediate in size. The range of farm size is greatest here: though the average was 40 acres in 1985, 19 percent of the farms were 50 acres or larger, 81 percent were under 49 acres, and 46 percent were under 15 acres. Japanese Americans comprise the largest segment of the grower population (46 percent). Together, Anglos and Japanese account for 74 percent of the growers and 88 percent of the acreage. Mexicans are the smallest group in size and acreage. Most occupy marginal land at the periphery of the valley and are minimally integrated into local farming networks. As we saw in Chapter 4, Japanese and Anglo growers in this area have the most experience farming berries and are the most cohesive. Farms here are, with one exception, owner-operated. Most are solidly financed—not because owners have extensive assets to invest, as do the large Salinas Valley corporations, but because they have farmed successfully for years and have accumulated savings and good credit ratings. Growers here are the most stable and conservative in their economic strategies. They borrow the least to support their ongoing operations and contribute the most to their own financing.[8] In contrast with growers in the North Monterey Hills, their loans generally come from established lending agencies. Not surprisingly, they have the lowest rates of turnover and bankruptcies. On the average, they invest the most per acre in their crops and are the most likely to concentrate on the high quality end of the fresh berry market—practices which their carefully tended fields reflect (see plate 11).

The level and stability of wages are also highest in the Pajaro region. Interviews revealed that hourly wages are on the average 23 percent higher than those in the Salinas Valley and 28 percent higher than those in North

[8]This pattern is influenced by the high proportion of Japanese growers in the area, but Anglos here also supply more of their own financing.

Plate 11. Berry harvest on the coastal bluffs, Pajaro Valley. Photo Jack Kelly Clark, courtesy University of California

Monterey County. Most growers here use the hourly-plus-piece pay method during the heart of the season. For growers, this method encourages high picking quality while maintaining incentives for speed. For workers, it moderates seasonal fluctuations in earnings and provides a relatively high floor for hourly wages. Most farms offer at least the minimum wage, overtime pay, and workers' compensation and unemployment insurance. Some still continue the health insurance and other benefits initiated during the peak of union pressure.

Employment opportunities are more restricted here than in the Salinas Valley but broader than they are in the North Monterey County Hills. Strawberry farms are the main employers of field workers, but bushberries, lettuce and miscellaneous vegetables, and apples also contribute. Canneries hire locally resident women for a season that conflicts with the strawberry harvest. The local presence of these industries expands workers' employment alternatives and reduces their reliance on strawberry employers. However, this expansion is less extensive than in the Salinas Valley, because alternative jobs are fewer and access to all positions is more restricted. Job access structures are the most closed in this microregion.

Berry jobs are exceptionally dependent on personal connections. Because growers are so concerned with harvest quality, most require new hires to have personal recommendations and experience. Berry growers here try hardest to use core workers for as many tasks as possible and to hire walk-ons and contracted crews only as a last resort. Entry barriers restrict access to nonstrawberry jobs as well. Bushberries are usually worked by carefully screened sharecroppers. Vegetable harvest jobs are relatively few in number and require personal connections to secure. Cannery jobs are unionized, so access to them is restricted. Because most labor contractors and vegetable companies are based in Salinas, vegetable thinning and weeding jobs are less accessible to Pajaro workers. Apple growers do hire for the harvest within the locality, but they rely on the recommendations of existing workers for new hires.

Employment Strategies

The employment strategies of workers reflect the opportunity structure of the microregion. Workers here are more dependent on strawberry employment than in the Salinas Valley, but less so than in the North Monterey Hills. Most try to maximize their employment in strawberries, spending the entire season with a single grower. The desired length of a worker's employment depends on whether he or she is based in Mexico or the United States. Workers based in Mexico generally prefer to return in September. Local residents often pick up important increments of income at the end of the berry season from the apple harvest and from unemployment insurance. Other crops play a relatively minor role in individual incomes. It is more common here than in the Salinas Valley for all working-age adults in a household to work in the strawberry industry. Industry crossovers—of the husband to a lettuce crew or a wife to a cannery—do take place, however. High strawberry pay rates, the hourly-plus pay method, restricted access to equally remunerative jobs such as the vegetable harvest, and the scarcity of such positions by contrast with the Salinas Valley, all encourage workers' reliance on strawberries. So do the paucity of locally recruiting labor contractors and the shortage of easily enterable piece-rate harvests that coincide with, immediately precede, or follow the strawberry peak. The apple harvest in late August or September is the main source of sequenced or competing employment for berry workers, but this competition is not usually problematic, because strawberry yields and labor demand decline at that time. The hourly-plus pay method discourages the Salinas employment strategy of combining peak-season piece-rate work in several crops, because it prevents the very high earnings that motivated piece-rate workers can earn at the peak. At the same time, hourly-plus encourages continuity with a single employer, because it distributes and stabilizes earnings over the season. Growers in this microregion are explicit about preferring such full-season workers, believing that they are more careful and reliable.

Production Relations

Pajaro Valley production relations combine aspects of those in the other two microregions. They are personalistic, as in North Monterey County, but based on U.S. standards of workplace justice, as in Salinas. Instead of the class-based polarity of Salinas Valley farms, we find here the dyadic dependencies of the North Monterey Hills. Yet the dependency and the intertwining of patrons' and clients' lives are less. In the Pajaro Valley, many facets of workers' lives fall outside the patron-client relationship. The social distance between growers and workers is intermediate, and considerable solidarity prevails among workers. Several factors contribute to this pattern, including the scale and structure of farming; the ethnic identity and resource level of farmers; the citizenship status, longevity in the system, and off-the-job community structure of workers; and the placement of the microregion vis à vis the centers of union pressure.

First, because most berry farms are small or midsized and are operated by their owners, the opportunities for social exchange between growers and workers are relatively frequent. Although on some large ranches workers only know their foreman, most interact directly with the farm owner in his role as employer, labor supervisor, production manager, or problem solver. Workers here tend to see the grower as their patron, with the status asymmetry that this relationship entails. But the local availability of job alternatives and the greater social distance between workers and their Japanese and Anglo employers, reduce workers' dependency on these patrons. The two do not share the language, cultural values, social networks, and experience that lend North Monterey County patron-client relations such intimacy and pervasiveness. Nor are patron-growers in the Pajaro region carriers of a cultural tradition of workplace justice derived from Mexico. Rather, they are U.S. nationals whose own notions of labor relations were forged in the crucible of the central coast. Though these notions assume status asymmetry between growers and workers, the disparity in status is much less marked.

Because workers here are the most likely to be documented and to have spent many years in the local system, their dependency on their immediate employers is less. Growers avoid hiring walk-ons; some have employed the same family networks for over two generations. Because most farms are worked by one or two family groupings, their potential for solidarity is considerable. As compared with the North Monterey Hills, Pajaro Valley workers tend to be more experienced; better aware of their alternatives; more thoroughly connected to jobs, employers, and workers in the area; more willing to speak out; and more in touch with the standards for labor treatment that have developed over the years of union struggle.

Workers' off-the-job community structure provides more physical and psychological separation from growers and more solidarity among workers than in North Monterey County, although less than in the Salinas Valley. It increases workers' willingness and ability to articulate interests counter to those of their employers, and their capacity to take action on these interests. Growers here rarely provide housing, although some own a garage or a small house that they rent to favored workers. Most workers find their own places to live in one of several labor camps on the outskirts of Watsonville or in the run-down houses and apartment complexes scattered around town. Farm worker populations are especially dense in several neighborhoods, providing contexts in which workers can interact and process the events of their days. Finally, because the locality is somewhat removed from the center of union pressure in Salinas but still strongly linked to it, workers tend to be at once aware of the issues, but not sharply polarized. Many participated in the 1970 strike and have attended rallies and marches over the years. But there have been no worker-initiated union contracts on berry farms here.[9] Generally workers know their legal entitlements and carry the UFW's vision of farm worker empowerment. They attend to labor victories on other central coast farms, and are quick to request comparable improvements for themselves.

Labor Resistance

What sets the Pajaro Valley apart from the other two areas is its personalistic, yet negotiative, pattern of workplace relations. In contrast to North Monterey County, where workers rarely if ever question the terms set by the grower, challenges of wage rates and unjust treatment are relatively frequent here. Yet these challenges are less confrontational than in Salinas, and much less likely to interrupt the course of work. Pajaro Valley workers

[9]At least one grower initiated a short-lived "sweetheart" contract with the Teamsters during the UFW insurgency of the early 1970s.

do speak up about breaches of the social contract during the seasonal transitions in pay methods, and they pressure growers to match wage increases on neighboring farms. But their discourse on such occasions tends to employ the consensual language of "fairness," rather than the oppositional language of "entitlement" familiar in the Salinas area. Pajaro workers are more inclined than Salinas workers to negotiate and factor the personal circumstances of the grower into the solutions they will accept. Their personal relationships with growers, the more limited and closed array of local employment alternatives, and the special measures that growers take to ensure labor compliance and commitment all encourage their accommodation.

This negotiative pattern of labor relations is also connected to growers' resource levels and production strategies. In the Pajaro Valley, as in other segmented labor markets (Doeringer and Piore 1971), high capital investment is correlated with high investment in labor control. Because growers here have the highest nonlabor investments in their crops per acre, and because they aim for high crop quality to recoup those investments with high market prices, careless picking and harvest disruptions are most costly to them. Because they invest the most in labor training, retraining is also the most expensive. As a result, growers here devote the greatest effort to ensuring the stability, care, and commitment of labor. Measures to increase and stabilize workers' incomes are at the heart of this investment. They include high wage levels, hourly-plus pay methods, and the most explicit policy of maximizing the employment of core workers. Growers here are the most likely to plant crops with a short-lived labor demand, such as peppers or squash, in order to provide work for their core workers during lulls in the strawberry harvest. Many adjust their planting and harvest schedules so that some or all of their workers can move on to the apple harvest or draw unemployment insurance. They experiment the most with combinations of summer and winter plantings and short-day and day-neutral varieties to lengthen and flatten their harvests, and thus workers' incomes. In the interviews, they were the most likely to spontaneously identify this experimentation as a means of increasing workers' job satisfaction. Growers in all microregions spoke to the importance of overseeing, reprimanding, and controlling workers, but Pajaro growers spoke the most about positively motivating workers.

The example of one Japanese grower—let us call him Hiroshi Takaki—illustrates the reflection and effort that go into achieving smooth labor-management relations in this locality. Nothing is as important as making sure that the workers are satisfied, Takaki insisted:

> A grower should exploit the market, the technology, and the plants, but not the laborers. North Monterey County growers are mistaken in thinking they can make the greatest profits by exploiting labor. Labor is the source of profit in strawberries and it has to be well done. But you can't get commitment with exploitation. . . . Growers can't afford to save money on wages. You have to pay at least the going rate. You can't afford to pay much more than that. So you have to give them things that will make them want to stay.

Takaki himself offered what he called "mental money" to increase workers' job commitment. This package included a variety of benefits that workers themselves said they appreciated: knee pads, overshoes, giving workers two ten-minute breaks a day in addition to the lunch break, allowing them to take home occasional boxes of berries, granting leaves to tend sick children or visit relatives, and helping workers in their contacts with local institutions. Takaki also managed his workers so as to get "the highest quality of life per person possible for the fewest number of workers." By tapping his workers' family networks, Takaki sustained a relatively small core of full-season workers while providing periodic employment for a wide range of their relatives. He aptly deployed the incentives of hourly and piece-rate pay methods over the season: customarily, he paid workers by the hour, which supported his demand for top quality; when the crop was heavier than his core workers could handle, he shifted to piece rate for a day or two and asked workers to stay later and bring their experienced relatives. Because the shifts to piece rate were for a limited duration and because reemployment was at stake, Takaki was able to insist on and get the quality he required on hourly pay. All in all he had one of the lowest ratios of per-crate labor costs to market price in the region.

Takaki also had a profit-sharing plan for his workers. He described it as an example of the "symbiotic relationship" between growers and workers: "I do my job keeping up on scientific developments in strawberry production, on seeing that they are marketed well, and they do their part picking and taking care of the plants . . . and we all benefit. We need each other." Takaki's plan put a certain part of the yearly profits in a profit-sharing pension fund in which all workers and the boss participated. This fund accumulated tax-sheltered interest to be used by participants on retirement. Workers qualified for the plan by staying with the company for seven consecutive years and working a certain amount each year. Their returns were based on the amount of time served. Workers who quit or otherwise withdrew early had to pay a penalty. Takaki treated workers who left work without permission as having quit. This plan discouraged unexcused absences and quitting and encouraged workers to maximize the number of years and months per year they worked for him. Although most workers did not understand it, and would have preferred direct pay, the plan appeared to reduce turnover and increase workers' experience and reliability.[10]

This plan illustrates the exceptional attention that growers in this area devote to enhancing the commitment of labor. Takaki and others insist that the kind of close working relationship that is necessary in strawberries cannot be accomplished on large farms. Growers vary as to their visions of the optimal size. Most say that thirty to forty acres is the watershed after which labor relations are likely to become conflictual. Takaki thought that anything over fifteen acres became "difficult." He himself had almost thirty acres and felt he was at the outer limit of efficient and peaceful operation. Beyond that, he thought, workers would start to shirk, come to work irregularly, and leave before the end of the harvest. At least as important, he feared "rumbles" in the fields.

Larger Pajaro Valley farms also invest in labor commitment, using measures like those of forward-looking employers outside agriculture. The case of Morris Edwards, a prosperous, large-scale Anglo grower descended from a long line of berry producers, illustrates some of these methods. Edwards' investment in labor performance and predictability is one of the highest in the area. It includes the employment of a professionally trained personnel manager whom I will call Susan Montgomery. In 1986, she described her goal as "to get people more efficient and satisfied, to get things to run more consistently, and to get people to work together better." To these ends she trained field supervisors separately and in small groups in "communication, motivation, progressive discipline, and how to deal with complaints." She ran an orientation program for workers when they were first hired and returned to work each year. In this program they met in groups of ten to review the rules and the benefits package, to fill out their insurance registration cards, and to meet the supervisors with whom they would be working. Ms. Montgomery also planned and implemented a large end-of-year ranch party for employees from all of this growers' ranches, complete with barbecue, Mexican music, and raffled prizes. The grand prize was a trip to Hawaii, which the woman who won did not want, or could not take, and Ms. Montgomery ended up taking by default.

To enhance the intimacy of production relations on Edwards' several 80-

[10]Many of Takaki's workers aspired to stay the seven years, but few expected to harvest berries until retirement. As could be expected, the plan is most valued by the locally resident workers who comprise the largest portion of his workforce. Some workers see it as taking their rightful wages from them and putting them into a pot from which their employer can dip as well.

to 100-plus-acre ranches, he initiated a crew system that vested considerable authority in direct labor supervisors. Each commercial ranch had a ranch manager and four crew bosses who supervised from twenty-five to thirty workers each. Upon the crew bosses' suggestion, their titles were changed from the common *surquero* (row boss) to the more authoritative *mayordomo* (majordomo). As an experiment, the crew bosses were given all the responsibility for hiring and firing workers for planting, weeding, and harvesting. In effect, the crew bosses became the effective *patrones* from workers' points of view, and the crews developed considerable solidarity. The crews chose names, such as Los Tigres and Los Latinos. The company erected signs in the fields to compare their weekly performance along three dimensions: the average number of crates picked per hour per person for the week (measuring speed), the number of days without producing the low-quality crates called "standards" (measuring quality), and the number of days without a workers' compensation claim (measuring overhead costs). This system increased productivity markedly: workers enjoyed its competitive, gamelike aspect and also their increased earnings. It also reduced workers' compensation claims because workers pressured each other not to report and claim restitution for accidents.

Not all Pajaro Valley growers have devoted as much attention or as many resources to increasing the motivation of their workers as Takaki and Edwards. Nonetheless, on the whole, growers here are the most actively involved in increasing their workers' commitment and in undermining sources of their opposition. They act not only individually, but collectively as well. As noted earlier, Pajaro Valley growers are the most cohesive and socially interconnected. Thus it is not surprising that they exhibit the greatest degree of collective involvement in solving labor problems. North Monterey County growers are isolated from one other and tend to solve their labor problems individually, through personal dialogue with particular workers. Salinas Valley growers are somewhat more collective in their responses. Some belong to the Western Growers and Shippers Association and the Salinas Valley Independent Growers' Association, which provide advice and political representation on the issue of unionization. Both organizations, however, are dominated by large vegetable companies and do not directly address problems of the strawberry industry. Only in the Pajaro Valley do industry-specific berry grower organizations actively engage in labor-management struggles.

Perhaps the most public example of Pajaro Valley growers' collective mobilization came during the 1970 general strike. As described in Chapter 3, after the strike broke out in late August 1970 and spread from Salinas to Pajaro Valley farms, the members of Naturipe and Watsonville Berry Cooperative, along with ten large independent grower-shipper companies who together comprised almost all of the berry producers in the microregion, banded together to negotiate with the UFW. Stalling tactics enabled them to wait out the season, and early the following spring they instituted a more permanent response by forming the Pajaro Valley Strawberry Growers' Association (PVSGA). This organization provided labor relations advice and employee benefits such as health, accident, and life insurance coverage comparable to those offered by the UFW. Whereas Salinas berry growers obtained some of these benefits through the large vegetable associations, PVSGA offered assistance tailored to strawberry problems. For a number of years in the early 1970s, PVSGA employed a Spanish-speaking "labor relations expert" who visited members' ranches to detect labor unrest, identify union organizers, and convince workers that they could resolve their problems without a union.

Throughout the tumultuous 1970s and into the 1980s, Pajaro Valley growers sustained collective discussions as to how to respond to union pressure and contracts. The marketing associations and the CSAB were the most frequent and influential fora for such discussions. During the peak of union pressure, these organizations reviewed prevailing field labor wage rates and "suggested" a pay rate that berry growers should offer to avoid labor unrest. So closely was this scale geared to rates established by UFW vegetable contracts that growers said they could anticipate their future wage rates from the annual step increases of union contracts. Although the grower associations had no means of enforcing their suggested wage levels, peer pressure to observe them was strong because they were seen as a means of stemming the tide of unionization. One Japanese grower explained:

> The union is teaching our workers bad things. They know all about union wages. When union contracts grant a wage increase over in Salinas, they [workers] are out in the fields the next day telling us about it. It's the workers not the growers who are in charge now. They all communicate. A couple of weeks ago the union gave a 40-cent raise and now we are forced to give one too. I know that my workers will walk off the ranch if I don't. Some of them have been with me for years. We [growers] are all in the same boat. We have to stick together. In the association [his marketing cooperative] we talk about what to do. There's a suggested wage each year we try to stick to, but we can't always do it. It's rough.

In fact, farm labor experts in the local employment office estimate that most Pajaro Valley berry growers adhered to the wage level guidelines in the mid- and late 1970s. Marketing cooperative members note that, while some members were still paying the previous year's suggested rate at the start of the 1979 season, by its end all were paying the recommended wage for that year. When the Sun Harvest contract was signed on August 31, 1979, Pajaro Valley growers anticipated a one-dollar-per-hour increase in strawberry wages by the start of the following season. Indeed, that is what happened. The exchanges through which these increases were initiated mirror those described between the Japanese grower and his worker in the vignette at the start of this chapter. Seven growers recounted similar encounters around the time of the Sun Harvest contract. Some were initiated by a spokesperson. Others were direct engagements between individual workers and their supervisors. All in all, growers here respond more quickly to initiated negotiations than do those in the Salinas Valley, so that labor-management frictions are less likely to disrupt the harvest and are more quickly resolved. Growers do not necessarily respond by immediately raising wages, however. They often appeal to their personal relations with workers and their more limited resources to gain workers' tolerance of a delay until the following season. As a result, wage increases in the Pajaro Valley lag behind those in the Salinas Valley, although in the long run they come to rest at a higher average level. Thus, growers here use the bonds of personalism to delay, but not to avoid, wage increases.

Time, Place, and Resistance

Thus patterns of production relations and the timing and extent of labor resistance are highly variable—both over time and across space. The cyclical rhythms of the harvest cycle create fluctuations in the power capacities of growers and workers and violations of implicit standards of worker reward. Workers' willingness and ability to oppose these violations are shaped by the local organization of production.

Strawberry workplace struggles unfold in three distinct microregions that provide different opportunity structures for the conduct of class relations at work. To summarize: in the Salinas Valley, more plentiful job opportunities and open access to jobs increase workers' leverage and decrease their dependence on strawberry employers. Production relations involve a high degree of social distance and weak personal ties between growers and workers, a U.S.-based reference point for workplace justice, and strong horizontal ties among workers. Here, workers' relatively autonomous community structures support more radical, oppositional relations with employers. All in all, production relations in this microregion help workers coalesce common interests counter to those of their employers, encouraging class polarities rather than dyadic dependencies. Not surprisingly, labor resistance is the most frequent and sustained in this microregion.

The local organization of production in the North Monterey Hills reinforces the dependency of workers. The mix of open and closed job access structures permits workers some economic mobility and independence. But the undocumented status of most workers, the isolation of farms, and the local paucity of other jobs make workers highly dependent on their immediate employers. Production relations here undermine workers' ability to collectively oppose the demands of their employers, creating dyadic dependencies rather than class-based opposition. Vertical bonds of patron clientage are strong, social distance between growers and workers is minimal, and horizontal solidarity among workers is weak. This area is distinguished by its Mexico-based standard of workplace justice and the extent to which the work and home lives of growers and workers are intertwined. The intertwining of the social lives of the two undercuts worker solidarity and reinforces deference and compliance. The lack of autonomy in workers' community structure supports labor-management relations that are deferential, personal, and particularistic. As a result, workers here rarely challenge the terms of their work.

In the Pajaro Valley, the local organization of production affords workers an intermediate degree of mobility and independence. Although the availability of nonstrawberry work falls between that of the other two areas, closed job access structures and high strawberry wages and incomes encourage dependence on a single strawberry employer. Production relations support a degree of maneuverability, however. The social distance between classes is moderate here, involving personal, patronal relations, separate work and home lives, and considerable solidarity among workers. Growers here invest exceptionally in production, and in labor compliance and commitment. The United States is the reference point for workplace justice, the tenor of class relations is negotiative and accommodating, and as workers speak quickly to perceived injustices, so do growers respond with alacrity, so that their frictions rarely disrupt work.

These local microregions importantly segment the regional commodity system and labor market. Contrasts in the interests, resources, values, and social relations of the local class populations, and in the array of job opportunities, entry and exit structures, and performance and reward standards, differentiate the operation of the labor market. In effect, the local organization of production filters regional political pressures, variously enhancing, diminishing, or transforming their impact. Thus the existence of political constraints in the region does not determine the extent or nature of their relevance in the locality. To put it another way, one cannot infer the character of local power relations from the array of power resources at the regional level. Although regional resources and constraints can potentially enhance or restrict the leverage of class members, class encounters always occur in a local context. Thus outcomes depend on the locally represented segments of regional class populations, the localized structures of economic opportunity, and the local patterns of social relationships. These specific contexts, as well as the interests, values, and alternatives of these particular actors, accord regional class resources their meaning. As a result, the impact of the political forces structuring the regional labor market depends on their utility and relevance at the local level.

Let us clarify the varying microregional patterning of political constraints by reference to the three most influential political forces: union mobilization, protective labor legislation, and immigration policy. First, unionization has a much greater impact on the valley floors than in the North Monterey Hills. Salinas and Pajaro Valley farmers are highly sensitive to union pressure, not only because of their physical proximity to union campaigns, but because the norms of workplace justice acknowledge union claims, the politicized and empowered workforce presses for them, and growers themselves pay a greater cost for harvest disruptions. By contrast, union mobilization has had little direct impact in the North Monterey Hills because the area is physically removed from the heat of the conflict and because workplace norms dismiss the union's claims, workers are unaware of or fearful to join the union, and the union avoids challenging employers who are its ethnic compatriots. Second, protective labor legislation also has limited impact in the North Monterey Hills. Few growers or workers push for enforcement, because workplace norms are unsupportive, because workers are uninformed and disempowered, and because growers are less able to and interested in paying such a commitment-enhancing fee. Growers and workers alike, however, take initiative to enforce labor laws on the valley floors. Workplace norms support these initiatives, as do greater exposure to enforcement agencies, the higher resource levels and greater quality concern of growers, and the greater economic and political empowerment of workers. Finally, border policy is exerted unevenly across the three localities. Because it stratifies the regional workforce along lines of citizenship, it creates the conditions for the spatial expression of this stratification. The most disempowered, undocumented stratum is channeled toward the North Monterey Hills, with its least desirable jobs and least likelihood of apprehension. Documented workers are channeled toward the valley floors, because jobs are more rewarding and because apprehension is more likely and costly to growers. Somewhat more documented workers are found in the Pajaro Valley, where pay and benefit levels are highest and growers have the greatest investment in labor performance.

In conclusion, unexpected openings for wage workers' resistance are created by swings in the industry's annual production cycle and contrasts in the local organizational bases of worker power. These openings and periodic upwellings of resistance, however, are fundamentally conservative. They are seasonal rituals which reestablish and reaffirm the legitimacy of the status quo. They do not, therefore, account for the reconfiguring of capitalist power relations represented by the return to sharecropping. How then do we explain the shift from wage labor to sharecropping in the mid-1960s, when the conventional explanations of world economic crises, core sector economic challenges and capacities, commodity-specific labor demand, and the power accorded workers by their skill and labor organizations, do not suffice?

[7]

Sharecropping and Labor Control: The Role of Politics

The labor market conditions most prevalent after the war included a negligible to moderate level of organized labor activity and legal restriction on growers' managerial authority, and a predominant surplus of noncitizen workers. Given this configuration of political forces structuring the labor market, wage contracts worked to growers' advantage and wage workers' opposition forced no restructuring of capitalist production relations, despite the supports for resistance inherent in the production cycle and the local organization of production. Yet for a period of time, power relations and labor processes were indeed restructured, but not as a result of workers' job-based pressure. Between the mid-1960s and the early 1980s, many growers returned to sharecropping, a labor process virtually nonexistent since the early 1950s.

Why the Resurgence of Sharecropping?

Sharecropping was the dominant labor process before World War II. Most sharecroppers were Japanese immigrants who were prevented by the Alien Land Laws from legally owning agricultural land. When these laws were repealed after the war, the Japanese moved on to independent farm operatorship. At the same time, labor and product markets matured, harvest yields and labor requirements exploded, and most growers turned to crews of bracero wage workers to bring in their crops.[1] In the mid-1960s,

[1]A few growers kept sharecroppers throughout the postwar period, because of loyalty to their sharecroppers and the inertia of custom. Most of these also started wage labor opera-

however, an unexpected thing happened: certain producers in Monterey and Santa Cruz Counties switched back to sharecropping. From the mid-1970s through the early 1980s, my research suggests, between 40 and 55 percent of the berry acreage in the two county region was sharecropped (Wells 1984a:4–5). At that point, sharecropping again began to decline: by 1988, it occupied only from 10 to 20 percent of the total acreage; by the early 1990s, even less.[2]

At first glance, these swings in the use of sharecropping are perplexing, for they fly in the face of economic arguments that sharecropping is inefficient and fated to disappear in mature capitalism (see Chapter 1). They also counter predictions of the progressive deskilling and disempowerment of workers, the simplification and bifurcation of class structures, and the polarization of class relations under capitalism. Finally, they challenge the notion that, as capitalism develops, "rational" bureaucratic links of superordination and subordination will replace "irrational" employment relations based on personal connection. Yet the empirical evidence does not confirm the inefficiency and universal dwindling of sharecropping. Much of the gain in U.S. agricultural productivity has occurred in areas where share tenancy is dominant (Bray 1963:25). Moreover, productivity may not differ significantly between rented and sharecropped land (Mangahas 1975:138; Roumasset 1976:91). How, then, can we account for its use?

Several explanations promise answers, one of which has to do with the labor demands of certain crops. That is, crop-specific labor demands that link outputs directly to the quality of labor—its pace, efficiency, timing, and inventiveness—may necessitate prohibitively high supervisory costs and thus benefit from the positive incentive of giving laborers a share of the output (Reid 1976, 1979). Strawberries possess such a labor demand profile, as do other crops that have historically been farmed on shares, such as tobacco, cotton, and snow peas in the United States, maize in Mexico, and cotton in Spain and Peru (Albert 1982; Caballero 1982; Reid 1976, 1979; Martinez-Alier 1974, 1977; Murrell 1983; Stiglitz 1974). Still, a survey of empirical research shows that crop characteristics are in fact an un-

---

tions in the 1950s and 1960s and expanded their sharecropping when the bracero program ended. At that point, they, like other growers, recruited Mexicans.

[2]Sharecropping also expanded in the Santa Maria Valley just to the south, though wage labor persisted in the rest of the state. Local agricultural commissioners report that none of the acreage in the one-third of the Santa Maria Valley falling in San Luis Obispo County was sharecropped, but that over three-fourths of the acreage in Santa Barbara County was sharecropped. The local farm adviser thinks that the proportion is closer to 100 percent. This region had two large established high-resource sharecropping operations, and many low-resource Mexican growers began sharecropping to expand the scale of their production.

reliable guide to the choice of agricultural contracts. The strawberry industry is not unique in its variable use of labor despite constancy of crop characteristics (Rao 1971). Why would sharecropping be chosen at one time and wage labor at another? Clearly, additional and changing factors must shape the profitability of share tenancy.

A second explanation, then, could be a shift in the world economy. Some analysts argue that falling profit rates spur employers to squeeze more from their workers, causing workers to resist and motivating employers to redesign labor processes in order to cheapen and control labor (Ehrensaft 1980; Gordon, Edwards, and Reich 1982; Kondratieff 1925). This argument suggests that the world economic downturn of the 1970s and 1980s could have stimulated the return to sharecropping. Yet, as we saw in Chapter 2, the California strawberry industry was buffered from the economic crises of that period, so they could not have caused the change in labor processes. A third explanation has to do with the resource complementarity of farm owners and share tenants. That is, sharecropping may be chosen by individuals who lack the means (e.g., capital, expertise, labor, access to markets) to farm on their own (Reid 1979; Hallagan 1978). However, resource pooling does not explain the bulk of postwar strawberry sharecropping in this area, since most growers had the wherewithal to farm directly with crews. A fourth explanation points to the risk-sharing advantages of sharecropping: both farm owners and tenants may prefer sharecropping when volatile market prices, crop fragility and perishability, and changeable climatic conditions increase production risk (Cheung 1969; Newbery and Stiglitz 1979; Reid 1976:575, 1979; Stiglitz 1974:219, 230). This account comes closer to the conditions of the strawberry industry, because it targets the potential impacts of risk and uncertainty. The sources of instability identified, however—market prices, climatic conditions, and crop characteristics—did not change radically during the period in question and could not have caused the restructuring of labor processes.

Labor process scholars offer another explanation. They argue that because direct coercive control methods elicit workers' resistance and reduce their motivation to perform, firm owners may adopt responsibility-expanding control structures to improve cooperation and productivity (Edwards 1979; Friedman 1977; Littler 1982). But it is firms in the monopoly core of the economy that these scholars believe likely to pursue this strategy, because their labor processes are more complex and can benefit from workers' initiative, because their workers are more skilled, unionized, and oppositional, because their greater size and complexity make them especially vulnerable to labor disruption, and because they have other means of increasing their returns. Therefore, they do not have to coerce the maximum from their workers in the short run and can afford the cost of expanded autonomy in the long run. Authors of this view expect that small firms in the competitive periphery of the economy, which cannot control input or market prices and which hire unskilled and nonunionized workers, will continue to exert coercive control. And, indeed, most strawberry growers have historically done so, without detriment to productivity. Thus this account, as well, is unsatisfactory.

In short, the usual explanations for this exception to predicted patterns of labor process change do not suffice. How, then, do we account for the resurgence and subsequent decline of strawberry sharecropping? Was it an historical anomaly—the brief resurfacing of an outmoded production form? Or do explanations for its reappearance inhere in the current dynamics of production? In this chapter, I argue that postwar sharecropping was primarily a response to changing political pressures on the labor market, pressures that were felt especially keenly by large growers in the Pajaro and Salinas Valleys. Three political developments were paramount: changes in border policy, the rise of agricultural unionization, and the increasing intervention of the state into the rewards and conditions of work. Together, these pressures shifted the balance of class power in the industry, radically increasing the costs and risks of production and making it hard for producers to control the timing, performance, and price of labor through wage contracts. For the vast majority of growers who returned to sharecropping, it was a means not only of dispersing but of actually reducing these politically generated costs and risks. Although this was the dominant motivational pattern behind the sharecropping revival—and is thus the pattern that receives most attention in this chapter—some producers had different concerns. For a handful of large growers in North Monterey County, sharecropping was a means of expanding the scale of production with limited capital and expertise. Although this pattern accounted for less than 10 percent of the sharecropped acreage, it is important for our argument because it demonstrates the crucial role of the local organization of production.

To develop these points, I first describe the task allocation and social relationships of pre-war sharecropping and then contrast it with the postwar form. Next, I explore the reasons for the sharecropping revival, both its advantages in the abstract and the two concrete motivational patterns of the growers who adopted it. Finally, I inquire more deeply into the dominant pattern—showing how it helped growers deal with the increasing political costs and risks of production.

Sharecropping before the War

Pre-war strawberry sharecropping differed importantly from the postwar form. Before the war, sharecroppers had substantial control over production decisions. Each family tended from two to three acres on ranches that ranged from twenty to over two hundred acres (Wilhelm and Sagen 1974:192–206). Farm owners recruited sharecroppers through the recommendations of existing tenants on the basis of farming experience and large family size. Written contracts were rare and the distribution of responsibilities was variable. In general, owners provided the land and all equipment, including mules at the outset and tractors later on. They prepared the land, dug the wells, and provided materials for irrigation flumes. Some sharecroppers were paid by the hour to build flumes, but all were expected to install them as part of the share agreement. Owners and sharecroppers shared the marketing of the crop and the provision of plants, water, and fertilizer, depending on the resources of each and the interest of the owner in farming. Some large ranches employed a sales agent and one or more foremen, but, by current standards, the extent of supervision ranged from negligible to moderate. Sharecroppers provided all labor from planting through harvest and were relatively free to carry it out as they pleased. Many lived on the ranch in barrack-style housing that the owner provided. Many had small plots on which they grew subsistence crops for themselves.

The degree of independence on some ranches was considerable. Many ranches resembled collections of family farmers who purchased supplies and marketed their product collectively. Share agreements usually lasted for four years, after which growers moved to a different plot of land because of the accumulation of diseases in the soil. Sharecropping was an entry-level subsistence base for new immigrants. Share farmers on a single ranch tended to be friends and relatives, often from the same prefecture in Japan. Families helped each other in planting and ongoing plot maintenance. At harvest time, most were able to bring in their crops with the help of one or two extra people, primarily "friends who weren't as busy as you were." Some small families had to employ a couple of workers at peak harvest—mostly recent Japanese immigrants. These were paid a low hourly wage, often supplemented by free housing, meals, and assistance in operating in the host society. The sharecropper population exhibited little turnover. Although not without friction, bonds between owners and share tenants were often personal and enduring. Even before the war, some owners loaned long-time tenants money to start their own farms.

In sum, before the war, sharecroppers engaged in a wide range of production activities, controlled many decisions, and provided many nonlabor inputs. Responsibilities were allocated through custom and personal negotiation, and sharecroppers were loosely connected aggregations of fairly independent operators joined primarily for access to land and markets.

Postwar Sharecropping

When sharecropping was reinitiated after the war, its task allocation and production relations were quite different. Owners set procedures and supplied nonlabor inputs, responsibilities were established by carefully worded legal contracts, and sharecroppers (or share farmers or share tenants as they were also called) were responsible primarily for hand labor. To understand why some growers found this form of sharecropping more advantageous than wage labor at certain points in time, and to explicate its role in evolving class relations, we must first characterize the legal form and working relationships of the system.[3]

The Legal Contracts

Sharecropping contracts reconfigured the rights and obligations of strawberry production. Between the mid-1960s and the early 1980s, most contracts in the region were modeled after the form developed by the large Watsonville-based grower-shipper company, Driscoll Strawberry Associates (DSA), which was the largest user of sharecroppers in the state during the 1970s.[4] These contracts were written in English, supplied by farm owners, and signed by sharecroppers without negotiation as a condition of employment. Their length and legal precision indicate the thought that growers put into this labor process. The standard contract was seventeen pages long and specific in its designation of the legal identities, rights, and responsibilities of the signing parties. Contracts generally lasted for a year but could be terminated within a period of several (typically five) days should the sharecropper default on any aspect of the agreement. They were usually renewed annually pending satisfactory performance.

[3]This characterization rests on interviews with industry leaders, farm advisers, agricultural commissioners, growers, sharecroppers, and wage workers, on my review of sharecropping contracts, and on my study of some of the court cases that addressed the employee status of sharecroppers (discussed in Chapter 8).

[4]Based on testimony presented in *Real* (1975) that DSA had two hundred sharecroppers, on the estimate of the CSAB president that there were about three hundred sharecroppers in the state in the early 1980s, and on the relatively constant incidence of sharecropping between those dates, it seems likely that DSA then employed about two-thirds of the state's sharecroppers.

Sharecropping contracts subdivided large farms, usually ranging from 50 to as many as 300 acres, into a series of smaller parcels of from 2.5 to 5 acres each. Each parcel was assigned to a sharecropper. The farm owner provided the land and retained title to the crop and the right to sell it.[5] As table 15 shows, the farm owner hired the labor and supplied the materials and equipment to prepare the ground for planting. He also provided the plants, determined the planting dates and procedures, and in most cases paid directly for planting outside the sharecropping contract. He provided the pipes and labor to sprinkle the fields after planting and then distributed the parcels to the sharecroppers. Sharecroppers were responsible for all hand labor necessary to weed, prune, manicure, and cut runners on the plants over the growing season, and to pick and pack the crop for harvest. They were also authorized to hire and supervise any workers beyond their immediate family members who were necessary to fulfill these obligations. They generally furnished their own hoes, shovels, pruning knives, and hand carts for picking the fruit. Most farm owners irrigated, fertilized, and inspected and sprayed the fields for pests—tasks which sharecroppers shouldered before the war, but which technological changes made increasingly capital intensive. Farm owners transported the filled crates of fruit to the cooler, arranged for their sale, and returned to each tenant his or her share of the market proceeds. In accord with their contracts, sharecroppers typically received from 50 to 55 percent of the proceeds from the sale of the crop. From this gross were deducted from half to all of the cost of the crates and boxes; half of the cost of precooling, loading, hauling, handling, and marketing; a per-crate assessment levied on all growers by the California Strawberry Advisory Board (CSAB) to pay for promotion and research; and, in the case of DSA sharecroppers, a plant patent fee. From their shares, sharecroppers paid for their hired labor, including all taxes and assessments imposed on employers by the government.

Sharecropping contracts defined sharecroppers as "independent contractors" rather than "employees." The DSA contract made this quite explicit, stating that neither the farm owner nor DSA "has assumed under this agreement any rights of supervision and control over the growing of the said strawberry crop." It went on to state that the sharecropper "is in no sense the representative, servant, or employee of (the farm owner and

[5]In the case of DSA, the grower-shipper organization comprised an additional layer of authority, since its grower-members use DSA's patented plant varieties. The DSA contract assigned farm owners the right to use the patented strawberry plants for a percentage of the market proceeds, and to subcontract the actual growing to sharecroppers, "subject to approval by DSA in each instance." The contract emphasized that at all times DSA retained ownership of both the plants and the crop derived from them.

Table 15. Division of responsibilities between farm owners and sharecroppers

Step	Work performed by	Worker employed by	Materials/ equipment used	Equipment owned/ supplied by
LAND PREPARATION				
Obtain land	owner	—	—	—
Rip subsoil	tractor drivers	owner	tractors	owner
Disk land	tractor drivers	owner	tractors	owner
Cultivate	tractor drivers	owner	tractors	owner
Plane land	tractor drivers	owner	tractors	owner
Survey land	supervisor/subcontr.	owner	transit or laser	owner
Cultivate	tractor drivers	owner	tractors	owner
Sprinkle	workers	owner	rented pipe	owner
Fumigate	workers/subcontr.	owner	plastic, chemicals	owner
Cultivate	tractor drivers	owner	tractors	owner
List	tractor drivers	owner	tractors	owner
Roll furrows	tractor drivers	owner	tractors	owner
Slice beds	tractor drivers	owner	tractors	owner
Mark beds for planting	tractor drivers	owner	tractors	owner
PLANTING				
Place plants in ground	cropper/workers	cropper/owner	hoes, trowels, plants, plant bags	cropper/owner
Roll beds	tractor drivers	owner	tractors	owner
Sprinkle beds	workers	owner	rented pipe	owner
MAINTENANCE				
Weed	cropper[a]	cropper[a]	hoes	cropper[a]
Prune	cropper[a]	cropper[a]	pruning knives	cropper/owner
Irrigate	1979: cropper[a]	cropper[a]	rented pipe	owner
	1979–present: irrigator	owner	drip system	owner
Fertilize	workers[b]	owner[b]	fertilizer	owner[b]
Spray/dust	tractor drivers/ airplane pilots	owner	tractors, airplanes, spray equipment, chemicals	owner
HARVEST				
Pick berries	cropper	cropper	carts, hands	cropper
Pack berries	cropper	cropper	crates, baskets	owner
Supervise	cropper/supervisor[a]	cropper[a]	judgment	cropper[a]
Grade berries	inspectors	owner	judgment	owner
Schedule truck pick-ups	supervisor	owner	trucks	owner
Transport berries	truck drivers	owner	trucks	owner
Market fruit	owner/salesman	owner	judgment	owner

[a]Some work hired by owner
[b]Some work done by sharecropper
Sources: 1986–87 interviews, field observations, and "Brief for Appellants," 23 June 1977, *Real v. Driscoll Strawberry Associates, Driscoll Berry Farms,* No. 77-1935, p. 5, United States Court of Appeals for the Ninth Circuit, San Jose, California.

Table 16. Background similarities of sharecroppers interviewed

Characteristic	Percentage of interviewees
Born in Mexico	95
Born in Jalisco or Michoacán	63
Parents were peasant farmers	60
Grandparents were peasant farmers	90
Prior work strawberry wage labor	75
Parents did strawberry wage labor	80
Got job through family, friends	95
Cannot speak English[a]	80

[a]The mean number of years of school was 6.

in growing the crop for the account of DSA shall be under the control of the (owner) only as to the result of the work assigned to be performed by him and not as to the means by which the results are to be accomplished."

The Working Relationships

As before the war, growers recruited sharecroppers whose other options were limited. The new sharecroppers were Mexican immigrants who, like pre-war Japanese sharecroppers, lacked capital and were mostly unable to speak English. Although, unlike the Japanese, Mexican sharecroppers were legally entitled to own land, attitudinal and institutional barriers constrained their access to land, capital, information, and markets (Small Farm 1977). As table 16 shows, the background characteristics of these sharecroppers were virtually identical to those of wage laborers: they had a mean of six years of formal education, almost all were born in Mexico, and most were involved in a family tradition of strawberry labor and came from the states of Jalisco or Michoacán, where unemployment and underemployment were rampant.

Sharecroppers got their jobs through personal connections. When growers first began to convert to sharecropping in the mid-1960s, many approached long-time harvest workers and offered to make them sharecroppers. As sharecropping became maturely established in the early 1970s, recruitment channels were regularized. New recruits were recommended by current sharecroppers or other growers. They were drawn from strawberry workers. The three most important qualifications that growers sought in a sharecropper were experience picking strawberries, a reputation for reliability, and access to labor. They also prioritized local residents who were citizens or legal immigrants to minimize difficulties with the *migra* and maximize the likelihood that sharecroppers would tend their plots year around. Once engaged, however, sharecroppers usually used their contracts as evidence of steady employment to obtain legal status, so that many were eventually documented. Finally, though growers preferred their sharecroppers to speak English, this ability was rare and unnecessary, since their supervisors spoke Spanish.

A few growers engaged sharecroppers who lacked immediate family but had wide interpersonal networks through which they could mobilize employees. Many engaged husband and wife teams as the core of family labor. Most, however, preferred large nuclear families in which the husband, wife, older children, and possibly other co-resident adults could provide unpaid labor. Unpaid family labor was important, since labor expenses could otherwise reduce sharecroppers' returns to the point that they abandoned their parcels in midseason. Growers preferred couples or families because they thought that their direct benefit from the quality of their work increased their motivation to perform and reduced the likelihood of complaint. Many large families supplied all labor from planting until harvest. With a harvest labor requirement of from 1.5 to 2 workers per acre, however, most sharecroppers in the Salinas-Watsonville area employed helpers during the harvest. Their hired workers were of two sorts. One set was drawn from the bottom stratum of the labor force—mostly recent illegal immigrants. Some of these were walk-ons; some were recruited through personal networks. They were the newest arrivals in the local labor market and had the least experience and the fewest contacts in the industry. Some were relatives, friends, and acquaintances from the sharecroppers' home villages in Mexico. The second set was recruited through personal networks and comprised of friends and relatives from the local area. Many were legal residents who were seeking extra income. Nuclear family members worked without pay, but more distant relatives were usually paid. Fewer than half of the families had another source of income to sustain them over the winter and through bad years. As might be expected from the fact that sharecroppers received only half the proceeds from the sale of their crops, they tended to pay the lowest wages in the industry and only sporadically observed costly labor-protective regulations.

The use of child labor varied considerably across the region, depending on the composition of the sharecropping unit (individual, couple, or family) and the standards of farm owners. The individual and couple units usually had only one or two unpaid family workers, a number of paid employees, and no under-age children. Family units varied in their use of under-age children depending on the ages of children available and on the supervisory efforts of growers. The major users of sharecroppers in the

Table 17. Advantages, disadvantages, and risks of sharecropping evaluated by croppers interviewed

Factor	Percentage of interviewees
Major advantage cited	
Possibility of higher household income	50
Possibility of greater independence/control	40
Major disadvantage cited	
Greater risk of income variation	90
Primary risk cited	
Production risk	40
Market risk	30
Partnership risk	30

Note: In conclusion, 100% of the interviewees said they would prefer sharecropping to doing wage work.

Salinas-Watsonville area were high-resource growers with stringent quality standards, and many of these forbade the use of under-age workers, in large part because their carelessness could damage the crop. Some of these growers were quite effective through supervision in ensuring that under-age workers did not harvest the crop. Low-resource owners, however, were not as particular, and some high-resource owners did not enforce this practice either. Moreover, families often brought younger children with them to the fields to watch over them, and it was hard for owners to tell which of them were working and which were not. In short, under-age children were part of the labor force, although their contribution seems to have been less significant than in other regions, industries, or historical periods.[6] From their early teenage years on, children usually worked on the family parcel after school, on weekends, and during the summers.

When asked about their major reasons for sharecropping, sharecroppers cited the opportunity for higher household income and greater on-the-job independence (see table 17). In relation to the first, they emphasized the frequent periods of unemployment which they and household members experienced as wage workers in the surplus labor market. Sharecropping

[6]As I observed more sharecropping operations and conducted more interviews, I came to recognize that child labor was more extensive in this region than my early observations and informants had indicated. Its use was highly variable across the region, however, and seems on the whole to have been less extensive than in cotton sharecropping in the American South, in contemporary pickling cucumber sharecropping in California and the Midwest, and in low-investment strawberry sharecropping in California's Santa Maria Valley. See Chapter 8, text and notes 8 and 11, for information on these contrasts.

enabled them to reduce such periods of unemployment and maximize the income-producing potential of all household members. They pointed out that this means of achieving a higher household income helped them bring family members from Mexico, live with their families without migrating, attain legal immigrant status through proof of a stable job, and offer their children uninterrupted schooling. It particularly helped women combine their dual roles as breadwinners and mothers. Some mentioned that sharecropping could be a stepping-stone to independent farming. And for some, as we have seen, it was. On the average, sharecroppers earned more as individuals and as families than wage laborers: those interviewed earned an average of $18,600 as individuals in 1985, almost three times the income of an average wage worker.

But sharecroppers' incomes were also more variable than those of employed wage workers: the household incomes of those interviewed ranged from a low of $4,000 to a high of $45,000. Not surprisingly, incomes were lowest and the risk of income variation was greatest for sharecroppers who worked for low-resource, low-investment growers. They sometimes made less than wage laborers and even lost money in bad years. Some survived from the off-farm income of family members; others abandoned their parcels and returned to Mexico. Sharecroppers viewed the risk of income variability as the major disadvantage of sharecropping. The primary sources of this variation were production risks such as cold weather, rains, and pest or disease infestations; market risks, such as low berry prices, crop damage prior to sale, or the lowering of sharecroppers' pooled returns because of the poor product quality of other sharecroppers; and partnership risks, that is, the risk that the farm owner would do his part poorly or dishonestly, for example, by misreporting market returns to cheat sharecroppers, by skimping on chemical applications, or by not maintaining irrigation systems.

Because sharecroppers did not always make more money than farm laborers, the anticipation of increased independence was especially important to them. They did have more control than wage workers over the daily process of work. Within limits, they chose when to start work, take breaks, and finish for the day. They could leave the ranch to tend a sick child, oversee their children in the fields, go to the doctor, or do the shopping. Sharecroppers could hire whom they wished and pay them what they wished, within the bounds of the law and its enforcement. They supervised workers on their own parcels and did not labor under the constant scrutiny of a foreman. Their autonomy should not be overrepresented, however. Sharecroppers themselves were supervised, as we will see, although less intensively than wage workers. Growers set out quite precisely the frequency and standards for parcel maintenance and fruit harvest. Although the contracts left the implementation of these specifications up to sharecroppers, growers hired checkers and supervisors to monitor the "result of the work assigned" to them. Growers engaged approximately one supervisor for every one hundred acres to manage sharecroppers, as opposed to one foreman for every fifty to sixty acres to manage wage workers. I discuss later the actual extent of direction that these supervisors exerted, but I would note here that the supervision of sharecroppers was a touchy and crucial matter: it had to respect their contractually stipulated independence while ensuring that they follow the procedures growers wanted.

Growers' Motivations for Sharecropping

Postwar sharecropping offered a number of potential benefits to strawberry growers. Growers differed, however, as to which of these they sought.

The Promise of Sharecropping

First, unlike the semifeudal sharecropping arrangements critiqued by Marx and Lenin, this form did not leave the tools and techniques of production in the hands of poor and uneducated direct producers. Rather, farm owners exerted relatively firm control over the methods and means of production. They supplied all inputs with the exception of the hand labor involved in the harvest and in maintenance, excluding pest control, fertilization, and irrigation. Although they assigned harvest labor recruitment, remuneration, and management to sharecroppers, they specified and monitored the procedures to be used. This form of sharecropping permitted, therefore, at least in theory, the optimal and scientific deployment of production factors. Second, it increased the intensity of labor management and the motivation for labor performance. Sharecropping subdivided large farms that used one manager for every thirty to thirty-five workers into small parcels on which a husband and wife sharecropping team supervised from four to ten workers. Often these workers were family members and friends, so personal relationships and the direct link of effort to reward enhanced their motivation to perform. By making each sharecropper into a labor recruiter, sharecropping also accorded growers access to a wide scope of personal recruitment networks. Because sharecroppers had less land to oversee than crew foremen did, and because they were directly rewarded for their careful stewardship of it, they were more likely than foremen to help growers tailor their farming practices to small differences in the production environment. For example, because a sharecropper, in one grower's words, "sets foot in every one of his rows several times a day, while a grower may never visit certain parts of his ranch," he could help identify pockets of pest infestation or areas of heavy soil that required less water.

Although sharecropping did improve labor management and motivation in these ways, it did not necessarily increase market returns. In fact, 68 percent of the growers said that crop *quality* actually tended to be lower with sharecroppers than with wage workers; 82 percent said that crop *quantity*, though roughly comparable, was more variable and could fall far below. The trends and variation in this matter seem to revolve around the issue of labor management. Almost 90 percent of the interviewees said that, although sharecropping increased the number of labor managers per acre, it also hindered the optimal implementation of some operations. For example, it was harder to coordinate whole-ranch procedures, such as aerial pesticide spraying, because of the varying paces and schedules of harvest workers. It was also harder to ensure sharecroppers' adherence to owners' standards and procedures, because sharecroppers were legally independent contractors and were entitled to some autonomy. Indeed, sharecroppers often resisted growers' attempts to instruct them. As neoclassical economists predict, they also responded to the fractional division of their returns by trying to minimize their labor inputs. Owners often complained that sharecroppers came to work later, left earlier, and picked less frequently than instructed. Preventing such behavior required constant vigilance, which sharecroppers resented. When monitoring was too loose, pilfering for home use and outside sale became a major problem. Though growers acknowledged that sharecroppers could "cover up the mistakes" of inexperienced or uninvolved growers by carrying out tasks according to general specifications, in the long run and under "peaceful" production conditions, experienced and conscientious growers could do better with crews.

There was, however, a third potential benefit to sharecropping: it reconfigured patterns of cash flow and capital demand in ways especially advantageous to certain growers. Share tenants were not paid for their work until the crop was sold, so that owners could delay payment for the labor involved in weeding, cutting runners, pruning, and manicuring the plants in the five to seven months between planting and harvest. Capital-poor growers benefited particularly from this arrangement, because it coordinated their payments for labor with their incomes from the harvest. Moreover, because sharecroppers were paid for maintenance on the basis of the job done, rather than the hours expended, sharecropping could significantly lower maintenance costs during cool or rainy seasons when runner production was high and clean-ups after inclement weather could be substantial.

Finally and most importantly, sharecropping offered growers crucial benefits in the post-1960s political climate. These had to do with the way that the organization and incentive structure of sharecropping undercut the solidarity and oppositional leverage of workers, and with the way that the legal status of sharecropping enabled growers to avoid the restrictions and costs of labor-protective laws.

The Two Patterns of Adoption

As might be expected, the contrasting economic, political, and demographic characteristics of the three production microregions affected growers' evaluations of the potential advantages of sharecropping. Two categories of growers turned to share farming after the mid-1960s: low-resource, large-scale growers in the North Monterey Hills; and high-resource, large-scale growers in the Pajaro and Salinas Valleys. The actual organization of share tenancy was the same in both cases, although the motivations for its adoption diverged.

Growers exhibiting the first pattern—which I call low-investment sharecropping—were responding to resource scarcity. This category represented a minor fragment of the sharecropping revival and involved only several ranches on the central coast. Farm owners in these instances were Mexicans with little capital or farming experience who began independent farming in the mid-1970s, and non-Mexican investors (one Anglo, one Chinese American) who wanted to minimize their involvement and expenditures in farming. For these growers, sharecropping was a means of expanding the scale of their operations with limited capital and expertise. It enabled them to capture the (albeit limited) production skills of sharecroppers, thereby reducing the need for their own expertise and involvement. It also sequenced their demand for cash outlay to coincide with the harvest income. These growers were not concerned with union pressure, because the union did not target ranches—especially Mexican ranches—in the North Monterey Hills. Nor were they mitigating the burdens of protective labor laws, since they unevenly observed them. Finally, because all these growers entered farming in the 1970s after the labor market had restabilized, they were not responding to the disorganization of recruitment networks occasioned by the end of the bracero program.

Growers pursuing this pattern were quite explicit about its advantages. As one Mexican grower put it, "sharecropping means you don't have to take out a loan for pruning or cutting runners before the season's income comes in." Another observed that his sharecroppers' knowledge of how to pick and recruit workers "helped (him) get started when (he) didn't know much about farming." An absentee investor commented: "The sharecroppers pretty much know how to do the job. With them and a good ranch manager, the business pretty much runs itself." In general, growers in this category invested less in the operations for which they were responsible, guided sharecroppers less in theirs, and achieved poorer crop quality, quantity, and prices.

Growers pursuing the second pattern—which I call high-investment sharecropping—were motivated mainly by changing political constraints. This pattern accounted for about 90 percent of the postwar sharecropped acreage. The farm owners involved in this pattern were large-scale Anglo and Japanese growers with ample resources, who were situated in the Pajaro and Salinas Valleys. These individuals were experienced and successful producers. Some were familiar with sharecropping through their use of Japanese sharecroppers before the war. They were not trying to minimize their involvement in the production process, and they were not particularly concerned about cash flow or management augmentation. In fact, if not for increasing political constraints on the use of wage workers, most would have stayed with crews.

Most of all, these growers appreciated the way that sharecropping helped them deal with the changing political environment. Their appreciation was directly related to the motivations, problems, and resources characteristic of large growers in the these microregions. As I noted in Chapter 6, growers in the Pajaro and Salinas Valleys were the most vulnerable to unionization and to the enforcement of protective labor laws and border regulations. By virtue of their high investments in crop quality, they were also the most concerned with harvest disruptions. Moreover, large farm size and the Anglo and Japanese identity of owners weakened personal bonds between them and their workers and increased their vulnerability to union organizers. Finally, because of their large size, these growers bore the heaviest burdens of labor recruitment and were the most destabilized by the end of the bracero program. Let us see how growers described these politically induced challenges, and the relief offered by sharecropping.

Sharecropping and the Political Construction of the Labor Market

The resurgence of sharecropping coincided with a three-faceted shift in the political construction of the labor market: the end of the bracero program, which both reflected and enhanced growers' diminishing control over border policy; the rise of agricultural unionization, which increased workers' leverage in society and at the point of production; and the increasing involvement of the state in restricting growers' managerial prerogatives and in supporting the subsistence of workers outside the wage relationship. These pressures were exerted most intensely from the mid-1960s through the early 1980s. In 1964, the bracero program was terminated and union organizing gathered force. In 1970, the union turned its attention to the central coast, and into the early 1980s this region was the primary focus of union militance. During the same period, laws protecting the rights and guaranteeing the subsistence of farm workers proliferated and were especially enforced in the heat of union struggle. Together, these developments transformed the context for labor deployment in the industry. The following accounts from the 1986–87 interviews express the weight of these concerns.

First, growers described the severe labor supply problems caused by the end of the bracero program. Not only was the program's recruitment and management structure dismantled, but its administrative cap on wage levels was lifted. Suddenly, growers were faced with the task of finding, training, and managing a large, seasonally variable, and semi-skilled workforce themselves, at a time when established labor market processes were in disarray. In addition, as the supply of braceros was cut off and as illegals took their place, growers faced the prospect of harvest disruptions through Border Patrol raids. This was a source of particular anxiety in the transitional years of the late 1960s, when it was unclear how rigorously border laws would be enforced. Growers' reminiscences indicate the crisis in labor recruitment and management they faced at that time and the respite offered by share tenancy:

> I remember the year before termination. Labor was all my father and his friends could talk about. We had never had to worry about labor before. All of a sudden we were all scrambling for workers. We didn't know where they were going to come from. There just weren't enough experienced workers. Growers tried everything. Some bussed bums down from San Francisco. One even tried Sioux Indians. My father flew to Mexico and Texas to recruit workers. Eventually we went back to share farming. It was something we knew. My father brought Japanese workers from Hawaii. A couple of them still work for us. (grower interview no. 16)

> We needed workers who were educated to take care of strawberries. Before the war we had them with Japanese sharecroppers. The braceros weren't that educated, but they were hard-working. When the program ended, Mexicans weren't reliable. They came and went as they pleased. As the years

went on, many workers got educated in berries. You got an experienced, qualified workforce. But in those years it was hit and miss. (grower interview no. 21)

We lay awake almost every night the year after the braceros stopped, wondering whether we would find workers. I cut my farm size in half for two years. My neighbor had decided to sharecrop and he always had workers. So I tried it too. (grower interview no. 8)

The braceros were legal, you know. They had the government's blessing. When they stopped we just had the wetbacks. We didn't know if that would be a problem. It made us very nervous. Sharecroppers were legal. They got their papers. Lots of their relatives were legal too. They were safer. (interview no. 12)

Small growers made out okay. They had a few braceros who had worked for them for years. They promised those guys papers in return for rounding up their aunts and uncles and wives and neighbors to come pick berries in Watsonville. It wasn't such a big job for them. Each one only had a little piece of land. But for me, I had 60 acres and it was just too much to handle. So I got sharecroppers to do it for me. (grower interview no. 44)

We switched from crews to sharecroppers in 1965. They were a way of dealing with recruitment headaches when the bracero program ended. Sharecroppers are pretty stable and so are their hired workers, because they are probably relatives. (grower interview no. 38)

Sharecropping meant that the grower didn't have to battle with the risk of getting workers, or battle with the workers once he got them. That was really a problem when the braceros stopped. In this day, workers come back season after season so sharecroppers are not so valuable. But they really helped back then. (grower interview no. 3)

Thus, sharecropping helped growers deal with the challenges posed by the end of the bracero program. By increasing the number of documented workers per acre and by subdividing large crews into small groupings that were present in the fields at varying times and in limited numbers, it reduced growers' exposure to Border Patrol raids. Even more important, given the uneven enforcement of immigration policy, it helped larger growers deal with the recruitment and management crisis that followed the dismantling of the bracero program. By delegating labor recruitment and management to sharecroppers on small parcels, growers replaced many of the functions formerly accomplished by the program. With more recruiter-managers per acre and fewer workers for each to deal with, the labor supply and management problems of large ranches were easily solved. The personal networks and loyalty bonds between sharecroppers and their workers facilitated recruitment and improved labor performance and stability as the labor market re-equilibrated in the late 1960s. By the early 1970s, these advantages dwindled in importance, because the labor market had adjusted to deliver a steady flow of immigrant workers to the area and because growers had developed their own means of labor recruitment and management.

At that point, a second and longer-lasting challenge confronted growers: the rise of agricultural unionization. The 1970 general strike ushered in more than a decade of intense union pressure. Most growers regard the UFW as the major cause of renewed share farming: not only did the union increase the enforcement of border regulations and labor laws, but it introduced an unprecedented tension and uncertainty into employment relationships. Union contracts and militance bolstered workers' bargaining power at the point of production and decreased growers' latitude in determining the terms of work. Even those with established labor forces were at risk. Growers' comments vividly portray the turmoil of this period and the haven offered by sharecropping.

> Sharecropping began to be popular again in the early 1970s, when Chavez was strong. With 60 acres and 120 pickers, one or two agitators could break up the whole thing. So the only way around it was to make workers their own bosses. You break up the ranch into 40 separate groups where their incomes are related to yours, and the union can't get organized. It's their own business then, and many of their own family members work, so they won't strike themselves. (grower interview no. 27)

> I began sharecropping right when I began growing berries in 1974. It was the norm for big growers then. It was real hard to get workers at that time—reliable workers, that is, workers you could control. It was the height of labor unrest with Chavez. Lots of growers would have both sharecroppers and crews for insurance. (grower interview no. 41)

> We started sharecropping in 1973–74. It was hard to get workers to work hard then. They took too long to do their work. It was the union trouble, that's why. So I made some of the illegals that had worked for me for a long time into sharecroppers. I hoped that with sharecroppers I'd have no worries about their performance or how long they took to do their work. (grower interview no. 33)

Sharecropping definitely began again in the early 1970s after the union came in. I began with half crew and half share in 1970. I drifted toward all share by 1975. That was so I'd have fewer problems with my workers. In those days there were always some workers agitating with a big crew. With sharecroppers I had small groups scattered. (grower interview no. 18)

Sharecropping was adopted because of the fear of Chavez. The union wouldn't touch sharecroppers, even when it was very active. Part of it was that the sharecroppers are Mexicans, just like union members. Sharecroppers are Mexican families trying to better themselves. Some growers made a big point of that. After the 1970–71 union trouble, some growers actually posted signs at the edges of their fields saying: "These fields are farmed by independent Mexican families." The signs were directed straight at the union and the Labor Commissioner, to keep them out. (grower interview no. 11)

If you're a big grower you're more at risk from the union and the Border Patrol. They go where they can make the biggest catch. It's more work for the union to go after sharecroppers because each unit is so small. It's not worth their while. They only go after the big guys. It's the same with the *migra.* It's not worth their while. (grower interview no. 5)

Thus, sharecropping protected central coast berry growers from the tensions, costs, and uncertainties associated with unionization. Far from being "irrational" in this context, the personal ties between sharecroppers and their workers and their personal investments in the quantity and quality of the harvest discouraged labor organizing and strikes. The small size of each unit and the Mexican ethnicity of sharecroppers prevented the union from targeting such ranches for organizing. Because sharecroppers hired, supervised, and fired their own workers, they could not join the union, and because sharecropping deflected the union's attention, it reduced growers' exposure to border regulations.

Sharecropping also reduced growers' vulnerability to the third political shift in the labor market—the expansion of protective labor legislation. Many growers bemoaned the burden of legislation, which grew heavier as laws proliferated and as UFW pressure increased the likelihood of their enforcement. With farm workers' inclusion under the Social Security Act and the Fair Labor Standards Act, they became less dependent on growers for survival. Unemployment and workers' compensation insurance and welfare programs gave them additional support outside the wage contract. The Agricultural Labor Relations Act (ALRA) supported their organizing and helped prevent dismissal. Together, these measures increased production costs, enhanced workers' leverage, and restricted growers' ability to deal with, deploy, and reward workers as they pleased. Growers expressed their frustration with this altered legal climate and described the relief offered by share farming:

> You wouldn't believe how the laws changed in the 1970s. It used to be it was just you and your workers in your field. You paid what you thought was a fair wage, you told them when and how to work, and mostly they did it. It was a business for a person who liked to go it on his own. Then all of a sudden you were out in your field with every politician and labor agitator on this side of the continent. You couldn't tell your workers to do anything without Chavez or Brown or some guy who sits in his office in Salinas having something to say about it. And then they began to charge you additional taxes for labor when you were already paying all you could afford. They call them payroll taxes. Farming's a politician's business now. (grower interview no. 7)

> The real problem came when the union came in. The union tells them they shouldn't work on Sundays and they shouldn't stay late. Now they insist on overtime pay. Not only that, but if a bunch of agitators comes in you have to sit down and talk with them. A berry farmer just can't operate like that. (grower interview no. 24)

> It's the labor costs that kill you. Not only have wages gone up, but now they have payroll taxes. An extra 17 percent of your labor tab comes from payroll taxes. With sharecroppers you don't pay those. It's up to them to take care of those things themselves. (grower interview no. 43)

These comments speak to the way that sharecropping benefited growers by distancing their workforces from the costs and restrictions of labor-protective legislation. I will develop this point in greater detail in the next chapter. For now, suffice it to say that sharecroppers fell into several legal categories which made them unlikely to be permitted to join the union or be covered by the ALRA, the Social Security Act (SSA), the Fair Labor Standards Act (FLSA), or workers' compensation or unemployment insurance. As a result, farm owners did not have to shoulder associated payments, and sharecroppers were more dependent than wage laborers on—and had fewer outside allies in—their relationships with their employers. Although sharecroppers' hired workers were covered by protective laws, and ranch owners were technically responsible for their contractors' observance of such laws, neither sharecroppers nor owners were in practice held accountable.

Political Pressure, Economic Organization, and Labor Market Power

Strawberry sharecropping was a response to distinctly contemporary political pressures: it was a means of dealing with a shift in the balance of class power occasioned by changing political constraints on the labor market—a shift that increased the costs and uncertainties of deploying wage workers. In this context, sharecropping enabled growers not only to share, but actually to reduce, their exposure to politically generated costs and risks. On a microregional level, the impact of political pressures varied. Growers were differentially responsive and vulnerable to the altered cost and risk environment occasioned by political pressures. This environment was most costly for large producers in the Pajaro and Salinas Valleys, and less so for those in the North Monterey Hills. Thus the decisive factors altering the configuration of class power in this case emanated from the labor market. Moreover, they were primarily political. For the most part, however, the influence of these pressures was exerted indirectly, through the standards of treatment and reward and the climate of public opinion they established in the region, rather than through their direct observation or contractual enforcement within particular firms. Here, it was wage workers' increased leverage and exchange value in the regional labor market that enhanced their potency at the point of production and motivated growers to reconfigure labor processes.

Despite ostensible advantages for growers, sharecropping did not provide a lasting solution, largely because sharecroppers' responses to it triggered the reconfiguration of legal constraints. To this process, and to the ways that sharecropping affected the initiatives of labor-suppliers and the broader course of class relations, we now turn.

[8]

Legal Conflict, Class Relations, and the Labor Process

When strawberry growers returned to sharecropping, they not only enhanced their stability and labor control in an increasingly restrictive political environment, they also reconfigured the playing field for class relations at work. They changed the organization and social relations of production, and they reduced workers' claims on the resources of the state. Sharecroppers were not passive pawns in this process. They and their allies assessed this reconfiguration and responded to it by challenging its legal characterization. The dynamic thus joined reveals the crucial interconnections among the law, economic organization, and social class.

Social Class and the Law

Social class is usually defined in terms of the relationship of a set of individuals to the economic means of production, but, in advanced industrial societies, class also defines and is defined by a relationship to legal-political categories. The laws and apparatuses of the state importantly influence the material and ideological dimensions of social class: they affect the resources and prerogatives attached to particular economic statuses, and they help shape individuals' perceptions of their roles in production. The law also affects the wider course of class relations: because the law is so closely involved in economic relationships, challenges to those relationships often build into challenges to the law, and, in the end, both can change. This chapter explores and documents these processes, revealing that the role of state apparatuses in economic relations is more intimate and dialectical than usually recognized.

The Role of Sharecroppers in Class Structure

Sharecropping altered labor-suppliers' economic and legal relationship to the means of production, creating new possibilities for class interest, identification, and action. Structurally, postwar sharecroppers partook of some of the prerogatives and responsibilities associated with capital, but they also experienced most of the dependency associated with labor. Their structural position in class relations was thus, on the face of it, indeterminate: their definition as proletarian or petty bourgeois depended on the boundary-defining criteria that observers or participants emphasized. In essence, these sharecroppers occupied a contradictory location in class relations (Wright 1976), for they were pulled in conflicting directions by the legal, economic, and ideological dimensions of their positions.

The Legal Position of Sharecroppers

When sharecropping was reinstituted after the mid-1960s, sharecroppers occupied a certain place in the body of labor-protective legislation that defined the legal status and protections of workers. As farm workers moved increasingly into the category of persons thought to merit legal protection after the war, the defining features of an agricultural employee were evaluated and refined. From the start, many protective laws excluded three specific categories of workers: independent contractors, supervisors, and sharecroppers. For differing reasons and to varying extents for varying pieces of legislation, sharecroppers could fit under all three. The point of departure for all protective labor laws was the philosophy voiced by the drafters of New Deal legislation: that the government had a responsibility to protect those whose ability to support and protect themselves in the market was particularly limited. Employees were seen as such individuals. Independent contractors, sharecroppers, and supervisors, depending on the statute involved, were not. The underlying contrast was the distinction between dependency and independence. The authors of New Deal legislation reasoned that because employees have no means of sustenance other than their ability to work and because they surrender this ability—and thus in an important sense, themselves—to the authority of their employers, they are distinctively dependent, and their livelihoods are especially precarious. The other three sorts of agents were often deemed more autonomous and active participants in the economy, able to do without extramarket assistance.

This notion forms the backdrop for the enforcement of New Deal and subsequent federal and state remedial legislation, but each law has its specific protective intention and history of enforcement precedents. As a result, laws vary in the ways they define employee status. The Fair Labor Standards Act (FLSA) has no specific sharecropper exemption. In fact, the congressional discussions in 1966 surrounding its amendment to cover agricultural workers made it clear that some sharecroppers were to be covered:

> It is intended that the minimum provisions of the Act be extended to certain sharecroppers and tenant farmers. The test of coverage for these persons will be the same test that is applied to determine whether any other person is an employee or not. . . . Coverage is intended in the case of certain so-called sharecroppers or tenants whose work activities are closely guided by the landowner or his agent. These individuals, called sharecroppers and tenants, are employees by another name. Their work is closely directed; discretion is non-existent. True independent-contractor sharecroppers or tenant farmers will not be covered; they are not employees. (H. Rep. No. 1366, 89th Cong., 1st Sess. 32 (1966))

Shortly thereafter, the U.S. Department of Labor adopted these directions regarding sharecropping into its guide to employment relationships in agriculture (DOL 1967), and hearings before the House Committee on Agriculture emphasized that sharecroppers who contribute only hand labor should be considered employees (U.S. Congress 1967:9).

The most inclusive exemption to coverage under the FLSA, the National Labor Relations Act (NLRA), and the Social Security Act (SSA) is that of "independent contractor." Because Congress enacted the FLSA with the broad purpose of remedying power inequities in employment relationships, it uses an inclusive definition of employee that tries to determine the extent of a person's actual economic independence or dependence. The cases defining coverage under the act have established that reliance on any single criterion in making that determination is inappropriate (*Rutherford v. McComb* 1947:722), and that the full economic reality of dependence in a particular case must be examined, to determine whether an individual falls within the category intended to be protected (*Bartels* 1947:126; *Rutherford* 1947:722; *Silk* 1947:704, 716). Six factors form the basis of the federal employment test for purposes of the FLSA: the extent of outside control over the worker; the worker's opportunity for profit or loss; the worker's extent of investment in the production facilities;

Table 18. Criteria defining independent contractor versus employee

Factor	Independent contractor	Employee
Degree of outside control over worker	lesser	greater
Opportunity for profit or loss	greater	lesser
Investment in the facilities	greater	lesser
Permanency of the relationship	lesser	greater
Skill required in the operation	greater	lesser
Extent to which work is an essential/integrated part of the business	lesser	greater

the permanency and exclusivity of the working relationship; the degree of skill required; and the extent to which the work is an integral part of the business (see table 18) (*Silk* 1947:716).

Depending on their intentions, other statutes have used a more limited definition of independence that revolves around whether workers personally control, or have a right to control, their work. California's Agricultural Labor Relations Act (ALRA) uses the "right of control" test used by the NLRA to establish independent contractor status. By this test, an independent contractor is one who completes a job by his or her own methods and is not subject to an employer's control over how the work is performed. If the individual *is* subject to an employer's control, or right to control, the result and means or method of conducting the work, he or she is deemed an employee. Over time, the NLRA has come to interpret independent contractor status more broadly, considering, first, the entrepreneurial aspects of the individual's business, including the right to control; second, the individual's risk of loss and opportunity for profit; and, third, the individual's proprietary interest in his or her dealership (Gorman 1976:28–30). In all of these distinctions, the issues of contribution to and control over production are paramount. Even if an individual is found to be an employee, that person may be excluded from coverage under the ALRA and the NLRA if he or she is determined to be a supervisor. Supervisory status is unlike most other designations in protective labor legislation, in that it is decided not by an evaluation of the full economic context, but by the presence of authority over *any one* (or more) of certain defining activities (*NLRB v. Edward G. Budd* 1948). According to the NLRA (Section 2 (11)), a supervisor is

> any individual having authority, in the interest of an employer, to hire, transfer, suspend, lay off, recall, promote, discharge, assign, reward, or discipline other employees, or responsibly direct them, or to adjust their grievances or effectively to recommend such action, if in connection with the foregoing the

exercise of such authority is not of a merely routine or clerical nature, but requires the use of independent judgment.

The distinction between an employee and a supervisor rests also on the issues of allegiance and interest. Because supervisors are hired by employers to represent them, they owe them their loyalty and should not be legally supported in allying with employees against them. Moreover, because supervisors perform some management functions, their interests diverge structurally from those of employees, and they therefore should not be included in the same union bargaining unit. The authority to hire and fire has become one of the most important criteria deciding supervisory status, along with the matter of how much independent judgment or discretion is involved in hiring, firing, and managing workers (Gorman 1976:36).

At the time that strawberry sharecropping was readopted, sharecroppers were treated as exempt from Social Security withholding under the Federal Insurance Contributions Act as well as from coverage under workers' compensation insurance. Moreover, as independent contractors, they were exempt from child labor laws that prevent minors under the age of twelve from working on farms at all and that limit the farm work of minors through the age of fifteen.[1]

In short, when sharecropping expanded in the central coast strawberry industry, sharecroppers occupied a legal position that was likely to exclude them from coverage under federal and state labor-protective legislation. Although sharecroppers' exclusion was not a foregone conclusion, in practice, employers' claims as to the legal status of their workers tend to be accepted until they are challenged in the courts. And indeed strawberry sharecroppers were initially treated as independent contractors and supervisors: the petty bourgeois agents of capital whose contracts accorded them some autonomy, who performed crucial functions for management, and who themselves employed and supervised workers. Viewed thus, they could not qualify for employee protections, and they could not join labor unions.

The Economic Position of Sharecroppers

If we look beneath sharecroppers' formal legal designation to their actual roles in the productive process, their petty bourgeois status appears less clear-cut. Let us examine this position in terms of the six "reality of economic dependence" criteria used to establish independent contractor

[1]Children are still required to attend school full time through the age of fifteen.

versus employee status under the FLSA (see table 18), which to a considerable extent coincide with the diacritica used by social scientists to determine petty bourgeois versus proletarian status (Poulantzas [1974] 1979; Wright 1976).[2] Here a landmark court case challenging the independent contractor status of sharecroppers, *Real v. Driscoll Strawberry Associates* (1975), is illustrative. First, we find that the degree of control that these sharecroppers exerted over the manner in which the work was to be done—including the amount of initiative, skill, judgment, or foresight required from them, and the amount of supervision and the "right to control" on the part of owners—was extremely limited. Although their contracts termed them "independent contractors," their ability to assign the means of production to given uses and to control the physical operation of production was highly constrained. Sharecroppers in *Real* experienced an additional level of bourgeois authority not exerted over all sharecroppers, in that the grower delegated a variety of research, production, and marketing functions to his marketing organization, Driscoll Strawberry Associates (DSA), which represented a differentiated function of capital. Sharecroppers in this case were formally responsible for planting, but in fact DSA's "Patent Sublicense and Subcontract" gave it "full and complete authority to determine the number of plants to be supplied per acre . . . to vary the variety to be supplied . . . and to reduce the acreage agreed to be grown hereunder." The ranch owner received DSA's directions as to how and when planting should be executed, and sharecroppers were expected to follow these specifications precisely. Sharecroppers were charged with dusting for mildew, applying extra fertilizer, weeding, and irrigating, and DSA's field agents regularly inspected the fields for pests, diseases, and the adequacy of water and fertilizer. They issued directions to the grower, and through his field supervisors to the sharecroppers, as to when and how these responsibilities should be carried out. Tellingly, although the grower portrayed his supervisor's instructions to sharecroppers as simply "advice," the supervisor said that sharecroppers had never disobeyed him (*Real*, Mukai 1976:16). The text of seven identical sharecropper affidavits shows the substantial extent of supervisory control:

[2]Poulantzas and Wright determine bourgeois status in terms of the extent of a worker's actual involvement in economic ownership and the extent of his or her actual control over production. Poulantzas holds that while the functions of capital may be assigned to different persons, its structural position is unitary, so that involvement in any part of it designates that grouping or individual as bourgeois ([1974] 1979:180–81). I disagree, because differentiated capitalist production relations generate divergent pulls for class identification and action, and because his characterization overemphasizes the role of structure to the detriment of class struggle, contingency, and agency.

> When it comes time to fertilize the strawberries, Kay [Driscoll supervisor Mukai] tells me when it is time to fertilize, either by leaving the fertilizer bags in the field near my plot or by telling me to get fertilizer from the storage shed.... It is very clear to me that I have no choice as to whether to fertilize or not, or when or what type to use. I do what Kay tells me. During the picking season, there are times when it is necessary for me to get additional help in the picking. I either hire more people or tell Kay that I have not been able to hire more people, as none are available. If Kay tells me to hire more people, I hire more people.
>
> The hours of picking are determined by Kay. If I do not arrive in the fields, Kay is on the telephone calling every five minutes to find out where I am. . . . Kay also determines the hours that we will pick by informing us that the last truck will pass through the fields at a certain time. Since the strawberries must be loaded onto the trucks, that determines when our picking day will end. I plant both summer variety and winter variety of strawberries. Kay tells me how many [of each] I will have in my plot, and which rows to put into [each]. Kay tells me how far apart to plant the plants in that a machine comes by and automatically makes a mark in the earth where the plants are to go. If any plant is out of order, Kay comes by, points to it and tells me to replant it, and I have to replant it.
>
> When it comes time for pruning . . . Kay calls me at home to tell me to come out and prune. He also calls me at home to tell me that my plot needs weeding. If I do not come out, he stays on the telephone and insists I come out. At the end of . . . the year when the plants are to be disked under, the only thing we know as to when disking will occur is that Kay tells us to get the irrigation pipes out of the fields, and then the disker comes and everything gets disked under. Those plants still have strawberries that we could pick and sell, but we are not permitted to do this. During every day's picking, a lot of strawberries are rejected, either for size or for shape, but that are otherwise very good berries to eat. I do not have the right to take these berries and sell them anywhere. I am instructed either to pick these berries and throw them in the trenches or to dump rejected crates of berries. I do not get paid for those berries.... Whenever I have tried to argue with Kay when he has told me to do something, like dusting or fertilizing or irrigating, or over the hours I work, he always lets me know that he can take the strawberries away from me and that I have to do what he says. It is my personal understanding that if Kay does not like the way I am using my plot, he can fire me.

As these statements reveal, these sharecroppers' actual independence and control were highly circumscribed and were held within the lines of technique established by the owner. To be sure, supervision was not always as intensive as on this ranch, but in most cases it went far beyond its contractual portrayal as involving only the "result of the work assigned to be performed . . . and not the means as to which the results are to be accomplished." Thus, though these sharecroppers did have more flexibility than wage workers in setting the hours, pace, and social composition of labor, and though they took on a management function by hiring and supervising workers, they were also personally subordinated to a supervisor in the process of production.

Second, in terms of sharecroppers' "opportunity for profit or loss dependent on [their] managerial skill," the owner in this case bore the full risk of loss since the monetary investment was his. Sharecroppers could do little to increase their opportunity for profit but to request a larger plot. Even then, the owner made the allocation, usually on the basis of family size. As a result, a sharecropper's profits relied mainly on his or her speed and efficiency as a pieceworker and on DSA's managerial skills and decisions regarding quality standards and the number and type of plants to be given sharecroppers (*Real,* Brief 1977:18; *Real,* Crowley 1976:5; *Real,* Summary 1979: 2894–95). Third, sharecroppers' investment in the facilities and materials required for their tasks was also extremely limited and was far outbalanced by the farm owner's provision of land, plants, chemicals, and substantial machinery and equipment. Sharecroppers supplied only simple tools and equipment, items that wage workers often provided as well.

Fourth, in terms of the skill involved in the operation, sharecroppers' tasks and skills, aside from those involved in recruiting and managing workers, were essentially those of wage workers. Fifth, as we have seen and as the evidence of *Real* confirmed, the work that sharecroppers do—planting, cultivating, and harvesting strawberries—is clearly an integral part of the farming business, as opposed to the sort of peripheral, separable service associated with an independent contractor. Finally, in terms of the permanency of the employment relationship, sharecroppers were engaged for a season at a time and hired repeatedly, like employees, rather than more briefly and sporadically, like independent contractors. The power to establish the terms of the relationship clearly belonged to owners, who unilaterally set its conditions and length and could terminate it at any time. Moreover, labor market surpluses and the immigrant and often undocumented status of workers further diminished their ability to bargain the terms of their contracts, ensuring that they would accept what was offered (*Real,* Brief 1977:17–18; *Real,* Summary 1979:2895).

In sum, sharecropping reconfigured the legal dimensions of class structure, but it changed its economic dimensions less substantially. Sharecroppers' actual economic roles involved almost none of the economic control, independence, or investment that one would expect from a petty bourgeois independent contractor. Rather, they reflected primarily the dependency and subordination that one would expect from a proletarian employee. Thus sharecropping did not significantly change the economic dependency that motivated the legal protection of employees. In this sense, there was reason to think that they would qualify as employees in terms of the binary categories of the law. Sharecropping did, however, alter economic structure in ways that affected intra- and interclass relations, for it fragmented the working class and instituted relations of exploitation within it that redounded to the benefit of capital.

That is, by replacing some of the wage labor on a ranch with unpaid family labor mediated by personal relationships, sharecropping enabled farm owners to profit from family members' self-exploitation. Indeed, according to sharecroppers and other observers, the hourly rate often fell below the legal minimum.[3] Sharecropping also enabled growers (and sharecroppers) to benefit from under-age workers. Furthermore, it fragmented the overall workforce into one set of workers (sharecroppers) who had the authority to hire and fire and the motivation to extract the most from their employees, and another (their hired workers) who had none of that opportunity or motivation. As the immediate directors of the production process and the dispensers of jobs, sharecroppers enjoyed some of the prerogatives and status accorded growers. Then, too, they were the legal agents (to some sharecroppers, the "partners") of growers, their fortunes rose and fell along with growers', and on the face of it, they were excluded from labor organizations. These facts distanced them from workers and encouraged their identification with growers. Together, these structural pressures could be expected to fragment and undermine the solidarity of the workforce by increasing sharecroppers' sense of common cause with growers and by driving a wedge between sharecroppers and hired workers. Yet other aspects of their positions worked against this fragmentation. Sharecroppers did manual work, they were supervised themselves, and they were often highly restricted in the exercise of their functions, which encouraged a concomitant identification with workers. Their employment of family members and friends and their sharing of ethnic history, traditions, and liabilities with their employees also fostered empathy with labor.

In short, sharecropping engendered a tension between sharecroppers' alleged (and initial) positions in legal structure and their actual roles in economic structure. Their economic positions themselves also created

[3]Melvyn Silver, the lawyer who represented the sharecroppers in *Real,* had his clients keep records of the investment of family labor on their parcels. In almost half of the years and cases documented, hourly wage rates were below the legal minimum—sometimes substantially so.

certain strains. Sharecroppers were not free wage laborers, although they performed proletarian functions within capitalist firms. Together, their economic and legal positions accorded them an objectively contradictory structural location within class relations.

The Ideological Position of Sharecroppers

How did the sharecroppers' positions in class structure affect their actual perceptions of self-interest, identification, and alliance? To get at this question, and at wage workers' perceptions of sharecroppers' class location as well, I asked both groups whether they thought a sharecropper was "more like a farm worker [*trabajador del campo*] or more like a farm owner [*agricultor, ranchero, dueño*]." I selected these terms after consulting with principal informants as to how participants would refer to these groupings. In the interviews, I first elicited spontaneous responses, then probed the reasons behind them, and finally explored the contradictions contained within them. For example, if a person answered "like a farmer," I would observe after his or her elaboration, "But can't the contracts of sharecroppers be ended at any time?" If the individual answered "like a farm worker," I would comment, "But don't sharecroppers hire farm workers themselves?" Interestingly, most of these probes elicited a reinforcement of the initial statement. A few interviewees switched from one or the other position to "both," offering clarification of their revised positions. No interviewee reversed a perspective initially offered, suggesting that the probe did not skew their responses.

Sharecroppers' responses reflected the contradictory pulls of their objective positions in economic and legal structure. Some saw sharecroppers definitively as growers, citing the attributes associated with this status: ownership *(dueño),* direction of production tasks *(agricultor, ranchero),* and authority and a right to deference *(patrón).* In this connection they emphasized sharecroppers' more flexible work hours and pace, their independence from the most coercive direct supervision, their sharing of some of the responsibilities, risks, and benefits of being a grower, and their belief that sharecropping could be a stepping-stone to independent farming. One former sharecropper who returned to farm labor when his sharecropping ranch shifted back to crews, attributed sharecroppers' petty bourgeois status to their involvement in guiding production:

> I was the *agricultor.* When I went out and saw the rows I was going to get, they were mine. I did the production. I was proud of the harvest. On a block there were many sharecroppers and we were in competition. I was proud

when I got a better crop than other sharecroppers because it was the same climate. The difference was, I was a better *agricultor.* (labor-supplier no. 57)

Another former sharecropper also saw himself as more like a grower, basing his assessment on his legal status, the fact that he shared with the grower a direct benefit from market proceeds, and the fact that he was less intrusively supervised:

> A sharecropper is a *ranchero.* He receives part of the profit and shares the cost with the *patrón.* When I was a sharecropper I was registered as a *ranchero* in Sacramento. The big difference is, no one orders you around. If you're late as a *trabajador,* the foreman fires you. If you are late as a sharecropper, he points it out to you. Of course as a sharecropper you often arrive even earlier, because you are responsible for the work and you want to keep the job. (labor-supplier no. 43)

A third emphasized his opportunity, as a sharecropper, to become an independent farmer:

> I'm learning as a sharecropper. *Señor* [X] has given me a chance to learn how to grow strawberries. We want to get a little ranch up there in the hills, like my cousin. He was a sharecropper first too. It's a chance to improve oneself. (labor-supplier no. 13)

However, some interviewees challenged these representations of sharecroppers' independence, emphasizing their actual dependency and common cause with workers.

> When we were sharecroppers they told us that we were *patrones.* They said we had the chance to make more money. But I did not feel like that. If we were *patrones,* why couldn't we even bring a box of berries home to eat? They never showed us the sales price that they got for the berries, so how could we know how much we should really be earning? How could we know what to do better? In truth, a sharecropper is only a *patrón* compared with a *trabajador.* He's a *peón* to the *dueño.* (labor-supplier no. 23)

> A sharecropper is more like a *trabajador* because, in reality, he is taking orders from another person, just like a *trabajador.* He has to work with his hands just like a *trabajador,* while the *agricultor* orders others to do the work. And he has the same problems—that he can be fired at any moment they want. [I probe: "Isn't it true that you can hire and fire too?"] Yes, we

can hire and fire our workers, but the *dueño* can fire us tomorrow as well. If I were really independent, who would be able to fire me? No one. That's why I'm more like a *trabajador*. (labor-supplier no. 10)

A sharecropper is more like a *trabajador* because he doesn't prepare the land. How can one be an *agricultor* if he doesn't even put a tractor in the earth, if he doesn't even know about the fertilizers, if he doesn't irrigate or spray? We can't even decide how to plant our plants. They do all of that. We know nothing about how to do it. They order their people to spray and we have to leave the fields. We only do what a worker does: we bring in the harvest and make sure that the plants are clean. It's true that we employ people. In this we have some control. But in the rest we're just *trabajadores del campo*. (labor-supplier no. 36)

A sharecropper is worse than a worker. A worker almost always gets his money and he can apply for [unemployment insurance]. As sharecroppers we can work all year and never get anything. My cousin and his wife had to go back to Mexico because the berries were not good enough to pay for the food and the rent. Some years are like that. And who takes care of us then? No one. (labor-supplier no. 16)

In some cases, the objective bases for divergent assessments were expressed in the same interview. For example, one husband-and-wife team who shared responsibility for their parcel, answered decisively in opposite directions (interview no. 63).

"Like an *agricultor*," she said.

"Like a *trabajador*," he said.

She elaborated: "We are like *dueños*. I can take the children to school or stay home with them when they are sick. I can go home to make lunch for them. We can work mostly as we want . . . slow, fast. As a *trabajador*, one always has to work fast. If the foreman tells you to, you have to go into the fields after a rain and get covered with mud. As sharecroppers, we stay home."

He interrupted: "But we aren't independent. If we don't work as they say, we could lose our parcel just like that. We worry ourselves sick about whether we'll have a job next year. But [he brightened visibly], it's true that the *dueño* depends on us to tell him if the plants are sick. We even have a key to the ranch!"

Almost 60 percent of the labor-suppliers interviewed responded spontaneously that sharecroppers were more like growers. But a substantial minority—27 percent—were less enamored with sharecropping and saw sharecroppers as comparable to wage workers, citing their limited freedom of action, job security, and production responsibilities. Not surprisingly, sharecroppers for low-resource, low-investment growers were concentrated in this category. If we add to this most disillusioned group those who affirmed that sharecroppers were in ways like both, the challenge to their petty bourgeois status is even greater. Initially, 13 percent insisted that sharecroppers were like farmers in some ways and like workers in others; after my probe, 49 percent said they were "like growers," 21 percent said, "like workers," and 30 percent said "both." Interestingly enough, sharecroppers and wage workers did not differ significantly in their responses, which is understandable given their common social origins and current networks, as well as individuals' movement back and forth between the positions.

The Role of Sharecroppers in Class Struggle

How did the reconfiguring of legal and economic structure and the consequently divergent pulls on class identification affect the actual relations between social classes? Did it, as one might expect, benefit growers by undermining the solidarity of the workforce, weakening labor organizations, and freeing growers from legally mandated costs and restrictions? In point of fact, this anticipated benefit did not universally materialize, both because of the contradictory pulls on class consciousness and because of the interplay between class initiatives and the law. In the end, the meaning of class structure took shape through the processes of class struggle, as these were played out in the fields and in the courts.

Class Struggle in the Fields

The institution of sharecropping produced a complex fabric of daily relationships among labor-suppliers. A sensitive and conflictual relationship linked sharecroppers with their supervisors, in which the supervision of the latter often violated the contractual autonomy of the former. In essence, these two agents of capital collided in the implementation of their formally defined roles. Sharecroppers' day-to-day relationships with their employees were more ambiguous. Because sharecroppers received only a fraction of the returns for their own labor, they had a reputation for "squeezing" their workers and paying the lowest wages in the industry. Their walk-on workers were especially dependent, since they lacked experience and connections to other work. Yet personal affections and affiliations mitigated workplace tensions as well: many employees were friends or relatives, and many workers were household members. Thus personal commitment coexisted with, and frequently softened, the strains generated by low wages and high performance pressure. Like growers in the North Monterey Hills, sharecroppers tried to smooth over frictions by calling their jobs "extra income" or "training" for those who took them. To my knowledge, concerted labor protest did not exist on sharecropping ranches: it was dispersed through personal negotiation and dampened by the dependency of unconnected workers, whose job tenure was especially short.

Sharecroppers' relations with the UFW were also ambivalent. As employers, they could be expected to oppose it; yet many had belonged to it in the past, sympathized with it in the present, and expected to join it in the future should they lose their positions as sharecroppers. Many had friends or relatives who were union members. Moreover, their economic dependency fostered a sense of common cause with wage workers. Finally, most sharecroppers perceived the UFW as it presented itself: not simply as a labor organization, but as an ethnic power movement—the advocate for Mexicans against Anglo and Japanese farmers. For its part, the UFW avoided sharecropping ranches, as it did those of Mexican growers, because they extended entrepreneurial opportunities to Mexicans. As union conflict intensified in the region, however, sharecroppers were drawn into the fray. During the 1970 general strike, many sharecroppers participated in rallies and marches. When Chavez urged local workers to organize and formulate their grievances against their employers, a group of Driscoll sharecroppers gathered to discuss their concerns. A primary complaint was that they ("the ones who do all the real work") were given such a small share of the market returns. This group of sharecroppers then approached Chavez, identifying their concern as one of the historical injustices against Mexicans which the UFW was dedicated to address. They asked him to form a special bargaining unit of sharecroppers within the union to represent their interests to growers. Chavez was sympathetic to the spirit of their request because his own family had been sharecroppers and he believed that sharecroppers were exploited.[4] Because they were employers, however, he could not admit them into the union. As a compromise, he assigned UFW spokeswoman Dolores Huerta to negotiate on their behalf with DSA growers. As a direct result of these negotiations, Driscoll sharecroppers received an increase in their share of the market proceeds from 50 to 55 percent. In short, although sharecropping generated some conflicts of interest among labor-suppliers and some shared interests between sharecroppers and owners, it

[4]Interview with Marshall Ganz, Pacific Grove, Calif., August 1986.

did not prevent sharecroppers from attempting to ally with the labor movement in a period of intensified class conflict and working class mobilization. Most significant in this context, was sharecroppers' awareness of the dependency and ethnic identity they shared with workers.

Class Struggle in the Courts

The resurgence of sharecropping was but one of several steps in the interplay between legal structures and class initiatives in the industry. First, growers responded to the changed legal—and broader political—climate by restructuring their labor processes, thereby altering the legal and economic dimensions of class structure. Second, by so doing, they introduced contradictory strains into the social relations of production, and into labor-suppliers' views of their economic roles. Third—and here we pick up our story—because the rights and obligations of sharecroppers were set out in a legal contract, disputes about the economic relationship were brought to the courts. Over the course of the 1970s, a new form of class conflict emerged on some ranches: lawsuits initiated by sharecroppers and their allies against farm owner-operators. These suits illustrate several aspects of court-based class struggles: the transformative interaction between the economic realities and legal definitions of work relationships; the active, even catalytic, involvement of advocates; and the impact on local class prerogatives and obligations of legal precedents and struggles that are temporally and geographically distant. Finally, the strawberry suits, along with those brought in different regions and crop industries, eventually altered sharecroppers' views of their roles in production, as well as the advantage of sharecropping under the law. When the political advantage of economic relations shifted, strawberry labor processes were again reconfigured. An examination of the processes of court-based class struggle clarifies this dialectical process.[5]

In 1975, about a decade after the resurgence of sharecropping began, fourteen sharecroppers working for Driscoll Berry Farms in the Salinas-Watsonville area initiated a suit jointly against this company and its marketing association, Driscoll Strawberry Associates (DSA) (*Real* 1975). The plaintiffs in *Real* expressed complaints that were common among strawberry sharecroppers and had been brewing for years. That is, when individuals initially became sharecroppers, they were excited by the prospect

[5]My understanding of the following cases is based on a review of the court records and material provided by the sharecroppers' attorneys in *Real, Álvara,* and *Borello;* interviews with growers, sharecroppers, wage workers, farm advisers, and others; study of the legal history and precedents affecting the strawberry cases; and talks and written exchanges with involved attorneys and labor organizers in the Midwest and Texas.

of the greater independence and autonomy their contracts offered them. Many took seriously their contractual characterization as independent contractors, and they thought of themselves as small-scale entrepreneurs. Although they did not expect the full freedom of action that entrepreneurs in other contexts might anticipate, they were frustrated by the actual extent of their subordination. They complained that they were too restricted in the exercise of their responsibilities, paid too little for their fruit, and that, because the company withheld sales information and required them to market the crop through it, they could not exercise their rights as independent contractors to seek the highest return for their product. After presenting these concerns to their supervisor to no avail, several sharecroppers approached a local community development corporation. There, a staff member urged them to sue DSA for constraint of free trade and monopolistic domination of the market and put them in touch with Melvyn Silver, a labor lawyer with the firm of Morgan, Beauzay, and Hammer.

Upon sharecroppers' initial instruction, Silver prepared a class action suit against DSA and Driscoll Berry Farms as joint employers, on behalf of the estimated two hundred sharecroppers who had signed DSA contracts in the state. The charges were antitrust damages, fraud, misrepresentation, and breach of contract. The initial six detailed causes of action accused the defendants of restraining free trade in the market by combining and contracting to establish an artificially low price to be paid to sharecroppers, by restricting the production of berries, and by controlling the quantity and price of berries in the market. In addition, the suit maintained that DSA withheld financial information from sharecroppers and in other ways restricted their "freedom to . . . conduct their business in a manner of their own choosing" (*Real* 1975:2–9). All of these actions, the suit declared, intentionally violated sharecroppers' contractual status as independent contractors.

After filing the case, Silver began to interview his clients to get a better understanding of the case. Within a week, he concluded that his clients were inadequately protected employees rather than unfairly restricted independent contractors. He presented this view to his clients with mixed results. Some were adamant about pursuing the vision of their roles as independent entrepreneurs whose freedom to conduct business was unfairly constrained by a large, monopolistic firm. Yet all also acknowledged their day-to-day dependency, and as their attorney emphasized this dimension of their positions, it became more salient in their eyes as well. In the end, they let him file a seventh cause of action charging that the DSA contract was a "sham" whose misrepresentation was "deliberate, willful, and intentional and was designed to mislead and did mislead plaintiffs into not understanding their true status as employees" (*Real,* Complaint 1975:3).

This charge importantly changed the legal conception of the case. It claimed unspecified damages for violations of the FLSA on the grounds that the relationship between the plaintiffs and defendants was one of employees to employers, because of the substantial control the defendants exerted over production. As the suit played out, this seventh cause of action was the one that prevailed. The defendants refused to answer many questions pertaining to their alleged monopolistic practices on the grounds that the information was privileged. In 1977, the U.S. District Court for the Northern District of California granted summary judgment in favor of the defendants, on the grounds that there was insufficient evidence to proceed. Attorney Silver decided that he did not have enough evidence to prove the antitrust case, but he did have enough to justify a reversal of the summary judgment and a retrial on the FLSA charge. He appealed the summary judgment of the seventh amended cause of action to the U.S. Court of Appeals for the Ninth Circuit. The appellate court dismissed several of the defendants' arguments as to why sharecroppers were independent contractors: because their contracts said they were, because they thought they were, and because they hired and fired helpers. Instead, it ruled that expanded definitions of employee and employer and the economic reality of the sharecroppers' positions as determined by the six-factor federal test of employment should be used to establish employment status, rather than the possession of a single defining feature, the common law usage of the terms, contractual labels, or the beliefs of participants (*Real,* Summary 1979:2888; *Real,* Brief 1977:14). In the end, the appellate court reversed the summary judgment and remanded the case to the lower court for further consideration, on the grounds that there was indeed sufficient dispute of material fact as to the potential employee status of sharecroppers to warrant reevaluation of the case. At that point, the defendants offered to settle out of court. Silver accepted their offer and, in March 1981, the case was dismissed.

Real, then, illustrates the chain of events set in motion by growers' resumption of sharecropping: first, sharecropping altered some aspects of workers' legal, economic, and ideological positions in class structure; second, the discrepancy between the ideal of their legal characterization and the reality of their economic experience engendered frustration; third, the fact that sharecroppers' economic rights were set forth in legal documents encouraged them to turn to the courts for relief; and, fourth, the process of litigation enhanced the felt salience of economic dependency and secured a ruling that changed the interpretation and application of the law.

The Aftermath

The legal-economic interplay did not stop here. The impact of *Real* went far beyond its immediate courtroom drama. Although the appellate court only reversed the summary judgment and did not rule definitively on the merits of the case, it clearly laid out an argument that supported sharecroppers' employee status. Moreover, because this ruling was published, it could be used as precedent in other cases. Central coast growers, farm workers, and sharecroppers had followed the case closely, as had the agents and agencies responsible for enforcing the law. In practice, *Real* established a legal precedent for the notion that California strawberry sharecroppers were disguised wage workers, and this elicited new responses from sharecroppers and growers alike. Beyond its impact on the central coast strawberry industry, *Real* became part of a wider state and national struggle between farm workers and their advocates, on the one hand, and growers and their spokespeople, on the other, concerning the legal designation and prerogatives of sharecroppers.

Central Coast Responses

For sharecroppers on the central coast, *Real* introduced one more element of confusion and contradiction into an already complex employment relationship. Some expressed resentment of *Real,* fearing it would mean the end of a valued job. Growers openly discussed this possibility with them. Some sharecroppers stated that *Real* had changed their understanding of their work, leading them to believe they were employees, and, as an expression of this conviction, they brought workers' compensation claims against farm owners. For owners, *Real* raised the specter of costly suits and fines. Growers recognized that, should they continue to engage sharecroppers as before, or should they be challenged on former practices, they could be liable for tremendous fines and back payments for payroll taxes and wages, not to mention charges of child labor law violations. News of the landmark case spread rapidly through the tightly knit central coast farming community. Local workers' compensation insurance companies began to informally require berry growers to insure their sharecroppers as if they were employees. Most growers quietly paid. Pajaro Valley growers met to discuss their alternatives, bringing in labor relations experts to clarify the legal consequences of *Real.* One such expert prepared a document that identified the "factors to be considered to prove that these individuals are share growers and not employees." The factors identified were the six criteria used in *Real.* The document went on to describe how the relationship between growers and sharecroppers should be structured and described to outside observers, and what costs and responsibilities should be shifted to sharecroppers so as to legally establish their independent contractor status.

In response to their recognition of legal vulnerability, some growers again began to restructure and redefine the working relationships on their ranches. One common practice was to retain sharecropping but to marginally increase sharecroppers' independence and contribution to production. In one such case, the grower gave his sharecroppers small pumps to inject fertilizer into the drip lines and loans to purchase small tractors that could be used for weeding, pruning, and cutting runners. He also required them to help pay for fertilizers and pesticide applications. The grower performed all the aerial spraying himself, but he let sharecroppers spot spray with backpack sprayers or go elsewhere to subcontract ground sprayings. He also instituted a joint sharecropper-management committee to set the timing of aerial spraying. Another strategy was to change the legal designation of sharecroppers to "foremen," identifying them and their families and hired workers as the grower's employees and granting foremen a bonus linked to market proceeds in addition to their wage. This arrangement retained the fundamental organization of sharecropping: the same parcels were worked in the same manner by the same individuals. It had the advantage of providing some of the performance incentives of sharecropping while permitting close supervision and ensuring that labor protections—for which farm owners were ultimately responsible—would be observed. In one such case, contracts assigned each foreman a specified parcel of land and authorized each to supervise and keep records of hours worked and crates picked for the workers necessary to tend the parcel. The grower provided all nonlabor inputs, marketed the fruit, and paid each foremen and his crew at certain (differing) wage rates. As an extra incentive, foremen were allowed to sell (on their own time) any fruit the grower had rejected. At the end of the season, each foreman received a "bonus" similar to the percentage received by sharecroppers.[6]

[6]That is, from the gross sales of berries harvested from that parcel, the grower deducted the cost of crates, baskets, and wires used, and he computed the foreman's share as a certain percentage (ranging from 43 to 51) of the amount of each variety of fruit picked on the parcel. From this share the grower deducted: gross wages for the foreman and his crew; the total employer's share of FICA; premiums for unemployment, disability, and workers' compensation insurance; and miscellaneous deductions for employee misuse or loss of equipment, tools, and supplies. The bonuses of foremen were in fact small under this system, but they tied the returns of a foreman to the value and efficiency of production on the parcel, thereby providing an additional incentive beyond that offered by a straight wage. Like sharecroppers, these foremen could increase household income by hiring family members, whereas stan-

In sum, *Real* had a major impact on the central coast strawberry industry. The growers involved in the dominant, high-investment pattern of sharecropping were the most responsive to its findings, because they were the most integrated into industry and political networks, the most aware of the consequences of legal infractions, and the most averse to unfavorable publicity. Some of them responded by increasing the independence of sharecroppers to make them more acceptable under the law. For most growers, however, the difficulties and risks of continuing to sharecrop appeared overwhelming. Grower after grower explained to me that the potential legal sanctions that could result from controlling sharecroppers, and the difficulty of achieving the level of adherence to technical specifications without close control, were too great. These growers, who had the capital and management expertise to farm with wage workers, began to shift back to wage labor after the early 1980s. By 1987, the proportion of sharecropped berry acreage on the central coast had shrunk from about 50 percent to about 10 percent.

The Wider Context

Real contributed to changes in legal standards and working relationships in other regions and industries as well. Here again, legal advocates and labor organizing played crucial roles in spurring adherence to the law. As in *Real,* some advocates were private lawyers; others were housed in the agencies charged with enforcing social-protective laws; yet others were members of the large and integrated national network of legal services attorneys.

California. First, *Real* played a role, albeit with varying local responses, in struggles over the legal status of sharecroppers elsewhere in California. To understand this variation, we must look more closely at crop-related and regional differences in the incidence and nature of sharecropping. When *Real* was settled, share arrangements were employed in a variety of other California crop industries. Throughout the state, as in the Midwest and elsewhere (Reed and Horel 1980; Reid 1979), cash grain and tree fruit and nut producers customarily had share agreements with landowners. Such arrangements differed substantially, however, from those in strawberries, in that share tenants were more genuinely independent, shouldered a significant proportion of production risk, performed a much wider

---

dard foremen were rarely allowed to comprise their crews entirely of relatives, due to the potential friction with other workers caused by perceptions of favoritism. This bonus arrangement buffered foremen from major risks, by giving them a base wage and by providing that the grower shoulder the burden of a negative cash flow.

range of (if not all) production tasks, and invested substantially in the business. Share contracts were also used in other labor-intensive fruit and vegetable crop industries in the state, and this form of sharecropping was more similar, in that sharecroppers provided the hand labor and farm owners generally financed and ran the business. Important pockets of this form of sharecropping were found in the production of bush berries in the Salinas-Watsonville area, pickling cucumbers in the Gilroy-Hollister area just to the east of our region, and snow peas, tomatillos, vine tomatoes, peppers, and baby vegetables in the Santa Maria Valley just to the south. By far the most important user of labor-intensive sharecropping, in terms of the acres, crop value, and labor-suppliers involved, was the Santa Maria Valley strawberry industry. According to the local farm adviser, almost 100 percent of Santa Maria strawberry and labor-intensive vegetable acreage was sharecropped until the appeals court decision in *Real*.[7]

Not surprisingly, share agreements in grains, tree fruits, and nuts were not disturbed by this case, because the sharecroppers involved were so much more independent. The first response to *Real* arose in the Santa Maria Valley strawberry industry. Like Salinas-Watsonville, Santa Maria was relatively distant from the border, destabilized by the end of the bracero program, and exposed to substantial UFW pressure over the course of the 1970s. The region differed from Salinas-Watsonville, however, in terms of the composition and motivations of its grower population, their links to the wider political economy, and the control relations on their ranches. Through the 1970s, berry production in the area was dominated by several large, high-investment sharecropping companies that had been in the business for years. One of these was a member of DSA. Between 1980 and 1990, however, strawberry acreage in the two-county area quadrupled (PSAB 1992). Most of the new growers were Mexican-origin former sharecroppers, many financed by independent shippers. A minority were nonfarming investors. Both categories of new growers used low-investment sharecropping to improve their cash flows and bolster their farm management resources. Neither was well integrated into the industry's local and statewide informational and political networks. The Mexican growers, especially, were relatively uninformed about the potential legal

[7]During the 1980s, shifts in the cost of capital, domestic farm support policies, and international market prices and supplies motivated the conversion of a large part of the acreage in Santa Barbara and San Luis Obispo Counties out of capital-intensive, low-value products such as grains and livestock into labor-intensive, high-value crops such as snow peas, baby vegetables, vine tomatoes, tomatillos, and grapes (Palerm 1984). Share contracts were used in many of these crops. Information about Santa Maria sharecropping comes from the local farm adviser, CRLA attorneys, sharecroppers, and the dissertation research of Teresa Figueroa (Department of Anthropology, University of California, Santa Barbara).

sanctions against sharecropping and unconcerned about the threat of unionization. In some cases, sharecroppers on their ranches were relatively independent.

In 1978, even before the resolution of the *Real* appeal, a Santa Maria Valley strawberry sharecropper, Martin Álvara, went to the local office of California Rural Legal Assistance (CRLA) complaining that his employer, a member of DSA, had fired him for attempting to organize his fellow sharecroppers into a union. In Álvara's view he was as vulnerable as a wage worker and should be entitled to form a union. CRLA, whose mission was to provide legal services to farm workers in California, activated its broad support network to get a perspective on the matter. It contacted its San Francisco office, which in turn consulted Migrant Legal Action Program, the national support center for legal services lawyers, situated in Washington, D.C. It also contacted legal services attorneys in Texas and the Midwest who had sharecropper concerns of their own. Finally, CRLA lawyers directly contacted the sharecroppers' attorney in *Real* and reviewed the briefs and the plaintiffs' files in that case.

Convinced by this research that Álvara's complaint had merit and convinced more generally that such sharecroppers were employees, CRLA filed a complaint on behalf of Álvara before the Agricultural Labor Relations Board (ALRB). This case, *Álvara v. Driscoll Strawberry Associates* (1979), charged that Álvara's dismissal was an unfair labor practice under Chapter 4 of California's Agricultural Labor Relations Act. The charge was first dismissed in 1981 by the Oxnard regional director of the ALRB on the grounds that, because Álvara had the authority to hire, discharge, reward, discipline, and direct employees, he was a supervisor rather than an employee for purposes of the NLRA and ALRA. Thus, he was not entitled to protections for organizing. CRLA then requested a review of the dismissal by the board's general counsel, but the general counsel upheld the ruling on the grounds that Álvara's supervisory status outweighed the mitigating circumstances presented. Although the general counsel's review did not constitute legal precedent, and another counsel might have accorded different weight to supervisorial status, *Álvara* showed that sharecroppers would not have the support of the ALRA in their efforts to organize against and bargain with farm owners at that time.

When *Real* was decided in 1979, one of the large, high-investment strawberry sharecropping ranches in Santa Maria with control relations comparable to those examined in *Real* shifted back to wage labor. The other two continued to sharecrop, but they modified their contracts to increase the relative contribution and autonomy of sharecroppers. The low-investment strawberry and labor-intensive vegetable growers in the area not only continued to sharecrop, but proliferated, their owners drawn by the promise of getting a toehold on the agricultural ladder by engaging sharecroppers. Observing that these growers suffered no legal sanctions for their practices, and experiencing financial difficulties from the previous crop years, one large grower who had shifted back to wage labor after *Real* returned to sharecropping in 1985–86. Meanwhile, large-scale pickling cucumber producers elsewhere in the state did not respond to *Real* at all, a situation that observers attribute variously to ignorance, to the inertia of custom, to growers' beliefs that cucumber sharecropping differed sufficiently from that in strawberries, and to the reinforcing experience of midwestern cucumber growers who had been using sharecroppers for years with little legal consequence. This pattern of response was by no means isolated. Growers were most likely to change their employment relationships in response to rulings when they grew the same crop, so that the "economic realities" of their working relationships were comparable, and when they operated in the same region, so that the orientations of legal actors and the organization and character of growers and workers were similar.

In 1985, another California suit arose, this time against a family-operated fruit and vegetable company that produced pickling cucumbers for Vlasic Pickle Company near the town of Gilroy.[8] This suit, *S. G. Borello and Sons, Inc., v. State Department of Industrial Relations,* began when the Department of Industrial Relations cited Borello for having under-age children working in his fields and for failing to provide workers' compensation insurance for the fifty harvesters working on his ranch. Borello responded that his harvesters were independent contractors and were thus exempt from employee protection laws. Although the labor commissioner initially ruled against Borello, his ruling was overturned by the state court of appeal. Then the California Supreme Court took the rare action of ordering review on its own motion and launched an investigation into the case itself. Whereas *Real* was fought in a relatively low-key way, *Borello* was

[8]The pickling cucumber industries of California, Texas, and the Midwest illustrate crop-specific variability in the utility of sharecroppers. Sequential ripening and the high prices paid for pickles of a small and uniform size are major barriers to mechanization in this industry. Cucumbers thus continue to be hand harvested. Because cucumbers are not as fragile as strawberries, handling requirements are not as stringent and children regularly work in the fields. The advantage of cucumber sharecropping is also related to a peculiarity of pickle pricing: pickling cucumbers are priced according to their size per hundredweight, with the smallest cucumbers receiving the highest market prices from processors. In this situation, paying workers a straight piece rate would encourage them to pick larger cucumbers in order to fill the hampers more rapidly. Tying workers' returns to the market proceeds through a share arrangement encourages them to pick the highest-priced cucumbers. From this vantage point, this form of sharecropping can be seen as a form of piece work.

bitterly contested and hit the headlines almost immediately. Attorneys for the Western Growers Association and the California Farm Bureau Federation submitted *amicus curiae* briefs supporting Borello. The Employment Law Center and CRLA filed a joint brief against him. From its experience with *Álvara* and with many other complaints that its Santa Maria office received from sharecroppers working in the area, CRLA had come to consider sharecropping one of the most serious violations of farm workers' legal rights in the state. As in *Álvara,* CRLA activated its national network to develop its case.

In late March 1989, the California Supreme Court ruled that cucumber sharecroppers should be treated as employees for purposes of workers' compensation law. In discussing the bases for the ruling, Justice David Eagleson asserted that, although the common law "right to control the work" test had been historically used by California courts to distinguish exempt independent contractors from covered employees for purposes of unemployment and workers' compensation insurance, this test was, in fact, too narrow. Instead, to identify the full class of individuals intended to be covered,[9] the court used the broader federal test of employment which acknowledged the full economic reality of dependence, including the relative bargaining positions of the parties involved, the class of persons intended to be protected, and the remedial purposes of the statute in question. The court concluded that Borello's sharecroppers were "obvious members of the broad class to which workers' compensation protection is intended to apply" (*Borello* 1989:345). It also explicitly laid out the implications of *Borello* for the coverage of sharecroppers under other labor-protective laws. In his closing paragraphs, Eagleson concluded that the practice of designating individuals who are essentially employees as independent contractors

> would suggest a disturbing means of avoiding an employer's obligations under other California legislation intended for the protection of "employees," including laws enacted specifically for the protection of agricultural labor. These include the Agricultural Labor Relations Act, . . . statutes requiring the licensure and bonding of farm labor contractors, . . . laws governing minimum wages, maximum hours, and . . . employment of minors, . . . the antidiscrimination provisions of the Fair Employment and Housing Act, . . . and provisions governing employee health and safety. (*Borello* 1989:359)

[9]The Workers' Compensation Act explicitly excludes independent contractors and inserts the control of work test in its statutory definition of them (*Borello* 1989).

The Supreme Court's ruling in *Borello* dealt what newspapers called a "stunning" blow to California growers.[10] It was estimated that the ruling could affect as many as twenty thousand farm workers in the state who had signed some form of share agreement. Whereas the decision applied directly only to farm laborers, attorneys on both sides of the dispute said that the legal standards it set could affect future cases in other sectors of the economy, from the garment industry to taxi driving and the computer business, where subcontracting and consulting arrangements were common. *Borello* especially alarmed growers in the multimillion-dollar Santa Maria strawberry and vegetable industries, most of whom used sharecroppers. According to CRLA attorneys, most large-scale, high-investment berry growers stopped sharecropping "immediately" after the *Borello* ruling. Observance in the mid-1990s is more scattered among the smaller, lower-resource berry and vegetable producers. Some have adopted new permutations of subcontracting which, like sharecropping, make it hard to identify the employees and employers. At least one important new sharecropper case has hit the courts. In Salinas-Watsonville, most of the remaining sharecropping operations have shifted to wage labor, on low- as well as high-investment farms.[11]

The Midwest and Texas. As the independent contractor status of sharecroppers became increasingly contested and politically sensitive in California, similar battles were being waged elsewhere. Sharecropping was common in the pickling cucumber industries in Ohio, Michigan, Illinois, Wisconsin, Iowa, Minnesota, Colorado, and Texas. In the Great Lakes region, braceros were the pickle pickers of choice from the mid-1950s until the end of the program. But when the program ended and growers were faced with the reality of workers' expanded coverage under labor-protective laws and with the rise of the militant Farm Labor Organizing Committee (FLOC), they increasingly turned to sharecropping. As in the case of strawberry sharecropping, their sharecroppers were contractually identified as "independent contractors."

In the mid-1970s, cases challenging or alleging the independent contractor status of cucumber sharecroppers began to hit the courts. Attorneys examined the California precedents in developing their arguments. Although the cases had varying success in establishing the employee status

[10]See, for example, "Court Deals a Blow to Growers on Issue of Share Farmers," *Los Angeles Times*, 24 March 1989, pt. I, pp. 3, 23.

[11]Interestingly, Santa Maria berry growers continue to lag behind those in Salinas-Watsonville in terms of their willingness to abandon sharecropping. A variety of factors come into play here: the greater independence of sharecroppers on some ranches, differences in the character of the grower populations, and differences in the local political economy. This contrast invites further research and demonstrates the local contingency of such processes.

of sharecroppers, the historical trend was toward their inclusion. In Ohio, *Sachs v. U.S.* (1976) found that workers who cultivated and harvested pickling cucumbers were exempt from coverage under the FICA because they shared some of the risks with the owner and were "share farmers," a status allegedly exempt under the Internal Revenue Code. In 1982, a Texas court disagreed, ruling in *Salinas v. U.S.* that comparable sharecroppers were employees for purposes of the same statute. In 1985, the Internal Revenue Service resolved the dispute by affirming in Revenue Ruling 85-85 that cucumber sharecroppers were to be treated as employees for purposes of the FICA.[12] Similarly, in 1982, *Donovan v. Gillmor* ruled that Ohio cucumber sharecroppers were covered employees for purposes of the FLSA. This ruling was challenged by a Michigan court in *Marshall v. Brandel* (1983), which held that pickle farmers were not responsible for the child labor violations of their pickers because they were not employees under the FLSA. This ruling was upheld by the Court of Appeals for the Sixth Circuit in the following year (*Donovan v. Brandel* 1984). In 1985, however, a case was filed in Wisconsin charging child labor and other violations under the FLSA (*Brock v. Lauritzen*). *Brock* was appealed to the Seventh Circuit, which emphatically rejected the arguments of *Brandel*, upheld *Gillmor*, and ruled that migrant farm workers were unequivocally employees under the FLSA, whatever the crop or contract in each case.[13]

Growers' responses to these precedential cases varied according to their proximity to the district within which the cases were tried, and to the strength of labor organizing. Not surprisingly, attorneys and labor organizers report that pickle sharecropping increased in Michigan after *Brandel* upheld the independent contractor status of pickle sharecroppers. It has declined sharply, however, in Michigan and Wisconsin, after the appellate court ruling in *Lauritzen* (1987). It persisted after *Gillmor* in Ohio, despite the finding that sharecroppers were employees. The FLOC decided to take matters into its own hands by targeting food processors and securing their agreement to require the growers who delivered cucumbers to them to treat their harvesters as employees. In 1986–87, the FLOC signed its first contracts with Heinz and Vlasic. These contracts, and their subsequent reformulations, included an agreement to phase out the treatment of sharecroppers as independent contractors and to eventually treat them as employees.[14] Thus, the cases brought in the Midwest, Texas, and

[12]Rev. Rul. 85–85, 1985–25 I.R.B. 9.

[13]*Secretary of Labor v. Lauritzen,* 835 F.2d 1529, 1545 (7th Cir. 1987).

[14]Estimating that sharecropping saved growers from 15 to 20 percent in payroll taxes, and concerned that its members not lose their jobs through grower bankruptcies, the FLOC did cost and productivity studies in order to design proposals that growers could live with.

California have reinforced each other in an increasingly effective campaign to establish the employee status of sharecroppers in labor-intensive crops.

Labor Processes, Class Relations, and the Law

The law plays a crucial role in the relations among socioeconomic strata, one that varies over time and across subsectors of the economy. The court cases examined in this chapter represent the overt courtroom stage of an ongoing economic struggle between growers and workers regarding the conditions and returns of work. The confrontations in the fields and those in the courts are all part of a larger picture. Their examination shows that the law is intimately involved in shaping workers' daily perceptions of their economic roles, and that its impacts are highly variable. In the present instances, the law not only helped engender workers' initial consent to the terms of their work; it also helped motivate their eventual resistance. Whereas at one point it sustained and helped mask the existing distribution of power, it later provided the impetus, the tools, and the forum for changing it. In this case, political and economic structures continuously shape one another, as do political-economic structures and grower and worker agency. The outcomes of such court-based struggles cannot be assumed, however, for historical contingency, human agency, and the contradictory pulls of new job categories may move them in unforeseen directions. Finally, the suits brought in this industry, along with those in other industries and geographical regions, are working cumulatively to change the law, by bringing emergent economic forms under the protective umbrella of historical legal intent. The issue at stake is the legal prerogatives of economic statuses.

It is important to acknowledge that the declining legal advantages and increased legal costs of sharecropping were not the only factors encouraging its discontinuation. Other changes in the political forces structuring the labor market combined with these specifically legal shifts to reduce the attractiveness of sharecropping. As detailed in Chapter 3, these changes included a state political climate increasingly sympathetic to growers, an even more stable and plentiful supply of farm labor, and a decline in the militance and efficacy of the UFW. In short, after the early 1980s, decreasing union influence combined with changes in the legal definition of sharecroppers' employment status, in the state's political leadership, and in labor supply conditions, to usher in a new labor market regime that tilted the balance of labor market power back again toward growers. By the mid-1980s, the turmoil of the previous decade persisted only in local lore. In this new political context, sharecropping lost its appeal.

[9]

Politics and Social Class at Work: The View from the Fields

Two puzzles engaged us at the beginning of this book: the bases of labor resistance and the causes of labor process change. No one who looks beneath the relatively calm surface of class relations in the central coast California strawberry industry would argue that the resurgence of sharecropping was a reversion to a less "advanced" form of production. Nor would those involved in the local system express surprise at the extent of wage workers' opposition, despite their lack of skill and unionization. This is because participants do not share the economic determinism and assumptions of unilinear development that dominate much scholarship on work.

Strawberry growers and workers are well aware of the political forces that envelop their work. When they look out over the terrain of production, they see not only its economic dimensions: the serrated furrows, the clusters of stoop-backed workers, and the fruit-laden trucks wending their ways to the market. They see also its political dimensions: the motorcycles and closed vans of the *migra* pulling up unexpectedly at the edge of the fields, the straggling lines of picketers along country roads, the union rallies and politicians' urgent commentaries on the evening news, and the white-shirted officials who stop by their ranches to check on the ages, or wages, or sanitary facilities of their workers. The state is not a distant abstraction in their eyes. It is concretized in the individuals, institutions, and rules that constitute their everyday lives. Even the identities of the participants are transformed by political forces. Thus workers are not simply Alma Martinez or Jorge Reguerín—persons with families and histories. They are also employees, supervisors, and sharecroppers, or alternatively citizens, green-carders, and *sinpapeles*—categories with a relationship to the state. Although growers attend to the rhythms of the crop and market, political changes often capture more of their concern because these are less predictable and more volatile. Both classes recognize that their economic action is inherently political. Whether they celebrate or bemoan that fact, they invariably plan around it. And in carrying out their strategies, they transform the terms of their work.

In this final chapter, I will connect these observations from the fields with a broader analysis of class struggle and workplace change in capitalist agriculture. My objective is to clarify the central role of political forces in these processes while building a deeper understanding of the historical, local, and industrial specificity of class relations and economic change.

Class Struggles and the Transformation of Work

Although recent studies of the labor process have usefully heightened our awareness of the power relations inherent in work, they do not effectively explain developments in contemporary capitalist agriculture. This book challenges the view contained in much of the literature that capitalist economic structure at the level of production determines class relations and labor process change, and that the development of capitalist systems will be uniform and unilinear. This perspective, as we have seen, conveys an excessively static and simplistic view of actual change processes: it not only prevents explication of the diverse ways in which economic systems evolve, but it obscures the full range of influences that establish class concerns and class leverage. I develop here an alternative perspective that explores the sources of unevenness in wider patterns of economic development and places special emphasis on the roles of civil society and the state. I have tried in this analysis to clarify the crucial involvement of class mobilization and struggle—to show how economic and political structures jointly shape the arenas of contestation in which owners and workers engage, and how the initiatives of both transform the structural constraints that surround them.

I want to consider more generally now the connection between labor resistance and labor process change. As the foregoing analysis indicates, both, in this case, are facets of workplace struggle. The first refers to the initiatives of workers—their individual and collective responses to the terms set down by employers. The second refers to the initiatives of owners—their restructuring of employment relationships to increase their control over labor. Thus the task created by our attempt to connect them is that of understanding the determinants and outcomes of class struggles and the goals and strategies of competing classes. In my view, a synthesis of resource mobilization theories of popular resistance and protest (Jenkins 1985; Snyder and Tilly 1972; Tilly 1978) and moral economy theories of class and popular consciousness (Bulmer 1975; Moore 1978; Scott 1985; Thompson [1963] 1966, 1971) can help elucidate these matters.

On the one hand, resource mobilization theory explains collective action in terms of the interplay between two determinants: a group's mobilization opportunity, based on the structure of power and threat, and its mobilization capacity, based on its resources and organization. This theory tends to treat interests as relatively constant or unproblematic and focuses instead on the ways that broader structural developments create openings for mobilization. In addition, because the central concern of this approach is the causes of mobilization, it tends to neglect the ways that mobilization and resistance reciprocally shape the structures of sentiment and opportunity around them. Craig Jenkins and Charles Perrow (1977; Jenkins 1985), for example, attribute the successes of the UFW in the mid-1960s to openings created by changes in the wider economic and political context, apart from the experiences or initiatives of protesters. David Snyder and Charles Tilly (1972) make a similar claim for popular protest in France between 1830 and 1960. The moral economy literature, on the other hand, makes the social construction of discontent its central focus, thereby challenging the traditional Marxist assumption that class interests are rooted in the organization of production, and exploring the social and historical forces that shape a group's willingness to resist. Thus E. P. Thompson ([1963] 1966, 1971) and James Scott (1985) show how local social organization and historical experience shaped popular consciousness and resistance in England and Malaysia. Similarly, Colin Bell, Martin Bulmer, Howard Newby, David Lockwood, Graeme Salaman, and others (Bulmer 1975; Newby 1979) show how different types of work and community structures affect the world views and social relations between English employers and workers.

The foregoing analysis demonstrates that, while both moral economy and resource mobilization theories are usually applied to the actions of the less powerful, they may also be directed to understanding the circumstances, goals, and strategies of the more powerful. I have shown that class concerns are variable and socially constructed, and that an explication of the means and methods that each class deploys must rest on an understanding of the forces that shape its interests, as well as of those that shape its capacities and opportunities. The reciprocal relationships between socioeconomic structures and human agency and among different levels and arenas of structure are crucial to explaining the constantly changing forms and outcomes of class struggle at work. Moreover, class interests, capacities, and opportunities are more geographically differentiated and diversely determined than customarily acknowledged. Certainly, capitalist property relations and the rhythms of the world capitalist economy importantly frame workplace struggles, but they are only part of the determining context in which such contests unfold. Three additional structures of influence crucially shape the contemporary transformations of work: those of politics, industry, and locality. These structures vary in inclusiveness and consequence. Political constraints are the most influential and overarching, because they can affect owners and workers in industries and localities throughout a nation-state. Industry and locality constraints are progressively particular and circumscribed; yet they too place limits on workplace relations and importantly mediate and modify the impact of political forces. Together with the human agency of owners and workers, these structural influences account for much of the extant variation in patterns of class relations and economic development. Let me briefly specify the impact of each.

First and most important, in the strawberry industry as in advanced capitalist societies more generally, political forces have significantly shaped the reconfigurations of labor processes and the mobilization bases and strategies of social classes. Contemporary economic relationships are thoroughly politicized: both the state and private interest groups are actively engaged in trying to shape the legitimate distribution of resources to economic actors. This book illustrates the local and sectoral consequences of a process noted by scholars from a range of analytical traditions (e.g., Burawoy 1985; Harvey 1989; Piore and Sabel 1984). That is, as class struggles have matured and workers have become more organized, vocal, and effective in mobilizing outside allies in the industrial cores of advanced capitalist societies, states have increasingly intervened to regulate and mediate class conflict so as to preserve the conditions of capital accumulation while supporting their own legitimacy as keepers of the peace and the representatives of all classes. In the case of labor-intensive agriculture in the southwestern United States, the most consequential state interventions are protective legislation and border policies. The former has increased the entitlements of citizen workers and reduced their dependency on the wage relationship; the latter have stratified and disempowered workers, disqualifying many from claims on the resources of the state. These political forces are neither distant nor abstract. They are present in the minds and actions of owners and workers as they hammer out their agreements about work. Whether or not they are directly incorporated into the bureaucratic structures of firms, they exert an overarching influence on the leverage of owners and workers in the labor market. I will return to this point later. For now, let me simply affirm that in contemporary capitalist societies, political forces join with—and may even outweigh—economic forces in shaping the relations between social classes at work.

Second, the commodities, technologies, production processes, and input and product markets of particular industries shape the interests, opportunities, and capacities of social classes. They restrict the ways that work can be organized and the social relations that grow up around it. These causal factors and the resulting industrial variance in patterns of workplace relations are missed by analyses that rest with the abstraction of "the capitalist firm" or with the power conferred on workers by their skill and labor organizations. Such industrial differences can affect the likelihood that workers will resist and that owners will restructure their labor processes as a weapon in class conflict.

Third, the local organization of production—the local-level social systems which, over time and through the conjuncture of contingent processes, have developed relatively bounded and differentiated structures of class composition, employment opportunity, and production relationships—also shape workplace relations. They are the immediate settings in which owners and workers interact, and therefore the jobs and social relations exhibited in each, and the goals, resources, and visions of workplace justice held by the segments of class populations engaged in each, can affect the likelihood—and even the possibility—of labor resistance.

Answers to the Puzzles

How do these three structures of constraint help explain the extent and variance of resistance by strawberry wage workers who lack the attributes of skill and unionization ordinarily thought to accord them power? How do they account for the resurgence and subsequent decline of sharecropping, when traditional economic theories predict a steady increase in the prevalence of wage labor and in the social class dynamics associated with it? In short, what do my findings have to tell us about the interplay among political forces, class relations, and the organization of work?

The Bases of Labor Resistance

On an empirical level, this analysis shows that the temporally and spatially uneven upwelling of wage workers' resistance in this industry was not explicable in terms of workers' levels of unionization, skill, or opposition to coercive control methods. Rather, it had to do, first, with sources of class leverage and vulnerability conferred by the industry. In essence, industry characteristics limited workers' skill-based leverage at the point of production but rendered their care, commitment, and reliability central to producers' profits. Unlike similarly concerned producers in the core of the economy, however, berry growers did not try to increase workers' commitment through high wages or formal guarantees of job security or advancement, primarily because low wages were also crucial to profitability and because the political construction of the labor market effectively undercut wage demands and undermined opposition in most years and at most points in each season. The supply features most influential in this process were the politically engendered labor surpluses and the enforced—even directly managed—circulation of noncitizen workers between the United States and Mexico.

But at two points in each season—during the build-up and decline of the harvest—the balance of workplace power shifted, disturbing the conditions that contained labor resistance. In effect, the peaks and valleys of the harvest periodically disrupted the accepted balance of returns to each class, thereby challenging the legitimacy of the employment relationship. At the same time, swings in labor supply and demand temporarily increased the leverage of workers and enhanced their ability to mobilize around their discontents. Berry workers did not respond uniformly to these temporal openings, however, and the unevenness of their response highlights the importance of locality. In practice, whether or not workers perceived grower practices to be unjust and whether and how this perception was expressed varied decidedly across the three production microregions. This difference was a result of the local organization of production which in some cases permitted, even encouraged, and in others undermined or dissipated, workers' abilities and inclinations to challenge the terms of their work. The three berry-producing microregions exhibited distinctive arrays of job alternatives and structures of job access and reward. They varied in the ethnic composition and resource level of growers and the citizenship status and recency of workers. They varied as well in the national reference points for norms of workplace justice, the extent of owners' and workers' investment in the employment relationship, the extent of solidarity within each class, and the extent of polarization and social distance between them. Together these contrasts affected the extent and form of labor resistance, fostering spontaneous direct opposition in the Salinas Valley, accommodating patronal negotiation in the Pajaro Valley, and deferential patronal compliance in the North Monterey Hills.

Even when workers did protest as a result of these seasonal legitimacy crises, however, they did not disturb the contours of capitalist power relations, for their protests were fundamentally conservative. They reasserted and reinstated a vision of workplace justice which accepted the property relations, coercive control methods, and limited worker autonomy that characterized this sector of capitalist enterprise. As a result, their resistance did not account for the restructuring of capitalist enterprise represented by the return to sharecropping.

The Causes of Labor Process Change

In reflecting on the causes of strawberry sharecropping, we should recall that workers lacked the skill-based leverage and level of unionization, and employers lacked the resources and economic circumstances, that fostered comparable increases in workers' autonomy and self-direction in the core of the U.S. economy. Nor can we account for the resurgence and decline of strawberry sharecropping by pointing to shifts in the world capitalist system, to the resource-pooling advantages of sharecropping, or to the way it responded to an industry-specific labor demand and distributed climatic and crop-related risk. Instead, sharecropping was a response to changing political constraints on the regional labor market. It was reintroduced by growers after the mid-1960s in response to a shift in the balance of class power in the labor market. Three political developments encouraged this shift: first, the termination of the bracero program, which disrupted recruitment networks and ended the advantageous system of government-managed labor; second, the increasing coverage of agricultural workers under labor-protective laws, which increased growers' labor costs and reduced their labor control; and third, the rise of agricultural unionization, which destabilized immediate production conditions and increased growers' accountability to the regulations of the state. Together, these changes generated a production environment in which sharecropping was advantageous not only to growers, but to the workers they engaged.

For growers, the new political context reduced their control over employees and increased the costs, unpredictability, and hazards of farming with wage workers. Sharecropping was thus partly a means of dealing with production risk and uncertainty, as suggested by recent contract theorists in their analyses of sharecropping elsewhere.[1] In this case, however, its

[1]Bardhan and Srinivasan (1971), Cheung (1969), and Reid (1976, 1979) argue that sharecropping can be freely chosen, fair, and efficient in competitive markets, given scarce individual resources, certain product characteristics, and high market and climatic risk. Newbery (1976), Newbery and Stiglitz (1979), and Otsuka, Kikuchi, and Hayami (1986) argue the same for imperfect or noncompetitive markets, when performance is hard to monitor and risk is high.

causes were not the crop-related, climatic, or market factors that such studies identify. Nor was sharecropping primarily a means of sharing risk, since sharecroppers bore few more risks than did wage laborers. Instead, it was an economic strategy initiated mainly by an especially affected category of large producers as a means of reducing their exposure to politically generated costs, controls, and risks. Sharecropping thus played a particular role in class struggle in this economic sector: it was a protective response by capitalists to the increased leverage of labor engendered by the union mobilization of existing proletarians after they had made gains in the political arena. In this context, the organizational principles of sharecropping were used by market-oriented firms to perform vital functions that could not be accomplished at the same cost using the expected labor process of wage labor.

Although sharecropping was initiated by growers, workers valued it as well. Here, as elsewhere (Lenin [1899] 1956; Reid 1976), sharecropping offered the promise of upward mobility and greater day-to-day flexibility to individuals whose economic alternatives were limited. It helped Japanese and Mexican immigrants increase their job and residential stability, gain access to the land, maximize the income-producing potential of household members, and overcome political restrictions on their economic options. In addition, post-1964 sharecropping depended on uneven development in the world economy and on the political forces that fostered and sustained that imbalance. That is, for sharecropping to be viable, sharecroppers and their hired workers had to accept the low returns enforced by the split in market proceeds. This acceptance was encouraged by the safety net of a subsistence base in Mexico, which subsidized the reproduction of the hired workforce, and by severe under- and unemployment in Mexico, which lowered the opportunity costs and thus the acceptable returns for sharecroppers and hired workers. Thus, economic underdevelopment in the Mexican periphery promoted the expansion and differentiation of capitalist agriculture in the U.S. core and simultaneously muted the conflicts arising from it.

Politics and Work

Stepping back from the empirical substance of this case, let us reflect on the broad processes connecting politics and work. In recent years, Michael Burawoy has entered an important challenge within the labor process literature to the conceptual separation between economic base and sociopolitical superstructure (1985). Yet Burawoy's work directs little attention to exactly how the two are connected. We are underinformed about how political pressures impinge on the daily processes of class formation, class relations, and labor process change, or how these in turn might shape surrounding institutional structures. One of the most significant findings of my investigation is that the economic and political systems *evolve together*, as they are engaged and challenged by the exchanges between social classes. Not only are economic organizations sometimes reconfigured in response to political pressures, but because the law so thoroughly pervades, defines, and circumscribes economic relationships, challenges to these relationships often involve challenges to the law. As individuals abide by or resist their economic roles, they simultaneously confront their legal statuses. These confrontations occur in the courts, as well as on the job. And in the process economic organization, social class, and the interpretation and application of the law may all be transformed.

This book demonstrates that political and economic systems are more fluid and mutually determinant than portrayed by Burawoy's analysis of the role of state intervention in certain stages of economic development (1985) or Thomas' study of the role of gender and citizenship in the lettuce industry (1985). State apparatuses do not simply limit the range of workplace struggles; they may also become the targets of such struggles and be reconstituted in the process. Nor are sociopolitical statuses simply developed separately in society or produced outside of participation in economic organizations, then used by the managers of those firms to further their own ends (Thomas 1985). Although relatively separate societal processes do help compose such statuses, they are also shaped and reshaped through their involvement in economic disputes. Some are indeed used by owners, but they can also be deployed by workers. Thus, sharecroppers' legal contention of their employment status actually transformed the meaning and implementation of the law. In short, this study suggests that sociopolitical and economic structures jointly and continuously shape one another and that they are joined by the process of class struggle.

Not only do economic and political structures co-evolve, but they do so in a way that reflects the distinctive constraints of particular industries and localities, the local configurations of labor market power, and the telling interplay between the law and social class.

The Local Industrial Bases of Class Mobilization

I have found here that the industry and local organization of production shape patterns of class mobilization by mediating the relationship between politics and work. As we have seen, local-level activity systems filter the influences of broader political and economic structures, variously enhancing, diminishing, or transforming their impacts. Thus the regulations and protections of the state were unevenly supportive of workers and unevenly disadvantageous for producers in the different berry-producing microregions. In fact, it was these immediate settings that gave the broader structures their local "meaning." The local interpersonal, communal, and cultural systems surrounding the production process contain varying norms of workplace justice and varying conventions and structures of workplace relations, all of which affect the likelihood and form of labor resistance. These processes are confirmed by historical studies of working class culture and protest in the United States and Europe as well (Aminzade 1981, 1984; Dawley 1976; Foster 1974; Gutman 1977; Hobsbawm 1964, 1984; Thompson [1963] 1971, 1966, 1975). In addition, workers' world views are much more heterogeneous at the local level than conventionally recognized, and their heterogeneity may be structurally generated by the immediate social systems within which workers operate. In general, my analysis suggests that relatively autonomous community structures bolster workers' solidarity and support more radical, oppositional relations with employers, whereas those structures in which the lives of employers and workers are interwoven undermine workers' cohesion and engender comparatively deferential and compliant class relations. Patterns of class relations in England documented by Colin Bell, Howard Newby, Roderick Martin, R. H. Fryer, and David Lockwood reinforce this conclusion (Bulmer 1975; Newby 1979).

The evidence of this case suggests an important emendation of resource mobilization analyses of social movements such as the UFW (cf. Jenkins and Perrow 1977; Jenkins 1985). It indicates that where the localized social systems that surround the production process support the development of more solidary, separate, and oppositional worker communities, union victories may be a result not only of the mobilization openings engendered by wider political-economic changes and the mobilization strategies pursued by the union, but of the self-organization and enterprise of potential members. In the case of the central coast strawberry industry, mobilization successes that are widely attributed to the initiatives of the union were, in fact, generated by workers and based in the local organization of production. Thus, though Jenkins and Perrow are undoubtedly correct in arguing that political and economic realignments after the mid-1960s fostered the organizing efforts and clout of the UFW, we do not yet know how much of its local following was gained through the largely independent initiatives and organization of workers.

In addition to the structure of local social systems, the differing characteristics of local industries generate the interests and strategies of social classes. This book challenges assumptions that class concerns and recourses are given by the structure and logic of capitalism, and it reinforces the finding of commodity systems studies that producers' strategies are, in important part, industrially specific (Friedland 1984a; Friedland and Barton 1975; Friedland, Barton, and Thomas 1981; Goldberg 1980, 1981; Griffith 1993; Thomas 1985). While producers of tomatoes and lettuce turned to product differentiation, mechanization, relocation, and vertical integration to deal with the increasing unruliness and cost of labor, central coast berry growers turned to sharecropping, in part because the other avenues were closed. In the strawberry industry, as in the British gas industry in the late nineteenth and early twentieth centuries (Hobsbawm 1964), the rootedness of production in a geographic locale, along with peculiarities of the technology and market, circumscribed the alternatives of firm managers and increased the leverage of workers. Hobsbawm's study supports another central finding here: that bottlenecks in the production process can improve workers' bargaining power regardless of their levels of skill. In sum, this book makes a case for a particular relationship between commodity constraints, production forms, and class struggles. Arguing against industrial determinism, it shows that although commodity characteristics help structure class interests and capacities and constrain the possible forms of production, the actual forms that production takes are established by the wider context of class struggle. Social conflicts give rise to forms of commodity production, not the reverse, but they do so in part within limits set by the industry.

Class Leverage and Labor Market Regimes

Another important aspect of the political-economic interplay has to do with the crucial role of the labor market. I have shown that politics affect workplace relations not only by shaping the practices of particular firms, but also—and in some cases more consequentially—by affecting the leverage of workers and employers in the labor market. Labor markets are more than the neutral sites of individual transactions: they are institutions that transcend such exchanges, both temporally and physically, and they have histories that involve the exercise and allocation of political power. Thus, at any point in time, labor markets are governed by distinctive political regimes that structure the leverage and relations of those operating within them. Moreover, the distribution of labor market leverage is not fixed: although in this case it usually privileged employers, it also sometimes aided workers. This study demonstrates that agricultural labor markets are more segmented than often recognized—not by the skill requirements of sought-after workers, but by the structures of local activity systems, personalized recruitment mechanisms, and the citizenship stratification of workers. In the strawberry industry, these factors generated semipermeable boundaries around localized market segments, which filtered the impacts of broader political constraints, causing microregional differences in the allocation of labor market power. This evidence offers an instructive counter to labor market segmentation theories which privilege the production process as the cause of market differentiation and attendant worker power (Edwards, Reich, and Gordon 1975; Edwards 1979; Gordon, Edwards, and Reich 1982).

The foregoing analysis indicates as well that the balance of class power in the labor market can significantly shape the organization of work. In the strawberry industry, it was a politically induced increase in the leverage of workers in the labor market, rather than a shift in the narrowly economic or technological bases of their power in the firm, that motivated producers to restructure their labor processes through the adoption of sharecropping. In effect, the increased exchange value and power of labor in the labor market destabilized production and augmented workers' leverage within the firm, motivating employers to reconfigure their deployment of labor. This association between work organization and the political construction of class power in the labor market is borne out by evidence from other crop industries as well. For example, Friedland and Barton show that mechanization in the California tomato industry was a response to the reduction in the supply of braceros and the rise of unionization (1975). Friedland, Barton, and Thomas (1981) and Thomas (1985) found that lettuce producers responded to these same challenges by mechanizing part of the production process and preferentially hiring women and illegals. Taken together, this evidence suggests that labor market leverage can be more influential than production-based leverage in shaping class relations at work, particularly in the case of unskilled workers in the competitive periphery of the economy, and in an era in which capitalist states are heavily involved in supporting the conditions of accumulation and mediating the encounters between social classes.

Of course, labor market conditions do not always outweigh workers' power bases at the point of production. As Edwards (1979), Friedman (1977) and Montgomery (1979) demonstrate, the production processes and economic circumstances of firms in the industrial core of the economy have, at certain points, accorded workers enough leverage to directly force labor process changes. But the conditions supporting this kind of influence are less and less characteristic of core sector industries in the United States

(Burawoy 1985; Harvey 1989; Piore and Sabel 1984). Moreover, with the expansion of employment in the periphery and the incoming waves of Asian and Latin American immigrants, more and more workers face conditions like those of strawberry pickers: they must compete for jobs in secondary labor markets, without skill or the benefits of citizenship, in a context of sustained labor surplus. In such circumstances, I suggest, the political regimes shaping the leverage of workers in the labor market are likely to be more determinant of working class power than are their power bases within the firm.

The Law and Social Class

By scrutinizing the legal conflicts that arose from strawberry work, this book elucidates important aspects of the role of the state in class formation and class struggle. The view of the legal system presented here counters the two perspectives that have dominated legal sociology and anthropology: the instrumental Marxist view that the law is a tool to maintain and promote dominant economic interests, and the structural functional notion that it is the concretization of the moral boundaries of a state, a way of ensuring social predictability and containing the tensions arising from resource scarcity (Collier 1975: Currie 1971; Moore 1970; Quinney 1974). This book reinforces emerging evidence that the link between legal systems and class struggles is more complex than these perspectives portray. It shows that the law is not mechanically or solely a tool of domination: rather, it can variously obscure, reflect, shore up, or undermine the existing distribution of power and privilege. It can be both a product and a cause of class conflict, as E. P. Thompson also found in his study of the Black Act in eighteenth-century England (1975). Although the legal system can indeed support the interests of the powerful, it can also—as other analyses confirm (Blumberg 1970; Dahrendorf 1968)—provide an institutional forum and identity to opposition groups in their efforts to change the status quo.

State apparatuses affect social class dynamics in at least three important ways: they shape the material consequences of class position, the ideological construction of class interests, and the social processes of class struggle. First, legal-political statuses and institutions affect the resources of class groupings. Legal distinctions are centrally involved in defining the types of participants in production—here citizens and noncitizens, employers and employees, as well as sharecroppers, supervisors, and independent contractors. They help establish the resources available to persons with particular relations to the means of production—to those who occupy specifiable locations within the class structure. Each category is associated with a set of legal rights and protections, as well as with limits on the behavioral options of members. Legal statuses do not simply identify the attributes of individuals; they also assert differences from and links to others. In this sense, they are fundamentally relational, and this recognition helps clarify their functioning. In practice, such identities make claims on other persons or entities: on the state, in the case of citizens; on the state and employers, in the case of employees. They also distinguish and often stratify the rights of certain groups with respect to others. Thus, in giving rights to citizens, the law heightens the power disparity between citizens and noncitizens. In this sense, struggles over the assignment and definition of legal statuses generate a politics of classification which establishes the legitimate claimants on public resources. Because the law is so involved in comprising the opportunity structures for social classes, class actors often position themselves vis-à-vis the legal framework in their efforts to gain advantage for themselves. Whatever overtly appeasing, restrictive, or supportive stances states may take toward class struggles, their laws and their judicial and regulatory institutions have become integral parts of the economic environments in which social classes operate. In advanced capitalist societies at the present time, then, social classes are not just positions in the economic hierarchy: they also define, and are defined by, their relations to legal-political categories and resources.

Second, this book has shown how the apparatuses of the state crucially affect the ideological dynamics of class relations. Because the law purveys society's vision of the nature and prerogatives of class position, it adds a distinctive dimension to the "manufacturing" (Burawoy 1979) of class consciousness and consent to economic arrangements. By setting forth the entitlements of and constraints upon certain class locations, legal distinctions shape individuals' understandings of their own and others' positions in the productive hierarchy. In this case, we have seen that the state does not simply set the distant regulatory framework constraining managerial prerogatives and labor entitlements in a given stage of economic development. Rather, legal distinctions permeate daily work life and shape the options and perceptions of economic actors. They help mold workers' experiences of common cause and opposition—their notions of workplace justice—as well as their beliefs about what is acceptable and what must be challenged.

This analysis leads to a conception of the law as an ideological resource for various classes, whose impacts take shape through the processes of class struggle. Employers may use legal statuses and contracts as a form of ideological manipulation to create the appearance of divisions in workers' interests, to disguise the real relations of production, and to win compliance with otherwise discordant economic arrangements. Subcontracting arrangements are especially useful in this regard, because they create contradictory class locations whose actual control relations are not immediately apparent. Their utility is evident in the international arena as well, where national governments and international investors often represent contract farming in populist terms to engender public and labor support for arrangements that accord little real independence to direct producers (Watts 1994:33–34). Such measures are not, however, invariably effective, for the law neither directly nor inevitably determines class consciousness or class action, and the forces shaping the construction and resolution of conflicts are multiple. Thus, although the legal characterization of sharecropping and the role differentiation it implemented fostered the fragmentation of the working class, these forces did not prevent some sharecroppers from perceiving their common plight with workers in the context of an intense unionization struggle which framed recruitment in inclusive ethnic terms, especially given the objective similarities between sharecroppers' and wage workers' economic roles.

Workers may also seize upon legal statuses and standards to define and legitimate their discontents. In the California strawberry industry, as in the struggles of small-town residents in California's Owens Valley against urban and national domination (Walton 1992), and in the popular resistance to the state's attempt to expropriate the forests in eighteenth-century England (Thompson 1975), the less powerful used legal standards of rights and obligations to articulate, publicly argue for, and ultimately further their interests. Thus some strawberry sharecroppers initially internalized their contractual representation as independent contractors, and this internalization helped define their resentments and motivate the form of their legal challenge. Once they entered the realm of legal contestation, however, it was not only they and their colleagues who were engaged in the puzzle of their position and entitlements. It was also their advocates and the courts. This process reveals an important aspect of the production of consciousness in the legal realm: the guiding, even transformative involvement of legal practitioners. It illustrates as well the close involvement of the law in perceptions of class interest. In the process of trying to convince sharecroppers to change their claims as to their legal status, their lawyer helped shift their perceptual emphasis in characterizing their economic positions. Moreover, the statutes he deployed in supporting their new claim reflected their revised view of their legal status. Thus did their law help define sharecroppers' contradictory location in class relations.

This observation brings us to a third way in which legal processes affect class relationships: they alter the dynamics of class struggle. As legal statuses have become part of class resources, class actors have been drawn into an arena of contestation and negotiation whose processes differ significantly from those unfolding in the fields and on the shop floors. Rather than involving individual claims on employers by workers—or collective claims and pressure by labor organizations aimed at firm owners, politicians, and the general public—court-based class struggles take place in the courts and lawyers' offices through the mediation of legal professionals. Instrumental views of the law represent such professionals as the servants of propertied classes, but they may also, as we have seen, champion the less powerful and play important roles in their views of the conflict. Court decisions concerning who falls into a particular legal category are quite different in kind and consequence from the evaluations of workers in the fields about who is part of their collective "we." The latter sort of discrimination is more situational, informal, and variable. The former posits a firmer set of diacritica that are determined by statutes and decisions far from the immediate setting, and whose ramifications affect the resources available to contestants who are temporally and spatially distant. As class struggles move out of the workplace and into the courts, they draw in new and distant audiences, they enforce new constraints on inter- and intraclass relations, and they bring new consequences whose outcomes work cumulatively to change the law. In effect, cases such as *Real* are establishing a legal perspective on a type of worker that did not exist when the laws were enacted. They are part of a larger process that is generating a legal position on the growing portion of the workforce that falls outside the purview of protective laws.

Legal protocols also shape the engagements of social classes through the conventional structure of legal contention. Arguments regarding the appropriate coverage of a worker under a law are conducted through a comparison between the formal diacritica of the legal status and the substantive realities of the economic relationship. The meaning of the legal status is established by the philosophy and wording of the initial statute, as clarified and applied to real-world exemplars through the accumulated precedent of case law. In this way, the conventions of legal contests involve an interplay between legal intent and socioeconomic practice, a process which, as this case has shown, can actually encourage a long-term convergence between the two. Indeed, sharecroppers, who to some extent accepted their contractual representation as independent entrepreneurs, first expressed their frustration in terms of a legal statute designed to protect small-scale capitalists. As they compared their legal characterization with their economic experience, however, they changed their views of their legal status and the terms of their legal action. Thus, the processes of court-based class struggle can be unmasking and transformative and in the long run can even subvert efforts to confound the implementation of the law. In the short run, however, producers' allegations as to the legal status of their workers tend to be accepted as fact, unless or until they are challenged. As a result, misrepresentations can offer considerable initial advantage, and sanctions against them are uncertain.

The conventions of legal discourse also place certain forms of pressure and argumentation out of bounds, thus circumscribing the weapons of class struggle. That is, in order to serve its function of legitimating state and class rule, the law must appear to be logical, unbiased, and equitable in its implementation (Thompson 1975:262–67). When strawberry and cucumber growers generated legal documents alleging that their workers were independent contractors, they signaled their agreement to engage in a logic and rhetoric of discourse in which the decision as to whether sharecroppers' claims would be honored would rest not on the relative economic power of the contestants, nor on the preferences of the more powerful, but on the "justice" of the situation as decided by its logical relation to the law. In this sense, the legal construction of class conflict helped protect the less powerful.

This book has shown, then, that sociopolitical statuses have no inherent economic meaning. Rather, their utility depends on the ways that industries, localities, and wider political-economic conditions shape the ends, means, and outcomes of class struggle. As my comparison of the lettuce and strawberry industries indicates, there is a difference between the general impact of such statuses on the labor market and their particular utility within the labor process. Thus, whereas citizenship stratification dampens resistance and undercuts wage demands in agricultural labor markets throughout the state, industries vary in the extent to which their production processes and economic circumstances make it useful to use citizenship—or gender or employee status—to differentiate their labor forces and labor processes in order to improve their direct labor control. These contrasts indicate that sociopolitical inequities do not translate directly or necessarily into economic inequities, and that the relationship between them is contingent.

On a general level, this study suggests that the involvement of the state in employment relationships tends to increase the heterogeneity of the working class and the complexity of class structures while reducing the polarity of class relations. As employers seek to distance their sources of labor from union mobilization and the state, they may develop new, interstitial categories of labor-suppliers who enjoy some of the prerogatives of capital, along with much of the dependency of labor. As we have seen, the economic reality and ideological presentation of these positions may engage workers' cooperation in their own exploitation. The prevalence of such jobs in the strawberry and pickling cucumber industries indicates that legal employment status may be especially determinant of work organization and class relations in labor-intensive industries whose alternative means of increasing profitability are limited and whose workers are becoming increasingly organized and resistant. In such instances, I suggest, legal distinctions are likely to foster more complex and less oppositional class structures, as opposed to the polarization and simplification predicted by Marx.

The Course of Economic Change

We are now in a position to assess the implications of this case for the broader sweep of economic change. The analysis presented here helps illuminate several facets of the wider picture: the reconfiguring of California's agricultural economy, the role of sharecropping in rural class relations, and the overall causes and trajectory of socioeconomic development. In all of these contexts, we observe that economic systems are being restructured as firms, workers, and direct producers struggle to gain advantage in a changing—and increasingly politicized—market.

Trends in California Agriculture

To what extent are the dynamics highlighted in this book exemplary of wider trends in California agriculture, especially as they have evolved since the completion of my core interviews in 1988? On the whole, recent developments have neither altered the basic features of farm labor supply and demand in the state nor reduced the sensitivity of perishable crop industries to political limits on the use of labor. If anything, the politics of identification—especially struggles over the public entitlements of employees and noncitizens—have intensified with the decline in economic prosperity. The result is an increase in economic restructuring whose forms and functions parallel those of strawberry sharecropping.

Economically, the national dominance of California agriculture continues to grow, as does the relative importance of high-value, labor-intensive crops. The number of farmers and unpaid family members working in agriculture declines steadily and the reliance on hired workers increases (Villarejo and Runsten 1993). Although the state's growing connection to world markets has seriously disadvantaged some fruit and vegetable producers, the competitive position of central coast berry growers remains relatively stable.[2] Meanwhile, the contracting state and national economies, the December 1990 freeze, and the state's prolonged drought have occasioned hardship, especially for producers of wine grapes and vegetables. Yet despite these economic challenges, farming in California continues to be highly profitable for most.[3]

Politically, union membership has continued to decline, and border policies have been reconfigured. With the death of Cesar Chavez in April 1993, the state's already-dwindling farm labor movement lost his unifying charisma (Breton 1992; Ferriss 1993). Fragmented labor organizations have sprung up in certain regions, and one important Teamsters local persists. Nonetheless, California farm employers in the mid-1990s are relatively unencumbered by union pressure.[4] At the same time, the Immigration Reform and Control Act of 1986 (IRCA) has restructured the apparatuses of citizenship. The IRCA imposes sanctions on employers who hire undocumented workers, and it extends amnesty to unauthorized workers who have lived and worked in the United States continuously since 1981. The act's Special Agricultural Worker (SAW) visa program offers legalization to those claiming to have worked in U.S. farm labor for at least ninety days in the twelve-month period ending 1 May 1986. It was not until 1989 that agricultural employers' compliance with the act began to be checked at even a minimal level. By the early 1990s, its impacts on the farm labor market were becoming clear. At the outset, growers feared that it would reduce the supply of labor, causing crop losses and wage hikes in labor-intensive industries, but this prediction has not come to pass. Instead, an unanticipated flood of undocumented workers have applied for and received authorization to work in U.S. agriculture through the act. Moreover, it sent the message to economically stressed foreigners that the best way to get legalized was to cross the border and live for a period of time in the United States. As a result, the IRCA-mandated legalization programs have actually expanded the flow of immigrants into and out of agriculture.[5]

[2]The production and export of strawberries, tomatoes, frozen broccoli, and cauliflower have risen on both sides of the California-Mexico border (Villarejo and Runsten 1993:1–4).

[3]California farm cash receipts and net farm income experienced a downturn in the first years of the 1990s comparable to that of the farm crisis years of the mid-1980s. A wave of bankruptcies, consolidations, and mergers has swept the vegetable and wine grape industries (Villarejo and Runsten 1993:8–11).

[4]As of January 1995, Teamsters Local 890 holds the largest agricultural union contract in the state—perhaps the nation—covering some 12,000 employees of Bud Antle, Inc. UFW membership is unofficially estimated at about 2,500.

[5]The INS initially anticipated that about 360,000 workers would qualify for permanent residency under the SAW program. In fact, it received 1,277,514 applications, 700,000 from the state of California. By mid-August 1992, 1,076,650 of these applications had been approved (U.S. Commission 1992:52; Villarejo and Runsten 1993:45).

On the whole, California farm workers have become more documented, more foreign-born, more numerous, and more ethnically diverse. Although most still come from the traditional mestizo sending communities of central Mexico, indigenous peoples from Mexico and Central America have been drawn into the flow (Cornelius 1989). Especially important are Mixtec Indians from the state of Oaxaca, who may number as many as 30,000 and comprise the newest cycle of disempowered labor and ethnic replacement in California agriculture (Ferriss 1993:6; Zabin et al. 1993). To date, Mixtecs have not had a serious impact on the central coast strawberry industry, however, perhaps due to the vitality of established recruitment networks. The 1990 National Agricultural Workers Survey (NAWS) concluded that fully 92 percent of California farm workers—a higher percentage than at any other point in this century—are now born outside the United States (Mines et al. 1993; Rosenberg et al. 1993; Runsten 1991). The proportion of undocumented workers has apparently fallen, but how substantial this reduction actually is—and whether it will last—are unknown. Thus while the NAWS concluded that only 9 percent of California's seasonal farm workers are now undocumented, recently published case studies of the fresh tomato, citrus, and raisin grape industries found that up to 35 percent of the workers interviewed admitted they were illegally in the country (*Findings* 1991:23; U.S. Commission 1992:74). Because of the thriving business in forged authorization papers and the reluctance of illegals to acknowledge their status, the actual percentage is probably higher. Over a million previously undocumented California farm workers have been legalized through the IRCA, but many of these have moved out of agriculture, and their children plan to seek nonagricultural work (U.S. INS 1992). At the same time, large-scale unauthorized immigration continues, and the number of illegals apprehended approaches the record level of the mid-1980s (Villarejo and Runsten 1993:19, 44). In short, there is every reason to expect that documented immigrants will continue to cycle through California agriculture and that the farm labor force will be reproduced outside the country. Finally, despite growers' initial fears, labor surpluses have, if anything, increased since the IRCA and are higher than ever ("Fields of Pain" 1991:4; Gunter, Jarrett, and Duffield 1992; "Too Many" 1990; Villarejo and Runsten 1993:19, 24, 44). Growers are hiring more workers per acre in order to lower their risks, thereby reducing the annual number of hours that individual workers are employed. Together with sharply falling wage rates, this practice has substantially cut average annual individual earnings, so that farm wages have hit a twenty-year low.[6]

[6]California agricultural wage rates of direct-hire employers have dropped from almost $8 an hour in 1978 to less than $6 an hour in 1993—a decrease of 25 percent (Villarejo and Run-

In this context of profitable but economically challenged labor-intensive agriculture, more numerous and dispensable workers, and new political constraints on labor deployment, the economic restructuring exemplified by strawberry, cucumber, and vegetable sharecropping has in fact spread. A variety of other crop industries have reorganized production to reduce the exposure of owners to political restrictions on labor. The dimensions and impact of this trend make it, in my view, the most significant development in California farm employment in the past twenty years. The use of farm management companies as employment intermediaries is part of this phenomenon, as are apparent bankruptcies by unionized firms and their reconstitution with nonunion workers. Its major contributor is the shift from direct-hire workers to the engagement of labor contractors. Although contractors have always been used to some extent in California agriculture, their use increased in the 1970s, motivated by some of the same forces that led to the resurgence of sharecropping: the end of the bracero program, the expansion of protective legislation, and the increase in union mobilization (U.S. Bureau 1972, 1984a). Since the IRCA, labor contracting has expanded even more markedly, this time as a means of incorporating new immigrants, of distancing and undermining the potential organizing of an increasingly legal workforce, of avoiding new sanctions on the employment of illegals, and of deflecting responsibility for the observance of labor protections in the face of a more intrusive regulatory apparatus. Some employers have used labor contractors to replace unionized and highly paid workers.[7] According to the state EDD's 882-A reports, currently at least 122,000 individuals—that is, one out of four California farm workers—report working for a labor contractor at peak season. Contractors are distributed unevenly across the agricultural economy. Direct hire still dominates the central coast strawberry harvest, although contracting has increased in the Salinas Valley. Vegetable growers have shifted decidedly away from direct hire and toward the use of contractors: in the San Joaquin Valley, most of the peak-season labor in fruit and vegetables is now managed by contractors (Villarejo and Runsten 1993).

---

sten 1993:24–25). Because this figure does not incorporate the much lower wages paid by labor contractors, the actual drop in California farm wages is undoubtedly much greater.

[7]When union contracts expired in the Coastal Growers' Association's citrus farms in Ventura in 1981, growers replaced their unionized harvesting associations with labor contractors whose employees were paid less and were almost entirely undocumented (Lloyd et al. 1987). I found this pattern of replacing direct-hire, largely legal, unionized workers with contracted, largely illegal, nonunion workers in the central coast vegetable industry as well. In one case, unionized workers making $7.25 an hour were replaced by labor contractors whose employees were paid $4.25 for the same work.

The political advantage of contracting is not immediately apparent, because it does not legally exempt workers from protective laws or farm owners from responsibility for their treatment. Legally, the workers hired by contractors are "employees," and the growers who engage contractors are "employers." In practice, however, contractors are poorly monitored and their social relations with workers discourage the report of abuses. Research shows that the use of contractors lowers wages and benefit levels, impedes labor organizing, increases worker dependency, and reduces the likelihood that employees will pursue their rights under the law. This situation results in part from the fact that contractors rely so heavily—sometimes exclusively—on illegals. In part, it is encouraged by contractors' paternalistic relations with employees (Cornelius et al. 1982; Hubner 1984:19; Mines 1985). Contractors pay their workers much less than do direct-hire employers—in some cases, only half as much. They are also less likely to pay employer taxes and observe protective laws. Inquiries into their operations reveal practices ranging from misrepresentation of the terms of employment, to dangerous and unhealthy transportation, living, and working conditions, to outright violence and underpayment and nonpayment of wages. Despite continued efforts to monitor their activities, farm labor contractors exercise arbitrary and largely unconstrained authority over their workers' employment—often over their very tenure in the country. Overall, regulatory agencies have been notoriously ineffectual at preventing contractors' use of illegals and mistreatment of workers. If anything, the abusive practices of contractors appear to have increased since the IRCA (EDD 1992; Rosenberg 1993; Vaupel and Martin 1986).

In sum, the economic circumstances of California agriculture have declined since the height of strawberry sharecropping, and growers' exposure to protective legislation has increased as the IRCA has eased the legalization of immigrants. As a result, more and more growers are turning to labor contractors to bring in their crops, even in the absence of union pressure. This measure undercuts labor mobilization and evades labor protections in ways not immediately apparent. In this context, farm labor contracting is a current means of accomplishing the goals intended by strawberry sharecropping. Moreover, like sharecropping, contracting is being subjected to efforts to bring it under the law. Meanwhile, the economic downturn in the state and nation, occasioned largely by the globalization of the economy, has moved the political definition of economic actors to the center of social debate. Political careers are being based on the issue of the political construction of the labor market—of just who are its legitimate participants and what are their entitlements. Previously accorded state supports for labor are being contested in favor of a less intrusive, more market-oriented regulatory regime. In California, increasing immigration and the IRCA's facilitation of citizenship have focused attention on immigrants as a cause of economic hardship for the populace as a whole. In 1994, this concern was vented through Proposition 187, which aimed to restrict public resources to undocumented immigrants. On all fronts, the political contention of economic statuses and practices has intensified.[8]

The Meanings of Sharecropping

What can we conclude about the role of sharecropping in agricultural development? Opinions diverge widely as to its causes, efficiency, and distributive justice. As noted, Marx and Lenin considered sharecropping to be incompatible with efficient capitalist production because it hampers the mobility of labor, fosters technological stagnation, and requires a repressive political system to hold it in place. Early classical and neoclassical economists agreed that it was inefficient and likely to disappear, in their case because of the incentive impacts of share contracts. Late twentieth-century microeconomists, however, argue that sharecropping can be efficient, equitable, and freely chosen in competitive markets, given certain commodity characteristics, individual resource scarcity, and high market and climatic risk. In this book, I have presented yet another perspective: that sharecropping is efficient and profitable for well-endowed producers of labor-intensive crops when politically induced market imperfections restrict the options of labor and impose substantial costs, constraints, and uncertainties on capital.

How can we resolve these divergent views? Their apparent contradictions disappear, I believe, if we recognize that a diversity of production arrangements have been treated under the rubric of sharecropping. In point of fact, empirical examples of sharecropping constitute quite different "forms of production" (Friedmann 1978), in terms of, first, the relations within the production unit, especially the distribution of control over the means of production and the social relations among participants; and, second, the economic, political, and ideological dimensions of the wider social formation. Thus, sharecropping has no single cause, organizational form, or role in economic development. This framework permits us to distinguish among the various empirical instances of sharecropping.

In my view, the form, context, and causes of the share tenancy employed

[8]In 1993, publicity about the practices of farm labor contractors motivated California legislators and agency administrators to pass a law that polices and sanctions the practices of contractors more closely and that requires them to educate their supervisors about the rights of employees.

in cash grain farming in the American Midwest in the latter half of the 1800s and in the production of tree fruit, nut, and grain crops across the United States in the 1990s generally bear out the allegations of the "efficiency/free choice" perspective. That is, these landlords and tenants chose sharecropping in relatively unencumbered competitive markets, basing their choices primarily on the risk environment and labor demand of the industry and on their own possession of human and physical capital. Such tenants are relatively independent agricultural entrepreneurs who provide or secure labor and capital themselves and who share production risks. Their operations tend to be productive and fully involved in the market. Sharecroppers in such situations are essentially capitalist producers with a share feature to their rental contracts.[9] By contrast, sharecropping in postfeudal Europe, in the most coercive pockets of the postbellum South, and in many Third World countries falls toward the "inefficiency/coercion" end of the continuum.[10] This form of sharecropping has many of the features expected to hinder economic efficiency: exploitive paternalistic dependence on a landowner, a mobility-preventing subsistence plot of land, a low and stagnant level of technology controlled by uneducated and impoverished direct producers, and underdeveloped factor and product markets in the wider society. Such sharecroppers are essentially household—usually peasant—producers, who have a share feature to their relations of servitude with their landlords.[11]

Post–World War II strawberry sharecropping differs from the previous two types in terms of the relations within the firm and the character of the wider social formation. Here, sharecroppers provide only labor and the simple equipment usually supplied by wage workers. Farm owners, by contrast, own or control the means and methods of production. This division of responsibilities prevents sharecroppers from underinvesting capital, while close supervision ensures adherence to prescribed techniques and prevents their

[9]See, for example, Bogue 1963, Cogswell 1975, Gates 1973, Hibbard 1911, and Winters 1978. See Wells 1987b for more thorough development of this analysis.

[10]Studies of sharecropping in the postbellum South reveal considerable temporal and regional variation in extraeconomic coercion, as indicated by the extent and enforcement of repressive legislation, the amount of terrorist intimidation, the tenancy status of freedmen, and the extent to which blacks had alternatives to sharecropping. There is also considerable variation, both spatially and temporally, in terms of the extent of supervision and direct control versus relative independence. See, for example, Alston and Ferrie 1985, DeCanio 1974, Foner 1983, Mann 1990, Royce 1993, Wiener 1978, and Wright 1982, as well as Wells 1987b.

[11]Friedmann distinguishes between simple commodity and peasant forms of household production according to the extent to which external relations are governed by competition and mobility of factors (1980:160–63). I observe that where sharecropping follows the coercive pattern, household producers tend to be minimally integrated into developed and competitive market systems.

underinvesting labor. This form of sharecropping is fully integrated into factor and product markets and is employed by the most highly capitalized, technologically sophisticated, and vertically integrated firms in the industry. These sharecroppers have no mobility-hampering subsistence plots of land. Their relations with landowners are often paternalistic, but in this way, sharecroppers differ little from hired workers. Moreover, the paternalism of these relations neither prevents sharecroppers from moving to better jobs, nor prevents owners from firing poor performers. Sharecropping of this sort is especially suited to firms producing labor-intensive commodities whose need for product quality would otherwise necessitate extensive supervision, whose production processes permit the subdivision of inputs and responsibilities, and whose deployment of employees is increasingly constrained by political forces. Sharecroppers in such cases are essentially employees with a share feature to their wage contracts.

These three forms of sharecropping, then, vary empirically in terms of the extent to which they are the result of individual free choice or of systemic constraints, are sustained by economic or by political forces, are efficient or inefficient, and are generally more coercive or more collaborative. More coercive systems appear to be distinguished by an important feature: the dependence of access to factors of production on the categoric identities of prospective tenants—such as their race, immigration status, or historical status of servitude—rather than on their changing personal circumstances. I suggest that where sociopolitical institutions and practices differentially benefit or burden certain sets of economic actors according to such identities, we may expect sharecropping to tend toward the coercion pattern. In such circumstances, sociopolitical factors are crucial to understanding the system. When such categorical discriminations do not significantly disadvantage share tenants, sharecropping is more likely to be relatively equitable and amenable to microeconomic analysis.[12]

The substantial differences among these forms demonstrate that we can come to no simple conclusions about the causes, efficiency, and distributional justice of sharecropping, nor about its role in economic development. We must instead construct our understandings of particular cases by examining the empirical relations within the firms involved and their links to the wider social formation. We can ask, however, whether the sort of politically motivated sharecropping found in U.S. fruit and vegetable indus-

[12]So marked are the differences among these three forms that future scholars may want to reserve the term sharecropping for the most paternalistic, coercive systems that gave rise to Marx's initial claims. The form of sharecropping found in cash grain, tree fruit, and nut production, meanwhile, may be better termed share tenancy, and the form used in labor-intensive fruit and vegetable crops could be called share labor.

tries has its counterparts in other places, periods, and industries. Here, our answers are limited by the nature of extant data. Because the majority of sharecropping analyses have been conducted by economists working within a microeconomic framework, most attend little to the roles of political constraints and class struggle. It is clear, however, that political limits on share tenants' resource acquisition and mobility did increase the utility of sharecropping to land owners and black tenants in the postbellum South, peasants in postfeudal Europe, and Japanese immigrants in the pre-World War II strawberry industry. Moreover, studies of sharecropping in Spain (Martinez-Alier 1974), Southeast Asia (Hart 1986; Popkin 1979), Peru (Albert 1982), Mexico (Finkler 1978), and agrarian societies more generally (Paige 1975) show that sharecropping has played a crucial role in rural class struggles in other times and places. If our present perspective is correct, exactly what that role is can only be determined by an examination of the particular organizational form and wider political-economic dynamics of each case.

Combined and Uneven Development

Finally, what does the analysis developed in this book teach us about the broader course and causes of world economic change? There was a time when scholars believed that we could develop a big picture of the development of capitalism: the organization of its firms, the deployment of its production factors, the social relations among its key categories of participants, the forms and functions of its ideologies and politics, and the evolution of its national and international economic systems. Recent decades, however, have raised doubts as to whether such large-scale models can predict or even describe the dynamics of actual capitalist economies. As the all-inclusive project of the "big story" has been discredited, we appear to be left with the option of many "little stories" of local cases set in particular temporal and material contexts. Not only has the goal of prediction been called into question, but, for some observers, all generalization has become suspect. In this book, I have charted a tack between these two positions. I have discarded the economism, the unilinearity, and the focus on structure at the expense of agency characteristic of most efforts to tell the big story of capitalist development. I have also challenged the notion that history has irrevocable economic laws. Yet I have tried to show that despite our acknowledgment of contingency, we observe and can attempt to explain socioeconomic patterning. Expansive structures and tendencies make a difference in the unfolding of local contests, and these local contests make a difference in the composition of wider structures. It is the interrelation of these two, I am convinced, which offers the most fruitful focus for social scientific analysis.

Economic Restructuring Revisited. This book provides a useful platform from which to evaluate the processes of economic restructuring in the late twentieth century. In recent years, a range of scholars have argued that capitalist enterprise is undergoing a qualitative global transformation (Aglietta 1979; Atkinson 1988; Harrison 1994; Harvey 1989; Metcalf 1986; Piore and Sabel 1984). That is, since the mid-1970s the post–World War II "Fordist" regime of accumulation based on mass consumption and production, dedicated machinery, large vertically integrated firms, and supportive state regulation has been disintegrating, and in its place a new "post-Fordist" regime of "flexible specialization" (Piore and Sabel 1984) or "flexible accumulation" (Harvey 1989) is taking shape. This emerging regime is characterized by smaller-scale and more flexible technologies and organizational units, decentralized global production systems, differentiated product and niche markets, and new kinds of state regulation which legitimate flexibility. The central causes of this watershed are thought to be global and economic: the increasing volatility and competitiveness of the world economy engendered by rising raw material and labor costs, floating exchange rates, saturated markets, and falling product prices. All of these changes, it is argued, have challenged the hegemony of U.S.-based producers and rendered flexible technologies and organizational forms particularly advantageous.

At the enterprise level, this transformation is reflected in the downsizing and decentralization of production and the replacement of permanent, full-time employees with temporary and part-time workers, contractors and subcontractors, at-home workers, leased employees, the self-employed, and firms that are too small to be covered by protective laws. Such persons are often termed "contingent workers," to emphasize the temporary and unprotected character of their work (Callaghan and Hartmann 1992). It is impossible to establish the exact amount of contingent employment, but observers agree that it has expanded since the mid-1970s in advanced capitalist countries and currently comprises the most rapidly growing source of work. Contingent workers account for about 25 to 30 percent of the civilian labor force in the United States. In California, they comprise about 25 percent of nonagricultural and over 30 percent of agricultural workers—including sharecroppers, contractors, their employees, and many small-scale contract farmers.[13]

[13]The variety of boundary criteria used, the often hidden character of the economic activity involved, and the lack of systematic data collection all prevent measurement of the con-

My analysis suggests that three serious shortcomings of mainstream portrayals of economic restructuring hamper our understanding of the unevenness inherent in the late twentieth-century economic landscape. First and most consequential, they present an overly simplistic view of the causes of current restructuring. In their assumption that changing world economic structure is the primary motivator of restructuring, these analyses overhomogenize the processes and outcomes of economic change. Their broad brushstrokes privilege global influences over local, economic forces over sociopolitical, and structure over agency. Yet in actual instances of restructuring, these neglected dimensions may predominate.

As this book has shown, the processes of economic development are highly specific to time and place and responsive to their immediate sociocultural environments. In practice, the shift to a contingent workforce may not be a means for capitalists to eliminate a ponderous organizational structure, foster technological innovation, respond to changing consumer demands, or exploit new market niches so as to compete more efficiently in the global economy. Rather, the shift may be primarily a means of reducing the burdens imposed by state regulation and labor militancy. Moreover, as we have seen, such burdens are by no means uniform, because localized activity systems importantly mediate the impacts of broader constraints. As a result, felt pressures toward restructuring are extremely variable and the motivations of local capitalists cannot be inferred from the overlay of national or regional institutional frameworks.

The role of social conflict is particularly underexamined in contemporary analyses of restructuring. The flexible specialization/accumulation literature portrays restructuring as a necessary means of improving a firm's efficiency in an increasingly changeable and competitive global economy. There is thus an implication of inevitability and value neutrality in these assessments of restructuring which masks both its intentionality and its distributional impacts. We are insufficiently informed about how class interests and class strategies figure into economic reconfigurations—how such changes affect the power relations between classes, how and to what extent the changes burden or benefit each, and what initiatives each class might take to encourage or even effect them. As the examples of labor-intensive fruit and vegetable sharecropping and labor contracting in the United States demonstrate, the resort to contingent employment may be an in-

tingent workforce. Moreover, most in-depth research on this topic has focused on manufacturing, leaving the substantial expansion of contingent employment in service and agriculture relatively unexamined. My estimates of its size are derived from Berch 1985, Callaghan and Hartmann 1992, Castro 1993, Dillon 1987, Morrow 1993, and Villarejo and Runsten 1993.

tentional weapon in class conflict. The primary motivation for it may not be the flexibility it offers within uncertain and rapidly changing global market niches but rather the control and cost reduction it offers in relation to local class contests. Moreover, my investigation shows that the agency of employers is not the only cause of restructuring: the reciprocal agency of workers can undermine the advantage that restructuring initially offered and lead employers to again reconfigure their firms. In short, and as other evidence attests, the processes of restructuring are much more bilateral and ongoing, and much more influenced by social institutions and power struggles, than the mainstream literature acknowledges.[14] Rather than as-

[14]For example, reduced exposure to social conflict clearly plays a role in the proliferation of subcontracting in the global agro-food system. In some cases, the dismantling of formerly centralized enterprises was a response to the changing global structure of costs, demand, and competition, but in others it was primarily a means of buffering large foreign capitalists from nationalist and labor opposition. Thus, United Brands and Standard Fruit turned to contract farming in their Central American banana operations when state-led nationalist pressure in the 1950s generated labor opposition on their plantations. In this context, the shift to smaller-scale farms owned by national contract producers reduced foreign capitalists' political visibility and helped them undercut unionization and evade protective legislation. Studies of the involvement of U.S. agribusinesses in Mexican agriculture reveal comparable motivations for the use of contract farmers there (see Friedmann 1991; Griffith 1993; McMichael 1994; Watts 1994).

Along a different tack, Peter Evans (1994) underscores the impact of varying state structures and roles on patterns of economic organization worldwide. The role of institutional structures is evident in Italy as well. Although authors such as Piore and Sabel argue that global economic shifts were the most decisive causes of restructuring in that country, their own and other evidence indicates that regional and national political structures, cultural traditions, and social networks encouraged—perhaps even made possible—Italy's decentralized system of economic organization. Class struggle played a formative role as well, in that decentralized production in Italy was initially a temporary expedient developed by the owners of large integrated firms in the 1960s as a means of regaining control over production and biding their time until worker militancy subsided (Piore and Sabel 1984:151–56, 215, 227–29; Putnam 1993; Sayer and Walker 1992).

Finally, the large literature on the "informal sector" or "informal economy" underscores the causal importance of avoiding state regulation and labor mobilization. This voluminous and diverse literature documents a larger and often differently motivated realm of activity than the one considered here: in addition to paid work, it includes illicit and nonmarket exchanges and individual survival strategies on the margins; in addition to forms of activity initiated by employers, it includes those initiated by workers and the unemployed. Moreover, the motivations for the initiation of informal activity vary widely, since much of it occurs in Third World countries whose socioeconomic conditions and challenges differ significantly from those in the core. Nonetheless, if we confine ourselves to the portion of informal sector activity emphasized in this book—the restructuring of paid work in advanced capitalist countries, including the casualization and apparent decentralization of employment relations in previously centralized firms and the proliferation of small-scale enterprises in new economic arenas and in those formerly dominated by larger companies—we find ample evidence in this literature that employers have turned to an externalized labor force in order to delay or evade unionization, wage gains, and state-enforced labor protections (see Ferman, Berndt, and Henry 1993; Portes 1983; Portes, Castells, and Benton 1989).

suming that global economic structure is causally primary, we need to explore directly the combination of influences that affect the local level, as well as the ways that local actors respond to and transform them. Only then will we be able to build accurate generalizations about the processes and outcomes of contemporary economic development.

A second and related shortcoming of the economic restructuring literature has to do with its portrayal of the expansion of contingent employment as a qualitative watershed in the structure of the global economy—a "second industrial divide" (Piore and Sabel 1984). The present study suggests that this representation exaggerates the homogeneity of current and prior regimes of accumulation and confuses situational adaptations with epochal transformations. To some extent, this exaggeration is fostered by the very terminology of the debate. As David Harvey (1989:174–76) and others point out, the language of "divides" presupposes the discontinuity rather than the continuity of developmental stages. Yet evidence is accumulating that industrial organization has been so heterogeneous in both the "Fordist" and "post-Fordist" eras that allegations that they comprise unitary regimes may be inappropriate (e.g., Goodman and Watts 1994). Moreover, as this book shows, local variation and fluctuation in form within a given regime are much more common and substantial than recognized. It would be impossible to argue, for example, that shifts in the use of strawberry sharecropping were caused by, or even associated with, watersheds in the global regime of accumulation. Rather, they were contextual and reversible responses to the mix of national and local political pressures that shaped the regional labor market. We must take care to distinguish between economic reconfigurations that are part of the "ordinary" functioning of a continuous regime and those that are part of a transition from one regime to another. Such distinctions cannot be made from the remove of an overview of world economic structure; they must be grounded in the particularities of local systems.

The imprecise use of the term "flexibility" also hampers our assessments of whether a regime shift has occurred. It is unclear in many discussions which dimensions of flexibility are involved in alleged exemplars of the qualitative watershed. Do we mean flexibility in the assignment of tasks, in the employment or deployment of labor, in product character or output volume, in machinery use, or in linkages within the commodity system (Sayer and Walker 1992:199)? I have demonstrated here that contingent production forms are not necessarily more flexible in these regards. Nor are "Fordist" organizational forms necessarily less flexible (ibid.: 193–94). In addition, formal structural evidence of downsizing and decentralization may conceal an actual continuity of organizational scale and central direction. We must not confuse romanticized representations of emerging jobs as bearing out Piore and Sabel's (1984) claim that work is becoming more whole and creative for workers with actual production relations in which work is highly fragmented and controlled. In fact, as we saw in the strawberry industry, contingent workers' relations of economic contribution and control may not differ substantially from those of direct-hire employees. On the whole, studies of contingent employment in the United States suggest that although some of the new "flexibly specialized" workers get higher wages and more opportunity for creativity, most are not only less protected—because of their exclusion from social-protective laws and union membership—but they are paid less and controlled comparably (Callaghan and Hartmann 1992; Dillon 1987; Rosenberg 1993). Clearly, we need to delve beneath the form of economic structure to the substance of economic relations to uncover the actual dimensions and functions of current restructuring.

A third shortcoming of dominant representations of restructuring has to do with their limited apprehension of industrial and sectoral differentiation. This book demonstrates abundantly that industry characteristics shape the vulnerabilities, resources, and strategies of owners and workers, and thus their responsiveness to local and extralocal influences. It suggests as well that agricultural industries may be particularly inclined toward uneven development. Observers have long remarked that agriculture is more flexible and variable than industry in its production organization and labor deployment (Kautsky 1989 [1899]; Mann 1990; Mann and Dickinson 1978; Pugliese 1991). This contrast is based in the distinctive characteristics of agricultural production—the facts that production time exceeds labor time, labor demand is shaped by biological growth processes, production is relatively tied to the land, and land markets impose distinct rigidities. Because multiple job holding and casualized work arrangements are so common in agriculture, one cannot tell from a surface glance whether they are a continuation of an old regime or a divide comparable to that alleged in industry. My analysis advises caution in assuming the latter.

Whereas some authors argue that capitalist accumulation processes are eliminating the distinctions between industry and agriculture (FitzSimmons 1986; Kenney et al. 1991; Kim and Curry 1993; Pugliese 1991), the present study and others attest that the progress of industrialization and globalization in agriculture is highly uneven, and that the structures of agricultural commodity systems remain remarkably heterogeneous (Buttel and Newby 1980; de Janvry 1981; Friedland 1984a; Goldberg 1980, 1981; Goodman and Watts 1994; Marsden et al. 1990). This unevenness has to do in part, I suggest, with the ways that agriculture's necessary and varying bonds to land and climate and its dependence on the not-entirely-overcome natural rhythms of biological processes affect the course of class relations. That is, agricultural producers are unevenly able to relocate to escape local social struggles or to achieve optimal pricing for production factors. They also vary in their abilities to eliminate bottlenecks in production and to achieve labor control through mechanization. As a result, they are especially rooted in local sociopolitical systems and vulnerable to local disturbances, and they are particularly inclined to reorganize production to buffer themselves from such constraints. Certainly, agricultural industries vary among themselves in this regard, and some extractive and service industries are tied to locale as well and thus are especially motivated to develop compromises with local challengers that may involve economic reconfiguration (Hobsbawm 1964; Yarrow 1979). Such persisting barriers to rationalization are much more common in agriculture, however, and may be one of the most important ways in which the processes of agricultural development remain particular.

The Long View. The discoveries I present here lead to the conclusion that the economic forms and relations that may prove of use to capital are much more diverse than Marx and Lenin recognized. Clearly, there is no unilinear progression away from the stage of decentralized petty commodity production toward the epoch of centralized modern industry and wage labor. Nor is there a single development away from employment relations rooted in personal acquaintance and the family toward more objective, instrumental links of superordination and subordination, more simplified and oppositional class structures, and more polarized class relations. Under certain conditions, social relations of production other than the free wage labor contract can more effectively control and cheapen labor, a conclusion underscored by recent analyses of the persistence of family and peasant farmers in the United States and developing countries.[15]

In this book, I have presented an argument for the likely persistence of precapitalist forms which is tied neither to the character of agriculture nor

[15]Alain De Janvry and Carlos Garramon (1977) argue, for example, that as capitalist agriculture has penetrated the Third World, it has not destroyed precapitalist formations such as the peasantry, but has rather strengthened them and turned them to capitalist use. Thus agribusinesses use the subsistence base of semiproletarian peasant workers to subsidize the reproduction of the labor force, a tack that is particularly advantageous given the sporadic and seasonal demand for labor. Susan Mann and James Dickinson (1978) make a related argument in relation to family farms in advanced capitalist countries, arguing that the distinctive nature of the productive process in certain spheres of agriculture—particularly those in which labor time and production time do not (yet) coincide—makes these spheres undesirable for capitalist penetration and encourages the persistence of family labor farms. Michael Watts (1994) points to the renewed utility of contract farming in the global agro-food system.

to the subsistence base of peasant producers. I have suggested that the changing political context of production has motivated an increase in legally-distanced labor in advanced capitalist societies, fostering the proliferation of subcontracting, putting-out systems, and cottage industries—production forms once thought to be characteristic of earlier stages of development. These forms exist alongside and in causal interconnection with the internal, formally-protected wage workforces of capitalist firms. Sociopolitical forces, which Marx and Lenin thought to be outside the causal dynamics of production, are major current causes of their development. Clearly, Marx and Lenin did not anticipate the political circumstances that could make subcontracting and personalized work relations of renewed advantage to capitalist producers. In fact, in arguing for the inevitable dominance of a certain form of production, they lost sight of their central insight: that the distinguishing objective of capitalist enterprise is profit. If the evidence of this book is to be believed, the press of capitalism is not to transform diverse social forms into a uniform proletariat, but rather to control and generate profit from the variety of forms that exist.

I must acknowledge, in these reflections, that Marx did provide some guidelines for making sense of contemporary changes. In his analysis of the transition from feudalism to capitalism, he suggested that sharecropping might shift in function despite its "medieval garb." Should it unexpectedly persist, he advised, we should inquire into its capitalist functions ([1894] 1977:3:788). Marx also cautioned at certain points that the processes of economic change do not necessarily eliminate the old. If we carefully examine his discussion of modern industry, for example, we find that he anticipated the incorporation rather than the supercession of earlier forms ([1867] 1977:1:312–70). History lends weight to this anticipation. Despite assumptions of a rapid and uniform shift to centralized industry and wage labor, decentralized forms of employment continued to be vital, indeed, they even proliferated, during the period of classic capitalism in Europe and the United States (Allen 1929; Ashton 1926; Osborn 1903; Rischin 1962; Samuel 1977). This book has demonstrated that diverse production forms coexist and interdepend within contemporary capitalist economies as well. Together, these discoveries suggest that we are faced not with random and anomalous economic survivals, but with a prevailing pattern of economic growth—what Trotsky termed "combined and uneven development" ([1932] 1937). This pattern is unfolding in parts of capitalist systems that are viewed as the most advanced, as well as in those seen as the most backward.

References Cited

Aglietta, Michel. 1979. *A Theory of Capitalist Regulation.* London: New Left Books.

Agricultural Labor Relations Board (ALRB). 1976–88. *Annual Reports, 1975–1987.* Sacramento: State of California.

Albert, Bill. 1982. *Yanaconaje and Cotton Production on the Peruvian Coast: Sharecropping in the Canete Valley during World War I.* Norwich, Eng.: University of East Anglia, School of Economic and Social Studies.

Albrecht, Don, and Steve Murdock. 1988. "The Structural Characteristics of U.S. Agriculture: Historical Patterns and Precursors of Producers' Adaptations to the Crisis." In *The Farm Financial Crisis,* edited by Steve Murdock and Larry Leistritz, 29–44. Boulder, Colo.: Westview Press.

Allen, G. C. 1929. "Methods of Industrial Organization in the West Midlands, 1860–1927." *Economic Journal, Economic History Supplement* 1, no. 4: 535–53.

Allen, Rutilus. 1934. "Economic History of Agriculture in Monterey County, California, during the American Period." Ph.D. diss., University of California, Berkeley.

Alston, Lee, and Joseph Ferrie. 1985. "Labor Costs, Paternalism, and Loyalty in Southern Agriculture: A Constraint on the Growth of the Welfare State." *Journal of Economic History* 45, no. 95: 109–15.

Aminzade, Ronald. 1981. *Class, Politics, and Early Industrial Capitalism.* Binghamton: SUNY Press.

Aminzade, Ronald. 1984. "Capitalist Industrialization and Patterns of Industrial Protest: A Comparative Urban Study of Nineteenth-Century France." *American Sociological Review* 49: 437–53.

"Amplia Huelga la Union de Trabajadores Agricolas Unidos." 1979. *El Sol,* 6 September, p. 1.

Ashton, T. S. 1926. "The Domestic System in the Early Lancashire Tool Trade." *Economic History, Supplement to the Economic Journal* 1 (January): 131–40.

Atkinson, John. 1988. "Recent Changes in Internal Labour Market Structure in the U.K." In *Technology and Work: Labour Studies in England, Germany, and the Netherlands,* edited by Wout Buitelaar, 133–49. Aldershot, Eng.: Avebury.

Auditor General of California. 1985. *The Agricultural Labor Relations Board's Administration of the Agricultural Labor Relations Act.* Report to the Joint Legislative Audit Committee. Sacramento: California Legislature.

Bach, Robert. 1978. "Mexican Immigration and the American State." *International Migration Review* 12 (Winter): 536–58.

Bain, Beatrice, and Sidney Hoos. 1963. *The California Strawberry Industry: Changing Economic and Marketing Relationships.* Giannini Foundation Research Report no. 267. Berkeley: University of California.

Baird, Peter, and Ed McCaughan. 1979. *Beyond the Border: Mexico and the U.S. Today.* New York: North American Congress on Latin America.

Banfield, Edward. 1951. *Government Project.* Glencoe, Ill.: Free Press.

Bardhan, P., and T. Srinivasan. 1971. "Cropsharing Tenancy in Agriculture: A Theoretical and Empirical Analysis." *American Economic Review* 61: 48–64.

Barlett, Peggy. 1993. *American Dreams, Rural Realities: Family Farms in Crisis.* Chapel Hill: University of North Carolina Press.

Bell, Colin, and Howard Newby. 1975. "The Sources of Variation in Agricultural Workers' Images of Society." In *Working-Class Images of Society,* edited by Martin Bulmer, 83–97. London: Routledge and Kegan Paul.

Bennett, John. 1969. *Northern Plainsmen: Adaptive Strategy and Agrarian Life.* Chicago: Aldine.

Bennett, John. 1982. *Of Time and the Enterprise.* St. Paul: University of Minnesota Press.

Berardi, G. M., and C. C. Geisler. 1984. *The Social Consequences and Challenges of New Agricultural Technologies.* Boulder, Colo.: Westview Press.

Berch, Bettina. 1985. "The Resurrection of Out-Work." *Monthly Review* 37, no. 6: 37–46.

Bernstein, Harry. 1975. "5 Named to New Farm Labor Unit." *Los Angeles Times,* 27 July, sec. 1, pp. 3, 32.

Bernstein, Harry. 1986. "Settlements with Two Growers Mark Policy Shift by UFW." *Los Angeles Times,* 30 July, sec. 4, pp. 1, 3.

Bernstein, Harry. 1987. "Workers Can't Expect a Fair Shake from the Farm Board." *Los Angeles Times,* 8 December, pp. 7, 13.

Bernstein, Irving. 1950. *The New Deal Collective Bargaining Policy.* Berkeley: University of California Press.

"Berry Growers Here Prepare for Battle." 1971. *Watsonville Register-Pajaronian,* 20 May, p. 1.

"Berry Mechanization Studied." 1977. *Packer,* 22 October, p. 12.

Blauner, Robert. 1964. *Alienation and Freedom: The Factory Worker and His Industry.* Chicago: University of Chicago Press.

Blue Book: A Credit and Marketing Guide. 1976, 1986. Wheaton, Ill.: Produce Report Company, Spring.

Blumberg, Abraham, ed. 1970. *The Scales of Justice.* Hawthorne, N.Y.: Aldine.

Bogue, A. G. 1963. *From Prairie to Corn Belt: Farming on the Illinois and Iowa Prairies in the Nineteenth Century.* Chicago: University of Chicago Press.

Boitano, David. 1987. "Chavez Brings Campaign to Tracy." *Pleasanton Tri-Valley Herald,* 14 January, p. 1.

Bonacich, Edna, and John Modell. 1980. *The Economic Basis of Ethnic Solidarity:*

Small Business in the Japanese American Community. Berkeley: University of California Press.

Brannon, Jeffery, Santiago Ibarreche, and Wilke English. 1984. *The Economy of Mexico: 1984 and Beyond.* Monograph no. 12. El Paso: University of Texas, Center for Inter-American and Border Studies.

Braverman, Harry. 1974. *Labor and Monopoly Capital: The Degradation of Work in the Twentieth Century.* New York: Monthly Review Press.

Bray, James O. 1963. "Farm Tenancy and Productivity in Agriculture: The Case of the United States." *Food Research Institute Studies* 4, no. 3: 25–38.

Breton, Marcos. 1992. "Fields of Betrayal?" *Sacramento Bee,* 23 February, pp. A1, A15.

Briggs, Vernon M., Jr., Walter Fogel, and Fred H. Schmidt. 1977. *The Chicano Worker.* Austin: University of Texas Press.

Brighton Labour Process Group. 1977. "The Capitalist Labour Process." *Capital and Class,* no. 1 (Spring): 3–26.

"Brown Appointees Still Hold an Edge on Makeup of ALRB." 1985. *Davis Enterprise,* 22 November, p. 20.

Brown, Jerald B. 1972. *The United Farm Workers Grape Strike and Boycott, 1965–70: An Evaluation of the Culture of Poverty Theory.* Ithaca, N.Y.: Cornell University, Latin American Studies Program.

Bulmer, Martin. 1975. *Working Class Images of Society.* London: Routledge and Kegan Paul.

Bunje, Emil. [1957] 1971. *The Story of Japanese Farming in California.* Berkeley, Calif.: U.S. Work Projects Administration Project; reprint, San Jose: R. and E. Research Associates.

Burawoy, Michael. 1976. "The Functions and Reproduction of Migrant Labor: Comparative Material from Southern Africa and the United States." *American Journal of Sociology* 81 (March): 1050–87.

Burawoy, Michael. 1979. *Manufacturing Consent: Changes in the Labor Process under Monopoly Capitalism.* Chicago: University of Chicago Press.

Burawoy, Michael. 1985. *The Politics of Production: Factory Regimes under Capitalism and Socialism.* London: Verso.

Burlingame, Bert, Delbert Farnham, and Arthur Greathead. 1969. *Strawberry Production Costs for Monterey and Santa Cruz Counties.* Berkeley: University of California, Agricultural Extension Service.

Buttel, Frederick. 1983. "Beyond the Family Farm." In *Technology and Social Change in Rural Areas,* edited by G. F. Summers, 87–107. Boulder, Colo.: Westview Press.

Buttel, Frederick. 1987. "The U.S. Farm Crisis and the Restructuring of American Agriculture: Domestic and International Dimensions." Paper presented at the Workshop on International Restructuring and the Farm Crisis, Centre for European Agricultural Studies, Wye College, University of London, December.

Buttel, Frederick, and Howard Newby. 1980. *The Rural Sociology of the Advanced Societies: Critical Perspectives.* Montclair, N.J.: Allanheld, Osmun.

Caballero, José M. 1982. "Sharecropping: A Review of Issues." Paper presented at the 44th International Congress of Americanists, Manchester, Eng., September.

California Agriculture: Statistical Review, 1986, 1987. 1987, 1988. Sacramento: California Department of Food and Agriculture.

California Agricultural Statistics Service. 1988, 1989. *Agricultural Commissioners' Data, 1987, 1988.* Sacramento: California Department of Food and Agriculture.

California and the 21st Century: Foundations for a Competitive Society. 1986. Vol. 1. A Report of the Senate Select Committee on Long Range Policy Planning. Sacramento: State of California, January.

California Department of Housing and Community Development. 1977. *California Farmworkers Housing Assistance Plan, 1977.* Sacramento: State of California.

California Department of Industrial Relations (CDIR). 1952–86. *Work Stoppages in California.* San Francisco: State of California, Division of Labor Statistics and Research.

California Gene Resources Program, National Council on Gene Resources. 1982. *Strawberry Genetic Resources: An Assessment and Plan for California.* Sacramento: State of California.

California Institute for Rural Studies (CIRS). 1985. *A Farm Crisis Hotline for California.* Davis: California Institute for Rural Studies.

California State Senate, Fact-Finding Committee on Labor and Welfare. 1961. *California's Farm Labor Problems.* Sacramento: State of California.

"California Strawberry Acreage." 1960–87. *California Vegetables/California Vegetable Review.* Sacramento: U.S. Department of Agriculture and California Department of Food and Agriculture, California Crop and Livestock Reporting Service.

California Strawberry Advisory Board (CSAB). 1965. *Agricultural Labor Requirements in the California Strawberry Industry, March 1965.* Watsonville: California Strawberry Advisory Board.

Callaghan, Polly, and Heidi Hartmann. 1992. *Contingent Work: A Chart Book on Part-Time and Temporary Employment.* Washington, D.C.: Economic Policy Institute.

Carter, Harold, ed. 1986. *Impacts of Farm Policy and Technological Change on U.S. and California Agriculture.* Davis: University of California, Agricultural Issues Center.

Carter, Harold, and Warren Johnston. 1978. "Some Forces Affecting the Changing Structure, Organization, and Control of American Agriculture." *American Journal of Agricultural Economics* 60: 738–48.

Carter, Harold, and Carole Nuckton, eds. 1987. *Marketing California Specialty Crops: Worldwide Competition and Constraints.* Davis: University of California, Agricultural Issues Center.

Castaneda, Laura. 1985. "Church Leaders Call on Farm Labor Counsel to Quit." *Sacramento Bee,* 22 October, p. B12.

Castles, Stephen, and Godula Kosack. [1973] 1985. *Immigrant Workers and Class Structure in Western Europe.* Oxford: Oxford University Press.

Castro, Janice. 1993. "Disposable Workers." *Time,* 29 March, 43–47.

"Caught off Balance." 1985. *Los Angeles Times,* 10 November, sec. 4, p. 4.

Chandler, Alfred, Jr. 1969. *Strategy and Structure: Chapters in the History of the American Industrial Enterprise.* Cambridge: MIT Press.

Cheung, Steven. 1969. *The Theory of Share Tenancy: With Special Application to Asian Agriculture and the First Phase of Taiwan Land Reform.* Chicago: University of Chicago Press.

Childers, Norman F., ed. 1980. *The Strawberry: Cultivars to Marketing.* Gainesville, Fla.: Horticultural Publications.

Clawson, Dan. 1980. *Bureaucracy and the Labor Process: The Transformation of U.S. Industry, 1860–1920.* New York: Monthly Review Press.

Cochrane, Willard. 1979. *The Development of American Agriculture: A Historical Analysis.* Minneapolis: University of Minnesota Press.

Cogswell, Seddie. 1975. *Tenure, Nativity, and Age as Factors in Iowa Agriculture, 1850–1880.* Ames: Iowa State University.

Collier, Jane. 1975. "Legal processes." *Annual Review of Anthropology* 4: 121–44.

Cornelius, Wayne. 1981. *Interviewing Undocumented Immigrants: Methodological Reflections Based on Fieldwork in Mexico and the United States.* Working Paper no. 2. La Jolla: University of California, San Diego, Program in U.S.-Mexican Studies.

Cornelius, Wayne. 1989. "Impacts of the 1986 U.S. Immigration Law on Emigration from Rural Mexican Sending Communities." *Population and Development Review* 15, no. 4; 1–21.

Cornelius, Wayne, Leo Chavez, and Jorge Castro. 1982. *Mexican Immigrants and Southern California: A Summary of Current Knowledge.* Working Paper no. 36. La Jolla: University of California, San Diego, Program in U.S.-Mexican Studies.

Coryn, Sidney. 1909. "The Japanese Problem in California." *Annals of the American Academy of Political and Social Science* 34 (September): 262–68.

Craig, Richard. 1971. *The Bracero Program.* Austin: University of Texas Press.

"Cultural Practices Gave One Grower 60 Tons Per Acre." 1978. *Western Fruit Grower* 98 (April): 13, 48.

Currie, Elliott. 1971. "Sociology of Law: The Unasked Questions." *Yale Law Journal* 81 (November): 134–47.

Dagodag, Tim. 1975. "Source Regions and Composition of Illegal Mexican Migration to California." *International Migration Review* 9: 499–511.

Dahrendorf, Ralf. 1968. *Essays in the Theory of Society.* Stanford: Stanford University Press.

Darrow, George. 1966. *The Strawberry: History, Breeding, and Physiology.* New York: Holt, Rinehart and Winston.

Dawley, Alan. 1976. *Class and Community: The Industrial Revolution in Lynn.* Cambridge: Harvard University Press.

DeCanio, Stephen. 1974. *Agriculture in the Postbellum South: The Economics of Production and Supply.* Cambridge: MIT Press.

de Janvry, Alain. 1981. *The Agrarian Question and Reformism in Latin America.* Baltimore: Johns Hopkins University Press.

de Janvry, Alain, and Carlos Garramon. 1977. "The Dynamics of Rural Poverty in Latin America." *The Journal of Peasant Studies* 4 (April): 206–16.

Del Vecchio, Rick. 1987. "Chavez Returns to Battle for His Union's Life." *San Francisco Chronicle,* 8 June, p. 6.

DePietro, Linda. 1987. "California Farms: Better Times Ahead?" *California Journal* 15 (August): 369–72.

Dillon, Rodger. 1987. *The Changing Labor Market: Continent Workers and the Self-Employed in California.* Sacramento: State of California, Senate Office of Research.

Dinerman, Ina. 1982. *Migrants and Stay-at-Homes: A Comparative Study of Rural Migration from Michoacán, Mexico.* Monograph no. 5. La Jolla: University of California, San Diego, Center for U.S.-Mexican Studies.

Doeringer, Peter, and Michael Piore. 1971. *Internal Labor Markets and Manpower Analysis.* Lexington, Mass.: D. C. Heath.

Dorel, Gerard. 1977. "Le Vignoble Californien." *Les Cahiers d'Outre-Mer* 117: 5–30.

Durrenberger, Robert. 1972. *Patterns on the Land: Geographical, Historical, and Political Maps of California.* 4th ed. Palo Alto: National Press.

Edwards, Richard. 1979. *Contested Terrain.* London: Heinemann.

Edwards, Richard, Michael Reich, and David Gordon, eds. 1975. *Labor Market Segmentation.* Lexington, Mass.: D. C. Heath.

Ehrensaft, Philip. 1980. "Long Waves in the Transformation of North American Agriculture: A First Statement." *Cornell Journal of Social Relations* 15, no. 1: 1–15.

Employment Development Department (EDD), Labor Market Information Division. 1992. *Farm Labor Contractors in California.* California Agricultural Studies, no. 92-2. Sacramento: State of California, July.

Erasmus, Charles. 1968. "Community Development and the Encogido Syndrome." *Human Organization* 27: 65–74.

Ericson, Anna-Stina. 1970. "The Impact of Commuters on the Mexican Border Area." *Monthly Labor Review* 93 (August): 18–27.

Evans, Peter. 1995. *Embedded Autonomy: States and Industrial Transformation.* Princeton: Princeton University Press.

"Farm Bureau Solution: Secret Ballot for Farm Workers?" 1973. *Christian Science Monitor,* 22 August, p. 2.

Farm Labor Report. 1942–88. Report 881-A. Sacramento: California Department of Employment Development. (Weekly.)

"Farm Workers Union Extends Its Reach into Rural Mexico." 1986. *Wall Street Journal,* 15 November, p. 1.

Farrell, Kenneth. 1987. "Marketing Challenges Facing California Agriculture." In *Marketing California Specialty Crops: Worldwide Competition and Constraints,* edited by Harold Carter and Carole Nuckton, 9–16. Davis: University of California Agricultural Issues Center.

Feder, Ernest. 1977. *Strawberry Imperialism: An Enquiry into the Mechanisms of Dependency in Mexican Agriculture.* The Hague: Institute of Social Studies.

Federal-State Market News Service. 1972. *Marketing California Strawberries, 1967–71.* San Francisco: U.S. and California Departments of Agriculture.

Fellmeth, Robert. 1973. *The Politics of Land.* New York: Grossman.

Ferman, Louis, Louise Berndt, and Stuart Henry, eds. 1993. *Work beyond Employment in Advanced Capitalist Countries: Classic and Contemporary Perspectives on the Informal Economy.* 2 vols. Lewiston, N.Y.: Mellen.

Ferriss, Susan. 1993. "Fields of Broken Dreams." *San Francisco Examiner,* 18 July, Image sec., pp. 3–15.

"Fields of Pain." 1991. *Sacramento Bee,* 8–11 December, Special Report, pp. 1–20.

Findings from the National Agricultural Workers Survey (NAWS), 1990. 1991. Research Report no. 1. Washington, D.C.: GPO, U.S. Department of Labor, Office of the Assistant Secretary for Policy, July.

Finkler, Kaja. 1978. "From Sharecroppers to Entrepreneurs: Peasant Household Production Strategies under the Ejido System of Mexico." *Economic Development and Cultural Change* 27 (October 1): 103–20.

Finney, Essex, Jr., ed. 1981. *Handbook of Transportation and Marketing in Agriculture.* Vol. 1 of *Food Commodities.* Boca Raton: C.R.C. Press.

Fisher, Lloyd. 1953. *The Harvest Labor Market in California.* Cambridge: Harvard University Press.

Fiske, Emmett. 1979. "The College and Its Constituency: Rural and Community Development at the University of California, 1875–1978." Ph.D. diss., University of California, Davis.

FitzSimmons, Margaret. 1983. *Consequences of Agricultural Industrialization: Environmental and Social Change in the Salinas Valley, California, 1945–1978.* Ann Arbor, Mich.: University Microfilms International.

FitzSimmons, Margaret. 1986. "The New Industrial Agriculture." *Economic Geography* 62, no. 4: 334–51.

Foner, Eric. 1983. *Nothing but Freedom: Emancipation and Its Legacy.* Baton Rouge: Louisiana State University Press.

Foster, George. 1965. "Peasant Society and the Image of the Limited Good." *American Anthropologist* 67: 293–315.

Foster, John. 1974. *Class Struggle and the Industrial Revolution: Early Industrial Capitalism in Three English Towns.* London: Weidenfeld and Nicolson.

Friedland, William. 1984a. "Commodity Systems Analysis: An Approach to the Sociology of Agriculture." In *Research in Rural Sociology and Development: A Research Annual,* edited by Harry Schwarzweller, 221–35. Greenwich, Conn.: JAI Press.

Friedland, William. 1984b. "The Labor Force in U.S. Agriculture." In *Food Security in the United States,* edited by Larry Busch and William Lacey, 143–81. Boulder, Colo.: Westview Press.

Friedland, William, and Amy Barton. 1975. *Destalking the Wily Tomato: A Case Study in Social Consequences in California Agricultural Research.* Research Monograph no. 15. Davis: University of California, Department of Applied Behavioral Sciences.

Friedland, William, Amy Barton, and Robert Thomas. 1981. *Manufacturing Green Gold: Capital, Labor, and Technology in the Lettuce Industry.* New York: Cambridge University Press.

Friedland, William, et al. 1991. *Towards a New Political Economy of Agriculture.* Boulder, Colo.: Westview Press.

Friedman, Andrew. 1977. *Industry and Labour: Class Struggle at Work and Monopoly Capitalism.* London: Macmillan.

Friedmann, Harriet. 1978. "World Market, State, and Family Farm: Social Bases of Household Production in the Era of Wage Labor." *Comparative Studies in Society and History* 20, no. 4: 545–86.

Friedmann, Harriet. 1980. "Household Production and the Natural Economy." *Journal of Peasant Studies* 7, no. 2: 158–84.

Friedmann, Harriet. 1991. "Changes in the International Division of Labor: Agri-Food Complexes and Export Agriculture." In *Towards a New Political Economy of Agriculture,* edited by William Friedland et al., 65–93. Boulder, Colo.: Westview Press.

Frobel, Folker. 1980. *Current Development of the World Economy.* Tokyo: United Nations University.

Fujimoto, Isao, and William Kopper. 1978. "Outside Influence on What Research Gets Done at a Land Grant School: Impact of Marketing Orders." In *Priorities in Agricultural Research of the U.S. Department of Agriculture, Part 2.* U.S. Congress, Senate Subcommittee on Administrative Practice and Procedure of the Committee on the Judiciary, Appendix 95, 1. Washington, D.C.: GPO.

Fuller, Varden. 1939. "Supply of Agricultural Labor as a Factor in the Evolution of Farm Organization in California." Ph.D. diss., University of California, Berkeley.

Galarza, Ernesto. 1964. *Merchants of Labor.* Santa Barbara: McNally and Loftin.

Gardner, Delworth, and Richard Howitt. 1986. "Modeling Production and Resource Interrelationships among California Crops in Response to the 1985 Food Security Act." In *Impacts of Farm Policy and Technological Change on U.S. and California Agriculture,* edited by Harold Carter, 271–90. Davis: University of California, Agricultural Issues Center.

Garoyan, Leon, and James Youde. 1975. *Marketing Orders in California: A Description.* Leaflet 2719. Berkeley: University of California, Division of Agricultural Sciences.

Gates, Paul W. 1973. *Landlords and Tenants on the Prairie Frontier.* Ithaca: Cornell University Press.

Geyer, William. 1970a. "Farm Labor Issue Enters New Phase." *California Journal* 1 (October): 282–83.

Geyer, William. 1970b. "Unity and Diversity in the Farm Bloc." *California Journal* 1 (October): 290.

Gliessman, Stephen, et al. 1990. "Strawberry Production Systems during Conversion to Organic Management." *California Agriculture* 44 (April) 4–7.

Goldberg, Ray. 1980, 1981. *Research in Domestic and International Agribusiness Management.* Vols. 1, 2. Greenwich, Conn.: JAI Press.

Goldschmidt, Walter. [1947] 1978. *As You Sow: Three Studies in the Social Consequences of Agribusiness.* Montclair, N.J.: Allanheld, Osmun.

Gonzales, Juan L., Jr. 1985. *Mexican and Mexican American Farmworkers, the California Agricultural Industry.* New York: Praeger Publishers.

Goodman, David, and Michael Watts. 1994. "Reconfiguring the Rural or Fording the Divide? Capitalist Restructuring and the Global Agro-Food System." *Journal of Peasant Studies* 22, no. 1: 1–49.

Gordon, David, Richard Edwards, and Michael Reich. 1982. *Segmented Work, Divided Workers.* New York: Cambridge University Press.

Gorman, Robert. 1976. *Basic Text on Labor Law, Unionization, and Collective Bargaining.* St. Paul: West Publishing.

Goss, Kevin, Richard Rodefeld, and Frederick Buttel. 1979. *The Political Economy of Class Structure in U.S. Agriculture: A Theoretical Outline.* University Park: Pennsylvania State University, Department of Agricultural Economics and Rural Sociology.

Gouldner, Alvin. 1954. *Patterns of Industrial Democracy.* New York: Free Press.

Gramsci, Antonio. 1971. *Selections from Prison Notebooks.* New York: International Publishers.

Granovetter, Mark. 1990. "The Old and New Economic Sociology: A History and an Agenda." In *Beyond the Marketplace,* edited by Roger Friedland and A. F. Robertson, 89–112. New York: Aldine de Gruyter.

Greathead, Arthur. 1971. *A Sample of Strawberry Production Costs for Monterey and Santa Cruz Counties.* Berkeley: University of California, Agricultural Extension.

Greene, Sheldon. 1969. "Immigration Law and Rural Poverty: The Problem of the Illegal Entrant." *Duke Law Journal* 3: 479.

Griffith, David. 1993. *Jones's Minimal: Low-Wage Labor in the United States.* Albany: SUNY Press.

Grindle, Merilee. 1983. *Issues in U.S.-Mexican Agricultural Relations: A Binational Consultation.* Monograph Series, no. 8. La Jolla: University of California, San Diego, Center for U.S.-Mexican Studies.

"Gross Values by Commodity Groups, California, 1984 and 1985." 1986. Summary of County Agricultural Commissioner's Reports. Sacramento: California Agricultural Statistics Service, August.

Gunter, Lewell, Joseph Jarrett, and James Duffield. 1992. "Effect of U.S. Immigration Reform on Labor-Intensive Agricultural Commodities." *American Journal of Agricultural Economics* 74, no. 4: 897–906.

Gutman, Herbert. [1966] 1977. *Work, Culture, and Society in Industrializing America.* New York: Vintage.

Hahn, Steven, and Jonathan Prude. 1985. *The Countryside in the Age of Capitalist Transformation: Essays in the Social History of Rural America.* Chapel Hill: University of North Carolina Press.

Haley, Brian. 1987. "Change in California Agriculture and Society: A Preliminary Case Study of the Santa Barbara County Wine Industry." Manuscript, University of California, Santa Barbara, Department of Anthropology.

Haley, Mary Jean, ed. 1982. *Strawberry Genetic Resources: An Assessment and Plan for California.* Berkeley: California Gene Resources Program.

Hall, Richard. 1989. "Tricks of the Trade." *California Farmer,* 2 September, pp. 8–9, 32.

Hardesty, S. D. 1986. *1986 Michigan Farm Finance Survey: Final Report.* Staff Paper no. 86-33. Lansing: Michigan State University, Department of Agricultural Economics.

Harrison, Bennett. 1994. *Lean and Mean: The Changing Landscape of Corporate Power in the Age of Flexibility.* New York: Basic Books.

Hart, Gillian. 1986. *Power, Labor, and Livelihood: Processes of Change in Rural Java.* Berkeley: University of California Press.

Hartman, David. 1964. *California and Man.* Dubuque, Iowa: William C. Brown.

Harvey, David. 1989. *The Condition of Post-Modernity.* Oxford: Basil Blackwell.

Hawley, Ellis. 1966. "Politics of the Mexican American Labor Issue." *Agricultural History* 40: 157–76.

Haydu, Jeffrey. 1988. *Between Craft and Class: Skilled Workers and Factory Politics in the United States and Britain, 1890–1922.* Berkeley: University of California Press.

Hightower, Jim. 1972. *Hard Tomatoes, Hard Times: The Failure of the Land Grant College Complex.* New York: Schocken.

Hobsbawn, Eric. 1964. *Labouring Men: Studies in the History of Labour.* London: Weidenfeld and Nicholson.

Hobsbawn, Eric. 1984. *Worlds of Labour: Further Studies in the History of Labour.* London: Weidenfeld and Nicolson.

Hubner, John. 1984. "The God of the Movement." *San Jose Mercury News, West,* 19 August, pp. 10–33.

"Inter Harvest Shut by Citizens' Pickets." 1970. *Salinas Californian,* 1 September, pp. 1–2.

Iwata, Masakazo. 1962. "The Japanese Immigrants in California Agriculture." *Agricultural History* 36 (January): 25–37.

Jenkins, Craig. 1978. "The Demand for Immigrant Workers: Labor Scarcity or Social Control?" *International Migration Review* 12 (Winter): 514–35.

Jenkins, Craig. 1985. *The Politics of Insurgency: The Farm Worker Movement in the 1960s.* New York: Columbia University Press.

Jenkins, Craig, and Charles Perrow. 1977. "Insurgency of the Powerless: Farm Worker Movements (1946–72)." *American Sociological Review* 42: 249–67.

Johnson, James, Kenneth Baum, and Richard Prescott. 1985. *Financial Characteristics of U.S. Farms, 1985.* Agricultural Information Bulletin no. 495. Washington, D.C.: U.S. Department of Agriculture, Economic Research Service.

Johnson, James, et al. 1986. *Financial Characteristics of U.S. Farms.* Agricultural Information Bulletin no. 500. Washington, D.C.: U.S. Department of Agriculture, Economic Research Service, 1 January.

Johnson, James, Mitchell Morehart, and Kenneth Erickson. 1987. "Financial Conditions of the Farm Sector and Farm Operators." *Agricultural Finance Review* 47: 1–18.

Jolly, Robert, and Alan Barkema. 1985. *1985 Iowa Farm Finance Survey: Current Conditions and Changes Since 1984.* ASSIST-8. Ames: Iowa State University, Cooperative Extension Service.

Jolly, Robert, et al. 1985. "Incidence, Intensity, and Duration of Financial Stress among Farm Firms." *American Journal of Agricultural Economics* 67, no. 5: 1108–15.

Jones, Lamar. 1970. "Labor and Management in California Agriculture, 1864–1964." *Labor History* 11 (Winter): 23–40.

Jones, Richard, ed. 1984. *Patterns of Undocumented Migration: Mexico and the United States.* Totowa, N.J.: Rowman and Allanheld.

Kader, Adel, et al. 1985. *Postharvest Technology of Horticultural Crops.* Special Publication 3311. Berkeley: University of California, Division of Agriculture and Natural Resources.

Kautsky, Karl. [1899] 1989. *The Agrarian Question.* London: Swan.

Kearney, Michael, and James Stuart. 1981. *Causes and Effects of Agricultural Labor Migration from the Míxteca of Oaxaca to California.* Working Paper no. 28. La Jolla: University of California, San Diego, Center for U.S.-Mexican Studies.

"Keep the ALRB, Drop Stirling." 1987. *Fresno Bee,* 3 August, editorial page.

Kenney, Martin, et al. 1991. "Midwestern Agriculture in U.S. Fordism: From the New Deal to Economic Restructuring. *Sociologia Ruralis* 29, no. 2: 131–48.

Kerr, Clark. 1950. "Labor Markets: Their Character and Consequences." *American Economic Review* 40, no. 2: 278–91.

Kim, Chul-Kyoo, and James Curry. 1993. "Fordism, Flexible Specialization, and Agri-Industrial Restructuring." *Sociologia Ruralis* 33, no. 1: 61–80.

Koch, E., P. Parsons, and A. Greathead. 1956. *Strawberry Cost of Production Study for Santa Cruz and Monterey Counties.* Berkeley: University of California, Agricultural Extension.

Koch, E., A. Shultis, and A. Greathead. 1961. *Strawberries: An Expensive Crop to Grow.* Berkeley: University of California, Agricultural Extension.

Kondratieff, Nicolai Dimitrievich. 1925. "The Long Waves in Economic Life" (in Russian). *Review* 2: 519–62.

Kushner, Sam. 1975. *Long Road to Delano.* New York: International Publishers.

Lantis, David. 1962. *California: Land of Contrast.* Belmont, Calif.: Wadsworth Publishing.

Lawrence, Steve. 1985. "Farm Labor Board: A Decade of Turbulence." *Davis Enterprise,* 22 November, p. 20.

Learn, Elmer, and Gordon King. 1986. "The Direct and Indirect Effects of Commodity Price Support Programs on California Agriculture." In *Impacts of Farm Policy and Technological Change on U.S. and California Agriculture,* edited by Harold Carter, 253–70. Davis: University of California, Agricultural Issues Center.

Lee, Alton. 1966. *Truman and Taft-Hartley.* Lexington: University of Kentucky Press.

Leholm, Arlen, et al. 1985. *Selected Financial and Other Socioeconomic Characteristics of North Dakota Farm and Ranch Operators.* Agricultural Economics Report no. 199. Fargo: North Dakota State University.

Leistritz, Larry, and Brenda Ekstrom. 1988. "The Financial Characteristics of Production Units and Producers Experiencing Financial Stress." In *The Farm Financial Crisis,* edited by Steve Murdock and Larry Leistritz, 73–95. Boulder, Colo.: Westview Press.

Leistritz, Larry, and Steve Murdock. 1988. "Financial Characteristics of Farms and of Farm Financial Markets and Policies in the United States." In *The Farm Financial Crisis,* edited by Steve Murdock and Larry Leistritz, 13–28. Boulder, Colo.: Westview Press.

Lenin, V. I. [1899] 1956. *The Development of Capitalism in Russia.* Moscow: Foreign Languages Publishing House.

Levy, Jacques. 1975. *Cesar Chavez: Autobiography of La Causa.* New York: W. W. Norton.

Lewis, Oscar. 1965. "The Culture of Poverty." *Scientific American* 215 (October): 19–25.

Liebow, Elliot. 1967. *Tally's Corner: A Study of Negro Streetcorner Men.* Boston: Little, Brown.

Light, Ivan. 1972. *Ethnic Enterprise in America: Business and Welfare among Chinese, Japanese, and Blacks.* Berkeley: University of California Press.

Linden, Tim. 1979a. "Ten More Firms Settle with UFW." *Packer,* 15 September, p. 1.

Linden, Tim. 1979b. "UFW Contracts Expected to Alter Vegetable Trade." *Packer,* 22 September, p. 1.

Lindsey, Robert. 1984. "Farm Workers Facing New Teamster Contest." *New York Times,* 10 October, p. Y10.

Littler, Craig. 1982. *The Development of the Labour Process in Capitalist Societies: A Comparative Study of the Transformation of Work Organization in Britain, Japan, and the USA.* London: Heinemann Educational Books.

Littler, Craig, and Graeme Salaman. 1984. *Class at Work: The Design, Allocation, and Control of Jobs.* London: Batsford Academic and Educational.

Lloyd, Jack, John Mamer, and Philip Martin. 1987. "The Ventura Citrus Labor Market." Manuscript. Davis: University of California, Department of Agricultural Economics, May.

Lockwood, David. 1975. "Sources of Variation in Working-Class Images of Society." In *Working-Class Images of Society,* edited by Martin Bulmer, 16–31. London: Routledge and Kegan Paul.

Lydon, Sandy. 1985. *Chinese Gold.* Capitola, Calif.: Capitola Book Company.

McConnell, Grant. 1953. *The Decline of Agrarian Democracy.* Berkeley: University of California Press.

McDowell, A., and H. Tilden. 1951. *Marketing California Strawberries, 1950 Season.* San Francisco: California Department of Agriculture and U.S. Department of Agriculture.

Mackie, W. W. 1910. *Soil Survey of the Pajaro Valley, California.* Washington, D.C.: U.S. Department of Agriculture, Bureau of Soils.

McMichael, Philip, ed. 1994. *The Global Restructuring of Agro-Food Systems.* Ithaca: Cornell University Press.

McWilliams, Carey. [1935] 1971. *Factories in the Field.* Santa Barbara and Salt Lake City: Peregrine Press.

Majka, Linda, and Theo Majka. 1982. *Farm Workers, Agribusiness, and the State.* Philadelphia: Temple University Press.

Mandel, Ernest. 1978. *The Second Slump.* London: New Left Books.

Mangahas, Mahar. 1975. "An Economic Theory of Tenant and Landlord Based on a Philippine Case." In *Agriculture in Development Theory,* edited by L. Reynolds, 138–61. New Haven: Yale University Press.

Mann, Susan. 1990. *Agrarian Capitalism in Theory and Practice.* Chapel Hill: University of North Carolina Press.

Mann, Susan, and James Dickinson. 1978. "Obstacles to the Development of a Capitalist Agriculture." *Journal of Peasant Studies* 5, no. 4: 466–81.

Mariategui, Jose. [1927] 1974. *Seven Interpretive Essays on Peruvian Reality.* Austin: University of Texas Press.

Marsden, Terry, Philip Lowe, and Sarah Whatmore, eds. 1990. *Rural Restructuring: Global Processes and Their Responses.* London: David Fulton.

Marshall, Alfred. [1890] 1964. *Principles of Economics.* 8th ed. London: Macmillan.

Marshall, T. 1965. *Class, Citizenship, and Social Development.* New York: Anchor Books.

Martin, Philip. 1987. *California's Farm Labor Market.* Davis: University of California, Agricultural Issues Center.

Martin, Philip. 1988. "Network Recruitment and Labor Displacement." In *U.S. Immigration in the 1980s: Reappraisal and Reform,* edited by David Simcox. Boulder, Colo.: Westview Press.

Martin, Philip, et al. 1984. "Changing Patterns in California's Harvest Labor Force." *California Agriculture* 38 (September): 6–8.

Martin, Philip, et al. 1985. "The Fragmented California Farm Labor Market." *California Agriculture* 39 (November–December): 14–16.

Martin, Philip, Suzanne Vaupel, and Daniel Egan. 1986. "Farmworker Unions: Status and Wage Impacts." *California Agriculture* 40 (July–August): 11–13.

Martinez-Alier, Juan. 1974. "Peasants and Laborers in Southern Spain, Cuba, and Highland Peru." *Journal of Peasant Studies* 1 (January): 133–63.

Martinez-Alier, Juan. 1977. *Haciendas, Plantations, and Collective Farms: Agrarian Class Societies—Cuba and Peru.* London: Frank Cass.

Marx, Karl. [1867] 1977. *A Critical Analysis of Capitalist Production.* Vol. 1 of *Capital.* New York: International Publishers.

Marx, Karl. [1894] 1977. *The Process of Capitalist Production as a Whole.* Vol. 3 of *Capital.* New York: International Publishers.

Massey, Douglas, et al. 1987. *Return to Aztlan.* Berkeley: University of California Press.

Meister, Dick, and Anne Loftis. 1977. *A Long Time Coming.* New York: Macmillan.

Metcalf, David. 1986. "Labour Market Flexibility and Jobs: A Survey of Evidence from OECD Countries with Special Reference to Great Britain and Europe." Discussion Paper no. 254. London: London School of Economics, Centre for Labour Economics.

Mill, John Stuart. [1848] 1915. *Principles of Political Economy.* London: Longmans, Green.

Millis, Harry, and Emily Brown. 1965. *From the Wagner Act to Taft-Hartley: A Study of National Labor Policy and Labor Relations.* Chicago: University of Chicago Press.

Mills, Herbert. 1979. "The San Francisco Waterfront: The Social Consequences of Industrial Modernization." In *Case Studies on the Labor Process,* edited by Andrew Zimbalist, 127–55. New York: Monthly Review Press.

Minden, Arlo. 1970. "Changing Structure of the Farm Input Industry: Organization, Scale, and Ownership." *American Journal of Agricultural Economics* 52, no. 2: 678–86.

Mines, Richard. 1985. "Employers and Workers in California Agriculture." In *California Farm Labor Relations and Law,* edited by Walter Fogel, 51–90. Los Angeles: University of California, Institute of Industrial Relations.

Mines, Richard, and Philip Martin. 1986. *A Profile of California Farmworkers.* Giannini Information Series no. 86-2. Berkeley: University of California, Division of Agricultural and Natural Resources.

Mines, Richard, Susan Gabbard, and Ruth Samardick. 1993. *U.S. Farmworkers in the Post-IRCA Period: Based on Data of the National Agricultural Workers Survey (NAWS).* Research Report no. 4. Washington, D.C.: U.S. Department of Labor, Office of the Assistant Secretary for Policy, March.

Mitchell, F., E. Maxie, and A. Greathead. 1964. *Handling Strawberries for Fresh Market.* Circular 527. Berkeley: University of California, Division of Agricultural Sciences.

Montana, Constanza, and John Emshwiller. 1986. "Staying Alive: Its Ranks Eroding, Farm Workers Union Struggles to Survive." *Wall Street Journal,* 9 September, pp. 1, 25.

Montgomery, David. 1979. *Workers' Control in America: Studies in the History of Work, Technology, and Labor Struggles.* Cambridge: Cambridge University Press.

Montgomery, David. 1987. *The Fall of the House of Labor: The Workplace, the State, and American Activism, 1865–1925.* Cambridge: Cambridge University Press.

Moore, Barrington, Jr. 1978. *Injustice: The Social Bases of Obedience and Revolt.* White Plains, N.Y.: M. E. Sharpe.

Moore, Sally Falk. 1970. "Law and Anthropology." In *Biennial Review of Anthropology, 1969,* edited by Bernard J. Siegal, 252–300. Stanford: Stanford University Press.

Morris, Austin. 1966. "Agricultural Labor and National Labor Legislation." *California Law Review* 54, no. 5: 1939–89.

Morris, Justin. 1978. "At Last: Strawberry Mechanization Is On Its Way." *Fruit Grower* (May): 26–28.

Morrow, Lance. 1993. "The Temping of America." *Time,* 29 March, pp. 40–41.

Mountjoy, Daniel. 1995. "Culture, Capital, and Contours: Ethnic Diversity and the Adoption of Soil Conservation in the Strawberry Hills of Monterey, California." Ph.D. diss., University of California, Davis.

Murrell, Peter. 1983. "The Economics of Sharing: A Transactions Cost Analysis of Contractual Choice in Farming." *Bell Journal of Economics* 14 (Spring): 283–93.

Newbery, David. 1976. *Risk Sharing, Sharecropping, and Uncertain Labor Markets.* Technical Report 202. I.M.S.S.S. Stanford: Stanford University.

Newbery, David, and Joseph Stiglitz. 1979. "Sharecropping, Risk Sharing, and the Importance of Imperfect Information." In *Risk, Uncertainty, and Agricultural Development,* edited by James Roumasset, Jean-Marc Boussard, and Inderjit Singh, 311–39. New York: Agricultural Development Council.

Newby, Howard. 1979. *The Deferential Worker.* Harmondsworth, Eng.: Penguin.

North, David. 1970. *The Border Crossers: People Who Live in Mexico and Work in the United States.* Washington, D.C.: TransCentury Corporation.

"Norton: Labor-Law Balance Poses Uphill, Essential Goal." 1980. *Packer,* 4 October, pp. 1AA, 3AA.

Office of Technology Assessment (OTA). 1986. *Technology, Public Policy, and the Changing Structure of American Agriculture.* Washington, D.C.: Office of Technology Assessment.

Osborn, C. 1903. "The Hand-Working and Domestic Industries in Germany." *Economic Journal* 13, no. 49: 133–36.

Otsuka, Keijiro, Masao Kikuchi, and Yujiro Hayami. 1986. "Community and Market in Contract Choice: The Jeepney in the Philippines." *Economic Development and Cultural Change* 3 (January): 270–98.

Packer Red Book. 1976. 71st ed. Chicago: Vance Publishing.

Padfield, Harland, and Jacqueline Greenleaf. 1985. "The Fate of the Northwest Strawberry Industry." *Proceedings of the 75th Annual Meeting of the Western Washington Horticultural Association,* 126–29. Olympia: Western Washington Horticultural Association.

Padfield, Harland, and Jacqueline Greenleaf. 1986. "Competing in Strawberry Production in the World Economy." In *Proceedings of the 76th Annual Meeting of the Western Washington Horticultural Association,* 34–38. Olympia: Western Washington Horticultural Association.

Padfield, Harland, and Helen Thaler. 1984. *The U.S. Processed Strawberry Market: An Analysis of Trends and Commodity Characteristics as They Impact on Oregon.* Circular no. 695. Corvallis: Oregon State University, June.

Paige, Jeffery M. 1975. *Agrarian Revolution: Social Movements and Export Agriculture in the Underdeveloped World.* New York: Free Press.

Palerm, Juan Vincente. 1984. "The Transformation of Rural California: Agribusiness, Farmworkers, and the Making of Chicano/Mexican Enclaves in the Agricultural Communities of Kern, Santa Barbara, San Luis Obispo, and Ventura Counties." Grant proposal submitted to University of California, Santa Barbara.

Parker, Earl S. 1921. "The Real Yellow Peril." *Independent* 105, 7 May, pp. 475–76, 499–500.

Perloff, Jeffrey. 1986. *Unions and Demographic Wage Hours, and Earning Differentials in the Agricultural Labor Market.* Working Paper no. 387. Berkeley: University of California, Giannini Foundation of Agricultural Economics.

Petrulis, M., et al. 1987. *How is Farm Financial Stress Affecting Rural America?* Agricultural Economics Report no. 568. Washington, D.C.: U.S. Department of Agriculture Economic Research Service.

Piore, Michael, and Charles Sabel. 1984. *The Second Industrial Divide: Possibilities for Prosperity.* New York: Basic Books.

Pollard, Vic. 1983. "Inept Leadership Caused Turbulent Past, Troubled Future." *California Journal* 14 (December): 443–44.

Popkin, Samuel. 1979. *The Rational Peasant: The Political Economy of Rural Society in Vietnam.* Berkeley: University of California Press.

Portes, Alejandro. 1983. "The Informal Sector: Definition, Controversy, and Relation to National Development." *Review* 7 (Summer): 151–74.

Portes, Alejandro, and John Walton. 1981. *Labor, Class, and the International System.* New York: Academic Press.

Portes, Alejandro, Manuel Castells, and Lauren Benton, eds. 1989. *The Informal Economy: Studies in Advanced and Less Developed Countries.* Baltimore: Johns Hopkins University Press.

Poulantzas, Nicos. [1974] 1979. *Classes in Contemporary Capitalism.* London: Verso.

Processing Strawberry Advisory Board (PSAB). 1986–92. *Annual Reports, 1985–1991.* Watsonville, Calif.: Processing Strawberry Advisory Board.

Przeworski, Adam. 1985. *Capitalism and Social Democracy.* Cambridge: Cambridge University Press.

Pugliese, Enrico. 1991. "Agriculture and the New Division of Labor." In *Towards a New Political Economy of Agriculture,* edited by William Friedland et al., 137–50. Boulder, Colo.: Westview Press.

Putnam, Robert. 1993. *Making Democracy Work: Civic Traditions in Modern Italy.* Princeton: Princeton University Press.

Quinney, Richard. 1974. *Criminal Justice in America: A Critical Understanding.* Boston: Little, Brown.

Raney, William. [1940] 1963. *Wisconsin: A Story of Progress.* Appleton, Wis.: Perin.

Rao, C. H. H. 1971. "Uncertainty, Entrepreneurship, and Sharecropping in India." *Journal of Political Economy* 79: 578–95.

Raup, Philip. 1985. *Structural Change in Agriculture in the United States.* Staff Paper no. P85-41. St. Paul: University of Minnesota, Department of Agricultural and Applied Economics.

Razee, Don. 1979. "Strawberry Industry Opposes Mandatory State IPM Program." *California Farmer,* 14 July, pp. 9–10.

Reed, Doyle, and Lynne Horel. 1980. *Leasing Practices for California Agricultural Properties.* Davis: University of California.

Reid, Joseph, Jr. 1976. "Sharecropping and Agricultural Uncertainty." *Economic Development and Cultural Change* 24, no. 3: 549–76.

Reid, Joseph, Jr. 1979. "Sharecropping and Tenancy in American History." In *Risk, Uncertainty, and Agricultural Development,* edited by James Roumasset et al., 283–309. New York: Agricultural Development Council.

Richardson, Len. 1990. "Sound as a Dollar, Ag Comes Back Strong after a Four-Year Slump." *California Farmer,* July, p. 7.

Rischin, Moses. 1962. *The Promised City: New York Jews, 1870–1914.* Cambridge: Harvard University Press.

Rodefeld, Richard. 1978. "Trends in U.S. Farm Organizational Structure and Type." In *Change in Rural America: Causes, Consequences, and Alternatives,* edited by Richard Rodefeld et al. St. Louis: Mosby.

Rodriguez, Rick. 1985. "ALRB to Bear Duke's Stamp." *Sacramento Bee,* 25 December, pp. A1, A12.

Rodriguez, Rick. 1986. "New ALRB Majority Boosts Stirling's Power." *Sacramento Bee,* 5 February, pp. B6, B8.

Rosenberg, Howard. 1993. "Contractor Crackdown." *California Farmer,* 3 January, pp. 19–22.

Rosenberg, Howard, et al. 1993. *California Findings from the National Agricultural Workers Survey: A Demographic and Employment Profile of Perishable Crop Farm Workers.* Washington, D.C.: U.S. Department of Labor, Office of the Assistant Secretary for Policy, March.

Roumasset, James. 1976. *Rice and Risk.* Amsterdam: North-Holland.

Rouse, Roger. 1989. "Mexican Migration to the United States." Ph.D. diss., Stanford University.

Roy, Donald. 1954. "Efficiency and the Fix: Informal Intergroup Relations in a Piecework Machine Shop." *American Journal of Sociology* 60: 255–66.

Royce, Edward. 1993. *The Origins of Southern Sharecropping.* Philadelphia: Temple University Press.

Rubel, Arthur J. 1966. *Across the Tracks: Mexican-Americans in a Texas City.* Austin: University of Texas Press.

Runsten, David. 1987. "Strawberries." Manuscript prepared by the Study Group on Marketing California Specialty Crops. Davis: University of California, Agricultural Issues Center.

Runsten, David. 1991. *Agricultural Labor Research Proceedings.* Napa: State of California, Employment Development Department.

Runsten, David, et al. 1987. "Competitiveness at Home and Abroad." In *Marketing California Specialty Crops: Worldwide Competition and Constraints,* edited by Harold Carter and Carole Nuckton, 49–67. Davis: University of California, Agricultural Issues Center.

Russell, R. 1938. *Climates of California* 2, no. 4. Berkeley: University of California Publications in Geography.

Sabel, Charles. [1982] 1985. *Work and Politics: The Division of Labor in Industry.* Cambridge: Cambridge University Press.

Salamon, Sonya. 1992. *Prairie Patrimony: Family, Farming, and Community in the Midwest.* Chapel Hill: University of North Carolina Press.

Salant, P., M. Smale, and W. Saupe. 1986. *Farm Viability: Results of the USDA Family Farms Surveys.* Rural Development Research Report no. 60. Washington, D.C.: U.S. Department of Agriculture, Economic Research Service.

"Salinas Valley Hit by Produce Strike." 1970. *Salinas Californian,* 24 August, pp. 1–2.

Sample, Herbert. 1987. "Controversy Is Farm Board's Steadiest Crop." *Sacramento Bee,* 16 August, p. A3.

Samuel, Raphael. 1977. "Workshop of the World: Steam Power and Hand Technology in Mid-Victorian Britain." *History Workshop,* no. 3 (Spring): 6–60.

Sayer, Andrew, and Richard Walker. 1992. *The New Social Economy: Reworking the Division of Labor.* Cambridge, Mass.: Blackwell.

Scher, Howard, and Robert Catz. 1975. "Farmworker Litigation under the Fair Labor Standards Act: Establishing Joint Employer Liability and Related Problems." *Harvard Civil Rights–Civil Liberties Law Review* 10 (Summer): 575–607.

Scholz, Jennifer. 1987. "Duke's ALRB: The Farmer's Friend." *California Journal* 18 (August): 375–77.

Schumpeter, Joseph. 1939. *Business Cycles.* New York: McGraw-Hill.

Scott, James. 1985. *Weapons of the Weak: Everyday Forms of Peasant Resistance.* New Haven: Yale University Press.

Seasonal Labor in California Agriculture. 1963. Berkeley: University of California, Division of Agricultural Sciences.

Seivertson, Bruce. 1969. "Pajaro Valley, California: The Sequent Occupance of a Coastal Agricultural Basin." Master's thesis, Chico State College, Chico, Calif.

Shepard, L., and R. Collins. 1982. "Why Do Farmers Fail? Farm Bankruptcies, 1910–78." *American Journal of Agricultural Economics* 64: 609–15.

Skocpol, Theda. 1980. "Political Response to Capitalist Crisis: Neo-Marxist Theories of the State and the Case of the New Deal." *Politics and Society* 10, no. 2: 155–201.

Small Farm Viability Project. 1977. *The Family Farm in California.* Sacramento: State of California, November.

Smith, Adam. [1869] 1937. *Wealth of Nations.* New York: Modern Library.

Snyder, David, and Charles Tilly. 1972. "Hardship and Collective Violence in France: 1830 to 1960." *American Sociological Review* 37 (October): 520–32.

Soil Conservation Service (SCS). 1984. *Strawberry Hills Target Area: Watershed Area Study Report, Monterey County, California.* Davis: U.S. Department of Agriculture, SCS.

Sosnick, Stephen. 1978. *Hired Hands: Seasonal Farm Workers in the United States.* Santa Barbara: McNally and Loftin, West.

Sowell, Thomas. 1981. *Ethnic America: A History.* New York: Basic Books.

Stiglitz, Joseph. 1974. "Incentives and Risk Sharing in Sharecropping." *Review of Economic Studies* 41, no. 126: 219–56.

"Strawberry Growers Switching to Drip." 1977. *Western Grower and Shipper* 48, no. 4: 13–14.

"Strawberry Harvesters Galore!" 1971. *American Vegetable Grower* (May): 28–30.

"Strike Tightens; Coolers Closed." 1970. *Salinas Californian,* 27 August, pp. 1–2.

Summary of County Agricultural Commissioner's Reports: Gross Values by Commodity Groups, California, 1984 and 1985. 1986. Sacramento: California Agricultural Statistics Service, August.

Technological Change, Farm Mechanization, and Agricultural Employment. 1978. Berkeley: University of California, Division of Agricultural Sciences.

Thomas, Harold. 1939. *The Production of Strawberries in California.* Circular 113. Berkeley: University of California, Agricultural Experiment Station.

Thomas, Harold, and Earl Goldsmith. 1945. *The Shasta, Sierra, Lassen, Tahoe, and Donner Strawberries.* Bulletin 690. Berkeley: University of California, Agricultural Experiment Station.

Thomas, Robert. 1985. *Citizenship, Gender, and Work: Social Organization of Industrial Agriculture.* Berkeley: University of California Press.

Thompson, Orville, and Ann Scheuring. 1978. *From Lug Boxes to Electronics: A Study of California Tomato Growers and Sorting Crews.* Davis: University of California, Department of Applied Behavioral Sciences.

Thompson, E. P. [1963] 1966. *The Making of the English Working Class.* New York: Vintage Books.

Thompson, E. P. 1967. "Time, Work-Discipline, and Industrial Capitalism." *Past and Present* 38 (December): 56–97.

Thompson, E. P. 1971. "The Moral Economy of the English Crowd in the Eighteenth Century." *Past and Present* 50 (February): 76–136.

Thompson, E. P. 1975. *Whigs and Hunters: The Origins of the Black Act.* New York: Pantheon Books.

Tilly, Charles. 1978. *From Mobilization to Revolution.* Reading, Pa.: Addison-Wesley.

Trotsky, Leon. [1932] 1937. *The History of the Russian Revolution.* New York: Simon and Schuster.

Tweeten, Luther. 1981. "Agriculture at a Crucial Evolutionary Crossroads." *Research in Domestic and International Agribusiness Management* 2: 1–15.

U.S. Bureau of the Census. 1947, 1952, 1956, 1961, 1972, 1974, 1980, 1984a, 1989. *U.S. Census of Agriculture, 1945, 1950, 1954, 1959, 1964, 1969, 1972, 1978, 1982, 1987.* Washington, D.C.: GPO.

U.S. Bureau of the Census. 1984b. *Farm Population of the United States, 1982.* Washington, D.C.: GPO.

U.S. Commission on Agricultural Workers. 1992. *Report of the Commission on Agricultural Workers.* Washington, D.C.: GPO.

U.S. Congress, House Committee on Agriculture. 1967. *The Application of Minimum Wages in Agriculture: Hearings before the House Committee on Agriculture.* 90th Cong., 1st sess. Washington, D.C.: GPO.

U.S. Congress, Senate Committee on Labor and Public Welfare, Subcommittee on Migratory Labor. 1969. *The Migratory Farm Labor Problem in the United States.* 91st Cong., 1st sess., 1969, S. Rept. 91-83. Washington, D.C.: GPO.

U.S. Department of Agriculture. 1979. *Structure Issues of American Agriculture.* Economics, Statistics, and Cooperative Service. Agricultural Economic Report no. 438. Washington, D.C.: GPO.

U.S. Department of Agriculture. 1957–90. *Agricultural Statistics, 1956–1989.* Washington, D.C.: GPO.

U.S. Department of Agriculture, Economic Research Service. 1986b. *Financial Characteristics of U.S. Farms, January 1, 1986.* Agricultural Information Bulletin no. 500. Washington, D.C.: GPO.

U.S. Department of Labor (DOL), U.S. Wage and Hour and Public Contracts Division. 1967. *A Guide to the Employer-Employee Relationship in Agriculture: Sharecropping Arrangements or Landlord-Tenant Agreements.* Pub. no. 1187. Washington, D.C.: GPO.

U.S. Immigration Commission. 1911. *Reports of the Immigration Commission.* Washington, D.C.: GPO.

U.S. Immigration and Naturalization Service. 1992. *Summary of SAWS Granted Status under IRCA.* Washington, D.C.: GPO, February 13.

Valenzuela, Louie, and Marvin Snyder. 1987. *California Strawberry Industry Trends, 1981–1986.* Santa Barbara and San Luis Obispo Counties: University of California, Cooperative Extension Service.

Vaupel, Suzanne, and Philip Martin. 1986. *Activity and Regulation of Farm Labor Contractors.* Giannini Information Series, no. 86-3. Berkeley: University of California, Division of Agriculture and Natural Resources, June.

Villarejo, Don. 1980. *Getting Bigger.* Davis: California Institute for Rural Studies.

Villarejo, Don. 1985. *Agricultural Land Ownership and Operations in the 49,000 Acre Drainage Study Area of the Westlands Water District.* Sacramento, Calif.: Assembly Office of Research.

Villarejo, Don. 1989. *Farm Restructuring and Employment in California Agriculture.* Working Group on Farm Labor and Rural Poverty. Working Paper no. 1. Davis: California Institute for Rural Studies.

Villarejo, Don, and Judith Redmond. 1988. *Missed Opportunities—Squandered Resources.* Davis: California Institute for Rural Studies.

Villarejo, Don, and Dave Runsten. 1993. *California's Agricultural Dilemma: Higher Production and Lower Wages.* Davis: California Institute for Rural Studies, December.

Vogeler, Ingolf. 1982. *The Myth of the Family Farm: Agribusiness Dominance of U.S. Agriculture.* Boulder, Colo.: Westview Press.

Voth, Victor, and Royce Bringhurst. 1958. "Fruiting and Vegetative Response of Lassen Strawberries in Southern California as Influenced by Nursery Source, Time of Planting, and Plant Chilling History." *Proceedings of the American Society for Horticultural Science* 72: 186–97.

Voth, Victor, and Royce Bringhurst. 1978. "Four-Row Beds, Drip Irrigation Advances Strawberry Production." *Western Fruit Grower* 98 (May): 12–13, 41.

Wagner, Diane. 1987. "Some Staff Attorneys Say the Farm Labor Board Now Favors Growers." *California Lawyer* (March): 23–26, 63.

Wallick, Philip. 1969. "An Historical Geography of the Salinas Valley." Master's thesis, University of California, Berkeley.

Walton, John. 1992. *Western Times and Water Wars: State, Culture, and Rebellion in California.* Berkeley: University of California Press.

Watsonville Chamber of Commerce. 1952. *Watsonville: The First 100 Years.* Watsonville, Calif.

Watt, D., et al. 1986. *The Financial Status of North Dakota Farmers and Ranchers: January 1, 1985, Survey Results.* Agricultural Economics Report no. 207. Fargo: North Dakota State University, Department of Agricultural Economics.

Watts, Michael. 1994. "Life Under Contract: Contract Farming, Agrarian Restructuring, and Flexible Accumulation." In *Living under Contract,* edited by Peter Little and Michael Watts, 21–77. Madison: University of Wisconsin Press.

Welch, Norman. 1989. *Strawberry Production in California.* Leaflet 2959. Berkeley: University of California, Cooperative Extension.

Welch, Norman, and James Beutel. 1987. "Winter Planted Selva." *Strawberry News Bulletin,* no. 1. Watsonville: California Strawberry Advisory Board, September 21.

Welch, Norman, and Arthur Greathead. 1976. *Strawberry Production in the Central Coast of California.* Berkeley: University of California, Agricultural Extension.

Welch, Norman, Arthur Greathead, and James Beutel. 1980, 1985. *Strawberry Production and Costs in the Central Coast of California.* Berkeley: University of California, Agricultural Extension.

Welch, Norman, et al. 1982. *Strawberry Production in California.* Leaflet 2959. Berkeley: University of California, Agricultural Extension.

Wells, Miriam. 1981. "Social Conflict, Commodity Constraints, and Labor Market Structure in Agriculture." *Comparative Studies in Society and History* 23 (October): 679–704.

Wells, Miriam. 1982. "Political Mediation and Agricultural Cooperation: Strawberry Farms in California." *Economic Development and Cultural Change* 30 (January): 413–32.

Wells, Miriam. 1984a. "The Resurgence of Sharecropping: Historical Anomaly or Political Strategy?" *American Journal of Sociology* 90 (July): 1–29.

Wells, Miriam. 1984b. "What Is a Worker? The Role of Sharecroppers in Class Structure." *Politics and Society* 13, no. 3: 295–320.

Wells, Miriam. 1987a. "Legal Conflict and Class Structure: The Independent Contractor-Employee Controversy in California Agriculture." *Law and Society Review* 21, no. 1: 49–82.

Wells, Miriam. 1987b. "Sharecropping in the United States: A Political Economy Perspective." In *Farm Work and Fieldwork: American Agriculture in Anthropological Perspective,* edited by Michael Chibnik, 211–43. Ithaca: Cornell University Press.

Wells, Miriam. 1990. "Mexican Farm Workers Become Strawberry Farmers." *Human Organization* 49, no. 2: 149–56.

Wells, Miriam. 1991. "Ethnic Groups and Knowledge Systems in Agriculture." *Economic Development and Cultural Change* 39 (July): 739–72.

Wells, Miriam, and Martha West. 1989. *Regulation of the Farm Labor Market: An Assessment of Farm Workers Protections under the California Agricultural Labor Relations Act.* Working Group on Farm Labor and Rural Poverty. Working Paper no. 5. Davis: California Institute for Rural Studies.

Wessel, J. 1983. *Trading the Future: Farm Exports and the Concentration of Economic Power in Our Food System.* Birmingham, Eng.: Third World Publications.

Wiener, Jonathan. 1978. *Social Origins of the New South: 1860–1885.* Baton Rouge: Louisiana State University Press.

Wilhelm, Stephen, and Albert Paulus. 1980. "How Soil Fumigation Benefits the California Strawberry Industry." *Plant Disease* 64 (March): 264–70.

Wilhelm, Stephen, and James Sagen. 1974. *A History of the Strawberry.* Berkeley: University of California, Division of Agricultural Sciences.

Winters, Donald. 1978. *Farmers without Farms: Agricultural Tenancy in Nineteenth-Century Iowa.* Westport, Conn.: Greenwood Press.

Wolf, Eric. 1966. "Kinship, Friendship, and Patron-Client Relations in Complex Societies." In *The Social Anthropology of Complex Societies,* edited by Michael Banton, 1–22. London: Tavistock.

Wood, Stephen. 1983. *The Degradation of Work? Skill, Deskilling, and the Labour Process.* London: Hutchinson.

Worster, Donald. 1985. *Rivers of Empire: Water, Aridity, and the Growth of the American West.* New York: Pantheon.

Wright, Eric. 1976. "Class Boundaries in Advanced Capitalist Societies." *New Left Review* 98 (July–August): 3–41.

Wright, Gavin. 1982. "The Strange Career of the New Southern Economic History." *Reviews in American History* 10, no. 4: 164–80.

Yarrow, Michael. 1979. "The Labor Process in Coal Mining: Struggle for Control." In *Case Studies of the Labor Process,* edited by Andrew Zimbalist, 170–92. New York: Monthly Review Press.

Zabin, Carol, et al. 1993. *Mixtec Migrants in California Agriculture: A New Cycle of Poverty.* Davis: California Institute for Rural Studies, May.

Zimbalist, Andrew. 1979. *Case Studies on the Labor Process.* New York: Monthly Review Press.

Zwerdling, David. 1980. "The Food Monsters." In *Crisis in American Institutions,* edited by Jerome Skolnick and Elliott Currie, 38–53. Boston: Little, Brown.

Cases Cited

Alvara v. Driscoll Strawberry Associates, Inc., Nos. 79-CE-1-SM, 79-CE-2-SM (Cal. Agricultural Labor Relations Board 1981).
Bartels v. Birmingham, 332 U.S. 126 (1947).
S. G. Borello & Sons, Inc. v. Dept. of Industrial Relations, 48 Cal. 3d 341 (1989).
Brock v. Lauritzen, 624 F. Supp. 966 (E.D. Wis. 1985).
Donovan v. Brandel, 736 F.2d 1114 (6th Cir. 1984).
Donovan v. Gillmor, 535 F. Supp. 154 (N.D. Ohio 1982), *appeal dismissed,* 708 F.2d 723 (1982).
Marshall v. Brandel, No. G76-393 CA6, slip op. (W.D. Mich. 17 January 1983).
NLRB v. Edward G. Budd Mfg. Co., 169 F.2d 571 (6th Cir. 1948).
Real v. Driscoll Strawberry Associates, Inc., No. C 75-661-LHB (N.D. Cal. filed 4 April, 1975); Deposition of Kazumasa Mukai (8 November 1976); Deposition of William J. Crowley (16 November 1976); Brief for Appellants (23 June 1977); Summary Judgment (23 February 1977); 603 F.2d 748 (9th Cir. 1979).
Rutherford Food Corp. v. McComb, 331 U.S. 722 (1947).
Sachs v. United States, 422 F. Supp. 1092 (N.D. Ohio 1976).
Salinas v. United States, No. B-82-140 (S.D. Tex. 1982).
Secretary of Labor, U.S. Dept. of Labor v. Lauritzen, 835 F.2d 1529 (7th Cir. 1987).
United States v. Silk, 331 U.S. 704 (1947).

Index

Anthropology of Contemporary Issues

A SERIES EDITED BY ROGER SANJEK

Chinatown No More: Taiwan Immigrants in Contemporary New York
by Hsiang-shui Chen
Farm Work and Fieldwork: American Agriculture in Anthropological Perspective
edited by Michael Chibnik
The Varieties of Ethnic Experience: Kinship, Class, and Gender among California Italian-Americans
by Micaela di Leonardo
Lord, I'm Coming Home: Everyday Aesthetics in Tidewater North Carolina
by John Forrest
Chinese Working-Class Lives: Getting By in Taiwan
by Hill Gates
Accommodation without Assimilation: Sikh Immigrants in an American High School
by Margaret A. Gibson
Praying for Justice: Faith, Order, and Community in an American Town
by Carol J. Greenhouse
Distant Companions: Servants and Employers in Zambia, 1900–1985
by Karen Tranberg Hansen
Rx: Spiritist as Needed: A Study of a Puerto Rican Community Mental Health Resource
by Alan Harwood
Dismantling Apartheid: A South African Town in Transition
by Walton R. Johnson
Caribbean New York: Black Immigrants and the Politics of Race
by Philip Kasinitz
The Solitude of Collectivism: Romanian Villagers to the Revolution and Beyond
by David A. Kideckel

Nuclear Summer: The Clash of Communities at the Seneca Women's Peace Encampment
by Louise Krasniewicz
Between Two Worlds: Ethnographic Essays on American Jewry
edited by Jack Kugelmass
American Odyssey: Haitians in New York City
by Michel S. Laguerre
From Working Daughters to Working Mothers: Immigrant Women in a New England Industrial Community
by Louise Lamphere
Sunbelt Working Mothers: Reconciling Family and Factory
by Louise Lamphere, Patricia Zavella, and Felipe Gonzales, with Peter B. Evans
Creativity/Anthropology
edited by Smadar Lavie, Kirin Narayan, and Renato Rosaldo
Cities, Classes, and the Social Order
by Anthony Leeds. edited by Roger Sanjek
Lesbian Mothers: Accounts of Gender in American Culture
by Ellen Lewin
Civilized Women: Gender and Prestige in Southeastern Liberia
by Mary H. Moran
Blood, Sweat, and Mahjong: Family and Enterprise in an Overseas Chinese Community
by Ellen Oxfeld
The Magic City: Unemployment in a Working-Class Community
by Gregory Pappas
State and Family in Singapore: Restructuring an Industrial Society
by Janet W. Salaff
Uneasy Endings: Daily Life in an American Nursing Home
by Renée Rose Shield
Children of Circumstances: Israeli Emigrants in New York
by Moshe Shokeid
History and Power in the Study of Law: New Directions in Legal Anthropology
edited by June Starr and Jane F. Collier
"Getting Paid": Youth Crime and Work in the Inner City
by Mercer L. Sullivan
Breaking the Silence: Redress and Japanese American Ethnicity
by Yasuko I. Takezawa
Underground Harmonies: Music and Politics in the Subways of New York
by Susie J. Tanenbaum
City of Green Benches: Growing Old in a New Downtown
by Maria D. Vesperi
Strawberry Fields: Politics, Class, and Work in California Agriculture
by Miriam J. Wells
Renunciation and Reformulation: A Study of Conversion in an American Sect
by Harriet Whitehead
Upscaling Downtown: Stalled Gentrification in Washington, D.C.
by Brett Williams
Women's Work and Chicano Families: Cannery Workers of the Santa Clara Valley
by Patricia Zavella